The *Tawhidi* Methodological Worldview

"Professor Dr. Masudul Alam Choudhury has written a thorough critique of the mainstream theory premised on trade-off between material and moral means of scientific investigation in order to make sense of our world from an Islamic point of view. To do so, he adopts a holistic and heterodox perspective in reference to the unifying power of the law of *Tawhid*, the unique cement of unity of 'everything' in Islamic belief, life and thought. His book comes to the forefront as the first of its kind in expounding the methodological worldview of monotheistic unity of knowledge and reconstruction of the design of the unifying world-sytem studied in its generality and particular. To do so, he merges economics, finance, science, and society by their interlinkages. Thus, his work can well be expected to pave the way for a new insight in studying the foundations of Islamic thought from a transdisciplinary and systemic perspective."

—Prof. Dr. Halis Yunus Ersöz, *Vice Rector, Istanbul University, Turkey*

Masudul Alam Choudhury
Editor

The *Tawhidi* Methodological Worldview

A Transdisciplinary Study of Islamic
Economics

 Springer

Editor
Masudul Alam Choudhury
International Chair, Postgraduate Program
in Islamic Economics and Finance,
Faculty of Economics
Trisakti University
Jakarta, Indonesia

ISBN 978-981-13-6584-3   ISBN 978-981-13-6585-0   (eBook)
https://doi.org/10.1007/978-981-13-6585-0

Library of Congress Control Number: 2019935552

This Springer imprint is published by the registered company Springer Nature Singapore Pte Ltd.
The registered company address is: 152 Beach Road, #21-01/04 Gateway East, Singapore 189721, Singapore

This book is dedicated to

Nuzhat
who single-handed raised a whole family of
her four boys and enriched us all by her
unfailing caring and resilient personality.

Nuzhat
is to us the Kosem Sultan, who was the most
illuminating Queen mother of the Turkish
Ottoman World-system, an astounding mark
of Islamic civilization.

Preface

It has now been 19 years since the birth of the unique educational institution of Postgraduate Program in Islamic Economics and Finance (IEF) now with the Faculty of Economics of Trisakti University, Jakarta, Indonesia. This institution (see online https://www.ief-trisakti.ac.id/) was established by its Academic Founders, Late Prof. Dr. Sofyan Syafri Harahap, Department of Accounting, Faculty of Economics, Trisakti University, and Prof. Dr. Masudul Alam Choudhury, Editing Author of this book. The specific objective behind this great educational project was to derive, develop and apply the methodology of *Tawhid* (monotheism as law) in the *Qur'an* and the *sunnah* (teachings of Prophet Muhammad) towards establishing the foundation of Islamic Economics and Finance and the socio-scientific nature of 'everything'. This erudite venture is lacked everywhere else among Muslims for a long time now.

Many other academic and government support in Indonesia were instrumental in establishing this postgraduate programme successfully. Ever since its establishment, IEF has flourished as a seat of advanced learning in the field of *Tawhidi* methodology and its application in training doctoral- and master-level students. In its nineteenth year now, IEF has over 100 students in the Ph.D. programme. IEF has graduated over 50 Ph.D. graduates who presently hold various academic and civil service positions in Indonesia. The academic advancement is progressing keeping the target of *Tawhidi* methodological worldview of unity of knowledge and its moral–material, abstracto-empirical embedding in diverse world-system studies in the socio-scientific forefront.

Thereby, the methodological formalism and application of the *Tawhidi* worldview have expanded into transdisciplinary fields. They overarch the theory of 'everything' including in it the socio-scientific fields of Islamic economics, finance, society and science.

This book is a manifestation of the depth and highly analytical nature of the study of *Tawhid* as the primal ontological law of monotheism. It uses a deeply *Qur'anic* exegesis, and mathematical, philosophical, and specialized socio-scientific approaches in deriving, developing, and empirically applying the imminent *Qur'anic* methodology of unity of knowledge and its consequential unified world-system in extensive diversity, by generality and particulars.

The approach of the study while being of *Qur'anic* ontological origin is also of a comparative nature. It is based on critical thinking. Educational faculty, advanced scholarly students, and the global academic forum are being educated substantively today in *Tawhidi* methodological worldview. The emergent approach is formalized in and by the modelling of the theory that is referred to in this book as *Tawhidi String Relation* (TSR).

The comprehensive moral and material embeddedness with abstraction and empirical inclusiveness of the nature of *Tawhidi* methodology of *Qur'anic* monotheism as law in relation to the unified world-system by way of organic unity of knowledge is explained by the two substantive parts. These are the *Qur'anic* exegesis on the study of ontology as the philosophical and mathematical socio-scientific origin of being and becoming of reality. Next follows the inquiry of the *Qur'anic* ontological foundation by the epistemology of derivation of knowledge and its nature and concrescence. Ontology and epistemology are followed by the study of phenomenology as the epistemic integration in reference to *Qur'anic* exegesis of emergent ideas in their generality and particulars. This integrative inquiry results in the pertinence of appropriate methods of analysis. Secondly, methodology thus leads into method of advanced analytical study and empirical application in a vast area of socio-scientific inquiry. TSR is thus rendered as the methodology combined with methods of advanced study of the theory of 'everything' in the socio-scientific domain.

This work along with many other ones by the author, while being derived from the ontological foundation of the *Qur'anic* worldview, further explained by the teachings of the Prophet Muhammad (*sunnah*), and discussion of the learned ones in the *Qur'an* and *sunnah* (*ulul-amr, ulul albab*), is a subtle extension of the meaning of *Tawhid* as a methodological worldview to a theory of 'everything'. The concept of 'everything' bears the meaning of universality and uniqueness of the generality and particulars of the world-system. The *Qur'an* refers to such a holistic domain as *a'lameen*. Its relational characteristics of systems, cybernetics, and analytical dynamics in the framework of complementary relationship between variables, all of the endogenous type, are described in the profundity of organic interrelations. The *Qur'an* refers to this property of the consciously evolutionary learning nature of the world-system in all its manifestations as both—organic interrelations between all things as created by the divine ordainment (*azwaja kullaha*) and the reoriginative phenomenon of evolutionary learning. Such *Qur'anic* constructs form the ever new and discoverable reality (*khalq in-jadid*) of experience.

The meaning of *Tawhid* is thereby much beyond simply a narrow understanding of divine oneness. It is subtle and richer than the mere traditional understanding. That is of *Tawhid* al-Rububiyyah (creatorship by Allah's sole Lordship as absolute and all-knowing) and of *Tawhid* al-Uluhiyyah (Allah being the sole owner of His attributes referred to as *Sifat*, and the beatific names referred to as Asma.). The conveying of *Tawhid* in the framework of its methodological worldview treats all of such divine properties as perfection that resides solely with Allah alone. They can only be invoked but cannot be manifestly comprehended in the worldly construction of the theory of evolutionary learning in unity of knowledge (divine oneness of knowledge) embedded in 'everything'. The principle of relational oneness as unity of knowledge and its worshipping form in terms of the unity of the world-system indeed are derived from the primal ontological basis of the *Qur'an*. The *Qur'an* (6:101) refers to this foundation of the theory of 'everything' as the 'primal origin': 'To Him is due the primal origin of the heavens and the earth: How can He have a son when He hath no consort? He created all things, and He hath full knowledge of all things'.

From the above discussion, we conclude that the inalienable perfection of *Tawhid* as law cannot be used for any form of worldly being for Allah has no exactness and similarity, no variability and no corporeality. These otherwise are signs of conceptual deficiency, whereas Allah is not deficient. He is all-knowing and all-hearing. Therefore, the primal origin of *Tawhid* in the *Qur'an*, and transmitted by the *sunnah* of Prophet Muhammad through his teachings and traditions, and further on explained by discursive function of the learned ones (*ulul-amr*), can only be used as ontological beginning to establish the nature of methodology of the *Tawhidi* worldview by unity of knowledge. Indeed, as pointed out by Morrow and Vittor (2009, p. 48): 'Although *Tawhid* is typically translated as 'oneness', the term derives from the Arabic root 'wahada' which means 'to unite, to join, to combine, and to gather'. Although Allah is absolutely and utterly One, and Islam adheres to the strictest and purest form of monotheism possible, *Tawhid* literally means 'unity' which means 'to bring together''. The organic relational essence of *Tawhid* as law is thereby central in understanding and applying the ontology of unity of knowledge in 'everything'.

The *Tawhidi* methodological worldview and thereby TSR that embeds 'everything' is a theory of *Tawhidi* unity of knowledge. It embeds and explains 'everything' in the order and scheme of the world-system. This comprehends the known and unknown with potentiality. TSR is a methodological way of explaining the derivation and functioning of the theory based on divine Oneness as explained by the derived theory of unity of knowledge in terms of abstraction, consciousness and application. The *Qur'an* explains all these functions of knowledge in socio-scientific inquiry and discovery in the midst of organic relations. Such complementarities explain inter-variable relationship in unity of knowledge. It is a property that prevails in the formalism of both knowledge (truth) and 'de-knowledge' (falsehood as avoidance). These two distinct truisms of total reality of *Tawhid* as law are explained by their own distinct systems and properties of inhering relations.

The study of TSR now commences as a theory of *Tawhidi* precept of unity of knowledge. The opposite to this worldview are the distinct properties and methods that arise from the same methodological origin of *Tawhid* as the primal law now invoking the distinctively opposite form of differentiation of knowledge and its consequences. Truth and falsehood as knowledge and 'de-knowledge', respectively, exist as opposite realities in 'everything' in respect of organic unity or as dialectical dualism and methodological individualism as differentiation, respectively.

The specific socio-scientific disciplines, such as economics, finance, science, and society are taken up for a uniform study within the transdisciplinary order and scheme of 'everything' as derived from *Tawhidi* methodological worldview. This universal and unique approach is that of the theory of unity of knowledge (truth and falsehood distinctly disparate). It remains embedded in explaining 'everything'. The emergent theory of the specific disciplines is thereby investigated uniquely, but with diversity of issues and problems, with the use of the ever-advancing supremely analytical rigour, richness, and critical realism. The emergent methodology thereby unifies the ontological, epistemological, phenomenological, and sustainability methods conforming strictly to *Tawhidi* methodology of unity of knowledge. These methods and the formalism arising from *Tawhidi* methodology are thereby complex and analytical in nature. Thereby, mathematical formalism becomes inevitably necessary to rigorously study the structural nature of this most original work on *Tawhid* and the abstract and applied perspectives of the emanating world-system.

Shari'ah and its components, *fiqh* and *fatawa*, are not foundational and therefore not methodological origins of *Tawhidi* worldview. *Shari'ah* and discourse on it make sense if they originate in *Tawhid* as the primal ontological law. *Shari'ah* then takes its different forms in accepting recommended choices and in avoiding false choices in the light of *Tawhid* as the Law with its foundational methodological worldview. This indeed is the inscrutable historical consciousness (Lucaks 1968) of *Tawhid* as law concerning 'everything'. This work intends to present the nature and analytics underlying *Tawhid* as the law of 'everything' in the light of the *Qur'anic* abiding consciousness.[1]

The approach of this work as an original one of its kind is a scholarly and critical inquiry into the true nature of Islamic law. That is of *Tawhid* and its relationship with the entirety of 'everything'. The critical and often contrary investigation of *Shari'ah* in all its forms is taken up in this work in this light of the *Qur'anic* primal position of *Tawhid* as ontological law along with its methodological consequences. In those choices that conform between *Tawhid* as law and the purpose and objective of *Shari'ah* in the light of *Tawhid* as law (*maqasid as-Shari'ah al-Tawhid*), it is to *Tawhid* that we must turn for the ultimate source of all legal and scholarly derivation of facts of reality out of discourse centring in the monotheistic unity of

---

[1]*Qur'an* (16:36): For We assuredly sent amongst every People a messenger, (with the Command), 'Serve Allah, and eschew Evil': of the People were some whom Allah guided, and some on whom error became inevitably (established). So travel through the earth, and see what was the end of those who denied (the Truth).

The ontological principle of historical consciousness further emanates from the *Qur'anic* verse (38:27): 'Not without purpose did We create heaven and earth and all between! that were the thought of Unbelievers! but woe to the Unbelievers because of the Fire (of Hell)!'

The philosophy of history along which the recurrence of continuously regenerating events describe the conscious historical path is distinct from the explanation given by Maritain (1973) and all of western interpretation of philosophy of history in that there is no interrelationship in these between divine law and worldly actions. Morality is understood as a secularized human interpretation that does not arise from the divinely ordained law. See, Maritain, J. (1973). *On the Philosophy of History*, ed. (J. W. Evans). Augustus M. Kelley Publishers, Clifton, New Jersey.

knowledge and overarching the theory of 'everything'. 'Everything' renders the generality and specifics of the world-system (*a'lameen*).

The mention of *Shari'atan* in the *Qur'an* as the way of moral guidance unequivocally appertains to the way towards *Tawhid* as the universal law. There is no constricted implication of the term *Shari'ah* in the *Qur'an* in any of its forms to jurisprudence as the ontological moral law and guidance. Since *Shari'ah* as jurisprudence has not been conveyed by the *Qur'an*, it could not have been conveyed by the Prophetic guidance of *sunnah* and by the discourse of the learned community (*ulul-amr*). The long history of *Shari'ah* as jurisprudence which Muslims and their religious leaders under different sects (*madhabs*) have preached as law is a great misunderstanding that goes against the worldview of *Tawhid* conveyed by the *Qur'an* in its entire embodiment. In this regard the *Qur'an* declares (21:22) declares: 'If there were, in the heavens and the earth, other gods besides Allah, there would have been confusion in both! But glory to Allah, the Lord of the Throne: (High is He) above what they attribute to Him!'

On the other hand, the objective of this work is on deriving and developing the methodological foundation of the *Qur'an* in its universality of the socio-scientific moral and material worldview of the unique groundwork of consilience of unity of knowledge. The result then is its abstracto-empirical sustained application in the world-system of 'everything'. Such a scholarly objective and its phenomenological abstracto-empirical study cannot be found in the field of *Shari'ah* as jurisprudence with its limited humanly innovative scope in *fiqh* and *fatawa*, meaning juristic interpretation and opinion, respectively.

We now commence this intellectual journey from theory to formalism to applications of *Tawhidi* methodological worldview. This study is carried out by the derivation and modelling of the most foundational supercardinal ontological premise of what it means by *Tawhid* in terms of its dynamics in the world-system and its sub-systemic multiverses. The primal ontological law of *Tawhid* is studied in its relationship with the unity of knowledge and unity of the knowledge-induced world-system.

The same methodological worldview applies as well as to 'de-knowledge'-induced dichotomy of the contrasting dualistic world-system and all that this has. The emergent path of the most original and contributory work in the world of learning presented in this work is thereby of a seriously mathematical, rigorous and analytical socio-scientific nature of the theory of 'everything'. It is governed by the *Tawhidi* methodological worldview as law by its model of *Tawhidi* String Relation (TSR).

This work and its erudition resemble the content of the book entitled *Relativity, the Special and the General Theory* by Albert Einstein (trans. R. Lawson, 1954). Yet by its originality of derivation strictly from the *Qur'an*, the present work is of a distinctly original nature. It confronts other theories of 'everything' by its subtle façade as contradistinction to the rationalist mind of space–time concept. The rationalist reasoning is thoroughly replaced by *Qur'anic* logical formalism in knowledge, space and time dimensions. In this regard, the whole complex system of events is induced by unity of knowledge.

In the same way, the primacy of *Tawhid* as Law is formalized analytically in this book to replace the narrow and constricted reasoning, erudition and domain of *Shari'ah* approach to the study of socio-scientific issues. In the uncompromising sense of universality and uniqueness of *Tawhid* as law of 'everything' with its distinctive features, the *Tawhidi* methodology represented as theory of TSR replaces both occidental rationalism and *Shari'ah* approach. The phenomenological understanding of methodology combines the primal ontological worldview of unity of knowledge with the imminent epistemology to construct the functional ontology and episteme in the ever-advancing evolutionary learning processes. Thereby, methodology comprises the formalism underlying continuous nexus of normative and positivistic worldviews into an organically unified one.

Reasoning and analysis thereby emanate from the embedded premise of the *Tawhidi* perspective of philosophy of science (Blaug 1993, Pheby 1988, Fox 1997). Such origination of reasoning and structure in logical formalism leads into the phenomenology and modulation of analysis. The consequential holism here is referred to as abstracto-empirical dimension of *Tawhidi* methodological worldview. Such an organically unified methodological worldview that is central to the *Qur'anic* organically unified universe, and its details was nonetheless not practised by Islamic thinkers by and large (see here the quote from Nusseibeh 2017). For instance, Ibn Taiymiyyah pronounced the baseless remark 'that Islam has no philosophers'. On the other hand, not only did Avicenna free himself from preset systems and styles, he also pursued reason until he arrived at its limits. The wholly peripatetic approach was also the exclusively speculative devotional methodology of Ghazali. To the present day, the singularly important theme of methodology that would apply universally to a theory of 'everything' in the individual (household) and socio-scientific domain has remained foreign to Muslim scholars (Al-Faruqi 1982a, 1982b; Al-Attas narrated by Daud 1998; Nasr 1978; Bakar 1991, 2014). All the contemporary ink of Islamicization and Gnosticism could not yield *Tawhidi* and thereby *Qur'anic* methodology in any substantive shape, form and schema. Consequently, the truly socio-scientific advancement receded into oblivion. In this respect, the project of Islamicization of knowledge remained ineffective. This observation was also made by Rahman (1988).

This book takes the viewpoint of logical formalism that if the *shari'ah* was to be enforced as the Islamic law, then the question is what then is the status of *Tawhid* as the ontological law of 'everything'? It is illogical that both of these premises would compete as the law and that the *Shari'ah* manifests *Tawhid* as law. The universe and the Prophet Muhammad and the conscious history of all the messengers of Allah were given the one law that ideally represents the totality of the *Qur'an*. The law was perfected and explained by the *sunnah* and the discourse of the learned (*ulul-amr*) based strictly on the *Qur'an*—not on Muslim sects (*madhabs*) and humanly interpreted reasoning in the first place.[2] It is regrettable that today

---

[2]*Qur'an* (69: 44-47): "And if he (Muhammad) had forged a false saying concerning Us (Allah), We surely should have seized him by his right hand (or with power and might), And then certainly should have cut off his life artery, and none of you could withhold Us from (punishing) him".

Muslims by and large neither invoke learning by discourse around *Tawhid* as the law and the world-system. The Muslim clergies do not devote to the study by engagement of the Islamic knowledge and practices arising from the penetrating depth of *Tawhid* and the world-system towards exciting Muslim erudition.

This work has advanced a step further than the earlier ones by this author on the role of knowledge induction in the attenuating multivariate system and the resulting empirical interpretations. This work has deconstructed knowledge into its interior component of belief. Thus, a good deal of analytical sections deals with the functioning of the belief-induced (denoted by $\{\varepsilon\}$) knowledge parameter in the form, $\{\theta(\varepsilon)\}$. Despite this, belief is treated as an inner dynamic force, not as an empirical effect as by knowledge parameter. Therefore, in this work, conceptual implications of belief-centred knowledge induction predominate in the methodological derivation revolving around *Tawhid* as law.[3]

Jakarta, Indonesia   Masudul Alam Choudhury

References

Al-Faruqi, I. R. (1982a). *Tawhid: its implications for thought and life*. Herndon, VA: International Institute of Islamic Thought.
Al-Faruqi, I. R. (1982b). *Islamization of knowledge: general principles and workplan*. Herndon, VA: International Institute of Islamic Thought.
Al-Shaykh al-Saduk (2009). In J. A. Morrow, A. R. Rizvi, L. A. Vittor, & B. Castleton (Eds.), *Kitab al-Tawhid, The Savor Foundation*, Paradstesh (pp. 177–180; 255–264; 265–280). Also see in this, Morrow, J. A., & Vittor, L. A. Tawhid in theological mode (pp. 35–49).
Bakar, O. (1991). *Tawhid and science, essays on the history and philosophy of Islamic science*. Kuala Lumpur, Malaysia: Secretariat for Islamic Philosophy and Science.
Bakar, O. (2014). *Islamic civilisation and the modern world*. Darassalam, Brunei: University of Brunei Darassalam Press.
Blaug, M. (1993). *The methodology of economics*. Cambridge, England: Cambridge University Press.
Daud, W. M. N. W. (1998). Metaphysical worldview. In *The educational philosophy and practice of Syed Muhammad Naquib Al-Attas, an exposition of the original concept of Islamization* (pp. 33–68). Kuala Lumpur, Malaysia: International Institute of Islamic Thought and Civilization.
Fox, G. (1997). *Reason and reality in the methodologies of economics*. Cheltenham, UK: Edward Elgar.
Lucaks, J. (1968). *Historical consciousness*. New York, NY: Harper & Row Publishers.
Maritain, J. (1973). *On the philosophy of history*, J. W. Evans (Ed.). Clifton, NJ: Augustus M. Kelley Publishers.
Nasr, S. H. (1978). *An introduction to Islamic cosmological doctrines*. Boulder, CO, USA: Shambhala.

---

[3] *Qur'an* (41:14): The desert Arabs say, "We believe." Say, "Ye have no faith; but ye (only) say, 'We have submitted our wills to Allah,' For not yet has Faith entered your hearts. But if ye obey Allah and His Messenger, He will not belittle aught of your deeds: for Allah is Oft-Forgiving, Most Merciful".

Nusseibeh, S. (2017). The nature of truth. In *The theory of reason in Islam* (pp. 167–168). Stanford, CA: Stanford University Press.

Pheby, J. (1988). *Methodology and economics, a critical introduction.* London, England: Macmillan.

Rahman, R. (1988). Islamization of Knowledge: A Response. *American Journal of Islamic Social Sciences, 5*(1).

Acknowledgements

Never-ending thanks are to Allah Almighty. He enabled a group of highly devoted intellectuals in Indonesia to commit them, firstly, in establishing the Idea of organizing the true foundation of the *Qur'anic* methodological worldview in the study of Islamic economics and finance. Included in such a study, there lies the foundational socio-scientific inquiry in its generality and particulars of a theory of 'everything'. These details of the learning world-system together comprise the theory of 'everything' in reference to the supercardinal worldview of the *Qur'an*. That is *Tawhid*, the Oneness of Allah as law and the role of the Prophet (*sunnah*) in conveying this irrevocable truth to 'everything'. Thereby, the upholding of the great *Tawhidi* methodological worldview by a group of intellectuals and senior students in Indonesia, followed by a systematizing of its erudition in the Faculty of Economics, Trisakti University, Jakarta, Indonesia, was a historical feat in contemporary Islamic studies covered in its wide perspective. Through this institutional achievement, an increasing number of students have pursued their graduate studies in the field of Islamic economics and finance. Many doctoral students are today seeking their postgraduate research pursuits in the application of the methodology of *Tawhidi* worldview to diversely many topics and problems. Many intellectuals in Indonesia and abroad have been instrumental in launching scholarly activities invoking the theory and application of *Tawhidi* methodological worldview.

In accomplishing such feats for the pleasure of Allah and the Prophet Muhammad in making the *Qur'an* and *sunnah* functional in world-system studies in the light of *Tawhidi* methodology, I highly acknowledge the contribution of my colleague, late Prof. Dr. Sofyan Syafri Harahap. His epistemological learning and organizational capability in accountancy enabled realizing the Postgraduate Program in Islamic Economics and Finance (IEF) in the Faculty of Economics, Trisakti University. I thank all faculty members of economics and management faculties in contributing to this great realization. Indeed, after a historical period of time in Islamic knowledge, IEF can be claimed to be the unique birth of the true foundation of *Qur'anic* methodology in Islamic economics, finance and socio-scientific fields. This reconstruction of Islamic knowledge is certainly different and in many cases distinct from the study of Islamic Economics and Finance within the pursuit of mainstream western ideas and the barren understanding of *shari'ah*, *fiqh*, *fatawa* in Islamic jurisprudence that has been constrained to earthly affairs alone (*muamalat*).

In the international context of intellectual pursuit, I have gained by the use of the famous Robarts Library in library research towards preparing this manuscript. In this regard, I thank the Social Economy Center of Ontario Institute for Studies in Education, University of Toronto, where I regularly spend every summer as Visiting Professor. I also thank various international forums where I have been able to present the emergent theory of *Tawhidi* methodological worldview in invited keynote lectures. In most recent times, these academic institutions were Seoul National University, Asia Center (2018); Department of *Shari'ah* and Economics (2016–2018), University of Malaya; SOACIS, University of Brunei Darussalam (2017); IKAM Research in Islamic Economics, University of Istanbul (2018); Minhaj University Lahore (2017); Istanbul Sabahattin Zaim University (2016–2017); Institute of Agriculture and Resource Economics, Faisalabad University, Pakistan (2016); Institute of Islamic Banking and Finance, International Islamic University Malaysia (2014); and several invited keynote lectures in Government Departments in Indonesia, Istanbul, and other global forums.

My gratitude is to the Department of Higher Education, Government of Indonesia, in supporting IEF all along in Trisakti University. In maintaining this collegial relationship, various Rectors of Trisakti University, Prof. Dr. Yuswar Basri, Director of IEF; Prof. Thoby Mutia retired Rector of Trisakti University; and Dr. Tatik Mariyanti, Secretary of IEF have played significant roles.

Thank you all.

Prof. Dr. Masudul Alam Choudhury

Contents

Part II Selected Abstracto-Empirical Applications of TSR

Prelude: Explanation of Selected Technical Terms

Abstracto-empirical

Organically unified embedding of abstraction with the empirical application of unity of knowledge based on the *Tawhidi* methodological worldview.

Being and becoming of reality

Things in their non-physical and physical forms exist (being) through a process of causality (becoming). Thus, all things and ideas are explained in and by the process of knowing by learning.

Consciously evolutionary learning nature of the world-system

The knowledge-induced processes of conscious learning are explained by evolutionary knowledge induction of the world-system over the conscious reality of history.

Conscious multiverse

The theory of 'everything' comprises the entirety between the heavens and the earth and all that lie over and under the earth. Such entirety exists by knowledge by learning and in knowledge-induced space and time. The continuous impress of unity of knowledge in learning thus forms the consciousness of history. History is thereby a conscious process of evolutionary learning.

Endogenous inter-causality

Evolutionary learning process in unity of knowledge forms a continuous inter-variable organic relationship in accordance with the dynamics of inter-causality. Such is the pervasive nature of the system of relations that evaluates the wellbeing function as objective criterion in the selected variables (*maslaha* function).

Episteme

This is the term used by Michele Foucault in his explanation of the architecture of knowledge as a continuous process of complete sequences of learning. Foucault writes: 'By *episteme* we mean … the total set of relations that unite, at a given period, the discursive practices that give rise to epistemological figures, sciences, and possibly formalized systems ... The episteme is not a form of knowledge (*connaissance*) or type of rationality which, crossing the boundaries of the most varied sciences, manifests the sovereign unity of a subject, a spirit, or a period; it is the totality of relations that can be discovered, for a given period, between the sciences when one analyses them at the level of discursive regularities'.

Epistemology
This term means the theory of knowledge in respect of the reasoning underlying the derivation of knowledge and its application towards structuring the functional ontology of explaining critical realism of existence of things pertaining to the reasoning.

Evolutionary convergence
This feature of evolutionary learning paths conveys a property of incomplete convergence and thereby of non-steady-state evolution of equilibriums by onto-logical and epistemological application of *Tawhidi* unity of knowledge in evolutionary learning. Thereby, steady-state equilibriums and optimality cannot logically exist in the emergent complex processes.

Evolutionary equilibriums
These are analytically derived in *Tawhidi* methodology of evolutionary learning worldview as non-steady-state equilibriums along the evolutionary learning path of temporary equilibriums.

Historical consciousness
History is described by paths of evolutionary learning of cause and effects of truth and falsehood. Consciousness thereby marks all events along historical continuity in the contest between truth and falsehood.

Meta-science
This comprises the supra-scientific inquiry using challenging new approaches to study all phenomena spanning systems in the heavens and the earth. The unique method-ology leading to the method used in the case of *Tawhidi* methodological worldview is the overarching complementary symbiosis of diverse systems in order to create a holistic approach to the study of such world-systems with universal and unique methodological inquiry. Yet problems under study will remain variously different.

Methodological worldview
This comprises all three in a continuous terrain of relationship. The interrelated sequences of theoretical derivation are primal ontological of *Tawhid* as Law, fol-lowed by *Tawhidi* epistemology, followed by phenomenology, and thereafter continuing with sustainability of these interactive and integrative evolutionary (IIE) learning parts always.

The meaning of 'worldview' in this book needs to be understood. This profound meaning is explicated in the light of *Tawhid* as the ontological law of 'everything'. The precept of *Tawhid* as the 'worldview' of unity of knowledge is explained within the singular most primal ontology. This is of the monotheistic oneness and its primal role in reasoning, socio-scientific formalism and the vastest field of applications in the generality and details of the world-systems. In the context of all these profoundest elements of belief, knowledge and thought, the term 'worldview' in this book applies to the central precept of divine oneness and how it is reflected in the manifest aspect of unity of knowledge as the *Qur'an* explains in terms of the extant of symbiotic pairing of the universe in all its details and in its generalized structure. It is this primal ontology of organic pairing (inter-causality) between all things that acquires equivalently the principles of complementarities, participation and thereby unity of knowledge (consilience). By its vastest extant of applications and explanatory power, this principle of pairing brings out the universally manifest meaning of *Tawhid* as the primal ontology of unity of knowledge through its methodological formalism and applications. They combine to establish the meaning of the 'worldview'. The worldview is thus inseparable from the underlying methodology of the organically paired meaning of divine unity and the universe as declared in the *Qur'an* (36:36).

Methodology and method do not bear the same meaning
The field of methodology comprises the progressive relationship in sustained continuity between, namely primal ontology, epistemology, phenomenology and sustainability. Methodology presents the unique and universal worldview of *Tawhid* as law premised in unity of knowledge with its properties of IIE-learning. On the other hand, method denotes a mechanism of applying the formal logic underlying the problem-solving in many ways. In the context of *Tawhidi* methodological worldview, the selected method of diversity must arise from, reflect and enable that methodology. Thereby, all analysis follows along lines of the results attained by the appropriate corresponding methods used.

Organic unity of knowledge (also organic interrelations, organic complementary between 'everything'), organic oneness as consilience of unity of knowledge
Organic unity of knowledge depicts in methodological ways the active properties of interaction, integration and evolutionary learning across historistic consciousness of sustainability. Thereby, morality and ethics in the central methodological stance mean continuous adherence to these values in respect of unity of knowledge between the good things of life while avoiding the bad choices that oppose organic unity of knowledge to establish pervasive complementarities (also participation = unification).

Pervasive and continuous complementarities
This terminology implies the conception and manifestation of pervasive organic unity of knowledge between the good things of life at the forbidding of the contrary kinds. These choices are explained by the *Tawhidi* law in respect of the principle of pervasive complementarities as unity of knowledge characterizing the totality of events governed across historical consciousness.

Physicalism and non-physicalism
These two aspects of meta-scientific inquiry include abstraction as conception of worldview and its application in the nature, order and scheme of 'everything'.

These two domains of inquiry are conjoint in the meaning of episteme in socio-scientific study.

Primal ontology

Tawhid in reference to unity of knowledge in the *Qur'an* is explained by the medium of Prophetic tradition (*sunnah*) and discourse of the learned ones (*ulul-amr*). In this way, the *Qur'an* and *sunnah* together form the primal ontology of the existence of Allah and the manifestation of the *Tawhidi* law in the order of 'everything'.

Phenomenology

This term is used to explain the theory of consciousness that embeds the total reality of being and becoming of phenomena. The study of phenomenology also assumes its application in applied mechanism the formalism and empiricism arising from the *Tawhidi* methodology of unity of knowledge.

Qur'anic ontological origin

This is the primal divine command of 'be and it is' (*kun fa-yakoon*) in the *Qur'an*. Its command assumes the totality of *Tawhid* as law and as corporeal law of the experiential universe and its details in 'everything'.

Supercardinality

This term signifies the incommensurable measure of *Qur'anic* domain of knowledge (Ω). It is analytically explained by the abstraction of mathematical topology (non-dimensional mathematical function) that establishes the following continuous functionals: (i) $S \subset \Omega$ by way of the reversible relational functional, $\Omega \leftrightarrow S$. (ii) Likewise, there exist the functionals, $S \leftrightarrow X$, and thus, $\Omega \leftrightarrow S \leftrightarrow X$. (iii) Therefore, the example of the organically unified domains of a priori and a posteriori multi-causal reversible relations are defined by knowledge flows according to unity of knowledge as interrelating organisms. The universal totality is mapped by the understanding and application of the *sunnah* as ontological mapping of the supercardinal domain of the divine law (*sunnat Allah = Tawhid*). Hence, a relational equivalence is established between the supercardinal domain of *sunnat Allah* through the medium of *sunnah* and the experimental world-system. All functions form interrelations. Such interrelations are inter-convertible by reversibility of knowledge production and its continuity involving simply the corporeal function and extension of the reading, understanding and applying of the monotheistic law (unity of knowledge) in the order of world-system in all its shapes and forms. This means extendibility across systems and their organic interrelations, meaning complementary multi-causal reversible relations. The property of multi-causal reversibility by the organic interrelations is that of continuity in knowledge, space and time.

Tawhidi String Relation (TSR)

This is an alternative terminology assigned to the system-oriented and process-driven outlook of the total delineation of the *Tawhidi* methodological worldview. It comprehends the holism of the dynamic relations in universal totality.

The experiential domain of *Tawhid* and the world-system comprises primal ontology of *Tawhid* in the *Qur'an*, the epistemological emanation of unity of knowledge as the foundational principle of unity as of the unified interrelations between *Tawhid* and the world-system and phenomenology as the study of moral consciousness that is embedded by *Tawhidi* unity of knowledge in the scheme and explanation of 'everything'. TSR is thereafter continued in sustainability across knowledge, space and time.

It is critical to understand what the term *Tawhid* means in the *Qur'anic* sense of monotheistic oneness of Allah and the generality and details of the world-system. In the *Qur'an*, the command of Allah at the infinitesimal moment of creation was *Kun fa-Yakoon*, meaning the divine command to Creation, 'be and it was'. At this very moment of creation, Allah by His command ordered the precept of *Tawhid* as divine oneness to be in two functional parts. They are not separable. Rather, they are intertwined in the order of functional relations between belief on the divine attributes (*sifat*), knowledge and the knowledge-induced world-system spanning over time. The nature of the first part of *Tawhid* is as the saying of the Prophet Muhammad declares: Allah held ninety-nine parts of his Mercy with Him to be bestowed at the Great Event of the Hereafter. The second one part Allah bestowed in the experiential world-system fully now and here. It is this one part that cor-poreality splendours on by its divinely ordained knowledge to the world-system. The first part is hidden in divine Mercy (*sifat*). But its human belief component affects the evidential world-system in subtle ways not precisely known. This second part embodies the signs of Allah (*Ayath Allah*). Signs of Allah are fully rendered to the functioning of the primal ontology (*haqq al-yaqin*), to knowledge formation (*ilm al-yaqin*), and finally to observation and creative investigation (*ayn al-yaqin*) across historical consciousness. It is this second part that belongs to knowledge functionally defined by the hidden belief in divine attributes (*sifat*). The first ninety-nine parts are metaphysical in nature. The second one part of God's Mercy is evident (ontic). We study in this work the *Tawhid* supplication of evidential (ontic) knowledge in its organically paired relations with the world-system in the extant of its sustainability over time.

Theory of 'everything'
The concept of 'everything' bears the meaning of universality and uniqueness of the generality and particulars of the world-system. The *Qur'an* refers to such a holistic domain as *a'lameen*. The theory of 'everything' carries with it the universal and unique methodological consequence of *Tawhidi* law as divine oneness. The premise of *Tawhid* as unity of knowledge is explicated in terms of its relationship with the world-system and the hereafter in generality and details. The theory of 'everything' premised in the primal *Tawhidi* ontology represents a formal and orderly body of socio-scientific knowledge derived from the *Qur'an* and *sunnah*. Its one of many other possible formal orientations is mathematical. Yet the mathematical approach here is beyond being a mechanistic tool. It is an explanatory and precise language of search, discovery and unravelling.

Unique and universal way

The methodology and meaningful overarching comprehension of *Tawhid* as the *Qur'anic* law are not to be found anywhere else. *Tawhid* as law is thereby for all and 'everything' for global learning and application. This is the attribute of corporeal law of *Tawhid* that is different from metaphysics. The latter inquiry does not bear any explainable and analytical methodology for conception, application and sustainability.

Unity of knowledge

The *Qur'anic* meaning of *Tawhid* is both transcendental in terms of the attributes of Allah, and it is corporeal in terms of its conception as methodology and its application that brings out the expatiation of monotheistic oneness in respect of the organic unity of knowledge in 'everything'. The distinct explanation of such participative unity of organism is explicated by the principle of pervasive complementarities between the good things of life at the rejection of the bad things of life that remain contrary to organismic unity of knowledge. The later kinds result in methodological individualism, independence and competition. Morality and ethics in the context of *Tawhidi* unity of knowledge remain benign in this contrary worldview.

Brief outline of the rigorous content of this book

This is a rare scholarly book in the principles of Islamic socio-scientific methodological worldview. The project based on the strict monotheism of the Oneness of Allah in the perspective of the *Qur'an* is yet an unrealized one in Muslim erudition in the light of its methodological worldview. The principal foundation of this law called *Tawhid* as the unravelled law of monotheism lends itself to every element of critical inquiry as the true *Qur'anic* law. The corporeal nature of such revealed law in cognizant reality with its ultimate extension in details of socio-scientific explanations of things forms the universal and unique worldview. It embodies its universal and unique methodology that explains and establishes the analytical nature of the moral and material details that are embedded in what is termed as the socio-scientific 'everything'. Thus, this book is the rare and scholarly work in the area of the ultimate theory of 'everything'. The study undertaken is thereby a boldly analytical one using advanced specialized fields of philosophy of science and advanced mathematics. These approaches generate the conceptual and formal modelling for doing imminent empirical work pertaining to the methodology of *Tawhid* as the primal law of oneness expressed as unity of knowledge. The conception and application of the precept of unity of knowledge in *Tawhid* as law with its exegesis in the *Qur'an* identify the methodological nature of *Tawhid* as law. The unravelling of the *Tawhidi* law of monotheistic oneness in its corporeal explanation of the nature of 'everything' is explained by relational organism as complementarities between the recommended choices mentioned in the *Qur'an* and by its exegesis. Such choices and symbiotic organism of participatory oneness are explained by complex and nonlinear mathematical formalism intra-systems and inter-systems.

The socio-scientific investigation is a bold and meaningful exercise in the quest for the theory of 'everything' that is embodied in *Tawhid* as primal law. Such an axiomatic study of the ultimate truth premise takes us into critical examination of the Muslim competing viewpoint of *shari'ah* as law. The study of the *Qur'an* and the analytical study of *Tawhid* as primal law of unity of knowledge in 'everything' lead into a reasoned and exegetic rejection of *shari'ah* as law. Thus, the arguments in this respect of the primacy of *Tawhid* lead us to keep the *shari'ah* and its various manifestations at bay within human concocted innovations contrary to the substantively original and complete nature of *Tawhid* as law.

The strictest abidance of this law with unity of knowledge in the extensively systemic inquiry causes us to view the consequential organic unity between things by their interrelations. These are sustained by what we refer to as inter-variable circular causality. The resulting model of embedded moral and material values and, thereby, the abstracto-empirical formalism is called the wellbeing objective criterion (*maslaha*). This formalism is derived from *Tawhidi* methodology of unity of knowledge by a critical rejection of *shari'ah*.

Contrary to *Tawhid* as the primal law of 'everything', *shari'ah* is shown to be methodologically benign in the light of the *Qur'anic* extensive exegesis of the symbiotic organic relationship of unity by participation and causality between entities and systems of 'everything'. The *Qur'an* generalizes these as all that span the heavens and the earth and all that lie between the heavens and the earth. Indeed, this entirety overarches below and above the vastest systems.

The partial equivalence between *Tawhid* as the super-encompassing law and *maqasid as-shari'ah* (purpose and objective of *shari'ah*) is found where there is commonality of the latter to *Tawhidi* law in the *Qur'an*. The extension of such derivations by the use of exegesis and *tawil* (extended interpretations) is possible only in respect of basing these on the *Qur'an* fully and then extending the interpretation to the body of *maqasid as-shari'ah* that is common to the *Tawhidi* law and its interpretive extension. The implication of this method of deriving a *maqasid* rule and its *Tawhidi* extension is that the worldly rule (*ahkam*) is derived not from *maqasid as-shari'ah*. Rather, the *maqasid as-shari'ah* refers always to the *Tawhidi* law for authenticity. Then, only the interpreted rule by the *Tawhidi* law is applied to the generality and details of the world-system in respect of the diverse issues and problems under study.

In the derivation of the formal model of *Tawhidi* unity of knowledge as participative organic interrelations between multivariate wellbeing functions (*maslaha*), strict abidance is maintained to the extensive exegetic meaning of precepts in the *Qur'an* and *sunnah*. The derivation of the entire formal model of *Tawhidi* unity of knowledge results in a consistent set of properties that abide continuously in the sustainability of knowledge and its induction of space and time dimensions. The properties of socio-scientific philosophy of science are of sequencing primal ontology, epistemology and phenomenology in overarching stages across continuums of sustainability defined by knowledge, space and time coordinates of all events. The events in their continuous occurrence by knowledge induction are caused by Interaction between entities represented by multivariables.

Interactions yield integration as consensus formed of interaction. Thereby, interaction and integration sequentially yield to continuous evolutionary learning processes in the knowledge, space and time dimensions of conscious historicism. Thus, the study of consciousness is realized in terms of the wellbeing evaluation, meaning estimation of nonlinear model with coefficients, subject to inter-variable circular causation. Such statistical evaluations explain the degrees of unity of organic interrelations between moral and material entities.

The emergent sustainability shown as continuity of evolutionary learning events in unity of knowledge across the knowledge, space and time dimensions is referred to as history. History is thereby marked by sustainable evolutionary learning events as coordinates. The resulting consequences are of reconstruction and continuity of heightened consciousness in the scale of learning in unity of knowledge. This attribute thereby marks the surest proof of the embodied effects and prevalence of *Tawhid* as law everywhere and in 'everything'. The subtle property of evolutionary learning in unity of knowledge across consciousness of history causes the advance from lower to higher degrees of attaining unity of knowledge. The consequential analytics defy the relevance of optimization at any event point of the experiential world-system.

Therefore, the relevance of sustained simulation over simulacra of possibilities results only in evolutionary convergences of equilibriums. Steady-state equilibriums are non-existent in the experiential world-system of evolutionary learning and continuous reconstruction towards ever heightened levels of consciousness of *Tawhid* and its implications.

This work shows the nature of learning institutions, organizational behaviour and dynamic preferences, and the whole gamut of variables in economics, finance, science and society to be characterized by the same kind of evolutionary learning properties across their conscious history of experiences. Nonetheless, the entire body of mainstream socio-scientific theory and application is derivable from the same *Tawhidi* methodological worldview either by assuming benignity of the episteme of unity of knowledge or by dialectical materialism.

The events continuously occurring along historical consciousness across knowledge, space and time dimensions thus undergo the following experiences. All these analytics are rigorously and elaborately explained in this book in the light of *Tawhidi* methodological worldview. This is a reality that transcends the benign methodological incompleteness nature of *shari'ah* in all its aspects. Although the details are elaborately and rigorously expanded in this book, we summarize the nature of the *Tawhidi* methodological formalism in the following figure. This schema conveys the pervasive experience of every continuous event point across historical consciousness by virtue of the induction of unity of knowledge in all such experiences of 'everything'. All events are complementary across intra-systems and inter-systems in the multi-world-systems in their generality and details. This is the derived consequence of participative organic unity of relations, positive or negative, as in and between truth and falsehood, respectively, and as pronounced by the *Tawhidi* law of 'everything'.

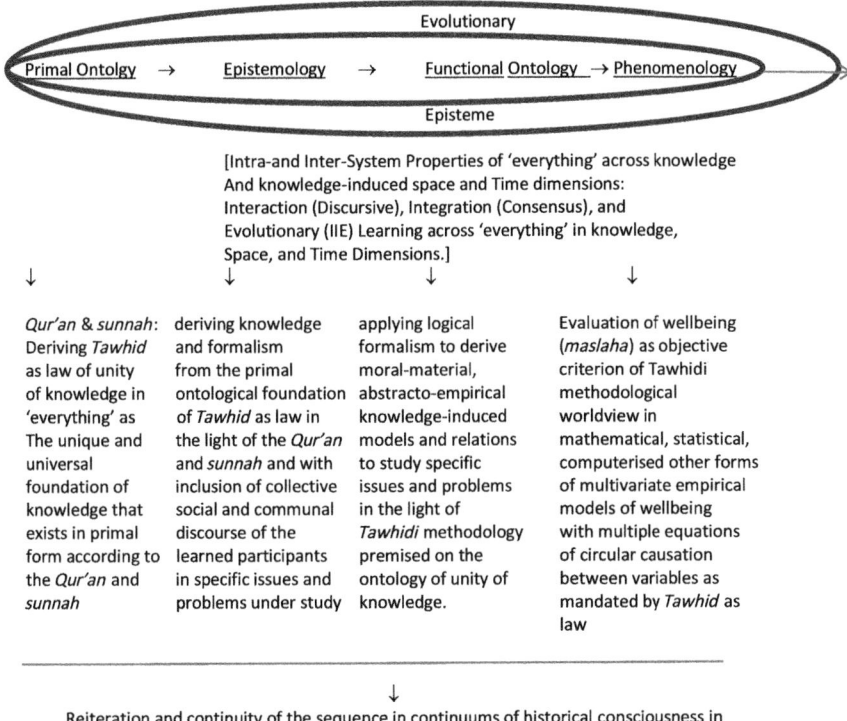

Qur'an & *sunnah*: Deriving *Tawhid* as law of unity of knowledge in 'everything' as The unique and universal foundation of knowledge that exists in primal form according to the *Qur'an* and *sunnah*	deriving knowledge and formalism from the primal ontological foundation of *Tawhid* as law in the light of the *Qur'an* and *sunnah* and with inclusion of collective social and communal discourse of the learned participants in specific issues and problems under study	applying logical formalism to derive moral-material, abstracto-empirical knowledge-induced models and relations to study specific issues and problems in the light of *Tawhidi* methodology premised on the ontology of unity of knowledge.	Evaluation of wellbeing (*maslaha*) as objective criterion of Tawhidi methodological worldview in mathematical, statistical, computerised other forms of multivariate empirical models of wellbeing with multiple equations of circular causation between variables as mandated by *Tawhid* as law

---

↓

Reiteration and continuity of the sequence in continuums of historical consciousness in
knowledge, and knowledge-induced space and time dimensions across complementary
intra-systems and inter-systems of multivariate world-systems: emergence of the
property of completely endogenous inter-variable circular causation relations

↓

SUSTAINABILITY AS CONTINUITY OF TAWHIDI UNITY OF KNOWLEDGE
IN MORAL-MATERIAL EMBEDDING

Unique and universal schema of *Tawhidi* methodological worldview of unity of knowledge in
'everything'

Explaining the transcendental and corporeal domains of *Tawhid* as law revealed on to the world-system

Tawhid as monotheistic oneness of Allah conveys its totality in two parts; yet each is linked with the other, working out in relation to the world-system of 'everything' in specific ways. *Tawhid* as the law of divine attributes of monotheistic oneness of Allah remains as the ultimate truth of reality. But such a case of incommensurable view of attributes is not corporeal in any ways. Yet they are cardinal articles of the Islamic faith arising from the *Qur'an*. We denote this part of the divine law in truth of unity of knowledge by the abstraction of the symbol $\{\varepsilon\}$. The second part of *Tawhid* as the supreme law is its universal corporeal functioning in relation to the generality and particularity of the world-system of 'everything'. It is this part of the *Tawhidi* law that enters inquiry and extensively possible substantiation by way of the *sunnah* and learned discourse (*ijtihad*). *Sunnah* comprises lessons of Prophet Muhammad's guidance as an ontological mapping of the *Qur'an* into the abstract and experiential cognizance of the unified world-system or otherwise. The commensurable measure of *Tawhid* as law applied to the abstraction and corporeality is denoted by the symbol 'θ'. The belief part embedded in the knowledge-induced part of *Tawhid* as law and its functioning as abstracto-applied measure of explanation in 'everything' is symbolized as $\{\theta(\varepsilon)\}$ in this work. Because of the incommensurable nature of $\{\varepsilon\}$, the total knowledge-induced 'everything' is simply denoted by consciously evolving events in the knowledge, space and time universe, $\{\theta, \mathbf{x}(\theta), t(\theta)\}$.

The ascription of the permanent presence of *Tawhid* as primal ontological law in 'everything' is uniquely caused by the principle of unity of knowledge. This is revealed in 'everything' by the pervasive principle of complementarity as unity of being and becoming. The same rule applies to accepting the good and eschewing the bad. This unique and universal principle is contrary to the postulate of marginal substitution (or trade-off) in mainstream economic thinking including the *shari'ah* allowance for this postulate in present-days' Muslim thought. The allowance is shown in so-called Islamic economics, finance, science and society. This case is the result of the axiom of economic rationality and the dialectical nature of competition due to methodological individualism that pervades all of mainstream socio-scientific thought. Such postulates are ingrained in Muslim thought as well due to the absence of a precise methodology in *shari'ah* such as of unity of knowledge conveying the *Qur'anic* monotheistic worldview of organic complementarities.

This book as the first ever of its kind in analytical disposition of the great meaning, methodology and application of *Tawhid* as Law contra *shari'ah* in all its forms brings out very many subtle details. The future generation of polymaths will recess deeper into these rich though intricate areas of search and discovery. One of the emergent formal implications concerning endogeneity and exogeneity of inter-entity relations between primal ontology and evolutionary learning processes in knowledge, space and time universe of 'everything' is explained as follow in a simplified way:

Let 'θ' be an ontologically derived knowledge-flow of *Tawhidi* unity of knowledge in $(\Omega,S) = \Psi$ in the *Qur'an*. In any given evolutionary learning process, let '$\mathbf{x}(\theta)$' denote an event in the conscious world-system. The two-ways θ-induced relations are explained by (i) above-mentioned Process 1: $\Psi \rightarrow \theta \rightarrow a(\theta) \rightarrow$ evaluation $\rightarrow$ evolution to new $\{\theta\}$; (ii) Process 2 in continuity to Process 1 across continuums: recurrent recalling of $\Psi \rightarrow$ new $\{\theta\} \rightarrow$ repeat the process, etc. Ψ is therefore the only exogenously original ontology that creates the entire endogenous inter-entity relations in continuums of world-systems. The cumulative nature of the knowledge flows in the structure of the evolutionary learning universe from the *Tawhidi* beginning to the *Tawhidi* end forms the supercardinal valuation of the *Tawhidi* universe of 'everything'.

The figure shown above by its details in tersely mathematical form is expanded in this book. Several moral/ethical formalisms are formulated and explained. An extensive range of abstracto-empirical work with statistical and computerized applications of the same methodological model is presented in a comprehensive way to bring out the holistic orientation presented in the figure. These together form the high watermark of scholarly originality of the field of *Tawhid* as the universal and unique law. This induces the methodological worldview in 'everything' as being induced by the *Tawhidi* precept of unity of knowledge. Many thanks are to my doctoral graduates and colleagues who have contributed to the modelling and statistical evaluation of the emergent model of TSR in various real-world problems.

Tawhidi methodology premised on the holism of primal ontology, epistemology, functional ontology, phenomenology and continuity by sustainability inheres in both the non-physical and physical reality as explained in this book. This accomplishment and great contribution to global learning in the socio-scientific field in contrast to the constrained and questioned field of *shari'ah* make it rise above the occidental ontology of rationalism and empiricism that are benign of moral values. The intrinsic moral values have been forgotten in the sheer space–time structure of explanation in the entire socio-scientific field. Contrarily, *Tawhidi* methodological worldview strictly derived from the *Qur'an* raises all of socio-scientific inquiry to the centricity of knowledge and knowledge-induced space and time structure in 'everything'.

The special focus on specific world-system study is given to economics, finance, science and society. The bold *Tawhidi* heterodoxy of non-physicalist and physicalist study introduces original and creative exegeses of the *Qur'anic* verses in the scheme and order of new evolutionary episteme. The emergent formalism is uniquely governed by the primal ontology of monotheistic oneness by virtue of the *Tawhidi* precept of unity of knowledge and its endowed applications in non-physicalism.

An anecdotal introduction to *Tawhidi* methodological worldview
The *Qur'anic* chapter on Noah (Chapter 71) conveys a cardinal lesson of the divine command given to all prophets as supreme teachers calling humankind out of the darkness of falsehood into the light of truth. These are lessons that are also cast in the recurrent lives of nations of peoples. We narrate one of these lessons in the mythology of Canadian natives, who in remote history surrendered to the one true God but then became oblivious, yet again to return to God the Creator and the Merciful. So we learn how the indelible lessons of divine truth reflect the supreme nature of *Tawhid* as divine law of monotheism in historical consciousness. That is how the monotheistic call of *Tawhid* as divine oneness as law survives permanently in 'everything'.

In many verses of the Qur'an Allah has thus commanded:

At length, behold! there came Our command, and the fountains of the earth gushed forth! We said: 'Embark therein, of each kind two, male and female, and your family—except those against whom the word has already gone forth,—and the Believers'. but only a few believed with him. (11:40)

So the Ark floated with them on the waves (towering) like mountains, and Noah called out to his son, who had separated himself (from the rest): 'O my son! embark with us, and be not with the unbelievers!' (11:42)

The son replied: 'I will betake myself to some mountain: it will save me from the water'. Noah said: 'This day nothing can save, from the command of Allah, any but those on whom He hath mercy!' And the waves came between them, and the son was among those overwhelmed in the Flood. (11: 43)

Then the word went forth: 'O earth! Swallow up thy water, and O sky! Withhold (thy rain)!' and the water abated, and the matter was ended. The Ark rested on Mount Judi, and the word went forth: 'Away with those who do wrong!' (11:44)

The word came: 'O Noah! Come down (from the Ark) with peace from Us, and blessing on thee and on some of the peoples (who will spring) from those with thee: but (there will be other) peoples to whom We shall grant their pleasures (for a time), but in the end will a grievous penalty reach them from Us'. (11: 48)

Such are some of the stories of the unseen, which We have revealed unto thee: before this, neither thou nor thy people knew them. So persevere patiently: for the End is for those who are righteous. (11:49)

And O my people! let not my dissent (from you) cause you to sin, lest ye suffer a fate similar to that of the people of Noah or of Hud or of Salih, nor are the people of Lut far off from you! (11: 89)

The law of XALS to Canadian Natives

A similar story abides in the conscious history of the godly 'Nexus' among the Canadian natives. God to the natives was named XALS. XALS blessed the land of the natives in remote history with plenty of food, security and promise. But the natives then forgot the remembrance of God in the midst of their godly endowed extravagance. XALS then punished them. The great flood overwhelmed the disobeying natives of the remote time. The exception was a tribe of natives called the LÁUWELNEW. They took to the mountains where a new nation of god-obeying native people arose in remembrance of XALS law on earth.

The storyteller, Gabriel Underwood (Thursday, 8 November 2018)[4] writes: 'We have emerged from the water to LÁUWELNEW (place of refuge), and we have been cleaned. We are not who we were. We are a new people. And we shall be known as the WSANEC (the emerging people)'.

'Greatly did the people, our ancestors rejoice. They thanked the land; they thanked the creator. They also thanked the trees they anchored to. They wanted to thank the tree, so from then on they remembered the tree, the great arbutus'.

Thus, we see the worldly experience in realizing the blessed world-system out of the remembrance and practice of the *Tawhidi* law. Such is the experience of the evolutionary world-system of permanence in God's remembrance premised on the unity of knowledge (consilience) in 'everything'. The *Tawhidi* law was bestowed on all as 'everything' as the *Qur'an* affirms.

---

[4]Underwood, G. (Thursday, November 8): '*Of the Land—local indigenous voices*: The story of the great flood', *Nexus*. Visited network story 13 Nov. 2018: http://www.nexusnewspaper.com/2016/06/15/of-the-land-local-indigenous-voices-the-story-of-the-great-flood/.

A poem regarding God's blessing: contemplative knowledge and the world-system
The poem is by Kassam, J. (2018), 'The aura of music' in *Stories from Another Universe*, Strategic Book Publishing & Rights Co., Singapore. The poem brings out the true reality of the contrasting world-systems in the mould of the divine entirety.

Out from the world so benign,
A world so unfeeling,
A world filled with fear,
To a world so intense,
A world so meaningful,
A world filled with courage,
Hope and faith of a world not so far from ours,
A world of the unimaginable,
Filled with countless possibilities and potential!

List of Figures

List of Tables

Prologue

اللَّهُ لاَ إِلَهَ إِلاَّ هُوَ الْحَيُّ الْقَيُّومُ لاَ تَأْخُذُهُ سِنَةٌ وَلاَ نَوْمٌ لَهُ مَا فِي السَّمَاوَاتِ وَمَا فِي الأَرْضِ مَنْ ذَا الَّذِي يَشْفَعُ عِنْدَهُ إِلاَّ بِإِذْنِهِ يَعْلَمُ مَا بَيْنَ أَيْدِيهِمْ وَمَا خَلْفَهُمْ وَلاَ يُحِيطُونَ بِشَيْءٍ مِنْ عِلْمِهِ إِلاَّ بِمَا شَاءَ وَسِعَ كُرْسِيُّهُ السَّمَاوَاتِ وَالأَرْضَ وَلاَ يَئُودُهُ حِفْظُهُمَا وَهُوَ الْعَلِيُّ الْعَظِيمُ

Allah—there is no deity except Him, the Ever-Living, the Sustainer of [all] existence. Neither drowsiness overtakes Him nor sleep. To Him belongs whatever is in the heavens and whatever is on the earth. Who is it that can intercede with Him except by His permission? He knows what is [presently] before them and what will be after them, and they encompass not a thing of His knowledge except for what He wills. His Kursi (Throne) extends over the heavens and the earth, and their preservation tires Him not. And He is the Most High, the Most Great. (*Qur'an*, 2:255)

Ayath al-Kursi

Part I
Analytical Derivation of *Tawhidi* Methodological Worldview: Theory of *Tawhidi* String Relation (TSR)

Chapter 1
Introduction

Masudul Alam Choudhury

Abstract This chapter explains the expanded understanding of *Tawhid* as the law of 'everything' in the framework of the primal ontology and imminent episteme of unity of knowledge between the details of world-system. The derivation of such a wide meaning of organic unity of knowledge as the foundation of explaining the primal ontology of *Tawhid* is from the *Qur'an*. The resulting derivation that overarches its meaning across the heavens and the earth and what lies below and above is explained to be universally unique. *Tawhid* as law is thus argued to be distinctly separate from the rules of *shari'ah*. The rules of *shari'ah* are constrained to the earthly domain, and then too in a limited way based on human concocted innovation. Thus the substantive premise of *Tawhid* as the sole law of the *Qur'an* in contrariness to *shari'ah* is explained. Details continue throughout this work.

Introduction

Since its inception over eighty years past, a self-professed field of Islamic Economics, and now the so-called Islamic Finance appeared. But they failed to render any degree of intellection for global learning and intellectual revolution. The reach of Islamic Economics and Finance has all along followed the mind-set and applications of mainstream economics in its microeconomic and macroeconomic garb lock, stock, and barrels (Tag el-Din, 2013). While there is now an inner questioning of the theory and methodology of mainstream economics by heterodox economic theory (Lee & Lavoie, 2013; Lawson, 1997), trying to raise new criticism in the field of epistemic and economics (Shackle, 1972), the self-claimed field of Islamic economics awaits methodological foundation. This quest requires renewal of thought upon the *Qur'anic* ontological, epistemological, and phenomenological grounds. The emanating methodological inquiry is thereby carried in diversities of issues and problems with problem-solving approach across its theory and applications in world-systems, in 'everything'.

M. A. Choudhury (✉)
Faculty of Economics, Trisakti University, Jakarta, Indonesia
e-mail: masudc60@yahoo.ca

© Springer Nature Singapore Pte Ltd. 2019
M. A. Choudhury (ed.), *The* Tawhidi *Methodological Worldview*,
https://doi.org/10.1007/978-981-13-6585-0_1

The problematique of emptiness of Islamic scholarship in respect of its failure to identify the methodological groundwork in reference to the essentials of the *Qur'an*, the *sunnah*, and learned discourse has remained a failure since the times of the *mujtahids* (learned scholars). The only limits to learned investigation and discourse in theological methodology that were marked by and now have reached enervating dogmatism are the fields of *fiqh* (jurisprudence) and *fatawa* (religious opinions by the clergy). The combination of *fiqh* and *fatawa* on a theocratic approach to the study of 'everything' comprising the world-system gave rise to the humanly concocted innovations of the *shari'ah*, conjured as Islamic law. *Shari'ah* subsequently came to be identified with its purpose and objective in a theocratic sense, called *maqasid as-shari'ah* (Ashur, 2013; Attia, 2008). This legal theocracy too in recent times has degenerated into the terminology and practice of *shari'ah-compliance*. While such intrusion of *shari'ah* in the entire Muslim thought since the tenth-century of the age of Islamic scholasticism intruded the field of Islamic economics and finance, and all of socio-scientific thought, there now remains misconstrued ideas as to what is truly the Islamic law and methodological worldview in 'everything'. The intellectual dynamics devoid of *shari'ah* exist. No true invoking of the *Qur'an* in rigorous intellectual thinking remains alive.

A Critique of *Shari'ah* as Islamic Law

Shari'ah has a variegated history of its emanation and practice. It was made as if identical to *Qur'anic* law by Islamic scholastic scholars, such as Imam Ghazali, Ibn Taimiyyah, Imam Shatibi, Ibn Qayyim, and later on by Imam Shafei according to edicts pronounced by them. *Shari'ah* thus became a law imposed by sects (*madhabs*), rulers and dynasties to prevail over society at large: "Sharia law started being forced and imposed upon society from above. That is because in Islamic jurisprudence it is not the society that molds and fashions the law but it is the law that precedes and controls society instead." (https://dailyhistory.org/How_did_the_Sharia_Law_develop%3F; visited Feb. 3, 2018). Along with the imposition of *shari'ah* open intellectual discourse based on the *Qur'anic* law and the world-system withered away from discourse concerning 'everything' in socio-scientific order. Ibn Khaldun (Mahdi, 1964) remarked that, the *shari'ah* despite being a best law was never to be found to prevail in a sustained way. Over its long span of outer meanings upon Muslims, *shari'ah* went into disparate interpretations under the warring Umayyad and Abbasid dynasties. Although the early learned Islamic scholars focused the emergence of *shari'ah* on the *Qur'an* and the authentic teachings of Prophet Muhammad (*sunnah*), this guidance faded away over time. In recent times *shari'ah* is fully in the grips of arbitrary interpretations made by innovative *fiqh* and *fatawa* and in reference to the sayings of certain learned scholars of Islamic scholasticism and more of those in recent times. Such references today frame the areas of *shari'ah-compliance*.

All attempts in unifying the different schools of *shari'ah* interpretations and their application by standardization of details of Islamic law have failed (Djibril et al., 2017).

What Truly Is the Conception of Law and Justice?

All shades of the development of *shari'ah*, *fiqh* and *fatawa*, once these distanced away from strict abidance by the *Qur'an* and *sunnah*, was left to human concocted innovations. These became whimsical discourses. In respect of the *Qur'anic* definition, law and justice are established upon the belief and practice of the most irrevocable and universal law in 'everything' of good and true to mankind over the span of historical consciousness.

The answer to the question: 'What is Law and Justice?' (Hart, 1994) is answered in a unique and universal way by the epistemology of unity of knowledge in reference to the phenomenological model of the unified worldview in 'everything'. In this case, the moral and normative law and justice take up center stage in social contract. Subsequently, ethics and the unified nature of the world-system are derived and explained on the basis of the primordial moral law. Such a total perspective of the phenomenological model of unity of knowledge resting in primal ontology is a thoroughly analytical and inferential socio-scientific project. The *Qur'anic* law of *Tawhid* is this unique and universal worldview. It is conceptualized and applicable in 'everything' across historical consciousness.

Tawhid as Law Contra *Shari'ah* as Law

In reference to the primal ontological, epistemological, and phenomenological contexts of the law of *Tawhid* arising from the *Qur'an* and the *sunnah*, and passed over into learned discourse by reference to every issue over space and time, the *shari'ah* cannot be the Islamic law. There is no praise of the utmost order for any aspect of the terminology of *shari'ah* in the *Qur'an*. The be-all and end-all of the *Qur'an* is devoted to *Tawhid*. This embodies the fullness of the divine law and the purpose, objective, and conduct of creation. Thus in one of many verses the *Qur'an* (45:36) declares: "Then Praise be to Allah, Lord of the heavens and Lord of the earth,- Lord and Cherisher of all the Worlds!" *Tawhid* as *THE LAW* represents the purity (*Iqlas*) of the *Qur'an* including the *sunnah* in the light of Allah as Creator and Sustainer of 'everything'. The methodological worldview of this foundational and pure law in Islam for 'everything' is established by the principle of pervasive and continuous complementarities governed by *Tawhid* as law in terms of the primal ontology and episteme of unity of knowledge.

There is yet another disabling problem caused by holding the *shari'ah* as law. This is its failure to comprehend and extend to the generalized universal systemic law of *Tawhid*, unity of knowledge in and between 'everything' between the heavens and the earth, and all that is below the earth and above the earth. In the sense of the objective and purpose of the *shari'ah* (*maqasid as-shari'ah*) this limited aspect of the *shari'ah* has failed to establish and render the universal precept of *Tawhid* as an analytical methodology of the episteme of unity of knowledge in 'everything'. By examining the limited scope of the *shari'ah*, we find that, there is no episteme in it to extend the meaning of *maqasid* to encompass the meta-science of the heavens and the earth as an overarching complementary symbiosis. The *maslaha* concept as wellbeing function could not be conceptualized and applied as a holistic criterion to explain the organic interrelationship of the heavens and the earth, which otherwise it is. Yet this is how the divine holism has been constricted by *fiqh* and *fatawa* into sheer earthly affairs (*muamalat*).

Yet on such matter there is the thoughtful depth of Kant's writing (Kant, trans. Friedrich, 1949, p. 261) that should be upheld as the widest scope of the universal law: "Two things fill the mind with ever new and increasing awe and admiration the more frequently and continuously reflection is occupied with them; the starred heaven above me and the moral law within me. I ought not to seek either outside my field of vision, as though they were either shrouded in obscurity or were visionary. I see them confronting me and link them immediately with the consciousness of my existence."

The *maqasid as shari'ah* has its very important status nonetheless. It is only as a codification and choice of the good things of life and identification for avoidance of the false and bad things of life that bring about no benefit and only harm to human kind and others, respectively. Yet all such originating foundation of goodness and evil lie in the primal ontological law of *Tawhid* as the sole law that emanates from the *Qur'an* along with its cardinal worldview of unity of knowledge is explained by relational and organic complementarities between the entities of 'everything'. Therefore, at best the *maqasid as-shari'ah* can be understood just as a learned discursive field of choices that are permissible or impermissible. This wide field of valuation is most grandly explained by the *Qur'an* and the authentic *sunnah* as the primal epistemic explication in the system of belief, knowledge, and learned discourse (*ulul-amr*) (Auda, 2008).

The result of origination and continuity of knowledge in the completeness and details of the learning and conscious multiverse is this: From the Glorious *Qur'an* (*Tawhid*) revealed to the Prophet Muhammad and explained by the *sunnah* to bring about knowledge, guidance, and goodness to mankind and to 'everything' across the relational multiverse (Kafatos & Nadeau, 1990; Elis, 2008). It would therefore be appropriate to use the differentiating terminology so as to place the ontological primacy of *Tawhid* first. Then only this would be followed subsequently by *maqasid as-shari'ah* as a subset; yet not as law. The reconstruction of thought may now be termed as *maqasid as-shari'ah al-Tawhid* (Choudhury, 2017).

There is no special place of importance and sanctity for the idea of *shari'ah-compliance*, as this is known to enact itself daily by human wishful accreditation. Rather, the usage of *shari'ah-compliance* in Islamic economics and finance has become an enormous game of legitimation of *fiqh* and *fatawa*, contrary to the primacy of *Tawhid* and the usage of *maqasid as-shari'ah al-Tawhid*. The sectarian groups (*madhab*) and their proponents in the form of movements, governments, and institutions remain the custodians of the utterance of the term *shari'ah-compliance*. The use of the preponderant meanings of *Tawhid* and its governance of the world-system in its generality and details; and of *maqasid as-shari'ah al-Tawhid* as a derived codification of choice, and a discursive set of guidance have been distantly abandoned by the 'Islamic' establishment over time.

Indeed, it is illogical to uphold the *shari'ah* as the Law in equivalence to *Tawhid*. The supremacy of *Tawhid* as the law explaining 'everything' across plurality of beliefs, cultures, and science is established by the *Qur'an* (1:1): "[All] praise is [due] to Allah, Lord of the worlds". The *Qur'anic* ultimate extant of 'everything' (Barrow, 1991) in conscious continuum of mind, matter, and universe, cannot allow for primacy of any other law to be more primal than *Tawhid* alone. If this was otherwise true, that would mean allowance for the Pure (*Iqlas*) Oneness of Allah to more than one divine law. That is unacceptable in *Qur'anic* terms. Thus, *shari'ah* cannot be a law competing with *Tawhid* as the law that remains universal and uniquely singular. The *Qur'an* (21:22) declares in this regard: "If there were, in the heavens and the earth, other gods besides Allah, there would have been confusion in both! But glory to Allah, the Lord of the Throne: (High is He) above what they attribute to Him!"

As it stands presently, *shari'ah* in all its vagaries is an incomplete body of thought that is not wholly supported by the *Qur'anic* worldview of *Tawhid*. Neither does *shari'ah* fully convey the worldview of *Tawhid* across 'everything'. The nature of the *Tawhidi* worldview derived and developed from the *Qur'an* and *sunnah* in this work avoids fully the metaphysical meaning found in Islamic theology. Instead this work adopts the worldview of *Tawhid* as the strictest ontological law of monotheism that explains the imminent methodology and formalism in conceptual, applied, and sustainable forms. The meaning of *Tawhid* in its dynamics is that of organic oneness as consilience of unity of knowledge in concert with the unified world-system in its generality and details. Such an explanation as theory of the *Tawhidi* methodological worldview is the socio-scientific objective of this original work.

An Example of Contrary Meanings of Market Pricing Between *Tawhid* and *Shari'ah*

An example will establish this fact. First, consider the failure of *shari'ah* in establishing the mapping relationship—*Tawhid* to *shari'ah*. *Shari'ah* as humanly concocted body of rules legitimizes financial 'mark-up' and rent (*ijara*) type pricing rules in Islamic economics and finance. Yet this is a pricing rule that contradicts the pure *sunnah* rule that, pricing is not legitimate for a fruit as long it is in the tree. A fish cannot be priced prior to its catch from the water and rendering to market process. Likewise, there exists no *ijara* rule (rent) of pricing risk before the occurrence of an exigency. Thus *Tawhid* as law of pricing of real contracts is contradicted by the humanly innovated edict of *shari'ah*. *Tawhid* does not lead into *shari'ah* in this case.

Secondly, consider these same pricing rules permitted by *shari'ah*. They violate the continuity rule of *Tawhidi* organic unity of knowledge as pronounced by the *Qur'an* (36:36). The *Tawhidi* methodology that combines discursive evolutionary learning (*shura, tasbih, khalq in-jadid*) establishes the formalism and application of the worldview of organic unity of knowledge in the form of inter-entity causality. *Shari'ah* therefore, cannot lead into *Tawhid*. A great deal of revisions and extensions remain unresolved in *shari'ah* to make it accord with the primal ontological law of *Tawhid* in completeness of 'everything'. This same argument abides in case of untennability of the claim of the mapping, *Shari'ah* to *Tawhid*.

Extendibility of *Maslaha* as Wellbeing

Such discontinuities between *Tawhid* as law and *shari'ah* in the subtleties of sustainability of continuums of evolutionary learning equilibriums between unity of knowledge and the world-system—as exemplified by the central pricing problem of episteme and economics and finance—have left the principle of wellbeing (*maslaha*) incomplete in *maqasid*. Some guess-works have been attempted, as by Qaradawi (Djibril et al., op cit) by including 'Freedom' in the edicts of *maqasid*; and by Omar et al. (2016) in the *maslaha* function. Yet such extensions are both exogenously assigned by the authors and by the choice of formal attributes. Such figurative assignments are simply randomly many possibilities that are arbitrarily assumed. They are not developed from algorithmic evaluations; then followed by humanly possible reconstructions. It is suggested that, to embody the *Tawhidi* law of unity of knowledge between formalism and practicum, a purely mathematical extension and enrichment can be applied by using generalized symbolism for analysis of *maslaha* with the generalized vector,

$$\mathbf{x}(\mathbf{\theta}) = \{x_1(\theta_1), x_2(\theta_2), \ldots, x_n(\theta_n), \mathrm{avg.}(\theta_1, \theta_2, \ldots, \theta_n)\} \qquad (1.1)$$

The above generalized analytical configuration leads to the endogenous evaluation (meaning estimation followed by simulation) of the *maslaha* function,

$$W((x_1(\theta_1), x_2(\theta_2), \ldots, x_n(\theta_n), \mathrm{avg.}(\theta_1, \theta_2, \ldots, \theta_n)), \qquad (1.2)$$

The evaluation of expression (1.2) is carried out subject to all the properties invoked by the *Tawhidi* methodology centred on unity of knowledge between the symbioses of good choices and avoiding the bad ones according to the *Tawhidi* reference. Such a generalized vector is denoted by $\{(x_1(\theta_1), x_2(\theta_2), \ldots, x_n(\theta_n), \mathrm{avg.}(\theta_1, \theta_2, \ldots, \theta_n)\}$. The generalized analytical study of the evaluation of *maslaha* function in the symbiotic meaning would then lead to the assignment of specific choices in the above-mentioned vector of variables. More is to follow in this in subsequent chapters.

The Primal Ontology of *Tawhid* as Law

Socio-scientific worldview must be constructed upon its ontological and epistemological origins, supported by formalism, and empirically evaluated for inferences by the phenomenological content. Following this there must be continuity of the proven worldview across knowledge, space and time dimensions with intensifying body of epistemic and analytical insight. The meta-socio-scientific worldview extends the socio-scientific methodology to sequential continuity by the wrapping of deductive with inductive to deductive recursively etc. reasoning across the ontological, followed by epistemological, and this followed by phenomenological domains of sustained analytical processes spanning across knowledge, space, time dimensions of 'everything'. In meta-socio-science definition the domain of methodology in spite of its prevalence in non-physicalist study, is wholly subject to rigorous study by logical formalism, analysis, inferences, and sustainable continuity over the domain of 'everything'. Thereby, the issues and problems of meta-socio-scientific study remain diversely different. Yet their reference to methodology is universally unique and identical by formalism and analysis across processes defined identically over knowledge, space, and time. Such a dimension encompasses events that are embedded in non-physicalism and physicalism. Thereby, every variable of the symbiotic vector $\mathbf{x}(\theta)$ is embedded by non-physicalism as of the moral and ethical or contrarily rationalist ontology, $\{\theta\}$, in material entities, $\mathbf{x}(\theta)$.

Moral-material embedding of the symbiotic type represents the endogenous organic complementarities between moral and material values; non-physicalism and physicalism; deductive and inductive reasoning; and between a priori and a posteriori[1] reasoning of unified moral-material imperative. We will soon explain such phenomena of circular causality in contrariety to Kantian methodology and its critique and prototypes. The *Tawhidi* methodological worldview worldview will thus be affirmed as being contrary to that of rationalism and the so-called 'Islamic' idea that affirms rationalism by its method of occidental imitation.

With the above definition of universality and uniqueness of meta-socio-scientific methodology, the definition of Law and Justice as provided in a previous section can be included within meta-socio-scientific methodology. Therefore, the methodology of primal ontology of moral law of unity of knowledge is firstly entrenched in *Tawhid*. Next, the ontological law is conveyed by unity of knowledge as the epistemic representation in the order and scheme of 'everything'. Sequentially, the ontologi-

---

[1] Kant wrote (see Friedrich, 1949, p. 25): "This, then, is a question which at least calls for closer examination, and does not permit any off-hand answer: whether there is any knowledge that is thus independent of experience and even of all impressions of the senses. Such knowledge is entitled a priori, and is distinguished from the empirical, which has its sources a posteriori, that is, in experience."

cal and epistemic premise is formally analyzed and inferentially tested in terms of phenomenology (Spenser, 2000). The process defined by the ontological, epistemo-logical, and phenomenological sequence is then continued in knowledge, space, and time dimensions. This totality of the *Tawhidi* ontological law is universally unique to all phases of meta-socio-scientific explanations despite diverse issues and problems of inquiry. By this implication thereby, the ontology of *Tawhid* as the singularly most pervasive law and justice explains the 'ought to be' as opposed to the presently existing 'as is' nature of *maqasid as-shari'ah* and its *shari'ah-compliance* prototype.

In reference to the *Qur'an*, the generalized meaning of Law and Justice is con-veyed by the principle of balance and moderation, which can be subsumed with the terms *mizan* and *al-wasatiyyah*, respectively. In the *Tawhidi* sense there is intimate relationship between the principles of organic symbiosis in the evaluation of the *maslaha* function. The dynamic terms as mentioned here, in as far as they convey the meaning of balance and order, and thereby the principle of unity of knowl-edge by pervasive inter-variable complementarities, are maintained by endogenous inter-causality between the variables $\{\theta, x(\theta)\}$. The interrelated meaning of organic causality between the good things of life is upheld by the property of complementary moral-material embedding. This property is conveyed by the principle of *Tawhidi* unity of knowledge and the endogenous inter-variable causality of the good things of life. Such relational meaning of unity of knowledge is explained by the stream, $[Qur'an \; \Omega, Sunnah \; S] \rightarrow f(\cup^{interaction} \cap^{integration} \{\theta, x(\theta)\}$ in the continuum of knowl-edge and knowledge-induced space and time. This expression is further explained as we proceed on.

There is no other law and worldview that embraces the universal principle of *Tawhidi* unity of knowledge and its meta-socio-scientific formalism and analytics in 'everything'. Thus, in the case of disjoint treatment of pricing theory in *ijara* (rent and deferred pricing) and *murabaha* (mark-up risk pricing for expected profits) types of financing as upheld by *shari'ah*, this rule contradicts the finance and real econ-omy rule of pervasive complementarities. *Shari'ah* therefore, does not analytically reflect the central principle of *Tawhidi* unity of knowledge and the endogeneity of continuously complementary relations between the choices while avoiding the false ones in establishing *Tawhidi* worldview of unity of systemic relations in the order and scheme of things.

Formalizing the *Tawhidi* Methodological Worldview

We can now write down the analytical conception of the originary nature of *Tawhid* as the law of 'everything' according to the *Qur'an*, and encompassing the meta-socio-scientific domains. The following symbols of the *Tawhidi* methodological worldview are defined.

Let Ω denote the supercardinal (Rucker, 1982a, b) domain of monotheism as abso-lute knowledge of 'everything' according to the *Qur'an*. This is explained by a super-cardinal topological mathematical domain as a non-dimensional and non-configured primal ontology. Its absolute and non-partnered status of full knowledge explains the divine creatorship and sustainership of 'everything'. Its property is understood wholly by this absoluteness of creatorship, sustainership, knowledge of monotheistic oneness. These attributes together convey the meaning of the absolute oneness of God as the absolute and non-partnered Creator and Sustainer of 'everything'. Hence, the underlying essence of monotheism defined by its supreme and singular essence of creatorship, sustainership, knowledge, and primal ontology is the supreme most law, referred to as *Tawhid*. There is nothing more fundamental and more reduced as this origin than itself as the absolute a priori overarching creation in all forms. *Tawhid* as the primal ontology explaining the nature of 'everything' as law is limitless in explanation of 'everything', but it remains uncreated and unbounded.

Thus *Tawhid* as law is of unbounded relational capability in explaining the unity of the multiverses. But by itself *Tawhid* as the essential attribute of Allah is characterized by nothing in comparison. *Tawhid* is thereby the pure and relational law of unity of being and becoming of 'everything'. In such a status of its supercardinal power, its domain over 'everything', and by its power of explication, *Tawhid* as primal ontological law defines the all-comprehensive nature of the Good, the Bad, the temporarily Undecidable. The Undecidables finally yield to either Good or Bad, Truth or Falsehood, as the worldly adherence to *Tawhid* as law deepens and enhances with evolutionary learning in reference to *Tawhidi* precept of unity of knowledge.

In spite of an increasing comprehension of the ultimate essence (*dhat*) of *Tawhid* as the monotheistic oneness of Allah and its primal ontological law of unity of knowledge in the extendible domain of being and becoming across consciousness, it defies a fullest human explication of monotheistic oneness in the midst of the purity of Allah as Being. Therefore, the perfection and completeness of being is only learnt in the evolutionary realm of relational continuity over emanating knowledge, space, and time by way of the relational holism of non-physicalism and physicalism as unified reality. This evolutionary learning experience (*tajdid*) continues from the Beginning to the End in the Hereafter (*Akhira*).

For the purpose of deriving the worldly methodology in respect of the worldview of unity of knowledge in the being and becoming across evolutionary learning domain of knowledge, knowledge-induced space, knowledge-induced time, we derive some essences to determine the *Tawhidi* methodological causation of the knowledge-induced world-system and the reasoning underlying the experiential world-system. This kind of abstracto-empirical reality that encompasses the expanding socio-scientific order comprises the phenomenological evolutionary knowledge-induced reality. Such reality of manifest oneness in terms of organic (relational) unity of knowledge emanates from the formalism derived from *Tawhidi* monotheistic methodological worldview. We formalize on the domain of the limited yet purposeful and experiential understanding of *Tawhid* as manifest law of 'everything'. The concurrent full and unbounded reality of the supercardinal and non-Cartesian mathematical representation is a central focus of this work. Without such a methodological approach it would be impossible to derive, explain, and apply *Tawhid* as manifest law in the universality of 'everything'.

Tawhid as Primal Ontological Law of monotheistic oneness of Allah's circum-scribing 'everything' in the unity of non-physical and physical domains is referred to as God's Essence of Purity (*Iqlas*) and as Law Giver (*Ayath al Kursi*), Allah's *Dhāt*. *Dhāt* is above all conditions. Imagination cannot soar up to it. In the second case, its existence is implied without further assertion. In the third case, something could be asserted about it (http://www.tajbaba.com/glimpse-of-tassawuf/49-dhat-and-sifat.html).

Allah's *Dhat* (Essence) envelopes the reality of the world-system and the precincts of Heaven and Hell in a purely exogenous mono-causal relationship; for Allah's *Dhat* is uncreated in every shape and form. This manifestation of ultimate reality of this world-system and the Hereafter is a finest articulation of the systemic embedding between non-physicalism and physicalism of interactive relations. Such exegetic meaning arises from the verses concerning the supercardinal extant of *Tawhid* and its *Dhat* and *Sifat*:

"He (Allah Most High) then firmly established (*istawā*) Himself over the Throne" (*Qur'an* 7:54): "Unquestionably, His is the creation and the command; blessed is Allah, Lord of the worlds." These verses are explained to mean, Allah firmly estab-lished Himself over the Kingly Throne and He began decreeing command of creation to the heavens and the earth.

It can then be inferred that, while *Dhat* governs the world-system and the Heaven and Hell as distinct realities, therefore, the causality flows between the earth and the domain of Heaven and Hell. This means that the relational order of worldly experience is determined by *Tawhidi* command as law; and in turn it determines human status in the Hereafter by the bliss of Heaven or the perdition of Hell, as the case would be. In the socio-scientific meaning this kind of unique relationship implies that, the Good and Bad, Truth and Falsehood of the world-system that is governed exclusively by the *Dhat* of Allah in the primal ontology of *Tawhid* as supreme most law governing 'everything' establishes human status in *Akhira*.

The determination is ascertained positively in the precincts of Heaven; negatively in the perdition of Hell. These two realities are disjoint all through from the world-system to the *Akhira*. Pickthall (2014) wrote that, the *Akhira* would not be created by Allah if the world-system was not there in the first place to test the widest conse-quences concerning Truth and Falsehood.

By the limits of human experience and the world-system comprehension of the *Dhat* of *Tawhid* as the singular primal ontological law of monotheistic unity of knowl-edge we can write the *Tawhidi* supercardinal non-Cartesian mathematical entity in Chap. 2.

References

Ashur, M. T. I. (2013). *Treatise on Maqasid as-Shari'ah*. U.S.A: International Institute of Islamic Thought, Herndon, VA.

Attia, G. E. (2008). *Towards Realization of the higher intents of Islamic law: A functional approach of Maqasid as-Shari'ah* (p. 2008). Herndon, VA: International Institute of Islamic Thought.

Auda, J. (2008). *Maqasid Al-Shari'ah as philosophy of Islamic law, a systems approach.* Herndo, Virginia: International Institute of Islamic Thought.

Barrow, J. D. (1991). *Theories of everything, the quest for ultimate explanation.* Oxford, Eng: Oxford University Press.

Choudhury, M. A. (2017). *A phenomenological theory of Islamic economics.* Kuala Lumpur, Malaysia: University of Malaya Press.

Djibrilla, M. M., Buang, A. H., & Olayemi, A. A. M. (2017). The challenges of shari'ah compliance in the Islamic banking practices: Whether Ibn Qayyim's principles of muamalat be the panacea? *Journal of Muamalat and Islamic Finance Research, 14*(1), 73–85.

Elis, G. F. R. (2008). Multiverses and ultimate causation. In F. Watts (Ed.), *Creation, law and probability* (pp. 59–80). Minneapolis, MN: Fortress Press.

Hart, H. L. A. (1994). *The concept of law* (p. 92). Oxford, England: Clarendon Press.

Kafatos, M., & Nadeau, R. (1990). Searching for the ground: Mutation, mind, and the epistemology of science. In *The conscious universe, part and whole in modern physical theory.* Springer: New York, NY.

Kant, I. (1949). In C. J. Friedrich (Ed.), *The philosophy of Kant.* New York, NY: Modern Library.

Lawson, T. (1997). *Economics and reality* (p. 25). London: Routledge.

Lee, F. S., & Lavoie, M. (2013). *In defense of post-Keynesian and heterodox economics* (p. 109). Abingdon, Oxford: Routledge.

Mahdi, M. (1964). *Ibn Khaldun's philosophy of history.* Chicago, IL: The University of Chicago Press.

Omar, M. (2016). The performance measurement of Islamic banking based on the maqasid framework. In Choudhury, M. A. (Ed.), *Islamic financial economy and Islamic banking.* Routledge, London, England.

Pickthall, M. M. (2014 reprinted). *Meaning of the glorious Qur'an,* Global Grey.

Rucker, R. (1982a). Large cardinals. In *Infinity and the mind,* Bantam Books: New York, NY.

Rucker, R. (1982b). Excursion I: The transfinite cardinals. In *Infinity and the mind* (pp. 239–286). Bantam Books, New York, NY.

Shackle, G. L. S. (1972). *Epistemics and economics.* Cambridge, England: Cambridge University Press.

Spenser, N. (2000). On the significance of distinguishing ontology and epistemology; contributed by Neville Spencer upon request, March 2000. See also *Critical realism and reality* by Andy Blunden, 2009. Internet version.

Tag el-Din, S. I. (2013). *Maqsid foundations of market economics.* Edinburgh, Scotland: Edinburgh University Press.

Chapter 2
Establishing *Tawhidi* String Relation as the Epistemic Foundation of *Tawhidi* Methodological Worldview

Masudul Alam Choudhury

Abstract An overview of the technical nature of the methodology derived from *Tawhid* as law of monotheism pertaining to the theory of socio-scientific 'everything' is presented. The technical nature of *Tawhidi* methodology is firstly cast in textual language. This is then followed by a degree of analytical depth. The objective thereby is to lay bare the nature of the *Tawhidi* methodological worldview of unity of knowledge meaning relational organic complementarities between the selected variables pertaining to *Tawhid* as the ultimate truth. The argumentation underlying such derivations in the light of the worldview of unity of knowledge as truth ingrained in the *Qur'an* and transmitted by the *sunnah* as Prophetic teachings is framed by the principle of universality and uniqueness in the context of pervasive complementarities between the inter-causal relations of selected variables. Just the contrary to all such manifestations of the technical dynamics of *Tawhid* as law contra *shari'ah* is the inhering law of opposites in marginalism and rationalism that the latter idea accepts but is logically untenable in the *Tawhidi* methodological worldview. Details along these directions in the subsequent chapters are thereby laid bare.

A Non-technical Overview of the Chapter

In every way concerning derivation of socio-scientific methodology from the *Qur'an* the law of *Tawhid* is distinct from the so-called Islamic law and jurisprudence of *shari'ah*. The latter belief has been mistakenly upheld by the Muslims over centuries. This perforation of Islamic thought by the notion of *shari'ah* in its various forms has caused debilitating effect on the rise of the truly *Qur'anic* methodological worldview in the socio-scientific theory of 'everything'. This latter essence of the holism of *Qur'an* is found in *Tawhid* as the true law contra *shari'ah* in all its forms.

M. A. Choudhury (✉)
Faculty of Economics, Trisakti University, Jakarta, Indonesia
e-mail: masudc60@yahoo.ca

© Springer Nature Singapore Pte Ltd. 2019
M. A. Choudhury (ed.), *The* Tawhidi *Methodological Worldview*,
https://doi.org/10.1007/978-981-13-6585-0_2

15

The *Tawhidi* methodological worldview of 'everything' is transcendental by being universal and unique in establishing the singularly most penetrating explanation of 'everything'. The domain of 'everything' encompasses the abstraction, the formal, and the phenomenological application in continuity of knowledge, and knowledge-induced space and time dimensions. A logical sequence of methodological derivation thus lays down the *Tawhidi* law. Such methodical derivation and sustained knowledge-induced evolution and application in 'everything' arising from *Tawhid* as law are essential. This analytical approach lies beyond sheer descriptive language so as to give the *Tawhidi* methodological foundation its rigorous abstraction and applications with sustained continuity. The result then is unification by the meaning of relational organic unity of knowledge between choices of the good things of life. The emergent inter-variable relations in unity of knowledge are analyzed by their inter-causal relations. Such organic inter-variable relations are termed as endogenous relations, and hence endogeneity. This methodological derivation of inter-variable circular causation relations is the opposite of the exogenous inter-relations and hence the property of exogeneity in inter-variable relations.

The endogenous kinds of symbiotic inter-variable circular causal relations convey the phenomenological explanation of the relational meaning of unity of knowledge. The ontological premise of unity of knowledge is thus the cause and effect circularly between the True choices; and oppositely between the False things of life. The nature of Truth and Falsehood is opposite manifestation of reality according to *Tawhid* as law.

Tawhid as law now signifies its two parts instilled in total reality at the moment of the divine ordainment to creation—'Be and it was' (*kun fa-yakoon*). The first part of *Tawhid* is its metaphysical essence that forms the indescribable, incognizant perfection of Allah's pure essence (*dhat*). This part of the exclusive universally overwhelming essence of the *Tawhidi* worlview comprehends belief. Belief is of an incognizant form and thereby incommensurate for socio-scientific inquiry. Yet belief forms the inner dynamics of conscious motivation that distinguishes Truth from Falsehood.

The other part of *Tawhid* is the divine ordainment to creation in its completeness in the form of cognizant law of 'everything'. This part of *Tawhid* as law is manifest in 'everything' as Signs of Allah in the forms of analyzable and comm5serate actions and responses in the order of 'everything'. Thus there are the *Qur'anic* terms: *Ayath Allah* (Signs of Allah), *Sunnat Allah* (divine law), and *A'lameen* (world-system). The result then is the conscious use of knowledge of the ontological Being of God as Truth of unity of knowledge (*Tawhid*) that fuses with the cognitive essence of *Tawhid* as law in the form of unity between the divinely moral and materiality in concrescence.

In the extant of *Tawhid* as law, which is measurable, analyzable, configured, applies, and sustainable by cognizance over the knowledge, space, and time dimensions the logical formalism of the philosophy of science takes its methodological roots. These elements of philosophy of science along with their mathematical analyses form the primal ontology of Being and monotheistic unity of knowledge in 'everything'. Primal ontology is followed by the crystallization of the law of monotheistic unity of knowledge in the form of interpretive and observant knowledge. This stage is of Epistemology. This functioning is realized by the medium of *sunnah* as topological mapping arising from the ultimate origin of the greatest cardinality. We refer to the greatest cardinality as the Being of the largest cardinal, which though is unbounded. In the fullest span of *Tawhid* as law spanning across all systems of multiverses from the Beginning to the End, this super-topological meaning establishes the mathematical meaning of Closure. Thereby, this epistemological stage of knowledge derivation forms the phenomenology of the *Tawhidi* knowledge-induced world-system in knowledge, space, time universe in Unbounded and Closed domain of total reality.

From Ontology to Epistemology to Phenomenology, this same sequence is carried over by evolutionary learning into simulacra of similar processes in Sustainability intra-systems and inter-systems. These stages altogether form the sequencing of the philosophy of science according to *Tawhidi* methodological worldview. The unification of knowledge intra-systems and inter-systems in knowledge, space, and time implies the transcendental existence of *Tawhid* as law everywhere and in 'everything'. The contrary worldview of Falsehood is found in pervasive differentiation of knowledge by marginalism, competition contra participative unity, and methodological individualism or dialectical materialism in 'everything'. In each of these opposite directions of reality, namely Truth (*maslaha*) and Falsehood (*mafasid*) the internal properties of the interactive, integrative, and evolutionary learning nature of *Tawhidi* methodological worldview of Truth opposite to Falsehood is carried through in Sustainability. Such logical form of methodological orientation of *Tawhid* as law for 'everything' has not been possible by *shari'ah*.

Introduction: The Primal Ontology of the *Qur'an* and the Epistemic Origin of *Sunnah*

Let Ω denote the non-Cartesian mathematical entity = {*Qur'an*; *Iqlas*; *Ayath al-Kursi*; Supercardinal (unbounded); Creatorship, Sustainership (Being and becoming of world-system); perfection in fullness of Knowledge; uniquely methodological (relational unity of knowledge in continuity of learning processes)}.

'S' denotes the *sunnah* as the teaching and guidance of the Prophet Muhammad in terms of *Tawhid* as the *Qur'anic* law of 'everything' (*Qur'an*, 53:3–4). 'S' is continuous and pervasive across the multidimension of knowledge, knowledge-induced space, and knowledge-induced time. 'S' is transmission mapping of the *Qur'an* into the world-system (*Qur'an*, 4:59). Its extension mappings into 'everything' is searched, discoursed, and discovered by carrying out authoritative research and authentic conclusions appertaining to the *Tawhidi* precept of 'everything'. This feat is accomplished by establishing and applying the principle of pervasive complementarities between the good things of life, while avoiding the bad things of life. On the other hand, differentiation and methodological or dialectical individualism and all that these contrareity cause mark the totality of explaining reality by the ontology of *Tawhidi* unity of knowledge. These contrasting attributes are uniquely explained by the foundational methodology of *Tawhid* as law and its worldview in applying to 'everything' of the socio-scientific generality and details.

The above-mentioned principle depicting the universality and uniqueness of *Tawhid* as ultimate law forms the methodological worldview of monotheistic unity of knowledge. This principle of universality and uniqueness is derived by the combination of the *Qur'an* and the *sunnah*. The precept of *Tawhidi* unity of knowledge is continuously premised on the distinct symbiosis of relations within and between selected entities separated between Good and Bad, Truth and Falsehood. Such exclusive symbiotic unification of inter-variable relations appears as biological and neurocybernetic type according to the *Qur'anic* worldview of organizing 'everything' in pairs (Wilson, 1998; Choudhury, 2010). Arising from such a primal ontological foundation of the *Tawhidi* worldview is established the nature of knowledge and learning according to the *Tawhidi* origin. Such primal ontological knowledge is mapped by the *sunnah* into the generality and details of the world-system.

The emergent process of methodological derivation of knowledge from the *Qur'anic* ontological origin comprises the first stage of intra-systemic learning by interaction (discourse) leading into the concomitant stage of integration (consensus); and thereby rising to evolutionary learning via interaction and integration across the pairing of entities of the multiverses. Such a tripartite comprising totality of dynamics and properties is sustained across historical consciousness of all events appearing and transforming in the kaleidoscope of unity in and across diversity (*mukhtalifan*) of knowledge, knowledge-induced space, and knowledge-induced time.

The primal ontology of *Tawhid* as law in the *Qur'an* and universally and uniquely in 'everything' is mapped by the epistemic origin of the *sunnah* as supercardinal mapping in well-definition and continuity across multidimensions of knowledge, knowledge-induced space, and knowledge-induced time configuring a subtle continuity. This is the continuity of primal ontology realized by the principal episteme of the *sunnah*. It forms strictly one-directional causality. That is from the primal ontology of *Tawhid* through the episteme of the *sunnah* and into the varieties of world-systems with their formalisms and diversity of interrelations in unity of knowledge comprising the unified nature of non-physicalism and physicalism. These two elements are inseparable. They together yield the permanent nature of knowledge and learning according to the *Qur'an*, *sunnah*, the discursive world-system and its continuity from the Beginning (*Tawhid*) to the End (Hereafter = *Tawhid*). The prevailing properties are of Interaction (I), Integration (I), and Evolution (E). We thereby abbreviate to (IIE)-process oriented learning in *Tawhidi* unity of knowledge intra-system and inter-system across multiverses.

The continuity of the one-directional causality from Ω to cognizant world-system via the mapping by 'S', that is the melding of episteme in primal ontology, forms a well-defined and exact mono-directional topological relationship of unity of knowledge from the ultimately exogenous worldview of self-determining *Tawhid* as law to 'everything' via the epistemic mapping of 'S'. This is the reality of Allah as Law-Giver to 'everything' in the world-system. Materiality cannot be mapped into divine essence. Allah is not cognizant of materiality.

Now only two possibilities can exist in the reverse mappings of 'functional' ontologies (Gruber, 1993 refers to this as 'portable ontologies') as systemic structures within IIE-learning processes in reference to *Tawhid* as law of unity of knowledge. Firstly, the reverse inter-causal relations of the world-system are continuously and pervasively circular and thus endogenous between representative variables of the Good. Such a structure of functional ontologies as topological mappings explains the nature of unity of knowledge between relations and entities (representative variables) that embed in them the *Tawhidi* law by its essence of unity of knowledge. This attribute establishes the realm of the Good. The contrary structure conveys the rationalist thought that embed methodological individualism and thus multiplicity of gods as the sign of Bad.

Figure 2.1 explains the two opposite kinds of world-systems explained by the universal and unique law of *Tawhid* and its formal structure governing the nature of Good (Truth) and Bad (Falsehood) (*Qur'an*, 25:1). The property of supercardinal topological ontology embracing the episteme of $[\Omega, S]$ implies continuously preserving relations across all possible functional ontologies compounded with $[\Omega, S]$ according to the dichotomous domains of *Tawhidi* law governing Good (Truth, Ω_1) and Bad (Falsehood, Ω_2). Such compounded functional ontologies on these opposite sides are denoted by $\{f \cdot S \cdot \Omega_1\}$ of Good (Truth) and $\{f' \cdot S \cdot \Omega_2\}$ of Bad (Falsehood). By allowing for the topological properties of these functional ontologies we can deduce that compound functions assume the following values: $\cap\{f\} \neq \phi; \cap\{f'\} = \phi$ along IIE-learning processes.

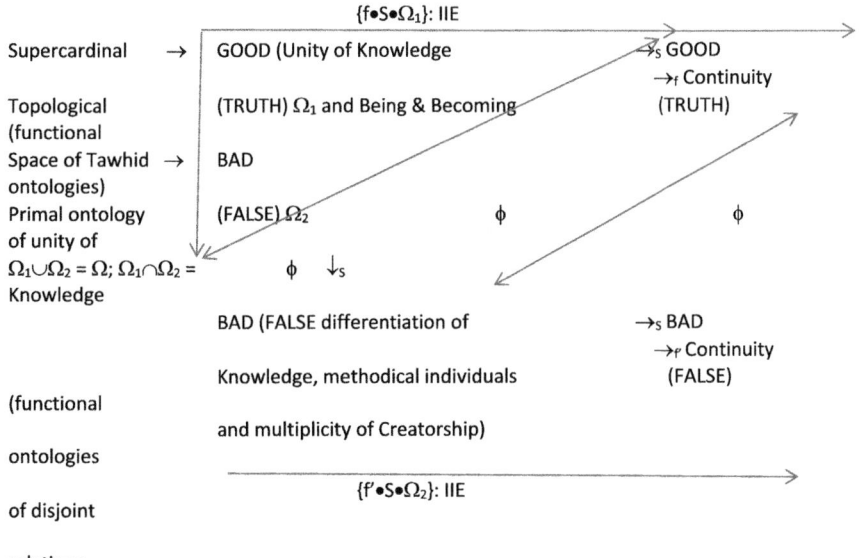

Fig. 2.1 *Tawhid* as the criterion of truth against falsehood in essence (*Dhat*) and the world-system

The IIE knowledge derivation and learning sequence

The methodological worldview of the relational unity of knowledge according to the *Qur'an* is derived in a systemic way by using the medium of the *sunnah*.

Intra-system (IIE):

Interaction, $i = 1, 2, \ldots, n$ leads into an integration. $\qquad$ (2.1)

Interaction to Integration, $j = (n_1\text{-interactions})[1], (n_2\text{-interactions})[2], \ldots,$

$(n_N\text{-interaction})[N]$, such that, $n_1 + n_2 + \cdots + n_N = n$; $\qquad$ (2.2)

with $i[j] = (1, 2, \ldots, n_1)[1], (n_1 + 1 \ldots n_2)[2], \ldots, n[N]$.

Interaction to Integration to Evolution,

$(i, j)[k] = (n_1\text{-interactions})(N\text{-integration})[1\text{-evolution}],$

$(n_2\text{-interactions})(N_2\text{-integration})[2\text{-evolution}], \ldots,$ $\qquad$ (2.3)

$(n_N\text{-interaction})(N\text{-integration})[N^*\text{-evolution}]$

This expression for IIE wholly can be simplified by assuming a probability limit converging by interaction over discourse into one integration, says N-number of interactions. Likewise, there can be one convergence of probability limit of integrations via interactions into one evolution, say N^*-convergence to probability limit following interaction leading to integration. Such is the case of various Islamic sects agreeing to an *ijma* (unique consensus though not unanimity). The IIE-learning process can then be characterized by its ontological and epistemic methodological foundations as follows below. The mathematical symbols so characterized can be identified by the superscript,

$$ijk; i = 1, 2, \ldots, n; j = 1, 2, \ldots, [N]; \ k = 1, 2, \ldots, [N^*]. \qquad (2.4)$$

The symbol [.] denotes the two possibilities. While this subscript symbolizes the entire process, sections of it can be denoted by the separated subscripts of i, j, k or suitable combinations of these as the case may be.

The end of an intra-system learning is followed by the emergence of the subsequent inter-system IIE-learning process. The inter-system continuity repeats the IIE-learning process evaluation of the intra-system now pertaining to the specific systemic processes.

$$[\Omega \to S] \to \{\text{knowledge formed by } (i, j, k) - \text{combinations in evolutionary learning processes}\} \qquad (2.5)$$

in IIE-learning processes specific to intra-systems that subsequently evolve into inter-systems.

A critical evaluation of the consistency of *Tawhid* contra *shari'ah*, as the onto-logical law of 'everything', can now be examined at this point. It is noted that, like any rule (*ahkam*), neither *Tawhid* nor *shari'ah* gives any formula to make a thing according to its precept. The ontology leads to the episteme as shown in the above expression as guidance of law and rules towards selection and organizing of the choices according to *Tawhid* as law and *shari'ah* as partial codification of the law.

From such fundamentals the subsequent functional ontologies and continuity of the deductive=inductive=deductive etc. continuity of reasoning prevails fecur-sively across IIE-learning processes. The reproductive inter-connectivity between a priori and a posteriori knowledge is carried along knowledge-induced sustain-ability of IIE-learning processes over knowledge, knowledge-induced space, and knowledge-induced time. Such continuity of reasoning along the unified plane of non-physicalism and physicalism can be derived only in the *Tawhidi* sense.

Such underlying dynamics of any imminent kind of methodology are not found in the *shari'ah*-based understanding of Islamic socio-scientific system. For instance, choices according to *shari'ah* are based on the predominance of contracts (*uqud*). Such contracts prevail only in the order of earthly *muamalat*. They do not extend to the realm of the heavenly subtleties. Consequently, the methodological depth of analytical socio-scientific worldview arising from the mathematical, ontological, and epistemic details of the principle of organic unity of knowledge and its constructs and explication of the world-system, are not to be found in the domain of *shari'ah*. Great limitations consequently arise from many such subtle absences in *shari'ah*. The limitations of *shari'ah* are otherwise completed by the supercardinal expanse of the *Tawhidi* methodological worldview in and across 'everything'. In many instances great gaps remain impending in the realm of *shari'ah*, while the meta-science of *Tawhid* leaves no shortfall and discrepancy in this monotheistic law of 'everything'. We refer to some examples here.

Examples of Limitations in *Shari'ah* Completed by *Tawhid* as Law

In financial economics, *shari'ah* has accepted and permitted the human concocted idea of speculative *ijara*-type pricing in everyone of the deferred financing instru-ments and businesses. Examples of these instruments are *murabaha* forward pricing of mark-up of assets. There is also the complete absence of intertemporal financ-ing of assets such as insurance (*takaful*), endowment (*waqf*), and deferred pricing. Contrarily, in the case of *Tawhidi* methodological approach of unity of knowledge in the good choices and the avoidance of the bad ones, all forms of pricing formu-las are established by derivations from the analysis of circular causation of inter-variable endogenous relations. Circular causation between endogenous variables is an approach that is objectively derived and established by the primal ontology across all functional ontologies. The emergent continuous sustainability projects the Hereafter onto the world-system just like *Tawhid* in the Beginning sustains its universal and unique mapping forward.

Another example is of an absence in *shari'ah* of intertemporal valuation of assets by an appropriate pricing formula. The emergent valuation formula pertaining to *Tawhidi* methodology uses observations and contingencies of occurrence of probabilistic events 'nearest' to the occurrence of contingencies for multivariables of the valuation model in the knowledge, knowledge-induced space of observations, and knowledge-induced moments of time of occurrence of the contingent events.

Valuation according to the *shari'ah* idea remains a periodic-based contractual approach (*aqd*). This is contrary to the intertemporal approach that must be compliant with the intertemporal theory of interest rates (*riba*). According to the *Tawhidi* asset valuation methodology over contingency and time a 'nearest' point of event-specific probabilistic evaluation can be done in the context of evaluation of the event-specific *maslaha* objective criterion. The probabilities associated with the emergences of contingent variables and events must be evaluated at points 'nearest' to the occurrences of the probabilities. This would reduce incidence of subjective probabilities and increase the degree of certainty of the probabilistic observations over knowledge, space, and time.

Contrary to the context of *shari'ah*, *Tawhidi* methodology of unity of knowledge in the symbiotic pairing of events in the multidimensions of knowledge, knowledge-induced socio-scientific space, and knowledge-induced time can explain complex reality in mathematical formalism. Study of such complexity can borrow from the methods of neuroscience and neurobiology with their many meta-scientific implications (Choudhury, 2010, 2017). In its contractual formulation, *maqasid as-shari'ah* cannot explain the complexity of the ecological universe with sheer human experience. Yet such investigations in respect of universal systemic pairing is of utmost importance in cybernetic study of meta-science that *Tawhid* as law comprehends. Consequently, the extensive improvising of the simple *maqasid as-shari'ah* idea that is independently structured on its mere five pillars of choices for wellbeing (*maslaha*), becomes a detailed mathematical and statistical problem in *Tawhidi* methodological worldview.

In conclusion, with respect to the inter-causal study of complementary relations, it is possible only for the *Tawhidi* ontological law to define the nature of *shari'ah*; and in doing so to reconstruct *shari'ah* in terms of the universality of the monotheistic knowledge and its scope in the order of unity of knowledge in 'everything'. But *shari'ah* is not found to be of this nature, even though human innovation calls *shari'ah* most incorrectly as Islamic law. It is equally impossible to go through any sensible mapping (relationship) from the level of *shari'ah* to imply *Tawhid*. That otherwise would make two contesting laws, *Tawhid* and *shari'ah*. How strange, abominable and illogical this would be—two gods rivaling in *Tawhidi* monotheism?!!!. Thus if there is the divinely One and only, then necessarily *Tawhid* as the ultimate law is irreplaceable by any human concocted idea of *shari'ah*.

Conclusion

In reference to Fig. 2.1 and its inner meaning of world-system induction done totally by *Tawhid* as law, there is no meaning in the mapping such as, 'from primal ontology of *Tawhid*, [Ω, S] onto *shari'ah*', unless this statement is understood as incremental evolutionary learning in the *Tawhidi* worldview of 'everything'. Yet *shari'ah* and its *maslaha* (wellbeing) implication have not proceeded in this holistic direction of 'everything' between the heavens and the earth. The universe of [Ω, S] is supercardinal in measure; whereas the domain of *shari'ah* remains contained and the *shari'ah* definition of *maslaha* remains incomplete.

The system of equations below shows the positioning of *maqasid as-shari'ah* in relation to [Ω, S] along the IIE-learning processes. It is noted that, [Ω, S] alone exogenously as the primal ontology-episteme of the IIE-learning process, determines the position and status of *maqasid as-shari'ah* (MQS) in 'everything'. *Maqasid as-shari'ah* is endogenously determined while [Ω, S] remains the absolute law of 'everything', where the search for the absolute reality lies.

$$\{\Omega \rightarrow S \equiv [\Omega, S]\} \rightarrow \{MQS\}_1 \equiv \{\theta^*, \theta\}_1 \text{ PROCESS 1}$$
$$\{\Omega \rightarrow S[\Omega, S]\} \rightarrow \{MQS\}_2 \equiv \{\theta^*, \theta\}_2 \text{ PROCESS 2}$$
$$\dots$$
$$\{\Omega \rightarrow S \equiv [\Omega, S]\} \rightarrow \{MQS\}_p \equiv \{\theta^*, \theta\}_p \tag{2.6}$$

$$\text{CONTINUITY} \Rightarrow \{\Omega \rightarrow S \equiv [\Omega, S]\} \rightarrow \cup^I \cap^J \{MQS\}$$
$$\equiv \{\theta^*, \theta\}\}_P; \ (d/d\theta)f_p[\{\cup^I \cap^J \{MQS\}\{\theta^*, \theta\}\}_P] > 0,$$

for evolutionary values of k, as was defined earlier. 'f(.)' denotes 'functional' ontology of the IIE-learning processes denoted by 'p'.

$\{\Omega \rightarrow S \equiv [\Omega, S]\}$ governs over all IIE-learning processes as exogenous ontology-episteme. Hence there is $\cup^I \cap^J$ followed by evolutions k = 1, 2, …, p, … universally over all processes. This unique and universal determination of *Tawhidi* methodological worldview over all processes means that, the ontology and epistemology convolution of $\{\Omega \rightarrow S \equiv [\Omega, S]\}$ singularly governs 'everything' from the Beginning to the End of creation in the form of Unbounded Closure of being and becoming of the *Tawhidi* world-systems in unity of knowledge. According to the inter-relational property of learning there exist formal inter-causal relations between $\{\theta^*, \theta\}$, such as $\{\theta^* \leftrightarrow \theta\} \cdot \{\theta^*\}$ denotes knowledge of various learned ulemas called *mujtahids* representing various schools of *fiqh* and *fatawa* referred to as *madhabs* (sects). Unfortunately, despite many attempts to unify the *madhabs*, they remain differentiated on many interpretations of *fiqh*, *fatawas*, and thereby aspects of *shari'ah* rulings.

Therefore, in the face of these problems of harmonizing *shari'ah* by its *fiqh* and *fatawas*, the knowledge-forming ought to be that of a truly discursive nature allowing for diversity of socio-scientific outlook within the context of *Tawhidi* unity of knowledge and this value-embedded world-system by its generality and specifics. Therefore, there is no compelling need to remain invariantly stricken to the rulings (*ahkams*) of different *madhabs*. Instead, it is necessary and sufficient to seek the origin of all knowledge ontology and epistemology on $\{\Omega \to S \equiv [\Omega, S]\}$. Such a society marked the practice of Prophet Muhammad who discussed matters with everyone regarding 'everything', seeking guidance by way of discussion and discourse. The *Qur'an* (4:59) declares in this regard of deriving knowledge from its originary sources.[1]

The entire system of continuity of IIE-learning processes denoted by 'p' covers all experiences of the learning world-system from the Beginning of its induction by $\{\Omega \to S \equiv [\Omega, S]\}$ until the End in the Hereafter (*Akhira*) (*Qur'an*, 57:3): "He is the First and the Last, the Ascendant and the Intimate, and He is, of all things, Knowing." Then there is the verse of the closure of being and becoming stating that Allah as Law Giver and *Tawhid* as law is the End and the Beginning just as the divine law is the Beginning and the End in its unbounded form (*Qur'an* 53:25): "Rather, to Allah belongs the Hereafter (End) and the first [life = Beginning]".

Thus the *Tawhidi* universe of totality of 'everything' as all multiverses in generality and details forms the nature of the Unbounded yet Closed Universe. This attribute of TSR forms the *Tawhidi* ≡ *Akhira* as the Great Closure in the IIE-learning processes from the Beginning to the End. The implication then is this: *Tawhid* as the sole law has given discursive power of unity of knowledge towards determining all knowledge and the organically symbiotic structure of world-systems by IIE-learning processes in and through intra-systemic and inter-systemic learning experiences.

Consequently, *maqasid as-shari'ah* is a partial rule of choices of the good things of life and the avoidance of the bad things of life as determined by the worldly manifestation of *Tawhidi* methodological worldview of unity of knowledge. The ontological law of unity is represented in the continuous and pervasive complementarities of the positive choices and oppositeky so across 'everything' in knowledge, and knowledge-induced space and time multidimensions.

Let us next consider a limiting point of the set of knowledge, $\{\theta^*, \theta\}$ derived from $\{\Omega \to S \equiv [\Omega, S]\}$:

plim $\{\theta^*, \theta\} = \{\theta\}$, without loss of generality in the symbol of knowledge according to the *Tawhidi* precept of unity of knowledge. Hereby, in the study of *Tawhidi* unity of knowledge and its induction of the unified world-system we will use the knowledge-induction symbol by 'θ'. The set of knowledge parameter that is ontologically induced by belief $\{\varepsilon\}$ is denoted by $\{\theta(\varepsilon)\}$.

---

[1] *Qur'an* (4:59): O ye who believe! Obey Allah, and obey the Messenger, and those charged with authority among you. *If ye differ in anything among yourselves, refer it to Allah and His Messenger, if ye do believe in Allah and the Last Day: That is best, and most suitable for final determination.*

References

Choudhury, M. A. (2010). A neurocybernetic theory of management system. In A. Gunasekaran & M. Sandhu (Eds.), *Handbook on business information systems.* Singapore: World Scientific Publications.

Choudhury, M. A. (2017). *A phenomenological theory of Islamic economics.* Kuala Lumpur, Malaysia: University of Malaya Press.

Gruber, T. R. (1993). A translation approach to portable ontologies Ontologiesontology. *Knowl Acquisit, 5*(2), 199–200.

Wilson, E. O. (1998). *Consilience.* Unity of Knowledge: Vantage Books, New York, NY.

Chapter 3
Tawhidi Structure of the Participatory World-System

Masudul Alam Choudhury

Abstract This chapter intensifies in further depth the structure of the analytical aspects of *Tawhidi* methodology in socio-scientific studies. The formal derivation and its conceptual extension of the sequencing of induction of unity of knowledge across various world-systems in respect of their knowledge induced events is established. Furthermore, the ultimate application of such sequences of knowledge-induced development of the *Tawhidi* world-system is explained. This invokes primal ontology leading to epistemology, then to phenomenology as the conscious application in the light of unity of knowledge. These three pronged states of every IIE-learning process is carried forward in continuous processes of sustainability. The extension of the intra-system formulation and application of the *Tawhidi* methodological worldview across conscious historicism is extended to multi-systems. Thereby, the nature of the inter-temporal evolution of multiverses of systems is formulated. Thereby, the mathematical properties of continuity, differentiability and sustainability of inter-causal relations of unity of knowledge are explained in the topological family of monotonic product functions with the same properties. The totality of such properties is explained to evaluate the wellbeing objective criterion with inter-variable circular causation relations signifying the endogenous nature of all variables under choice by the *Tawhidi* law of unity of knowledge arising from primal ontology. The actual empirical evaluation of the coefficients of the wellbeing function and its system of non-linear organic relations between endogenous variables is left for exclusive chapters.

A Non-technical Overview of the Chapter

Underlying the deepening analytical formulation of the single system and multi-various systems of intra-system and inter-system interactive, integrative, and evolutionary learning across sustainability of process in time it is necessary to derive the formal and empirical nature of *Tawhidi* methodology. While the actual evaluation

M. A. Choudhury (✉)
Faculty of Economics, Trisakti University, Jakarta, Indonesia
e-mail: masudc60@yahoo.ca

of the wellbeing function is not carried out in this chapter, its knowledge-induced evaluation is explained. The threshold of estimation and simulation of the coefficient of the system of complex organic relations between knowledge-induced variables is explained. The actual evaluation in the empirical form of the wellbeing function (*maslaha*) is postponed for the later chapters.

Along the direction of explanation of the widest possible formulation and application of the multivarious system of intra-systemic and inter-systemic wellbeing functions in reference to the sequences of *Tawhidi* methodology, it is explained how *maqasid as-shari'ah* and *Tawhid* are contrary perspectives of the methodology of 'everything'. Thereby, references are made to the works in *maqasid as-shari'ah* that nonetheless fail to convey the completeness of *Tawhidi* methodology. Instead, by and large the systemic and relational perspective of inter-variable causality in complex compounding of wellbeing functions (*maslaha*) is never appropriately studied in the literature on *shari'ah*.

The complex family of process-oriented IIE-learning systems in simple and extended forms of multiverses needs to be formalized in the mathematical form to bring out the embedded nature of knowledge-driven evolutionary processes in knowledge, space, and time dimensions. Only by such subtle formalism and the depth of analytical possibility the abstracto-empirical nature of the wellbeing function can be evaluated and rendered to critical reconstruction into the unified world-system in terms of the inter-variable causality.

Formal Symbolism of the *Tawhidi* Methodology and Its Functioning

The continuous intra-system and inter-system of IIE-learning processes are premised on the ontology and epistemology of unity of knowledge. This is the precept explained by complementarities in the form of unified learning between all choices. The choices are determined as good things of life (*halal at-tayabah*) and the avoidance of the bad ones. The continuity of determining such choices forms sustained learning processes in the knowledge, and knowledge-induced space and time dimensions. The resulting world of objective reality is defined by its evaluation of the spanning domain denoted by, $\{\theta, \mathbf{X}(\theta)\}$. Here $\{\mathbf{X}(\theta)\}$ is the complementary vector of variables, $\mathbf{X}(\theta) = \{x_1, x_2, \ldots, x_n\}[\theta]$, induced by the common averaged parameter of unity of knowledge, 'θ'.[1]

---

[1] An example of averaging is parameterization of the ranks of each variable in terms of its induction by the rank signifying interrelationship between the variables in terms of the ranks. A ranked variable computed in a simple way, but not limited to this way of averaging is this: Assign the value 10 (say) to the best value of each of the variables, denoted by $x^*(\theta = 10)$, in its column. The rest of the column parametric values are computed as, $\theta_i = (10/x^*) \cdot x_i$. Thereby we record the values of $\{x_i(\theta_i)\}$. Finally, the average value of $\{\theta_{ij}\}$ is obtained across columns (i) for each row (j). The resulting parametric value is the average value of various 'θ's' in the data-base.

The above parameterization method is more appropriately used for time series data. For the survey data we proceed along the following parameterization method: In the survey case, (row $\times$

$$\theta = \text{plim}\{\theta\} = \text{Average } \{\theta_1, \theta_2, \ldots, \theta_n\}. \tag{3.1}$$

The functional ontologies of the $\{\theta\}$-induced coordinates of the world-system preserve the topological character of monotonic mappings (Henderson & Quandt, 1980). This result is found in the following statement of a theorem: A monotonic positive transformation of a utility function (topological mapping) is a utility function (topological functional). Such monotonic positive transformations preserve the properties of the principle of complementarities that reflects the precept of *Tawhidi* unity of knowledge, which is universally conveyed by $\{\Omega \rightarrow S \equiv [\Omega, S]\}$ in expression (2.8). The transformations occur both intra-systems and inter-systems in reference to multivariate functions.

In its relationship to $\{\Omega \rightarrow S \equiv [\Omega, S]\}$ and the universality and uniqueness of process relations shown in expression (2.8) the essential properties of the imminent functional ontologies are preserved. That is, the functional ontologies all together and in each of the intra-systems and inter-systems are characterized by the properties of endogenous inter-variable circular causal relations in learning domains induced by parameterized θ-values of $\{\boldsymbol{\theta}, \mathbf{X}(\boldsymbol{\theta})\}$. We write the derived system of interrelations of $\{\boldsymbol{\theta}, \mathbf{X}(\boldsymbol{\theta})\}$ with the generic properties of IIE derived from *Tawhidi* methodology as follows:

$$x_i(\theta) = f_i(\theta, x_j(\theta)), \text{ with } i, j = 1, 2, \ldots, n; i \neq j. \tag{3.2}$$

$x_j(\theta)$ denotes the vector excluding ith-variable and including the rest of the variables of the vector $\mathbf{x}(\theta)$-variables. It is recommended to take the system of Eq. (3.2) in the natural loglinear form of the variables. This form would easily yield the values and signs of the coefficients, which yield the partial elasticity coefficients of $x_i(\theta)$ with respect to $\{x_j(\theta)\}$. Besides, the logarithmic form of the interdependent relations between these variables explains the degree of inter-variable interdependence for the good choices as opposed to the bad choices. The partial elasticity coefficients between the variables have their Bayesian probability distribution functions in respect of the embedded θ-parameters with the variables.

We note for instance, a specific form of expression for the system of Eq. (3.2).

The circular causation relations of expression (3.2) form estimable structural econometric equations. Because these are separable estimable equations, the problem of multicollinearity arising from interdependence between the endogenous variables in the structural equations is reduced. The coefficients of estimated equations point out the degrees of complementarities between the interdependent variables of the circular causation relations by their positive signs and marginal substitution by their negative signs.

---

column) responses of each respondent across survey questions form the Likert parametric weights. No further weighting, as in the case of time-series data is required. Averaging across responses would yield the θ-values of the data-base.

The ontology of the unified world-system in the light of the *Tawhidi* framework of unity of knowledge as expressed in expression (2.8) is written in the empirical explanatory form as follows:

$\{\Omega \to S \equiv [\Omega, S]\} \to \{MQS\}_1 \equiv \{\theta^*, \theta\}_1 \to plim\{\theta\} = \theta_1 \to \{X(\theta)\}: (\theta, X(\theta))_1$ PROCESS 1

$[\{\Omega \to S \equiv [\Omega, S]\} \to \{MQS\}_2 \equiv \{\theta^*, \theta\}_2 \to plim\{\theta\} = \theta_2 \to \{X(\theta)\}: (\theta, X(\theta))]_2$ PROCESS 2

$\ldots$

$[\{\Omega \to S \equiv [\Omega, S]\} \to \{MQS\}_n \equiv \{\theta^*, \theta\}_n \to plim\{\theta\} = \theta_n \to \{X(\theta)\}: (\theta, X(\theta))]_n$ PROCESS n

CONTINUITY:

$$\{\Omega \to S \equiv [\Omega, S]\} \to \{MQS\} \equiv \{\theta^*, \theta\} \to plim\{\theta\} = \theta \to \{X(\theta)\}: (\theta, X(\theta)) \quad \substack{\text{CONTINUED} \\ \text{PROCESS}} \tag{3.3}$$

$$\Rightarrow \{\Omega \to S \equiv [\Omega, S]\} \to \cup^I \cap^J \{MQS\} \equiv \{\theta^*, \theta\}\}_P = \ plim\{\theta\} = \theta; \tag{3.4}$$

$$(d/d\theta)f_p[\{\cup^I \cap^J \{MQS\} \equiv \{\theta^*, \theta\}\}_P = plim\{\theta\} = \theta] > 0, \tag{3.5}$$

The above expressions hold up for evolutionary values of k, as was defined earlier. 'f(.)' denotes functional ontologies of the IIE-learning processes 'p'. The expressions (3.3)–(3.5) establish the universal and unique meaning that the *Tawhidi* ontology and its epistemic transformation in unity of knowledge is conveyed by the *sunnah*. Thereby, all monotonic positive transformations are unravelled by the precept of unity of knowledge as pervasive inter-variable MQS-complementarities of *Tawhidi* world-system. This nature of the world-system denoted by $\{(\theta, X(\theta)\}$ remains invariant across evolutionary learning processes. This feature of the continuous world-system governed by *Tawhid* as law of the methodological unity of knowledge determined by choices in MQS indeed also conveys the meaning of continuous sustainability in knowledge, and knowledge-induced space and time.

Tawhidi World-System (*a'lameen*)

Lastly in this section we note that the meaning of world-system according to the *Qur'an* comprehends 'everything' (*a'lameen*). It is thereby implied that, in the context of the participatory nature of all elements of world-systems of every kind, there are intrinsic symbiotic relations of unity of knowledge (*tasbih*) that bring to bear the encompassing methodological worldview conveyed by expressions (3.3) and (3.5).

We thereby comprehend the multidimensional extensions of the tripartite reality. These tripartite realms of reality are Allah, the Mind, and the diversity of World-Systems. Except for the exogenous primal ontology of Allah according to the *Quran*; and with it the epistemological mapping of the *Qur'anic* knowledge via the *sunnah*, all other patterns of Mind (Reasoning) and the World-System are diversely many in nature in their abstracto-empirical concresence. Consequently, the nature of MQS that is determined by the primal ontology of *Tawhid* as the singularly universal and unique law must be diversely many. Yet this worldview is neither found in nor conceptualized by MQS in itself.

The absence of the *sunnah* mapping from MQS to [Ω, S], there being only one-way mapping as shown by an arrow, causes impossibility of inter-causal relations like f5 and f6 in respect to [Ω, S]. Thereby, f3, f4 do not exist with respect to [Ω, S]. On the other hand, f1, f2 and 'S' are relationally admissible as shown in respect of [Ω, S]. Thus, the implication of such composite relations is that, MQS is valid within worldly relations only, (f3–f8); but not so in primal relationship with [Ω, S]. There is no logical reverse relations from MQS to [Ω, S] in the largest scale of creation to Hereafter. The possibility of multidimensional extendibility is caused by [Ω, S]. Inter-causality exists only in the world-system under the primal ontological and epistemic effect of [Ω, S].

Essential Participatory Nature of the *Tawhidi* World-System in Unity of Knowledge

These relational contrariness between *Tawhid* as the monotheistic law of unity of knowledge and MQS is represented universally and uniquely by the principle of pervasive complementarities. The principle of pervasive complementarities in this sense manifests the cardinal essence, which is the nature of the *Tawhidi* participatory world-system in its full domain of 'everything'. The good choices contrast the bad ones that do not manifest and explain monotheistic unity of knowledge in the relational way of symbiosis by divine purity (*Iqlas*).

Figure 3.1 points out the singularly unique and essential mapping from [Ω, S] to MQS. Yet there cannot be a reverse mapping to complete the composite inter-causality among the functional ontologies shown by f's and 'S'. But, if contrarily in the presently mistaken way, MQS is considered as an originary Islamic law that cannot and does not imitate the *Tawhidi* law, then two disjoint sets of conjoint composite relations occur. These are f1, f2, S for [Ω, S] triangle; f3–f8 for MQS being disjoint from [Ω, S].

A serious mistake is pervasive in Auda's (2008, slightly modified) categorization of *shari'ah* contra *Tawhid* in his following words: "*Shari'ah*: The revelation that Muhammad had received and made practicing the message and mission of his life, i.e., the *Qur'an* and the Prophetic tradition." In these words, *shari'ah* has been identified with *Tawhid*, and then also identified with the *sunnah*. A vastly erroneous meaning has been painted. *Tawhid* is the injunction of the *Qur'an* transmitted by the *sunnah* of the Prophet Muhammad for the explicit and complete expression and explanation of *Tawhid* as the primal ontological law of unity of knowledge by systemic integration and continuity of relationships between the good things of life and avoidance of the bad things of life. What is yet unknown between this foundational basis of knowledge and reasoning as undecidable knowledge (*mutashabihat*) is reformed by reference to the *Qur'an* and *sunnah* with the discourse of the learned Islamic community.

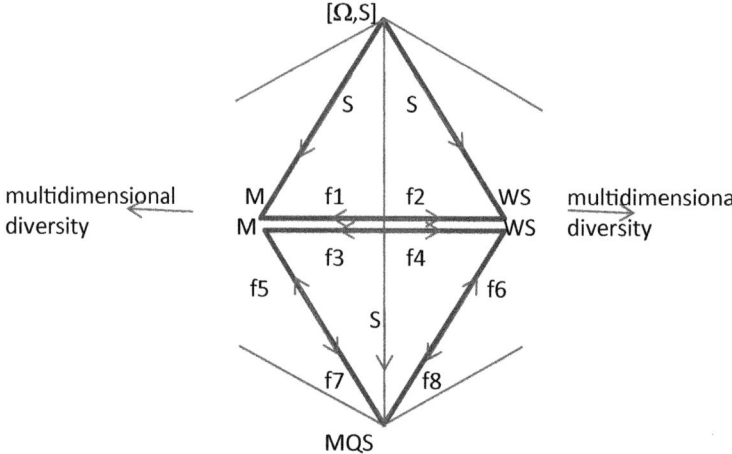

Fig. 3.1 The singularly universal and unique nature of *Tawhid* as Law; no reverse causality from MQS to *Tawhid*

In regards to this total picture, *Tawhid* as law embraces 'everything', the domain of ever-evolving knowledge that system-wide comprehends all of non-physicalism and physicalism, and the abstracto-empirical totality of phenomenological study of the multiverses. As an example, while *shari'ah* conveys a humanly concocted idea of justice, and even though some have tried to study this as balance, moderation, and codification of law, the greater understanding of all such attributes is in terms of methodological worldview of unity of knowledge. This takes up a systemic study of inter-causality and a unified study of the knowledge-induced wellbeing criterion function (*al-maslaha wal-Tawhid*) in terms of the principle of complementarities that characterizes the being and becoming of 'everything'.

Without such an overwhelming inclusive understanding of knowledge there is no substantive content as to how the shar'iah is explained in the following directions (Auda, op cit): That is as, "*Maqasid* is also the group of divine intents and moral concepts upon which the Islamic law is based, such as, justice, human dignity, free will, magnanimity, facilitation, and social cooperation. Thus, they represent the link between the Islamic law and today's notions of human rights, development, and civility." There is no methodological depth in any and all of such noble claims. For *Tawhid* the centrepiece is to understand all such attributes as substantive and functional structures of systemic inter-causality embedded in the ever-broadening domain of evolutionary learning pertaining to the monotheistic precept of unity of knowledge. Such evolutionary learning processes concerning being and becoming of 'everything' span the historical consciousness extending from aye to eternity. The

Qur'an (57:3) declares: "He is the First and the Last, the Ascendant and the Intimate, and He is, of all things, Knowing." *Maqasid as-shari'ah* lays its sole focus on certain partials of earthly affairs alone. It does not have the dynamics either to comprehend the vastness of the multiverse systems of interrelationships or to be even complete in itself and with much of the study of wellbeing left out.

Figure 3.1 establishes the above-mentioned points by means of its sole primal dependence upon *Tawhid* as the ontological law; and the absence of a reverse originary mapping from MQS to $[\Omega, S]$. It is therefore incoherent for MQS to supersede $[\Omega, S]$ in the methodological explanation of divine unity of knowledge as the participatory worldview of 'everything' that is relational and extensively learnt by interaction, integration, and evolution. Because of this incompleteness on the part of MQS to treat the five goals of *maslaha* (masalih) as interconnected holism by the *Tawhidi* primal ontology of unity of knowledge, the five goals have remained independently poised. They form independent elements of a social contract (*aqd*) by being absent of a relational order created by means of them. The need for complementarities by inter-causality between the MQS goals not being there, so also any development of the goals remains independently distributed elements of the wellbeing criterion. Likewise, morality/ethics and materiality remain exogenously treated. A theory of endogenous inter-causal relations of the morality/ethics and the world-system remains unknown among *shari'ah* scholars. *Mujtahids* such as Ibn Taimiyyah, Ibn Qayyim, and Muhammad Asad considered justice in a pedagogical sense of state function. A theory of consciousness in its endogenous induction of justice as natural liberty among people and 'everything' could not be propounded (Rahman, n.d. internet version).

In conclusion to this section we note that, although *Tawhid* as law of 'everything' in unity of knowledge ought to overarch the scope of MQS, yet this is not the case in reality. MQS is a very incomplete field of knowledge and world-system. This is a great limitation of MQS in respect of *Tawhid* as the primal ontological-epistemic law of symbiotic oneness. The matter is similar to what the sages have always asked: What truly is justice (Kant trans Friedrich, 1949; Hume, 1988; Rawls, 1971; Nozick, 1974)? While the Occidental philosophers have not been able to liberate them by any adequate answer because of their persistent culture of Rationalism as a bounded ontology; so also the MQS-gurus have not been able to establish an abstracto-empirical phenomenology of the theory of justice from the *Qur'an* (Coulson, 1984; Hallaq, 2005, 2009; Hassan, 2002). To date all studies on justice in Islam is simply an enunciation of the values that justice in Islam propounds (Ashur, op cit; Attia, op cit; Kamali, 2008). The greater role of consciousness to sustain justice, as according to the principle of justice as balance and unity of knowledge, has not been developed in a scholarly way except for the intellectual project taken up by Auda (op cit.). See also Choudhury (forthcoming in Azid).

Organizing the Participatory Nature of the *Tawhidi* World-System in Its Generality and Specifics

By generality of systems we mean multidimensional integrated systems by way of intra-system and inter-system complementarities between their representative variables. By specifics we mean each specified intra-system. This is the treatment in its account of relational unity of knowledge. This is the intra-systemic case of a specified chain of inter-causality between variables. Therefore, as shown below the distribution of the $\{\theta\}$-values is in association with the corresponding $\{X(\theta)\}$-values, as shown in expressions (3.10, 3.11, 3.12). Expressions (3.7) and (3.8) are for generality of inter-systemic cases, each having its own intra-system dynamics in $\{\theta, X(\theta)\}$-domains. Thus there appear the k-subscripts to identify the inter-systems. The symbol Π_k denotes the compounded number of inter-systems each having its (i, j) in the IIE-learning processes.

These multilayers of systems form multidimensional IIE-learning systems ensemble.

$$\{\Omega \rightarrow S \equiv [\Omega, S]\} \rightarrow \{MQS\} \equiv \{\theta^*, \theta\} \rightarrow \text{plim}\{\theta\} = \theta \rightarrow \{X(\theta)\} : (\theta, X(\theta))_p \tag{3.7}$$

$$\Rightarrow \{\Omega \rightarrow S \equiv [\Omega, S]\} \rightarrow \Pi_k \cup^I \cap^J \{MQS\}_k \equiv \{\theta^*, \theta\}\}_{P,k} = \text{plim}\{\theta\}_k = \theta; \tag{3.8}$$

$$(d/d\theta)f_p[\Pi_k\{\cup^I \cap^J \{MQS\}_k \equiv \{\theta^*, \theta\}\}_{P,k} = \text{plim}\{\theta\}_k = \theta] > 0. \tag{3.9}$$

Organizing the Learning Parameterization of $\{\theta, X(\theta)\}$

The correspondence between $\{\theta, X(\theta)\}$-variables parameterized by θ-values in reference to *Tawhidi* unity of knowledge as methodology of the construction and empirical evaluation of the *maslaha* criterion is now formalized as follows. We use the properties of topological sets and mappings (Maddox, 1970) for a generalized mathematically continuous, differentiable, invertible function as by the Jacobian (Hogg & Craig, 1965) and order-preserving (monotonicity) mappings 'f' from the open set of $\{\theta\}$ to the open set of $\{X(\theta)\}$, such that, $\{\theta\} \rightarrow {}_f\{X(\theta)\}$. There also exist one-to-one correspondence, $f(\theta) = X(\theta)$. These notations could be of vectors, matrixes, and tensors.
Thereby,

$$f(\theta) = \{\theta_1, \theta_2, \ldots, \theta_n\} = \{X_1(\theta_1), X_2(\theta_2), \ldots, X_n(\theta_n)\} \text{ in the vector form.} \tag{3.10}$$

In the matrix form a similar notation of one-to-one correspondence is

$$[\theta_{ij}] = \{[X_{ij}(\theta_{ij})]\}, i = 1, 2, \ldots, m; j = 1, 2, \ldots, n. \tag{3.11}$$

In its more explicit form, expression (3.11) is written as follows and for any monotonic transformation of the same in the topological context:

$$
[\mathbf{X_{ij}(\theta_{ij})}] =
\begin{array}{l}
\text{Observe } 1-m \\
\text{of variable 1} \\
\text{as acceptable} \\
\textit{Tawhidi} \\
\text{choice}
\end{array}
\begin{array}{l}
\text{Observe } 1-m \\
\text{of variable 2} \\
\text{as acceptable} \\
\textit{Tawhidi} \\
\text{choice}
\end{array}
\ldots
\begin{array}{l}
\text{Observe } 1-m \\
\text{of variable n} \\
\text{as acceptable} \\
\textit{Tawhidi} \\
\text{choice}
\end{array}
\begin{array}{l}
\text{corresponding} \\
\text{weights/ranks} \\
\text{of acceptable} \\
\textit{Tawhidi} \text{ choice} \\
\text{(calculated)}
\end{array}
$$

$$
[\mathbf{X_{ij}(\theta_{ij})}] =
\begin{vmatrix}
x_{11}(\theta_{11}) & x_{12}(\theta_{12}) & \ldots & x_{1n}(\theta_{1n}) \\
x_{21}(\theta_{21}) & x_{22}(\theta_{22}) & \ldots & x_{2n}(\theta_{2n}) \\
\ldots & \ldots & \ldots & \\
x_{n1}(\theta_{m1}) & x_{n2}(\theta_{m2}) & \ldots & x_{nn}(\theta_{mn})
\end{vmatrix}
\Leftrightarrow
\begin{vmatrix}
\theta_{11} & \theta_{12} & \ldots & \theta_{1n} \\
\theta_{21} & \theta_{22} & \ldots & \theta_{2n} \\
\ldots & \ldots & \ldots & \\
\theta_{m1} & \theta_{m2} & \ldots & \theta_{mn}
\end{vmatrix}
= [\theta_{ij}]
$$

$$(3.12)$$

By examining the elements of these matrices cross-wise we note the probability limits that are determined in the following way across variables: $\text{plim}_j\{\theta_{ij}\} = \{\theta_i\}$. One such set of values could be the average of $\{\theta_{ij}\}$ across $j = 1, 2, \ldots n$ for different values of $i = 1, 2, \ldots, m$. The respective values of $\{\mathbf{X_{ij}(\theta_{ij})}\}$ with the $\text{plim}_j\{\theta_{ij}\} = \{\theta_i\}$-values are $\{x_{ij}(\theta_i)\}$ across j-values, given different values of $i = 1, 2, \ldots, m$.

More on the use of expression (3.12) in empirical evaluation of the wellbeing criterion will follow starting Chap. 13.

References

Auda, J. (2008). *Maqasid Al-Shari'ah as philosophy of Islamic law, a systems approach*. Herndo, Virginia: International Institute of Islamic Thought.

Choudhury, M. A. (forthcoming). A theory of justice in Islam. In Azid, T. (Ed.), *Justice in Islam*. London, UK: Routledge.

Coulson, N. J. (1984). *Commercial law in the Gulf States: The Islamic legal tradition*. London, England: Graham & Trotman.

Hallaq, W. B. (2005). *The origins and evolution of Islamic law* (p. 182). Cambridge, UK: Cambridge University Press.

Hallaq, W. (2009). *Shari'a: Theory, practice, transformations*. Cambridge, England: Cambridge University Press.

Hassan, H. (2002). Contracts in Islamic law: The principles of commutative justice and liberality. *Journal of Islamic Studies, 13*(3), 257–297.

Henderson, J. M., & Quandt, R. E. (1980). *Microeconomic theory*. New York: McGraw Hill, Inc.

Hogg, R. V., & Craig, A. T. (1965). *Introduction to mathematical statistics*. New York, NY: Macmillan Co.

Hume, D. (1988). *An enquiry concerning human understanding*. Buffalo: Prometheus Books.

Kamali, M. H. (2008). *Shari'ah Law: an introduction*. Oxford, UK: Oneworld Publication.

Kant, I. (1949). In C. J. Friedrich (Ed.), *The philosophy of Kant*. New York, NY: Modern Library.

Maddox, I. J. (1970). *Elements of functional analysis*. Cambridge, England: Cambridge University Press.

Nozick, R. (1974). Distributive justice. In *Philosophy and public affairs* (Vol. 3).

Rahman, T. (n.d.). *Social justice in western and Islamic thought (A comparative study of John Rawls's and Sayyid Qutb's theories of social justice, n.d. internet version).*
Rawls, J. (1971). *A theory of justice.* Cambridge, MA: Harvard University Press.

Chapter 4
Wellbeing Objective Criterion (*Maslaha*)

Masudul Alam Choudhury

Abstract Contrary to various maximization objective criteria in mainstream and orthodox economics centered in the axioms of economic rationality, the objective criterion of the *Tawhidi* methodological worldview rests fully on the evolutionary learning process of unity of knowledge. The resulting evolutionary learning world-system in its generality and details cannot logically yield to optimization. Instead, the method of estimation and simulation in repeated processes takes over. These methods are then applied to the *Tawhidi* objective criterion of wellbeing index to determine the existing level of inter-variables causality and raise better reconstruction based on the 'as is' result changing to the 'as it ought to be' result. This chapter constructs the formal properties of the wellbeing function in terms of the belief-centered knowledge-induced *maslaha* objective criterion. The inner properties and abstracto-empirical embedding in the formal evaluation of the *maslaha* objective criterion are explained. The resulting approach to make policy-analysis, draw inferences, and continue in processes of sustainability over knowledge, space, and time dimensions is set up in a formal way to lay down the empirical details that follow.

A Non-technical Overview of the Chapter

Tawhid as law extends over the domain of abstraction, logical formalism, and abstracto-empirical embedded evaluation of the objective criterion of wellbeing in the extant of knowledge, space, and time dimensions. The rigorous set-up of the various aspects of evaluation of the wellbeing function is explained in terms of the most critical reference point of unity of knowledge. This criterion is the surest sign of *Tawhid* as law.

The inner dynamics of causality and motivation commence from belief-attribute. The belief-attribute is embedded in knowledge formation. Yet it is knowledge that attenuates to abstracto-empirical configuration of inter-causal embeddedness. The relationship between belief, knowledge and reasoning, and practical implications

M. A. Choudhury (✉)
Faculty of Economics, Trisakti University, Jakarta, Indonesia
e-mail: masudc60@yahoo.ca

need to be understood in a comprehensive sense to bring together the total *Tawhidi* methodology on applied issues of a problem-solving nature.

Examples that lend to such abstracto-empirical problem-solving outlook are legion in their otherwise way-laid treatment by *shari'ah* of problems of partitioned contracts of Islamic economics and finance. Debt-liquidation, and the role of inter-action, integration, and evolutionary learning in sustainability processes over knowl-edge, space, time dimensions are among some of the examples that are studied by means of the dynamics of unity of knowledge a la *Tawhid* as law contrary to the methodologically benign approach of *shari'ah*.

An important example of a social asset in the wider field of valuation of the good things of life for the common benefit of all is *waqf*. *Waqf* as perpetual charity for attaining wellbeing (*maslaha*) is thus treated as a continuously sustainable experi-ence in moral-material coterminous causality. In the same way, the *Tawhidi* law of evaluation of the state of the socio-scientific order evaluates by a unique and uni-versal formal approach. The *Tawhidi* methodology is fed into the outlook of *waqf* as perpetual charity. The approach of *shari'ah* to the *waqf* problem is differently viewed as endowment. The results of such dual perspectives show up between *waqf* as perpetual charity according to *Tawhid* as law ontologically premised in unity of knowledge and endowment premised in the exogenously centered meaning of contracts in *shari'ah*.

The wider field of unified moral-material valuation of issues and problems accord-ing to their generalized and detailed aspects takes up two distinctive scenarios that are important in studying the intra-systemic and inter-systemic nature of valuation. This substantive and propertized nature of sustainability in intertemporal valuation is approached by deconstruction of the wellbeing function in terms of detailed val-uation problems and then combining them in the form of a compounded wellbeing model. The results are then both a particularized and a generalized world-system integrated worldview in accordance with the *Tawhidi* law of unity of knowledge as explained by the organic inter-causality between the variables.

In the end it is noted that, the rich phenomenological study of *Tawhidi* law premised in monotheistic unity of knowledge comes to a confluence in the evaluation of the wellbeing function in each stage of evolutionary learning across sustainability in knowledge, space, and time dimensions. Each such process-oriented evaluation of the wellbeing function converges into the primal ontological, epistemological, phe-nomenological, and sustainability attributes of the entire process-oriented *Tawhidi* methodological worldview. The wellbeing objective criterion function thus unifies in the monotheistic form along the entire realm of sustainability of evolutionary learning processes with intertemporal causality.

The resulting explanation of the generalized *Tawhidi* methodology of monothe-istic unity of knowledge makes an unbridgeable partition between *Tawhid* as the monotheistic primal ontology of *Qur'an* and *sunnah* on its own right. On the other side lies the philosophy of rationalism in the occidental philosophy of science. The foundation of *shari'ah* being devoid of the overarching methodological worldview of *Tawhid* as law is also not distinct from rationalism. The *Tawhidi* reconstruction of the world-system is thus the pressing need for rejuvenating Islamic thought along its continued line of revival called *tajdid*.

Introduction

The climax of the application of *Tawhidi* methodology in the building blocks of the participatory and morally/ethically embedded world-system governed by the primal ontology and epistemology of unity of knowledge is reflected in the objective criterion of such a unified, permanently complementary structure of the world-system. This is a novel and path-breaking socio-scientific concept. It annuls the core assumption of scarcity of resource allocation as in mainstream economics and 'everything' else.

First therefore, we define the nature and form of the wellbeing objective criterion (*maslaha*) in reference to *Tawhidi* methodological worldview. Secondly, the empirical goal followed by the method to evaluate the wellbeing criterion in the light of *Tawhidi* methodological worldview is established in reference to the inter-variable circular causality between the critical variables, and thereby extended. Thirdly, as explained in the expressions (3.11), (3.12), the evaluation of the wellbeing criterion of the specifically and generally addressed world-system under study is sustained along continuums of knowledge and knowledge-induced space and time dimensions.

There is a distinct contrast in the theory, formalism, and applications of the wellbeing (*maslaha*) criterion and the mainstream maximization goals. Essentially, this contrast rests on the evolutionary learning worldview of *Tawhidi* precept of unity of knowledge on the one side, and the contrarily the end of novelty by assuming the goal of optimization in mainstream socio-scientific disciplines (Shackle, op cit).

The Concept of Evolutionary Wellbeing in {Knowledge, Space, Time} Dimensions

The simulated world in its ontological generality from which is derived the particulars of functional ontology as designs of a transformed world-system yields the methodological and applied form of the wellbeing criterion in the knowledge, space, and time dimensions. This idea is of a singularly revolutionary kind in the history of socio-scientific thought (Kuhn, 1970).[1]

The resulting conception of the wellbeing criterion that is premised on the primal ontology of unity of knowledge as law, as in the monotheistic systemic meaning of oneness (*Tawhid*) by organic interrelations, brings out its applications at each step of

---

[1] Kuhn (1970, p. 152) writes: "… scientific revolutions are here taken to be those non-cumulative developmental episodes in which an older paradigm is replaced in whole or in part by an incompatible new one".

the model formalization. In this way, the methodology of the unique and universal law of unity of knowledge premised on the primal ontology of monotheistic oneness is shown to apply cognitively at every point of the theory of wellbeing criterion, its formulation, and its application all along the continuity of the knowledge, space, and time trajectory. Likewise, the emergent wellbeing criterion, which is premised on the methodology and application of the primal ontology of unity of knowledge followed by the derived epistemological and phenomenological constructs, is also capable of explaining the rationalistic epistemological origin and nature of the earlier mainstream wellbeing concepts of space-time genre (Einstein, 1954).

With this introduction, we now formalize the wellbeing function for the generality and particulars of the world-system under study as premised in *Tawhidi* methodological worldview of unity of knowledge. To formulate the wellbeing function in its analytical form for methodological and empirical study we note that the Fixed Point Evolutionary Equilibrium (Kakutani, 1941; Nikaido, 1987) result in $\{(\boldsymbol{\theta}, \mathbf{X}(\boldsymbol{\theta}))\}$ and in each of these topological sets of variables taken up in their functionally related forms. Besides, the topological properties of the functional ontology suggests that, monotonic transformation of the $\{(\boldsymbol{\theta}, \mathbf{X}(\boldsymbol{\theta}))\}$-set would satisfy the same properties. We therefore denote the wellbeing function defined on the Fixed Point Evolutionary Equilibrium caused by $\boldsymbol{\theta}$-knowledge parameters as monotonic transformation as follows:

$$W(\theta) = W(\theta, \mathbf{X}(\theta)) \qquad (4.1)$$

The properties of continuity, differentiability, well-definition of functional transformations, and the invertibility of the monotonic functions so that the Jacobian of the functions exist, and altogether establish the derivation of the following type:

$$\theta = F(\mathbf{X}(\theta)) \qquad (4.2)$$

Note further the methodological meaning embedded in these expressions. The primal ontology of unity of knowledge in *Tawhid* as the Islamic law of 'everything', imparts this participatory and complementary worldview through the IIE-learning processes formed and sustained by θ-knowledge parameter as this is derived from the *Tawhidi* primal origin. Reference is made here to the system of ontological and epistemological relations. The pervasiveness of θ-values in continuum of knowledge and knowledge-induced space and time dimensions sets the properties of non-null continuous differentiability and invertibility of monotonic transformations that establish the Fixed Point Theorem but in the topology of unbounded and open space of intra-system and inter-system IIE-learning in unity of knowledge.

Without the universal and unique and singularly outstanding premise of *Tawhid* in its primal ontology of unity of knowledge, the above analytical properties would not be possible. Thereby, the functions (4.1) and (4.2) would not be possible. Let us investigate this corollary.

The Ontology of Rationalism

Contrary to *Tawhidi* primal ontology is the ontology of Rationalism. It dichotomizes a priori reason of the moral imperative from a posteriori reason of the sensate world-system. Thereby, the rationalist differentiation between these two ontologies of reasoning, namely $R_{apriori}$, $R_{aposteriori}$ is annulled. The expression $\{\Omega \rightarrow S[\Omega, S]\}$ is replaced by the disjoint relationship, $\{R_{apriori}\} \cap \{R_{aposteriori}\} = \phi$; $\{R_{apriori}\} \cup \{R_{aposteriori}\} \subseteq \{R_{aposteriori}\}$, which conveys a totally sensate material explanation of the world-system having no necessary moral imperative, although much desired in the Kantian ontology; but not so in Hume's ontology.

Consequently, the rationalist a priori domain comprehending God and the unified world-system is replaced by the inclusion of the moral imperative within the rationalist a posteriori domain. Consequently, a unique and universal role of the a priori ontology determining the a posteriori domain in terms of the precept of unity of knowledge as a participatory world-system ceases to be explanatory. The differences in the ontological precepts and their epistemological transformation in terms of competition contra complementarity (participation) by unity of knowledge causes loss of well-definition, continuity, differentiability, and existence of the Jacobian matrix of the multivariate wellbeing function. The knowledge embedded expressions (4.1) and (4.2) would not exist.

Circular Causation Between Variables in IIE-Learning Processes

The IIE-learning processes in the formation of $\{(\theta, X(\theta)\}$ tuples of morally/ethically embedded multivariates have been explained to be formed in stages of intra-systems evolved into inter-systems across the continuum of knowledge and knowledge-induced space and time. The IIE-learning processes thereby exist pervasively across continuums. Thereby, the continuity, differentiability, invertibility, and well-definition properties of the functional transformations in $\{(\theta, X(\theta)\}$ towards explaining the endogenous nature of interrelating variables through IIE-learning processes. Such endogenous relations in $\{(\theta, X(\theta)\}$ are expressed by testable degrees of complementarities between the variables in system of circular causation relations. They are as many as the variables are. Plus there is the additional quantitative equation of wellbeing in the whole vector of variables.

The degrees of complementarity between the pairing (participatory) variables are indicated by the coefficients of the variables. Positive signs of the coefficients imply positive complementarities between the good choices according to the precept of unity of knowledge between the endogenous variables. Negative signs of coefficients imply partial marginal rates of substitution between the endogenous variables as in the case of marginal rate of substitution in neoclassical economics. The last of the equations is the expression (4.2) as a quantitative transformation of the conceptual form of the wellbeing function given by expression (4.1).

The estimated followed by the simulated coefficients, and thus the evaluated coefficients of the various variables in relation to 'θ'-endogenous variable can be interpreted. The sum of such evaluated coefficients would then imply the state of economies of scale of the wellbeing function or otherwise. The *maslaha* indicator is thus determined along with the weights of the various variables in relation to 'θ'-knowledge variable in the quantitative form of the conceptual wellbeing function. The particular way of such evaluation of the wellbeing function that is evaluated subject to the system of circular causation equations, will be shown in empirical examples commencing from Chap. 13. It is convenient to take each of the equations in the natural loglinear form. This form in the conceptual and evaluated forms yield interpretations to the coefficients as partial elasticity coefficients of the wellbeing index (criterion). These technical concepts are explained later on in this manuscript.

Contrary to the wholly endogenous nature of all variables expressed through their functional relations, the mainstream and the existing Islamic economics pursued independently of *Tawhid* as the primal ontological law, treats inter-variable relations in various exogenous forms. See almost every presently falsely designed macroeconomic and econometric models of *shari'ah* imputation in so-called 'Islamic' economics and finance. Examples are of Munawar Iqbal on a feigned conception of money in Islam; M. Kabir Hassan & Lewis on so-called Islamic banking and mainstream econometric modeling without foundational Islamic methodology; and Ishaq Bhatti on an incorrect use of mainstream econometric models in so-called Islamic finance. Thereby, the relational property of the complementary variables is denied for the sake of an anchor of given variables for solving or estimating the system of equations with number of variables being higher than the number of observations (Johnston, 1984). In the *Tawhidi* String Relation the only most essential exogenous primal origin is the primal ontology of *Tawhid* as the sole and complete law of 'everything'. This foundational premise never changes as explained in the expressions (3.11), (3.12). The foundational methodological premise establishes the only existent exogenous, universal, and unique absoluteness of *Tawhidi* primal ontology and episteme for effectiveness in modeling the generality and particulars of the world-system.

Two questions remain to be answered now: Since 'θ' representing knowledge-flow of unity of knowledge is derived from the primal ontology of *Tawhid*, is it therefore an exogenous variable? The answer is in the negative, since 'θ' is derived discursively through the passage of 'θ^*' (of *ulul-amr*) through (θ^*, θ) into the world-system and then is subjected to empirical evaluation in the wellbeing function, subject to circular causation relations.

The second question is this: Are the categorically denied choices called *haram* exogenously determined once and for all in the abstracto-empirical formalism of the *Tawhidi* world-system? The law of *haram* and its mandated elements remain permanently denied in the *Tawhidi* law. Yet this status of *haram* is established discursively by learning and wisdom according to the *Qur'an*. The *Qur'an* declares (16:114) in verses the presence of the underlying discourse to determine the *haram* contrary to the permissible, *halal*: "Therefore, you shall eat from God's provisions 'everything' that is lawful and good, and be appreciative of God's blessings, if you do worship Him alone." Thus the universe of good choices is abundant, excluding the marginal number of prohibited ones.

Note also the variable-symbolizing in the evaluation of the wellbeing function with the choice of all positively complementary variables as ordained by *Tawhid* as law. If some *haram* indicators are present, such as *riba* (interest rate, 'i'), then we invert the variable (1/i) to combine with rate of return (r). The entered variable of the wellbeing function then is (r/i). The implication is that, although *riba* is absolutely prohibited in the *Qur'an*, its persistent existence in 'everything' means that *riba* must be phased out to the best possible instant, while trade is promoted (r). Yet another example is of forbidden consumption. In this case too, the symbolic inversion applies, for although *haram* is forbidden, yet avoidance of compulsion in religion means that *haram* will exist although eschewed.

The TSR Epistemic Definition of Islamic Economics as an Example of Endogenous Inter-variable Relational Dynamics

Mainstream version of Islamic economics, which has become a fashion in present times, has failed to give an intellectual groundwork to Islamic economics and has thereby contributed nothing to the worldview of creative learning. Contrary to this failed status of mainstream terminology of Islamic economics, the ontological and epistemic foundation of truly Islamic methodological worldview offers the following topological orientation to the field of Islamic Economics, $E(\theta)$:

$$E(\theta) = E\{(\theta, p, x, R, \wp, t)[\theta]\} = \{E(\theta, Space, Time)[\theta]\}. \quad (4.3)$$

Because of continuous evolutionary learning by $\{\theta\}$, dynamic preferences are formed discursively as a decision-making behavior. Therefore, if a society has m-number of individuals, then social preference ($\wp_{soc}$) is formed by the IIE-aggregation of organic unity of knowledge:

$E(\theta) = E\{(\theta, p, \mathbf{X}, \mathbf{R}, \wp, t)[\theta]\}$; with p denoting price vector; $\mathbf{R}$ denoting resource vector; $\wp$ denoting discursively determined collaborative preferences over choices with social valuation. All the variables are induced by unity of knowledge as the ontological-epistemic factor over knowledge 'θ', and knowledge-induced space and time $(t(\theta))$. The knowledge-dynamic nature of preferences maps over events across time is explained by, $(d/d\theta)[\wp_{soc} = \cup_k^{i=interaction} \cap_k^{j=integration} \{\wp_k\}][E(\theta)]] > 0$, across specified set of events, $\{E(\theta)\}$. $k = 1, 2,..., m$; i, j denote as many interactions (i) leading to integration (j) with simulated consensus, followed by evolutionary learning denoted by the differential $(d/d\theta)[.]$.

We note also that the vector, $E(\theta, p, \mathbf{X}, \mathbf{R}, \theta, t)[\theta]$ is endogenous in its elements by virtue of their systemic discursive nature of inter-causal relations implying inter-variable complementarities ensuing from the property of unity of knowledge of *Tawhidi* methodology. The continuously differentiable property in respect of 'θ'-induced variables conveys sustainability of the episteme of unity of knowledge.

An Example of endogenous versus exogenous variables in Tawhidi economic relations

In the epistemic definition of Islamic economics and finance, government expenditure is changed to endogenously determined spending variable. Now a complementary relationship exists between public and private sectors by way of agents in these sectors discursively unifying as decision-makers to nurture a market economy in the good things of life (life-fulfillment needs). Thereby, 'θ'-parameter representing unity of knowledge, induces the spending variable in life-fulfillment goods.

Contrarily, in mainstream macroeconomics and in mainstream Islamic economics, government expenditure is treated as an exogenous variable. Thereby, all macroeconomic policies are treated exogenously. On the other hand, all policies are endogenous in *Tawhidi* Islamic economics and finance by virtue of such policies being endogenously derived by discourse and systemic participation in the economy and society wide aggregation. Because participatory decisions are micro-preferences leading into aggregate preferences formed by the IIE-learning processes, say between households, private sector, and public sector in the *Tawhidi* Islamic economy, therefore, the compounded social preference and policy vector can be written as $\mathbf{P}(\theta)$:

$\mathbf{P}(\wp_{soc}(E(\theta))) = \cup_k^{i=\text{interaction}} \cap_k^{j=\text{integration}} \{\mathbf{P}\{\wp_k\}[E(\theta)]; k = 1, 2, ..., m; i, j$ denote as many interactions (i) leading to integration (j) (simulated consensus) with evolutionary learning denoted by,

$$(d/d\theta)[\mathbf{P}\{\wp_{soc}\} = \cup_k^{i=\text{interaction}} \cap_k^{j=\text{integration}} \mathbf{P}[\{\wp_k\}[E(\theta)]] > 0. \qquad (4.4)$$

Furthermore, because of the endogenous possibility of monetary policy vector as in the Quantity Theory of Money and in Money-Commodity-Money (MCM) model, and the endogenous nature of fiscal variable as spending in a market transforming economy, therefore, both of these policy vectors complement endogenously.

The TSR as Formalism to Evaluate the Wellbeing Objective Function: The *Maslaha* Criterion

The complete evaluation system of TSR objective of wellbeing, subject to circular causation explaining pervasive endogeneity between variables is now formulated.

Expression (4.5) is a universal formalism that can be applied to all fields of abstracto-empirical investigation. It can be applied to morally inclusive socio-scientific studies as well as to issues of ethically differentiated systems (Holton, 1992). The difference between these two applications is only this: The *maqasid as-*

Solely Exogenous Permanence of

Tawhidi primal Ontological Law
and *sunnah* as epistemological
mapping of *Tawhidi* law onto the
learning world-system
$\{\Omega \rightarrow S \equiv [\Omega,S]\}$
⇓   (4.5)

The Complete Endogenous
World-System across
Knowledge and knowledge-induced
Space and Time Dimensions

                                    PEOCESS 1
──→
                                                              CONTINUITY

Deriving reasoning in epistemic knowledge
$\{(\theta^*,\theta)\}$: MQS
⇓

Evaluation of generality and particular
of World-System
⇓

Evaluate (estimation Followed by Simulation)	$W(\theta) = W(X(\theta))$ Wellbeing (*maslaha*) in conceptual form	$x_i(\theta) = f_i(\theta,x_j(\theta))$ $i,j=1,2,...,n; i{\neq}j$ system of n-number of circular causation equations in the endogenous variables, $\{(\theta,X(\theta))\}$. This sequenc of variables forms the specific world-system under study.	$\theta = F(X(\theta)) \longrightarrow$ quantitative form of the wellbeing function, $W(\theta)$, which is the conceptual form deriving from *Tawhidi* primal ontological and epistemological premise.

Fig. 4.1 The *Tawhidi* string relation in one process (finite knowledge and knowledge-induced space and time dimensions)

shari'ah al-Tawhid premised on the monotheistic unity of knowledge as the *Tawhidi* ontological and epistemic origin of knowledge in the good things of life (*halal at-tayyabah*) forms the choices of the wellbeing objective criterion (Fig. 4.1).

Contrarily, the bad choices are identified in the *mafasid*-function as a utilitarian welfare criterion with marginalist contest of individualism and independence by social differentiation between the varioussocio-scientific systems and their variables. Still, the differentiated identities between the good and the bad together are determined by the attributes of the unique and universal law of *Tawhid* that dichotomizes within its unified scope the meanings of good and bad. This is the consequence of the foundational ontological law that applies the unique law of unity of knowledge in the following ways:

$$\cup^{\text{interaction}} \cap^{\text{integration}} \{(\boldsymbol{\theta}, \mathbf{X}(\boldsymbol{\theta})) = \text{Good}\} \neq \phi; \cup \cap \rightarrow \{(\boldsymbol{\theta}', \mathbf{X}'(\boldsymbol{\theta}')) \text{Bad}\} \neq \phi; \tag{4.6}$$

$$\lim_{\theta}[\{(\boldsymbol{\theta}, \mathbf{X}(\boldsymbol{\theta})) = \text{Good}\} \cup \cap \{(\boldsymbol{\theta}', \mathbf{X}'(\boldsymbol{\theta}')) = \text{Bad}\}][\theta, \theta'] = \phi;$$

$$\lim_{\{\theta\}}[\{(\boldsymbol{\theta}, \mathbf{X}(\boldsymbol{\theta})) = \text{Good}\} \cup \cap \{(\boldsymbol{\theta}', \mathbf{X}'(\boldsymbol{\theta}')) = \text{Bad}\}][\theta, \theta'] = \phi. \tag{4.7}$$

Analytical Formulation of the *Tawhidi* String Relations as the Framework of *Tawhidi* Abstracto-Empirical Methodology in Respect of Application to *Waqf*, Perpetual Charity

We now refer to the formulation of TSR with application of its system nature of global inter-causality to the topic of *waqf*, perpetual charity in Islam. The general idea of perpetual charity is explained in the beautiful exegesis of the verse of the *Qur'an* (2:265).[2] Out of such exegesis of *Qur'anic* verses arises the general theory of charity, productiveness, plenty, and life-fulfillment. All these attributes combine organically in the wellbeing criterion (*maslaha*) of the generalized system of inter-causal relations between the multivariates. This representation is formalized below. *Waqf* in such a kind of the general theory of the common good and social capital is to be understood in the system meaning of *Tawhidi* unity of knowledge. This meaning bears on the principle of pervasive complementarities between the good things of life defined by their inter-causal nature of pairing (consilience as complementarities). Likewise, as pointed out in expressions (4.6) and (4.7), TSR-methodology also applies to the bad choices in terms of their mathematical union by way of independently distributed and aggregated functional forms.

Application to the good choices pointed out by pervasive complementarities between the good things of life brings about wellbeing (*maslaha*). Application to the bad choices in the form of their disjoint and independently distributed utilitarian functional aggregation is the permanent sign of moral and social differentiation. The morality and ethics manifested by inter-causal relations between vastly endogenous sets of variables is the sure sign of the blessed functioning of organic and symbiotic consilience (Wilson, 1998). In such relational functioning positive complementarities are realized. When negative complementarities exist, the meaning then is of

---

[2]And the example of those who spend their wealth seeking means to the approval of Allah and assuring [reward for] themselves is like a garden on high ground which is hit by a downpour—so it yields its fruits in double. And [even] if it is not hit by a downpour, then a drizzle [is sufficient]. And Allah, of what you do, is Seeing.

marginalism and systemic differentiation. In the disjoint case as of utilitarianism with its lateral and vertical aggregation, the *Qur'anic* pairing worldview dissolves into non-connectivity of inter-variable relations. Such functional independence between the linearly related endogenous and exogenous variables is explained by the constant estimated nature of the coefficients of the evaluated model.

We formalize these relations in the following way in terms of the wellbeing function with circular causation relations between two sets of variables in the vector, X $= \{x_w, x_p, x_g\}$, with x_p and x_g being independent of each other.

Consequently, let the *waqf* related wellbeing function (*maslaha*) be denoted by $W(x_w, x_p, x_g)$. Here x_w denotes financial value of *waqf*; x_p denotes private sector donation; x_g denotes government donation on *waqf*. Thus government control of *waqf* $W(.)$ is estimated by the circular causal equations.

For instance, government expenditure in social directions including *waqf*-type charity is exogenous in nature, not invoking moral, ethical, and social consciousness. On the contrary, spending in charity as of *waqf* by the micro-entrepreneurial private sector is an endogenous variable caused by its system-causal interactive nature. It invokes consciousness by system-causality in respect of unity of knowledge in the world-system of *waqf* as perpetual charity.

Figure 4.2 can now be formulated in the form of the *Tawhidi* String Relations in Fig. 4.3, in a one-process and one string of evolutionary learning system with continuity across the historical consciousness, HH: $\{\theta, \mathbf{X}(\theta), t(\theta)\}$. This entirety comprehensively overarches the full *Tawhidi* methodological worldview of unity of knowledge in 'everything' taken up here in a single stage. This formalism is later on expanded to multi-systems.

An Exemplification of One-Stage TSR in Regards to *Waqf*

We now exemplify the one-stage TSR-learning process model by the *Tawhidi* meta-science relationship of perpetual charity as *waqf*. In the context of the *Qur'an* (2:261), the properties of perpetual charity inter-causally connected with wellbeing presents an appropriate example of an entity of meta-science in *Tawhidi* methodological perspective. In this meta-science perspective of *Tawhidi* unity of knowledge, *waqf* is defined by the following vector: $\{x_1 =$ value of asset, $x_2 =$ value of specific purposes $(1, 2, \ldots, n)$ by x_{2i} items (e.g. poverty alleviation, education, medical, microenterprise, charitable donations, etc.), employment generation, income generation, productivity, etc. $i = 1, 2, \ldots, m))$, and parameterized wellbeing contribution by unity of relations between these $\{x_{ki}\}$, $k = 1, 2 \ldots, n$; $i = 1, 2, \ldots, m$. Thus this vector is induced by the wellbeing parameter $\{\theta_{ki}\}$ in reference to the inter-variable unity of knowledge. Thereby, the wellbeing vector is denoted by, $\{x_{ki}(\theta_{ki})\}$.

The applied section of this work will point out the computational aspect of determining the representative best-value as prorata ranks, say by $\theta = 10$. Thereby the prorated $\{\theta_{ki}\}$–values by variables in respect of the representative best-values of the data-columns are computed to represent the parameterized $\{\theta_{ki}\}$–values. The data-

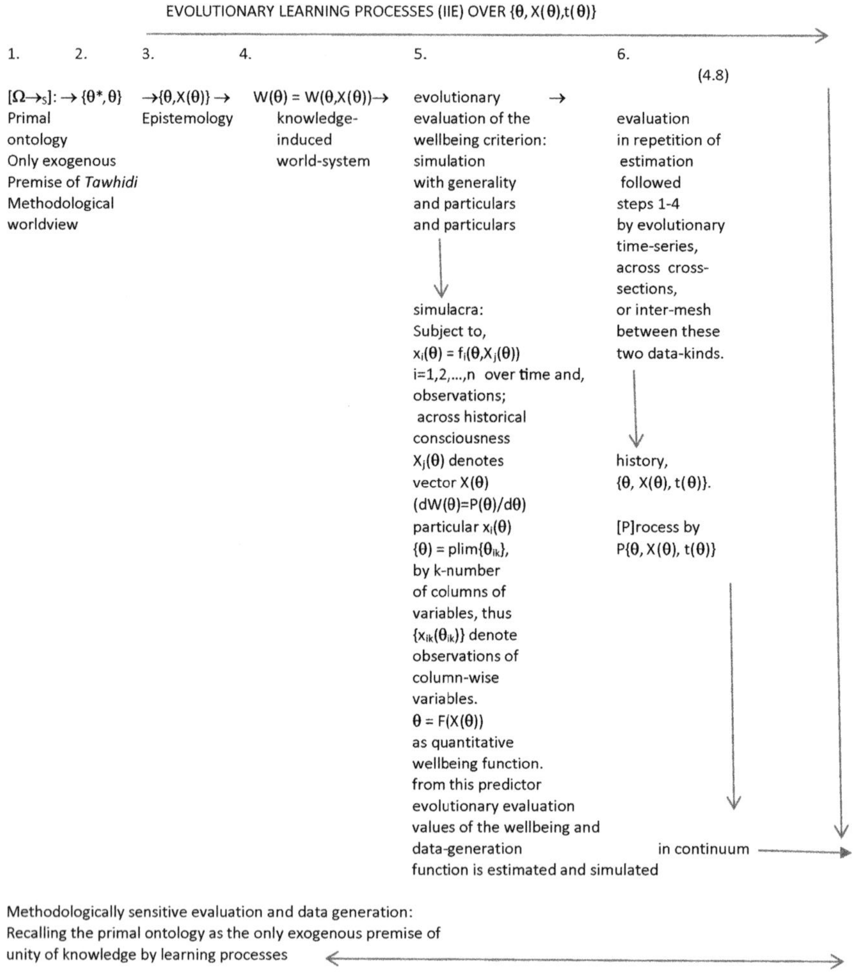

EVOLUTIONARY LEARNING PROCESSES (IIE) OVER {θ, X(θ),t(θ)}
1. 2. 3. 4. 5. 6.
(4.8)
[Ω→s]: → {θ*,θ} →{θ,X(θ)} → W(θ) = W(θ,X(θ))→ evolutionary →
Primal ontology Only exogenous Premise of Tawhidi Methodological worldview
Epistemology
knowledge-induced world-system
evaluation of the wellbeing criterion: simulation with generality and particulars and particulars
simulacra: Subject to, xi(θ) = fi(θ,Xj(θ)) i=1,2,...,n over time and, observations; across historical consciousness Xj(θ) denotes vector X(θ) (dW(θ)=P(θ)/dθ) particular xi(θ) {θ) = plim{θik}, by k-number of columns of variables, thus {xik(θik)} denote observations of column-wise variables. θ = F(X(θ)) as quantitative wellbeing function. from this predictor evolutionary evaluation values of the wellbeing and data-generation function is estimated and simulated
evaluation in repetition of estimation followed steps 1-4 by evolutionary time-series, across cross-sections, or inter-mesh between these two data-kinds.
history, {θ, X(θ), t(θ)}.
[P]rocess by P{θ, X(θ), t(θ)}
in continuum
Methodologically sensitive evaluation and data generation: Recalling the primal ontology as the only exogenous premise of unity of knowledge by learning processes

Fig. 4.2 *Waqf* in the TSR methodological fold

1. 2. 3. 4. 5.

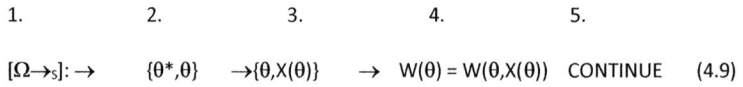

$$[\Omega \to_S]: \to \quad \{\theta^*, \theta\} \quad \to \{\theta, X(\theta)\} \quad \to \quad W(\theta) = W(\theta, X(\theta)) \quad \text{CONTINUE} \qquad (4.9)$$

Fig. 4.3 *Waqf* as moral-material unified event in *Tawhidi* unity of knowledge in sustainability of continuum of evolutionary learning processes of IIE(θ)

set is thus established with the $\{x_{ki}, \theta_{ki}, \text{averaged } \{\theta_{ki}\}\} = \theta$-values by respective data columns.[3]

The permanent ontological and epistemological presence of item (1) in the TSR-model (4.8) acting across continuums of the unitary knowledge-induced systems (2)–(4) and beyond, brings out the substantive nature of *waqf* in the *Qur'anic* and *sunnah* meanings of perpetual charity (*Qur'an*, 2:261). This derivation of the wider nature of *waqf* establishes the socially inclusive and development system of *waqf* as a process-based learning organism that pairs with the good things of life (*Qur'an* 36:36). The meaning so conveyed by the socio-cybernetic implication of *waqf* as a symbiotic system with sustainable continuums makes the underlying idea to be of the epistemic nature.

This kind of implication is not how *waqf* is implied according to present-day practices. Consequently, in the absence of the wider field of valuation of *waqf* as a socially inclusive, developmental, and sustainable idea, the history of *waqf* is a sorry affair (Joseph, 2014). This decline is noted particularly after the nineteenth century, when *waqf* was taken over by state control. Thus the holistic interactive, integrative, and evolutionary learning worldview of *waqf* has lost its fervour ever after the prophetic and classical period of Islam. Now if there is a future for *waqf* as a truly Islamic institution with its worldview centered in IIE-learning processes, then it must return to the classical understanding of the underlying principles.

In order to revive the classical *waqf* tradition in the framework of social capital, the TSR methodology invokes the following approach of its study: *Waqf* is governed by the ontological law of *Tawhid*. *Waqf* thereby becomes a case of particular world-system that exhibits in its moral-material perspective the unity of knowledge as blending of relations of embedding of circular causality between moral and material representations of variables. Besides, such a dynamic nature of moral-material embedding represented by *waqf* extends over the historical consciousness of {knowledge, knowledge-induced space and time}. The systemic phenomenology of *Tawhidi* unity of knowledge as marked by positive complementarities between the good things of life and the avoidance of the bad things of life is thereby quantitatively evaluated by the wellbeing function, subject to the properties of inter-variable endogeneity and the inter-variable causality between them. In all of these properties the attributes of learning processes characterized by interaction, integration, and continuous evolution spans over the multidimensional domain of {knowledge, space and time}[θ] in the disjoint cases of the Good and Bad. Sustainability follows in continuum over such multidimensional domains. Like all charitable gifts endowed in the name of Allah for the sake of generating wellbeing (*maslaha*), *waqf* also establishes unifying synergy in system-symbiosis representing the living and learning experience of *Tawhidi* unity of knowledge in the dynamics of being and becoming.

Coming to the case of *waqf* in the form of cash or fixed assets, which has been debated by Muslim clergy, we can resolve such a debate by the use of the wellbeing

---

[3]In reference to $\theta = 10$ for the best-value of $\{x_{ki}{}^*(10)\}$ by rows and columns of data, we obtain the computed $\{\theta_{ki}\}$–values: $(10/x^*(10)) \cdot x_{ik} = \{\theta_{ki}\}$. Thereby, plim $\{\theta_{ki}\}$ = Average $\{\theta_{ki}\}$ across columns $\{\theta\}$ by rows of the $\{x_{ki}(\theta_{ki})\}$-variables.

evaluation of the *waqf* system. *Waqf* is understood as a vast nexus of interrelated variables of the *waqf* associated wellbeing function that embeds moral-material inter-causality out of a vast and evolving system of endogenous variables. The above-mentioned delineation of such a system of endogenous variables in the wellbeing function defines the systemic inter-causality. The idea of *waqf* is thus not restricted to cash and fixed assets and institutional forms. Instead, *waqf* is a forceful idea and an institution with careful organization of its plenitude to convey wellbeing to an increasing domain of entities as social capital. We can now fit this principle of unitary social capital in the *maslaha* objective criterion in expression (4.8) to yield expression (4.9).

Generalization of 'Everything' in the TSR-Model

What is true of *waqf* as the idea of perpetual charity is a landmark of the general theory of charity, sharing, and moral-material sustainability at the grassroots, meaning life-fulfillment total sustainability. All such forms of charitable undertaking are understood in the light of the grand objective of wellbeing (*maslaha*) as defined within the *Tawhidi* precept of unity of knowledge. Therefore, the general theory of charity and shared distribution though not emanating from the side of *waqf*, is still formalized on the basis of *Tawhidi* methodological worldview of unity of knowledge and its functioning in the generality and details of the world-system evaluated by *maslaha* in the continuum of knowledge, space, and time dimensions.

In relationship to Fig. 4.4, while replacing the reference of *waqf* to the general theory of charity in the context of the objective goal of *maslaha*, the derived Process explained in Interaction, Integration, and Evolution (IIE) formalizes the generalized theory of 'everything'. The IIE- learning process in unity of knowledge of stages 2–5 with unchanging *Tawhidi* ontological origin of stage 1,[4] and repetitive continuity by stage 6 formalizes the generalized theory of 'everything' in the *Tawhidi* mould.

It is noted that every point of conscious historical trajectory HH is identified by complex compounding of Events comprising stages 1–5 of Fig. 4.4. There remains the ultimate exogeneity of the *Tawhidi* ontological law as in stage 1 for all evolutionary learning processes like 2–5 by repeated occurrence of the stages across stage 6. The ultimate point of optimal knowledge and its induced universe marks the reappearance of the *Tawhidi* ontological law in its manifest form in relation to the Great Event of Hereafter (*Akhira*). Hence the evolutionary learning universe of unity of knowledge has the two identical Closures of *Tawhid*. These are firstly the Beginning as the ontological law and the End, both reflecting each other. The Closure is of the Unbounded *Tawhidi* learning multiverses enveloped by the universe (*a'lameen*) between the conscious expanse between the Beginning and the End.

---

[4]*Qur'an* (48:23): [This is] the established way of Allah which has occurred before. And never will you find in the way of Allah any change.

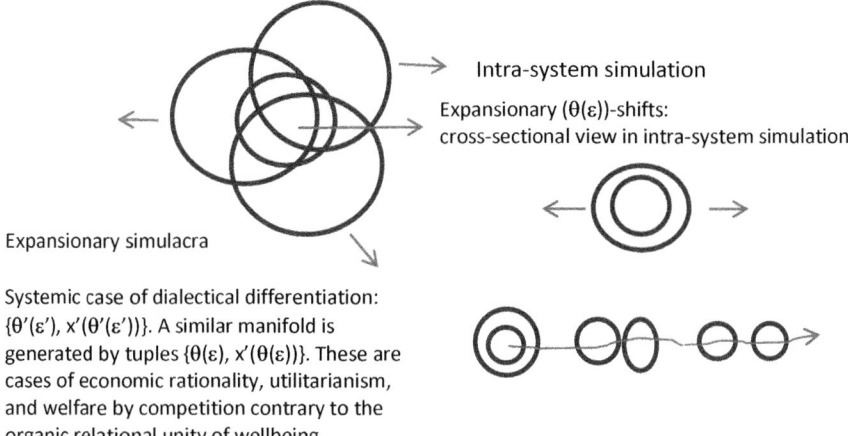

Intra-system simulation

Expansionary ($\theta(\varepsilon)$)-shifts:
cross-sectional view in intra-system simulation

Expansionary simulacra

Systemic case of dialectical differentiation:
$\{\theta'(\varepsilon'), x'(\theta'(\varepsilon'))\}$. A similar manifold is
generated by tuples $\{\theta(\varepsilon), x'(\theta(\varepsilon))\}$. These are
cases of economic rationality, utilitarianism,
and welfare by competition contrary to the
organic relational unity of wellbeing.

Fig. 4.4 Intra-system effect of simulacra by ($\theta(\varepsilon)$)-shifts and contrariwise

The methodological delineation of the *Tawhidi* evolutionary learning process-centered universe is compacted by the following expression:

$$\text{Process: } P[W(\theta(\varepsilon), \mathbf{x}(\theta(\varepsilon))): \vartheta(\theta(\varepsilon)) = F(\mathbf{x}(\theta(\varepsilon))); \text{ subject to, } x_i(\theta)$$
$$= f_i(\theta(\varepsilon), \mathbf{x_j}(\theta(\varepsilon)))] \rightarrow$$
$$\text{Continuum} \qquad (4.10)$$

The imputation of 'ε' in θ-parameter is implied, as in the case of belief-inducing attribute.

The Learning Nexus

The Process delineation of conscious historicism along the IIE-learning universe implies the fullest extent of inclusiveness of the stages 1–5 followed by stage 6 and onwards until the End in Hereafter. At the point of stage 6 and similar completion of given events and the imminent rise of subsequent events of similar type we define the evolutionary learning point. Thereby, the continuation of events of points like stage 6 and similarities, the following evaluation applies (expression 4.11):

$$dP(..)/d\theta > 0. \qquad (4.11)$$

This is a general-system property involving 'everything'.[5] The implication of this formula is a substantive one: It conveys the fact that, the *Tawhidi* epistemic foundation with its ontological law and its explicatory transmission by means of the epistemology of *sunnah* makes up the permanent commencement of 'everything'. Therefore, this foundational commencement of the learning multiverses (*a'lameen*) comprising the ensemble of these particulars is referred to as the universe in its completeness. The universe of the *Qur'an* explicated in details by the *sunnah* and these together making up the discursive nature of the knowledge derivation and its induction of 'everything' is the *a'lameen*. Furthermore, the depiction of such a continuum of multiverse comprising the universe in its completion, extending thereby from the Beginning to the End, encompasses the inter-relational unity of all such universes.

Such relational meaning of unity of knowledge in the order of being and becoming is evermore characterized by the continuous properties of Interaction (*Qur'anic* pairing), integration (signs of unity read by the worshipping world, *tasbih*), and continuously evolved by learning (reoriginative systemic inter-causality between events, *khalq in-jadid*). Let this holism and relational completeness by continuity be called Nexus. The completeness of the nexus is in terms of moral-material abstracto-empirical reality that is explained fully by the *Tawhidi* ontological law of unity of knowledge mapped by the *sunnah* as the permanently unique foundation; and the circular causation of IIE-relations of inter-variable causality between all cognitive entities. The nexus spans the all-comprehending universe as topological entirety. In this topological conception, extended to the supercardinal case of *Tawhidi* reality, the world-system and the heavens and the earth; the Good and the Bad, truth and falsehood; the Heaven and the Hell; the all-comprehending Throne of Allah (*Arsh al-Azim*); are all candidates for the study of total reality.

The expression (4.11) now formulates in its extended meaning the all-inclusive total reality in the following way: We put the wellbeing and circular causation equations in their derivative form:

$$\theta = F(\mathbf{x}(\boldsymbol{\theta}(\varepsilon))); \text{ yielding, } dF(.)/d\theta = \sum_i (\partial F(.)/\partial x_i) \cdot (dx_i/d\theta) \neq 0 \quad (4.12)$$

$$x_i(\theta(\varepsilon)) = f_i(\theta(\varepsilon), \mathbf{x_j}(\boldsymbol{\theta}(\varepsilon))); i = 1, 2, \ldots \text{ yielding, } dx_i/d\theta$$

$$= \sum_{I,j} [(\partial f_i/\partial \theta) + (\partial f_i/\partial x_j) \cdot (dx_j/d\theta)] \neq 0 \quad (4.13)$$

---

[5]Such a property of convergence by unity of knowledge along the IIE-learning process path is also where individuals, agencies, and diversity of forms are interwoven in evolutionary learning symbiosis. Elickson, Grodal, Scotchmer, and Zame (2006, p. 150) characterize a similar endogenous group phenomenon of inter-relations in the following words: "A group is determined by the characteristics of its members, by the inputs it uses and the outputs it produces, by the services it provides, to its members, its infrastructure, and its governance or organizational structure." In the formalism of TSR, groups are very many in systemic diversification but all are organically unified by evolutionary learning. The result is complex abstraction, formal learning forms, and their abstracto-empirical examination using phenomenological approach.

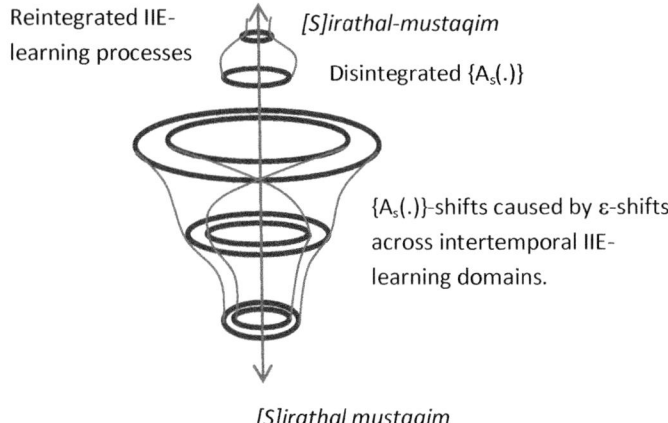

Reintegrated IIE-
learning processes

[S]irathal-mustaqim

Disintegrated {$A_s(.)$}

{$A_s(.)$}-shifts caused by ε-shifts
across intertemporal IIE-
learning domains.

[S]irathal mustaqim

Fig. 4.5 Wrapping of conscious historicism in the total reality of nexus, {$\theta(\varepsilon)$, $x(\theta(\varepsilon))$, $F(.)$} and contrariness

Continua of evolutionary learning paths,{$\theta(\varepsilon)$,$x(\theta(\varepsilon))$,$t(\theta(\varepsilon))$}, from events of intra-systems to inter-systems

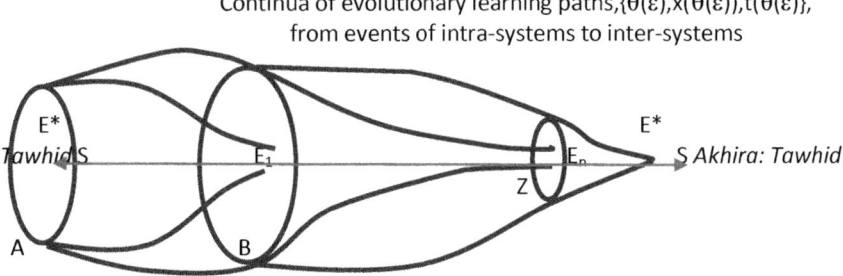

Fig. 4.6 Evolutionary convergence around the straight path of historical consciousness, SS

The imputation of 'ε' in θ-parameter is implied, as in the case of belief-inducing attribute.

These expressions are positive identically by terms in the two cases of 'θ' as knowledge parameter corresponding to the good choices (morally prescribed) {$x_i(\theta)$}; or oppositely corresponding to the choices of bad (morally forbidden) with 'θ' as 'de-knowledge' parameter; or by {$\theta'(\varepsilon)$, $x(\theta'(\varepsilon'))$}.

With these specifications, expressions (4.12) and (4.13) have important explanations: In either of the above two opposite cases, the tuples {$\theta(\varepsilon)$, $x(\theta(\varepsilon))$}, $F(.)$} generate families of positively sloped surfaces in multidimensional historical trajectories. This is true of either knowledge driven 'θ'-parameter or 'de-knowledge' driven parameter as the case may be, with shifting parametric effect of belief-attribute 'ε' as shown in the tuples. Figures 4.5 and 4.6 show the wrapping of the surfaces of the tuples {$\theta(\varepsilon)$, $x(\theta(\varepsilon))$}. The component trajectories that mark the path of historical consciousness are shown. The ensemble of such trajectories forms the totality of 'everything' as the nexus.

In the construction of the nexus we consider the interaction (I_n) between $A_s = \{\theta(\varepsilon), x(\theta(\varepsilon))\}, F(.)\}_s$, 's' denotes systems of such topological domains. Interaction is thereby denoted by the union of possible relations between elements of such collective domains. However, this does not mean the participatory, that is, established complementary inter-relations between all elements of the universal topological set of the domains. Interactions as inter-relations between possible elements of the A_s-domains are denoted by,

$$\text{Interactions} = \cup^{In}\{A_s\} \tag{4.14}$$

Next, interactions as so defined by possible composite complementary relations between A_s-domains are followed by the intersected topological set where integration as established complementary inter-domain relations is attained. Thereby, interactions are followed by integration as established complementary relations. We denote the learning process by way of interactions leading into integration (I_g) by the force of learning out of discourse in the midst of unity of knowledge with heightened wellbeing, both together comprising $\{\theta(\varepsilon)\}$ and its relational induction in $\{A_s\}$.

$$\text{Thus Integration}(I_g) = \cap^{Ig}\{A_s\}. \tag{4.15}$$

Thus, interaction (In) leading to integration, is denoted by,

$$\cup^{In} \cap^{Ig} \{A_s\}_{In,Ig} \tag{4.16}$$

Figure 4.5 configures the intra-systemic process of interaction leading to integration ($II(\theta(\varepsilon))$). Take s = 1, 2, 3. This figure applies equally well to the case of unity of knowledge between the complementary good things of life (*halal at-tayyabah*) and the differentiated dialectical processes between the competing false things of life (*khabisa*). The viewed difference in the figure is that in the second case, intra-system change by 'de-knowledge' marked by $\{(\theta'(\varepsilon'))\}$ applies. This causes opposite change in the expansionary ($\theta(\varepsilon)$)-shifts as cross-sectional view in the resulting differentiating intra-system simulation, as shown.

Intra-systemic simulations over time lead to evolutionary learning inter-systems, as shown in Fig. 4.6. This case is also implied by the mathematical time-differentiation of expressions (4.12) and (4.13). In the case of topological structures of $A_s(\theta(\varepsilon), x(\theta(\varepsilon)))$ in all cases of knowledge and 'de-knowledge' inductions with their corresponding kinds of ε-shifts occur continuously over time. The form of the evolutionary $A_s(.)$-wrappings are worth noting. In the continuous topological mapping of intra-system $A_s(.)$-relations connected with the inter-system evolutionary $A_s(.)$-stages, the stages 1–6 repeat themselves in continuous evolutionary fields of learning. Thereby, the properties of all monotonic transformation, such as $H(A_s(.))$ along the historical ensemble HH are preserved. Likewise, the discontinuous monotonic relations of dialectics and systemic differentiations between intra-systems $\{A_s(.)\}$, as in Fig. 4.5, are preserved in all such different cases. The critical distinction between domains of knowledge and 'de-knowledge' are thus established, implying thereby, the ultimate oppositeness of truth and falsehood in total reality. Indecisive cases disappear in the limiting cases by learning reverting to unity of knowledge. This is explained by, $\text{plim}\{A_s((\theta'(\varepsilon'), \theta(\varepsilon)), x((\theta'(\varepsilon'), \theta(\varepsilon)))\} = \{A_s(\theta(\varepsilon), x(\theta(\varepsilon)))\}$ (Choudhury, 2011).[6]

In Fig. 4.6 the straight path of historical consciousness SS (*Sirathal mustaqim*) is unattainable in intertemporal domain. It is attainable as multidimensional event on SS in the Hereafter, the ultimate unboundedness of closure in the End as in the Beginning. Such an attainment by $\{A_s(.)\}$ is ruled out beause that would otherwise mean the completion of IIE-learning universe in finite term either by truth or falsehood, unity of knowledge or systemic differentiation. SS is thereby the unique and universal path of historical consciousness defining the perfect criterion of truth versus falsehood. These universal attributes of reality are the incessant properties of the learning IIE-universe in temporality; but perfectly attained only by the *Tawhidi* ontological law of $[\Omega, S]$. The probabilistic variable nature of the event-paths as shown, with all forms of knowledge and 'de-knowledge' and their reversions in the inter-temporal domain are caused by the shifting ε-parameter.

The most central example of such parameters in the generality of the intra-system and inter-system universe encompassed by IIE-learning processes is spiritual belief. In the *Tawhidi* methodological worldview the spiritual belief is of monotheistic unity of knowledge. It is fully attainable by $[\Omega, S]$ in the Beginning and End of SS by determination of Truth and Falsehood, Good and Bad.

Measuring ε-Shift Effects on $\{a_s(\theta(\varepsilon))\}$

The level of belief $\{\varepsilon\}$ is socially effective but it is not socially measurable. This is contrary to the case of knowledge, which is a measure associated with the degree of unity of knowledge $\{\theta(\varepsilon)\}$. This in turn explains and assigns ordinal measures by ordinal levels of complementarities between the good things of life at the negation of bad things (differentiating) of life in a data-base. But despite its immeasurability, the ε-shifts as belief convey the inner dynamics of shifts inducing $\{A_s(\theta(\varepsilon))\}$. In a social sense of measuring attributes, observations on data regarding spirituality and pious behaviour can be calibrated by Likert-type scales to configure effects of such good belief-attributes. Thereby, in the case of deconstructing the inner dynamics of the

---

[6]$A_s\{\theta'(\varepsilon'), \theta(\varepsilon)), x((\theta'(\varepsilon'), \theta(\varepsilon)))\}$ can be organized in terms of $x(\theta(\varepsilon))/x'(\theta'(\varepsilon'))$ as $(x/x')(\theta(\varepsilon)/\theta'(\varepsilon'))$. An example of such a variable-reconstruction is rate of return as a relative to the rate of interest. Now as $(\theta(\varepsilon)/\theta'(\varepsilon'))$ increases, implying the intensifying of good over bad; truth over falsehood, just as the consciousness of *halal* spending to the *haram* of interest deepens, so also the relative value of rate of return in the good things relative to the rate of interest increases as bad, increases. Likewise, $(x/x')(\theta(\varepsilon)/\theta'(\varepsilon'))$ increases in circular causality between $(\theta(\varepsilon)/\theta'(\varepsilon'))$ and $(x/x')(.)$ increases. In the limiting case of $x'(\theta'(\varepsilon'))$ tending to zero, $\text{plim}[A_s\{\theta'(\varepsilon'), \theta(\varepsilon)), x((\theta'(\varepsilon'), \theta(\varepsilon)))\}] = A_s(\theta(\varepsilon))$, $x((\theta(\varepsilon))$. In the converse case of transformation to a non-*Tawhidi* worldview it can be proved that, $\text{plim}[A_s\{\theta'(\varepsilon'), \theta(\varepsilon)), x((\theta'(\varepsilon'), \theta(\varepsilon)))\}] = A_s(\theta'(\varepsilon')), x'((\theta'(\varepsilon'))$.

Table 4.1 Estimating circular causation with $\{\theta(\varepsilon)\}$ in quantitative-qualitative framework

Time-series (quantitative)	θ-estimation (quantitative) over time	Questionnaire survey (qualitative) over time for $\{\theta_1(\varepsilon_1)\}$	θ-estimation (quantitative–qualitative) with ε-shifts
t_0	θ_0		
t_1	θ_1	$\Delta\theta_1 = \theta_1(\varepsilon_1)$	Estimate by suitable statistical methods
t_2	θ_2	$\Delta\theta_2 = \theta_2(\varepsilon_2)$	
.	.	.	
t^*	θ^*	$\Delta\theta^{**} = \theta^{**}(\varepsilon^*)$	A further step in estimating circular causation equations and thereby the $\{\theta(\varepsilon)\}$-shifted wellbeing Function (*maslaha*) can be actualized
.	.	.	
.	.		
t_n	θ_n	$\Delta\theta_n = \theta_n(\varepsilon_n)$	

Table 4.2 Quantitative θ-estimation over time

t:	1	2	...	n	t:	1	2	...	n
x_1	x_{11}	x_{12}	...	x_{1n}	θ_1	θ_{11}	θ_{12}	...	θ_{1n}
x_2	x_{21}	x_{22}	...	x_{2n}	θ_2	θ_{21}	θ_{22}	...	θ_{2n}
....					....				
X_m	x_{m1}	x_{m2}	...	x_{mn}	θ_m	θ_{m1}	θ_{m2}	...	θ_{mn}

$$\theta_{ij} = (x_{ij}/x^*) \cdot 10 \text{ corresponding to } x^* \tag{4.17}$$

$$\text{Arithmetic Avg}_{j=1,2,\ldots,n} \{\theta_{ij}\} = \{\theta_i, i = 1, 2,\ldots m\} = [\Sigma^n_{j=1}(x_{ij}/x^*) \cdot 10)/n] \text{ or the geometrical average.} \tag{4.18}$$

knowledge-induced generality and particulars of the world-system the **ε**-attributes are significantly studied. But in the case of studying the dynamics of the aggregate knowledge parameters the **ε**-attributes can be subsumed in the treatment of $\{\theta\}$ and its induced embedding in variables. The example is similar to the effect of trust on indicators of social advancement and the rise and sustainability of civilization (Feiwel, 1989). Trust is the inner attribute of social conduct. Its social lubricating effect causes a good society and civil order to exist. So is also the manifestation of the good society by its inner dynamics of belief.[7]

Techniques of ordinal measurement of ε-shift effects on $\{A_s(\theta(\varepsilon))\}$ involves collation and use of three kinds of data on $\{\theta(\varepsilon), x(\theta(\varepsilon))\}$ as follows Tables 4.1, 4.2, 4.3 and 4.4.

---

[7]*Qur'an* (49:14): The desert Arabs say, "We believe." Say, "Ye have no faith; but ye (only) say, 'We have submitted our wills to Allah,' For not yet has Faith entered your hearts. But if ye obey Allah and His Messenger, He will not belittle aught of your deeds: for Allah is Oft-Forgiving, Most Merciful."

Table 4.3 Qualitative $\{\theta\}$-computation cross-sectionally

Attributes	1 2 3 ... m					(4.19)
Observations						
	A_1		A_2	A_3	...	A_m geometrical mean of observations
1	a_{11}	a_{12}	a_{13}	...	a_{1m}	across attributes as
2	a_{21}	a_{22}	a_{23}	...	a_{2m}	θ-measures
i	$a_{i1}{}^*$	$a_{i2}{}^*$	$a_{i3}{}^*$	...	$a_{im}{}^* \rightarrow$	as wellbeing function, say θ^* by
'	....					estimation using suitable statistical
n	a_{n1}	a_{n2}	a_{n3}	...	a_{nm}	method. Circular causation relations are estimated by the estimation of the equations, $A_i(\theta) = f_i(A_j(\theta))$

Table 4.4 Data meshing: quantitative-qualitative computation of $\{\theta(\varepsilon)\}$ over time inter-system

Time series		Intermeshed attributes $\{\theta^*(\varepsilon)\}_{it} = Avg_t\{\theta_i\}_t + \Delta\{\theta_{it}\}$
'		
1	$\{\theta^*(\varepsilon)\}_{11} = Avg_1\{\theta_1\}_1 + \Delta\{\theta_{11}\}$	$\{\theta^*(\varepsilon)\}_{21} = Avg_1\{\theta_2\}_1 + \Delta\{\theta_{21}\}$ ... $\{\theta^*(\varepsilon)\}_{m1} = Avg_1\{\theta_m\}_1 + \Delta\{\theta_{m1}\}$
2	$\{\theta^*(\varepsilon)\}_{12} = Avg_2\{\theta_1\}_2 + \Delta\{\theta_{12}\}$	$\{\theta^*(\varepsilon)\}_{22} = Avg_2\{\theta_2\}_2 + \Delta\{\theta_{22}\}$ ... $\{\theta^*(\varepsilon)\}_{m2} = Avg_2\{\theta_m\}_2 + \Delta\{\theta_{m2}\}$
.	....	....
n	$\{\theta^*(\varepsilon)\}_{1n} = Avg_n\{\theta_1\}_n + \Delta\{\theta_{1n}\}$	$\{\theta^*(\varepsilon)\}_{2n} = Avg_n\{\theta_2\}_n + \Delta\{\theta_{2n}\}$ $\{\theta^*(\varepsilon)\}_{mn} = Avg_n\{\theta_m\}_n + \Delta\{\theta_{mn}\}$

θ^* - $Avg_t\{\theta_i\}_t = \Delta\{\theta_{it}\}$ (any sign applies). Thereby, $\{\theta^*(\varepsilon)\}_{it} = Avg_t\{\theta_i\}_t + \Delta\{\theta_{it}\}$, i = 1, 2,...
m; t = 1, 2,..., n   (4.20)

Computing $\{\theta(\varepsilon)\}$-Parameters in Terms of Endogenous Quantitative and Qualitative Observations

The estimation of ε-shifts and the attribute induced knowledge parameters in terms of unity of *Tawhidi* knowledge, $\{\theta(\varepsilon)\}$ and all of $\{A_s(\boldsymbol{\theta}(\boldsymbol{\varepsilon}), \mathbf{x}(\boldsymbol{\theta}(\boldsymbol{\varepsilon}))\}$ compound the moral and material complementarities as in the abstracto-empirical learning system. Therefore, there exists a degree of subjectivity by historical inferences conveyed by factual references to past and ordinal implications in the events that move over {knowledge, space, time}-dimensions. In the pure theoretical implications, the moral-material shifts explain the TSR-dynamics in multidimensional and multisystem case across evolutionary inter-systems. Intra-systems explain inter-variable circular causation relations. Therefore, ε-attribute shifts need not be manifest in quantitative measurement.

On a simpler note the averaging formula of expression (4.20) can be applied to the final average column of expression (4.19) upon the completion of geometrical mean (or simple arithmetic average) of the attributes over time.

We now examine the generalization of the TSR-methodological worldview in the multisystem and multidimensional case. An example of such an extension of TSR-methodology is the study of the heavens and the earth in res extensa and res cogitans of $\{A_s(.)\}$ (Choudhury, 2015). This precept of generality of world-systems as multiverses comprising the holistic universe (*a'lameen*) is unique to the *Tawhidi* worldview. It differs substantively from the concept and practice of contractual views relating to *aqd*-based events, instruments, and ownership in the application and legitimizing by *shari'ah*.

A Mathematical Consonance of 'Evolutionary Convergence' Towards—yet Away from *Sirathal Mustaqim*, the Straight Path of Monotheism of Truth Against Falsehood (Logical vs Illogical, Resp.)

Underlying each and every intra-systemic and inter-systemic evolutionary emergence of socio-scientific events by virtue of *Tawhidi* unity of knowledge there exists the property of a degree of dissonance away from the straight path of truth (*sirathal mustaqim*). This property appertains to the fact that, every $\{A_s(\theta(\varepsilon))\}$ is continuously subject to shifts caused by evolutionary but incomplete learning. This attribute of evolutionary learning by ε-shifts can attain its perfect optimum only in the great event of the Hereafter. In the temporal conscious historicism of unity of knowledge, no perfect convergence is possible, which otherwise would be contrary to the evolutionary learning multiverse (*a'lameen*).

The ultimate socio-scientific formalism of TSR results in the continuous evaluation (estimation and simulation) of the wellbeing function (*maslaha*), subject to the system of non-linear circular causation relations, finally resulting in the quantitatively measured form of the conceptual wellbeing function. The extended *maslaha* function evaluated subject to attribute-induced knowledge flows, as is the case of belief embedded knowledge parameter in the precept of unity of knowledge, is now formalized as follows:

Quantitative form of wellbeing function: $\vartheta(\theta(\varepsilon)) = F(x_1, x_2,..., x_n)[\theta(\varepsilon)]$; $\vartheta(.)$ being a non-linear and complex function F(.) of the variables as shown.

Circular causation relations interrelating all the endogenous $\{\mathbf{x}(\theta(\varepsilon)\}$-variables are given by,

$[-x_1 + a_2 \cdot x_2 + \cdots + a_n x_n + \delta_1 \cdot q](\theta(\varepsilon)) = 0$ system of circular causation between the endogenous

$[b_1 \cdot x_1 - x_2 + \cdots + b_n x_n + \delta_2 \cdot q](\theta(\varepsilon)) = 0$ variables

. . . .

$[c_1 \cdot x_1 + c_2 \cdot x_2 + \cdots - x_n + \delta_n \cdot q](\theta(\varepsilon)) = 0$

$[\gamma_1 \cdot x_1 + \gamma_2 \cdot x_2 + \cdots + \gamma_n \cdot x_n - \vartheta(\theta)](\theta(\varepsilon)) = 0$ quantitative form of wellbeing function

$$(4.21)$$

The generalized matrix form of expression (4.21) showing the ε-attribute effect is this:

$$
\begin{vmatrix}
-1 & a_2 & a_3 & \ldots & a_n & \delta_1 \\
b_1 & -1 & b_3 & \ldots & b_n & \delta_2 \\
\ldots & \ldots & \ldots & \ldots & \ldots & \ldots \\
c_1 & c_2 & c_3 & \ldots & -1 & \delta_n \\
\gamma_1 & \gamma_2 & \gamma_3 & \ldots & \gamma_n & -1
\end{vmatrix}
\cdot
\begin{vmatrix}
x_1 \\
x_2 \\
\ldots \\
x_n \\
\vartheta
\end{vmatrix}
= -I \cdot x(\theta(\varepsilon)) + A \cdot x(\theta(\varepsilon)) = B \quad (4.22)
$$

That is, $(I-A) \cdot x = B$, with every symbol being a function of $\{\theta(\varepsilon)\}$. This is re-written as,

$$x(\theta(\varepsilon)) = (I - A)^{-1} \cdot [B]\{\theta(\varepsilon)\} \qquad (4.23)$$

Here,

$$
A\{\theta(\varepsilon)\} =
\begin{vmatrix}
0 & a_2 & a_3 & \ldots & a_n & \delta_1 \\
b_1 & 0 & b_3 & \ldots & b_n & \delta_2 \\
\ldots & \ldots & \ldots & \ldots & \ldots & \ldots \\
c_1 & c_2 & c_3 & \ldots & 0 & \delta_n \\
\gamma_1 & \gamma_2 & \gamma_3 & \ldots & \gamma_n & \vartheta
\end{vmatrix}
= [\theta(\varepsilon)];
$$

$B\{\theta(\varepsilon)\}$ denotes the vector of circular causation relations intertemporally across evolutionary inter—systems wherein $\{\theta(\varepsilon)\}$ apply.

Diagrammatic Explanation of the Property of 'Evolutionary Convergence'

The moral attribute-shifts denoted by $\{\theta(\varepsilon)\}$ point to the upward evolutionary learning shifts of increasing belief towards *sirathal mustaqim* (SS), yet not perfectly converging on SS. Every event along the path of historical consciousness is thereby a movement into certainty gained by the attribute shifts. On the other hand, the

Fig. 4.7 Non-compact
depiction of the topology of
evolutionary equilibriums
across knowledge, space,
time dimensions intra-system
and inter-system

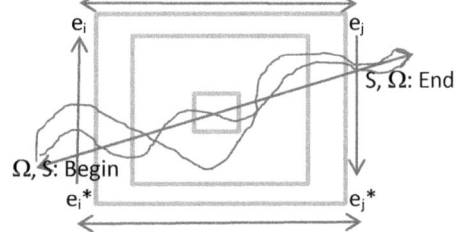

degenerating state of moral and social differentiation explained by continuous individualism and self-interest and their concomitant axioms of economic rationality, socio-scientific Darwinism, and dialectical conflict and re-emergence (Buchanan, 1999), are altogether dissociated, exogenous states of self-interest (Holton, 1992).

The above feature of 'evolutionary convergence' is depicted by the plethora of continuums in the circular relational paths across intra-systems and inter-systems. This is shown by Fig. 4.7.

Legend: SS is the straight path of perfection in evolutionary learning from the *Tawhidi* beginning to *Tawhidi* End in Hereafter.

A, B, C etc. are intra-systemic interaction leading to integration.

E* is the perfect equilibrium at the *Tawhidi* beginning in S.

E_i, i-1, 2,... are sets of Fixed Point equilibriums attained temporarily at evolutionary equilibriums by various emergent paths of evolutionary learning following up from interactions and integrations. Thus E_i's are evolutionary equilibriums along various conscious historistic paths of unity of knowledge as explained by the continua of evolutionary learning paths, $\{\theta(\varepsilon), x(\theta(\varepsilon)), t(\theta(\varepsilon))\}$ (Burstein, 1991; Hawking & Mlodinow, 2010).

The Density of Equilibriums in Non-compact Sets of Evolutionary Convergences

For any of the evolutionary convergent trajectories of the continua of evolutionary learning paths of historical consciousness the following condition must apply:

$\left| e_i - e_i^* \right| > e_i$, a small positive number indicating the degree of convergence for the equilibrium point e_i towards e_i^*, for various points i = 1, 2...

Similarly for equilibrium points e_j to e_j^* we note, $\left| e_j - e_j^* \right| > \varepsilon_j$

We can write thereby, $\left| (e_i - e_i^*) - (e_j - e_j^*) \right| = \left| (e_i - e_j) - \{ (e_i^* - e_j^*) = e^* \} \right|$

$$> \varepsilon_1 - \varepsilon_j. \qquad (4.24)$$

This can be a positive number or a negative number, according to as the evolutionary convergence takes place around SS. The implication of the result in expression (4.24) is that, everywhere in the continua of evolutionary convergences, the intra-system containing evolutionary points do not result in compact (closed and bounded) limit points (Maddox, op cit). Therefore, steady-state equilibriums with perfect convergence cannot exist anywhere in the continua of TSR evolutionary learning across historical consciousness. The deflections of evolutionary convergences of non-steady-state equilibriums around SS are narrated in the following Prophet's hadith (saying). Abdullah ibn Mas'ud reported: The Prophet, peace and blessings be upon him, drew a square and in the middle he drew a line which poked out the ends. Across the middle line he drew some smaller lines. The Prophet said, "This is man and the square surrounding him is death. The middle line is his hopes and the smaller lines are his troubles. If this one misses him, another will distress him. If that one misses him, another will distress him." (Source: *Sahih Bukhari* 6054).

The above formalism of evolutionary convergences with non-compact equilibrium points strewn around SS can be delineated in Fig. 4.7.

The multiplicity of trajectories of historical consciousness as mapped in Fig. 4.7 and previous to these, imply that, if any particular trajectory say $f_1(\theta_1, \mathbf{x_1}(\theta_1), t(\theta_1))$ applies to the theorem of IIE-learning processes with its characterizing evolutionary convergence as the ever-learning evolutionary gap, so also all monotonic positive functional transformations form similar functions in the open and unbounded topology of the entire continua of evolutionary learning trajectories. Consequently, the full representation of any sub-space of the topology of the continua reflects itself to all other monotonic positive learning sub-spaces of similar trajectories. The properties of IIE-learning processes and the principle of universal complementarities (participatory feature) fully define the whole topology and its sub-spaces in the closed and unbounded paired universe. This is the permanent and universal character of the learning universe of relational unity of knowledge. It is the sure expression of *Tawhid* at work in the order of the intra-world-system and inter-world-system covering all of extendible knowledge, space, and time dimensions. All are induced by the precept of unity of knowledge engineered with the full TSR methodology in its conceptual and applied forms.

References

Buchanan, J. M. (1999). The domain of constitutional economics. *The Logical Foundations of Constitutional Liberty*. Indianapolis: Liberty Fund.

Burstein, M. (1991). History versus equilibrium: Joan Robinson and time in economics. In I. H. Rima (Ed.), *The Joan Robinson legacy* (pp. 49–61). Armonk: M.E. Sharpe Inc.

Choudhury, M. A. (2011). On the existence of evolutionary learning equilibrium. *Sultan Qaboos University Journal for Science, 16,* 68–81.

Choudhury, M. A. (2015). Res extensa et res cogitans de maqasid as-shari'ah. *International Journal of Law and Management, 57*(6), 662–693.

Einstein, A. (1954). The problem of space, ether, and the field in physics. In C. Commins & R. N. Linscott (Eds.), *Man and the universe: the philosophers of science*. New York: The Pocket Books Inc.

Elickson, B., Grodal, B., Scotchmer, S., & Zame, W. R. (2006). The organization of production, consumption and learning. In C. Schultz & K. Vind (Eds.), *Institutions, equilibria and efficiency* (pp. 149–185). Berlin: Springer.

Feiwel, G. R. (Ed.). (1989). *Arrow and the foundation of the theory of economic policy* (pp. 179–221). London: Macmillan.

Hawking, S. W., & Mlodinow, L. (2010). Alternative histories. In *The grand design* (pp. 80–82). London: Transworld Publishers.

Holton, R. L. (1992). *Economy and society*. London: Routledge.

Johnston, J. (1984). The k-variable linear model. *Econometric methods* (pp. 193–198). New York: McGraw-Hill Book Co.

Joseph, S. (2014). *Waqf* in historical perspective: Online *fatāwā* and contemporary discourses by muslim scholars. *Journal of Muslim Minority Affairs, 34*(4), 425–437.

Kakutani, S. (1941). A generalization of brouwer's fixed point theorem. *Duke Mathematical Journal, 8*(3), 457–459.

Kuhn, T. S. (1970). *The structure of scientific revolution*. Chicago: University of Chicago Press.

Nikaido, H. (1987). Fixed point theorems. In J. Eatwell, M. Milgate, & P. Newman (Eds.), *The new palgrave: General equilibrium* (pp. 139–144). New York: W.W. Norton.

Wilson, E. O. (1998). *Consilience, unity of knowledge*. New York: Vantage Books.

Chapter 5
Examples of Dynamic Learning Shifts in Simulated Computational Generalized Equilibrium Systems

Masudul Alam Choudhury

Abstract The model of wellbeing (*maslaha*) comprising the wider field of valuation using inter-variable interaction, their integration and evolutionary learning (IIE-learning processes) is extended from single stage to multiple stages of evolutionary learning processes. This involves a formal understanding via relevant analytics concerning intra-system and inter-system sustainability across intertemporal IIE-learning processes. Throughout such formal modeling of compounded wellbeing functions the episteme of unity of knowledge abides. Important economic and financial implications are derived as in the case of intra-system and inter-system meanings of interest rates and rates of return in reference to the *Qur'anic* meaning of avoidance of interest rates and the pursuit of morally acceptable and productive possibilities concerning trade. Similar applications can be made using the inter-system formalism of the wellbeing function (*maslaha*) in *Tawhidi* knowledge-induced space and time dimensions. Examples given in this case are of the socioeconomic development indexes found in the UNDP literature.

A Non-technical Overview of the Chapter

Shari'ah literature from its very beginning has not been able to formalize the *maslaha* function in a way that would address its widest field of meaning involving intra-system and inter-system meanings of inter-causal variables. Consequently, the *shari'ah* study in the case of dynamic inter-system nature of the wellbeing function (*maslaha*) has not been possible in Islamic economic and finance literature and in socio-scientific field. The emergence of these fields in the *Qur'anic* methodological worldview conveyed by *Tawhid* as law has thereby failed in and by *shari'ah*. Yet without this highest level of intellectual calling the truly *Qur'anic* methodological worldview through *Tawhid* as law of monotheistic unity of knowledge cannot be realized. Therefore, Islamic economics, finance, and the socio-scientific erudition could not be and will not be actualized in the absence of a methodological invoking

M. A. Choudhury (✉)
Faculty of Economics, Trisakti University, Jakarta, Indonesia
e-mail: masudc60@yahoo.ca

© Springer Nature Singapore Pte Ltd. 2019
M. A. Choudhury (ed.), *The* Tawhidi *Methodological Worldview*,
https://doi.org/10.1007/978-981-13-6585-0_5

of *Tawhid* as law. The mistaken pursuit of *shari'ah* as a static explanation of atemporal intra-systemic relations and contracts (*aqd*) will continue causing limitations in Islamic intellectualism.

In the absence of the methodological foundation and formal development and evaluation of the inter-system interrelations between the diversely representative wellbeing functions, as is the case of *shari'ah*, it is impossible to actualize the abstracto-empirical function of the *maslaha* criterion. In the case of *Tawhidi* methodological foundation it is possible to formalize the wellbeing function as *maslaha* index concerning development planning and financial-economic relations. The meaningfullness of such a methodological approach by *Tawhidi* law and the world-system is centered in the completely endogenous inter-variable circular causal continuity in the IIE-learning processes across phases of sustainability.

The primal ontology of systemic unity of knowledge is premised on to establish the complex and compounded formulation of multi-stage wellbeing criteria across diverse world-systems and thereby their inter-causality. The resulting micro-wellbeing criteria and their aggregation by the IIE-evolutionary learning processes in respect of unity of knowledge become sensitive to *Tawhidi* methodology. Such micro-macro interface of the wellbeing criterion is possible for utilization in the widest range of evaluation by the convergent phenomenological model in the framework of evaluative formal model of wellbeing (*maslaha*). This model named as *Tawhidi* String Relation (TSR) carries the abstracto-empirical possibility centered in *Tawhidi* methodology, and thus based on monotheistic unity of knowledge across knowledge, space and time dimensions.

Introduction

1. *Technological change*

Take the case of environmental biodiversity as a continuously diversifying method of increasing environmental related complementary resources that permanently recycle, reuse, and reproduce resources as regenerated inputs and outputs in the joint production function (Henderson & Quandt, 1980). In such a case of continuously reproduced biodiversity, every event like $E_i(P_i = t_i)$ in Fig. 4.7, yields the complete set of activities denoted by $\{\theta_i, \mathbf{x}_i, \mathbf{y}_i, t_i\}[\theta_i]$, with $\mathbf{x}_i(\theta_i)$ denoting the vector of interrelated inputs, like pairing of seeds and specimen of technology to produce interrelated outputs of the vector, $\mathbf{y}_i(\theta_i)$. Thereby, across every process by simulation we obtain the class of extendible biodiversity input-output results by the circular causation relations:

$$\text{Input}-\text{output system, } x_{ij}(\theta_i) = f_{ij}(\mathbf{x}_{ij'}(\theta_i), \mathbf{y}_i(\theta_i); P_i(\theta_i)), \qquad (5.1)$$

Here, 'i' denotes specific process (or time) of intra-system simulation along the inter-system evolution across interconnected processes. 'i' = 1, 2, ..., P_j.

'j' denotes jth element of the vector, $x_i(\theta_i)$. 'j' = 1, 2, ..., n for numbered elements of $x_i(\theta_i)$-vector.

$x_{ij'}(\theta_i)$ is the vector $x_i(\theta_i)$ excluding the endogenous jth variables in particular circular causal relation, $f_{ij}(..)$.

The relational disaggregation of $y_i(\theta_i)$ is expressible by the equation,

$$y_{ik}(\theta_i) = f_{ik}(y_{ik'}(\theta_i), x_i(\theta_i); P_i(\theta_i)). \tag{5.2}$$

'k' = 1, 2, ..., m for numbered elements of $y_{ik}(\theta_i)$-vector.

For all of the variables pertaining to specific 'i' the same (geometric) computed average 'θ_i'-knowledge parameter apply expression (4.19). Thus there are the two expressions of the wellbeing (*maslaha*) criterion function—the theoretical ($W(\theta_i)$) and the empirical versions ($\vartheta(\theta_i)$), as given below:

$W(\theta_i) = W(\theta_i, x_i, y_i, t_i)[\theta_i]$ is the conceptual form of the wellbeing function (*maslaha*)

$\vartheta(\theta_i)$ may be taken in the non−linear natural logarithmic form of $\{\theta_i, x_i, y_i, t_i\}[\theta_i]$. (5.3)

Thereby, $\ln(\theta_i) = A(\theta_i) + \Sigma_{ij}a_{ij}(\theta_I). \ln(x_{ij}(\theta_i)) + \Sigma_{ij}b_{ij}(\theta_I). \ln(y_{ij}(\theta_i))$, at specific time 't' (process 'i').

The above formal study can be extended by treating attribute-shifts of knowledge-parameters, $\{\theta(\varepsilon)\}$ and their inter-variable induction. The complex and non-linear form of the wellbeing function, simulated subject to assigned process-based 'θ'-parameters, is caused by the evolutionary learning nature of these parameters in the variables and estimated coefficients. Estimation followed by simulation is referred to as evaluation of the generalized simulation wellbeing model. That is for every process (time-period) there is evaluation of wellbeing by expression (5.3), subject to circular causation computational generalized systemic evolutionary equilibrium in expressions (5.1) and (5.2).

These circular causation relations of the input-output type characterize the joint production relations of biodiversity. Thereby, endogenous technology and policy variables could be represented as additional vectors of biodiversity along with the list of input and output vectors. The wellbeing evaluation system with the generalized list of inter-causal relations of computational generalized evolutionary equilibrium system is further extended. In this way of extension, the computer-assisted evaluation and data-bank information are made amenable. Innovative statistical software and mathematical creativity are extended. The further study of the generality and details of the world-system in the light of TSR is continuously enriched. Some such dynamic forms of endogenous input-output relations will be explained in the Applied Part II of this study.

2. *Extended evaluative relations relating to trade and riba: exegesis of the trade-riba Qur'anic verse (2:275)*

To formulate the extended relationship between trade and all forms of rates of returns contra interest rates in the IIE-learning processes and with deepening consciousness or otherwise to premise the Islamic financial economy we proceed as follows:

The *maslaha* vector of inter-causal variables is,

{**Trade**, real output (**Y**), rate of return (r)/interest rate (i) (**r/i**), $\theta(\varepsilon)$}[$\theta(\varepsilon)$].

The existence of 'i', even so in a state of improving transformation into a more Islamic state of erasing interest rate and enhancing real rate of return 'r', implies variations in ε-attribute in uncertain degrees. Yet it is the real state of the financial world wherein interest necessarily exists for the worse. This is despite the continuous pursuit of the Islamic belief to phase out interest and raise the real rate of return. The evolutionary learning process of such Islamic reconstruction is possible by the evaluation of the wellbeing function subject to the system of inter-causal relations between the selected *maslaha* variables. Imperfection of the positive complementarities between the permissible choices is caused due to the creeping continuation of interest rate, despite the increase in (r/i).

The system of endogenously interrelated circular causation relations between the variables in the vector {**T**, **Y**, r/i, $\wp$, $\theta(\varepsilon)$}[$\theta(\varepsilon)$], with $\wp(\theta(\varepsilon))$ denoting technology, preferences, and the like; cannot avoid the influence of 'i' in all the variables including itself. The implication then is that, ε cannot ever reduce to a constant by a perfect convergence on SS. Thereby, 'evolutionary convergence' always remains. Interest-free policies and demands or desire for transformation should realize that in the largest scale of events, observing Islamic relations with non-Islamic states of existence, there would not be a prospect for complete abolition of 'i'. However, the reduction of the interest rate towards zero would prevail as the ideal moral and material condition of perfect attainment of unity of knowledge between the variables in the *maslaha* function.

The conditions of financial transactions under *shari'ah-compliance* make it impossible to reduce interest rate to zero across inter-system intertemporality. Thereby, the social and financial state of interest-free economy can never be attained under the existing human concocted attitude to Islamic economics and finance under *shari'ah* rules. The adverse conditions so raised are absence of correct *riba*-free approach to financial transactions, asset valuation, and intertemporal pricing (as in *takaful* premium) in the absence of formula pricing of any deferred things, as in *ijara* (rent), *murabaha* (mark-up pricing, and *sukuk* (bond pricing). Then there is the absence of Islamic monetary system that would otherwise create the situation of zero debt, which otherwise *shari'ah* ruling does not consider (Choudhury, 1987, 2018; Choudhury & Hoque, 2017).

These are indispensable reasons why the TSR methodologically induced methods of evaluating the wellbeing function in all cases of Islamic study must be used under the precept of unity of knowledge (consilience), subject to circular causation relations between selected variables suitably organized in the wellbeing function. Contrary to this *Qur'anic maslaha* (*sunnah* followed by learned *ulul-amr*) approach, the Islamic-compliance has relented to mainstream models that remain devoid of an appropriate Islamic methodology and emergent analytical methods according to *Tawhid* and the unified world-system.

The *shari'ah-compliance* approach legitimates fractional reserve requirement by not attenuating to 100% reserve requirement monetary system based on the gold standard as the monetary numeraire. *Tawhidi* approach of unity of systemic knowledge to money (banking), spending (finance), and real economy cannot logically accept the fractional reserve requirement monetary system. In fact, this approach is untenable in the 100% reserve requirement monetary system in the TSR methodological worldview, wherein money in circulation equates to national spending in the recommended choices.

In the *shari'ah-compliance* approach to money and real economy, interest-rate abolition is enforced as an exogenous case. Contrarily, according to the *Tawhidi* methodological worldview, all variables including 'i' in 'r/i' are endogenously interactive. The abolition of 'i' arises from the endogenous resource flows in the money-finance-real economy circular relations with the ever-extended embedding of the degrees of consciousness of $\{\theta(\varepsilon)\}$ along the IIE-learning processes over knowledge, space, time. In the case of technological induction of the vector of selected variables, the topological property of the wellbeing function and monotonic positive transformation of every trajectory as in Fig. 4.7), implies that, the same properties of the IIE-learning processes concerning (r/i) and the rest of trade-versus-*riba* extended by vector of circular causation variables prevails.

Hence, technology, institutions, and programs, that today comprise the idea underlying *shari'ah-compliance* product development for attaining forlorn goals of financial and economic efficiency as static concepts; and mistaken understanding of sustainability in the absence of endogenous circular causation relations (Myrdal, 1958; Hayek, 1990) have deprived the Islamic reconstructive transformation of its potentiality. This is further testimony to the fact that, Islamic socio-scientific inquiry under the premise of *shari'ah* in every form of socio-scientific intellection is devoid of analytics and methodological worldview of sustained and overarching power. Consequently, no intellectual contribution could be made of the *Qur'an* and *sunnah* through *shari'ah*, as these primal sources are otherwise so richly endowed in the discovery and advancing study of *Tawhid* and the world-system of 'everything'. Thus the *shari'ah* origin of Islamic socio-scientific thought is contrary to *Tawhid* and its ontological worldview wherein superbly rich methodological and analytical wholeness lies. The *Tawhidi* worldview of expanding knowledge of unity is ever learnt but is never spent in learning.

Technology continues to be exogenous artefact of product development as in the case of its exogenous nature found in neoclassical economics. Islamic economics under the fold of neoclassical economics and its offshoots has remained a deepening technological orientation of the postulates of economic rationality, a most misguiding direction in the theory of 'everything'. This result is contrary to the universality and uniqueness of the *Tawhidi* episteme of unity of knowledge, wherein every variable is of endogenous nature and thereby complementary by degrees.

Multi-system Extension of TSR and Its Analytical Methodological Worldview

The generality and particulars of forms of the events defining the entirety of the conscious historical trajectories of knowledge, space, and time along the IIE-learning processes as of Fig. 4.7 and by its nature of incomplete convergence to SS by the property of evolutionary convergence implies the non-Cartesian[1] multiverse of systems and cybernetics.

The formal TSR expression to merely explain, but not to depict the continuous topological reality, is presented by the complex inter-system wrapping with inter-causality.

From the pervasively relational essence of the knowledge-centered world-system we can formalize the *Tawhidi* general-systems methodology. Toward formalizing the general system model we consider the following expression:

$$F_1 \Leftrightarrow F_2. \tag{5.4}$$

F_1 and F_2 are two knowledge-forming processes (IIE-learning process = discursive precess = the *shuratic* process; with interactive, integrative, evolutionary learning properties) for the *Tawhidi* world-systems 1 and 2.

Below, the symbol ‖ denotes lateral and vertical interaction by corresponding categories in any two inter-systemic IIE-learning processes as shown. The wrapping and intermeshing between the systems by virtue of their multiple IIE-learning processes and ever-changing evolutionary convergences in multiple systems of $\{A_s(\theta(\varepsilon))\}$ cause the wellbeing functions to compound in the form of a generalized system wellbeing model.

$F_1:[\Omega \rightarrow_S:(\Omega,S)]\{\theta_1:\theta^*(\varepsilon),\theta_1(\varepsilon)\} \rightarrow_f\{x_1(\{\theta_1(\varepsilon)\})\} \rightarrow \downarrow \rightarrow Process2 \rightarrow continuity \rightarrow [\Omega,S]$

... =Hereafter

$\downarrow$

Evaluate $W(\theta_1,x_1(\theta_1))[\varepsilon]$ $\qquad\qquad\qquad\qquad$ (5.5)
In IIE-learning processes
subject to circular
causation relations.

---

[1] We term the nature of conscious historical trajectories as formless mathematical realities where the analytics are governed by the following properties: topological continuity in complex interrelated forms of inter-variable circular causality; thus monotonic continuity of particular complex forms describing events. Thus continuity means sustainability over knowledge, space, time dimensions causing moral-material inter-causal synthesis endlessly from Beginning to End of $\{A_s(\theta(\varepsilon))\}$. Non-Cartesian geometrical forms make it possible to formalize TSR structures in multidimensional systems and cybernetics of IIE-learning processes across knowledge, space, time dimensions.

$$F_2:[\Omega \rightarrow_S:(\Omega,S)]\{\theta_2:\theta^*(\varepsilon),\theta_3(\varepsilon)\}\rightarrow_f\{\mathbf{x}_2(\{\theta_2(\varepsilon)\})\}\rightarrow\downarrow\rightarrow \text{Process2}\rightarrow\text{continuity}\rightarrow..[\Omega,S]$$
$$=\text{Hereafter}$$
$$\downarrow$$

$$\text{Evaluate } W(\theta_2,\mathbf{x}_2(\theta_2))[\varepsilon] \qquad\qquad (5.6)$$
In IIE-learning processes
subject to circular
causation relations.

Between expressions (5.5), (5.6) we obtain the following multi-system IIE-learning interrelationships, which are uniquely governed by the fundamental epistemology of *Tawhid*, $[\Omega, S]$. We suppress 'ε' in 'θ' hereafter:

$$\rightarrow \quad \{\theta_1\}\rightarrow_{f1}\{\mathbf{x}_1(\{\theta_1\})\}\rightarrow\downarrow_{f3}\rightarrow\text{Process 2}\rightarrow\text{continuity}\rightarrow$$
$$\downarrow$$
Evaluate $W(\theta_1,\mathbf{x}_1(\theta_1))$
subject circular causation
relations.

$$\uparrow \qquad\qquad\qquad\qquad\qquad\qquad\qquad\qquad\qquad\qquad\qquad \downarrow$$
$$[\Omega,S]: \qquad \| \quad \| \quad \| \qquad\quad \| \qquad\qquad \| \qquad \Omega=H \qquad (5.7)$$
$$\downarrow \qquad\qquad\qquad\qquad\qquad\qquad\qquad\qquad\qquad\qquad\qquad \uparrow$$
$$\rightarrow \quad \{\theta_2\}\rightarrow_{f2}\{\mathbf{x}_2(\{\theta_2\})\}\rightarrow\downarrow_{f4}\rightarrow\text{Process 2}\rightarrow\text{continuity}\rightarrow$$
$$\downarrow$$
Evaluate $W(\theta_2,\mathbf{x}_2(\theta_1))$
subject circular causation
relations.

By the complex disaggregation of relations in expression (5.7) we note that the complex of non-Cartesian ensemble of IIE-learning processes across conscious histories of TSR trajectories is exemplified by,

$$\{\theta_i\}\rightarrow_{fi}\{\mathbf{x}_i(\{\theta_1\})\}\rightarrow\text{Evaluation of wellbeing (}maslaha\text{)}\rightarrow\text{Process2}\rightarrow\text{continuity}\rightarrow$$
subject to circular causation   Hereafter
relations $[\Omega,S]$

$$\uparrow$$
$$[\Omega,S] \qquad\qquad\qquad\qquad\qquad\qquad\qquad\qquad\qquad\qquad\qquad (5.8)$$
$$\downarrow \qquad \| \quad X \quad \| \quad X \quad \| \quad X \quad \| \quad X \quad \|$$

$$\{\theta_j\}\rightarrow_{fj}\{\mathbf{x}_j(\{\theta_j\})\}\rightarrow\text{Evaluation of wellbeing (}maslaha\text{)}\rightarrow\text{Process2}\rightarrow\text{continuity}\rightarrow$$
subject to circular causation relations   Hereafter $\approx[\Omega,S]$

$i, j = 1, 2, \ldots$ of IIE-learning TSR trajectories.

Here, 'X' denotes *crosswise* inter-systemic interaction. Such an interaction is extensive in nature and can be worked out even from this simple disaggregation to when it is extended to second and higher degrees of evolutionary learning sustainable processes. The functional mappings existing between extensive interactions, as shown, generate compound non-linear and complex functions.

The following three paragraphs are abbreviated from Choudhury's work. The wellbeing criterion function resulting from pervasive interaction across the interactive, integrative and evolutionary (IIE) branches of (5.5) and (5.6) is the non-linear and complex aggregation of the separate wellbeing functions belonging to these branches at their adjoining nodes. One such non-linear functional form would be the product function of complementary variables with knowledge-induced indexed coefficients of the elasticity of wellbeing with respect to the variables of the wellbeing function. The resulting non-linear aggregation of the wellbeing function conveys a cardinal measure of complementarities among the various variables and their relations appearing in the formation and measurement of the wellbeing function. The example of the quantitative form of the conceptual wellbeing function is shown in expression (4.1–4.2). Among the variables of this criterion function are technology, policy, behavioral and institutional ones. These imply the necessary conditions of participation among agents in the underlying decision-making process.

The joint result of interaction among the variables and their relations leads to the compound form of the branches of the trees configured in expressions (5.7) and (5.8). Such a compounding of mappings and relations is thus seen in terms of variables, their relations, the resulting wellbeing functions corresponding to such branches, and their representation in the resulting wellbeing functions. In this way, the attainment of complementarities among entities, agents, variables and their relations signifies the meaning of integration by degrees following interaction among the entities.

Finally, from the continuously dynamic nature of knowledge-flows affecting decision-making, variables and their relations, there emanate the evolutionary processes of further knowledge-flows and the knowledge-induced entities of the world-systems. The evolutionary nature of the interactive and integrative processes at each stage, as shown in expressions (5.7) and (5.8), brings out the importance of a simulation method of quantitative analysis in this interactive, integrative, and evolutionary learning worldview. The emerging method here suggests replacement of all steady-state equilibrium points by multiple evolutionary knowledge-induced equilibriums (Osborne & Rubinstein, 1994). We referred to this property of ensembles of IIE-learning processes denying perfect convergence to SS as 'evolutionary convergences'. Consequently, optimization as a method of holding the variables in an assumed end-state of equilibrium on SS by controlled movement in the variables and made possible through trade-offs among them is totally untenable in the pervasively complementary nature of the IIE-learning system.

There are two approaches to constructing a multi-system TSR wellbeing function(s) as the *maslaha* function. Firstly, with the following system-specific wellbeing functions like,

$$W(\theta(\varepsilon), \mathbf{x}(\theta(\varepsilon))) = \prod_{s=1}^{N} W_s^{a_s(\theta(\varepsilon))}(\theta(\varepsilon)_s, \mathbf{x_s}(\theta(\varepsilon)_s), \tag{5.9}$$

with $\theta(\varepsilon)$ as the computed average (arithmetic, geometric) of the vector $\{\theta(\varepsilon)_s\}$; and the corresponding variables-vector, $\mathbf{x}(\theta(\varepsilon)) = \{\mathbf{x_s}(\theta(\varepsilon)_s)\}$. $\{a_s(\theta(\varepsilon))\}$ denote the knowledge-induced dynamic coefficients.

In each of the multi-system cases in expression (5.9) the whole sequence of evaluation of the wellbeing functions in their quantitative forms, subject to the system of circular causation relations for every wellbeing evaluative function, is done. In such a case, each evaluated wellbeing function, subject to its system of circular causation relations of the specific variables of the particular wellbeing index. The evaluated wellbeing functions are then compounded together with their respective dynamic coefficients to form the final non-linear wellbeing function. The dynamic coefficients are denoted by $\{a_s(\theta(\varepsilon))\}$.

An example of such compounding of wellbeing functions is of interactively integrating the indexes such as Millennium Index with Human Development Index, Multidimensional Poverty Index, Gender Empowerment Index, and Corruption Index. The quantitative measurement of each of such indexes as wellbeing indexes, subject to its vector of variables, implies an explanatory nature of the separate indexes in forming the generalized index. Yet this is not the way that the UNDP indexes are calculated as independent parameters of sustainable development.

The other way to evaluate the generalized wellbeing index as a compounded index is to treat it as the wellbeing of the vector of all the inter-system wellbeing functions evaluated in their own right. The list of variables and the corresponding number of circular causation equations between the variables may become very large as a single bloc of wellbeing function that is evaluated in its quantitative functional form, subject to all the circular causation equations of the multi-system variables. The non-linearity and complexity of the functions remain because of the dynamic induction of the inter-variable coefficients by $\{\theta(\varepsilon)\}$. The nature, though not the evaluated value of the coefficients of the above two cases of relational aggregation, remains similar.

The statistical results in the above two cases of evaluation of the generalized wellbeing function may not be the same. They are expected to be similar in terms of the various variables. Thereby, we deduce the following result:

$$W(\theta(\varepsilon), \mathbf{x}(\theta(\varepsilon))) = \prod_{s=1}^{N} W_s^{a_s(\theta(\varepsilon))}(\theta(\varepsilon)_s, \mathbf{x_s}(\theta(\varepsilon)_s)$$

$$= A(\theta(\varepsilon)) \cdot \prod_{s=1}^{M} \mathbf{x_s}^{b_s(\theta(\varepsilon))}(\theta(\varepsilon))_s \cdot \theta_s(\varepsilon)). \qquad (5.10)$$

Expression (5.10) is the evaluated quantitatively by,

$$\vartheta(\theta_s(\varepsilon)) = [\prod_{s=1}^{N} W^{a_s(\theta(\varepsilon))}(\mathbf{x_s}(\theta(\varepsilon)_s)],$$

for each of the singular but relational inter-systems denoted by 's'

For the systems 's' taken up collectively we obtain,

$$\vartheta(\theta_s(\varepsilon)) = A(\theta(\varepsilon)) \cdot \prod_{s=1}^{M} \mathbf{x_s}^{b_s(\theta(\varepsilon))}(\theta(\varepsilon))_s. \qquad (5.11)$$

The circular causation between endogenously related inter-variables in their equations can be generated as usual with $\{\mathbf{x_s}(\theta(\varepsilon)_s)\}$, with $s = 1, 2, ..., N$ for each system (wellbeing indexes) taken separably; and $s = 1, 2, ..., M$ number of vectors of variables in the integrated inter-systems.

Conclusion

Expressions (5.10) and (5.11) in their details, form the widest extant of the *maslaha* objective criterion as the wellbeing function. The formulation of such *maslaha* functions forms much wider methodologically derived objective criterion of *Tawhidi* evaluation than the ones in the literature either in the classical sense or the recently extended cases. The principal difference between our methodologically derived *maslaha* function in the endogenous variables and the other ones is the use of individually and institutionally imposed forms with exogenously assigned coefficients and linear terms in the latter case. In our case, the coefficients of the non-linear complex forms of the *maslaha* functions in their single and multi-system stages are endogenously derived by virtue of the *Tawhidi* methodology applied in generality and particulars for the multiverse. Such a wellbeing (*maslaha*) objective criterion is both multivariate and intra-systemic evolving into inter-systems in the knowledge, space, and time dimensions.

References

Choudhury, M. A. (1987). *Money in Islam*. London, England: Routledge.

Choudhury, M. A. (2018). The ontological law of Tawhid contra shari'ah-compliance in Islamic portfolio finance. *International Journal of Law and Management, 60*(6), 1–22.

Choudhury, M. A., & Hoque, M. N. (2017). The future of monetary reform and the real economy: An Islamic problem of exchange versus interest. *ACRN Oxford Journal of Finance and Risk Perspectives, 6*(4), 37–52.

Hayek, F. A. (1990, reprint). The use of knowledge in society. In M. C. Spechler (Ed.), *Perspectives in economic thought* (pp. 183–200). New York, NY: McGraw-Hill.

Henderson, J. M., & Quandt, R. E. (1980). *Microeconomic theory*. New York: McGraw Hill, Inc.

Myrdal, G. (1958). The principle of cumulation. In P. Streeten (Ed.), *Value in social theory, a selection of essays on methodology by Gunnar Myrdal* (pp. 198–205). New York, NY: Harper & Brothers Publishers.

Osborne, M. J., & Rubinstein, A. (1994). *A course in game theory* (pp. 219–222). Cambridge, MA: The MIT Press. Read the chapter on knowledge and game theory.

Chapter 6
An Observation on the TSR Versus *Shari'ah* Models of Asset Valuation

Masudul Alam Choudhury

Abstract The important topic of asset valuation could not be encapsulated in its holistic approach of cash-flows and inter-causal interdependence of decision-making by choices of the market-institution interrelated variables. Neither mainstream financial economics nor non-*Tawhidi* approach in so-called Islamic economics of *shari'ah* could accomplish this very important task of analytical modeling. The consequence thus has been insensitivity of 'everything' in the socio-scientific world-system to the moral-material embedded endogeneity of the constituent variables. The richness of inter-variables causality has been rendered oblivious. Thereby, the ontological essence of *Tawhidi* unity of knowledge has been avoided in both mainstream and *shari'ah* based financial economics, Islamic economics, finance and socio-scientific inquiry has thus failed to be sensitive to its most central and indispensable foundation. That is of incorporating *Tawhid* as law in the methodological worldview of monotheistic unity of knowledge. *Tawhid* and *shari'ah* thereby exist as disparate ways of understanding the nature and logic of the primal ontology of unity of knowledge and its methodological implications of diversity of the world-systems.

A Non-technical Overview of the Chapter

The asset-valuation idea and its *Tawhidi* methodologically derived model is a non-linear, complex, and rich study in interaction, integration, and evolutionary learning according to *Tawhidi* methodological worldview. Contrarily, the same exercise in *shari'ah* perspectives is of a linear nature. Such a *shari'ah* based modeling relents on methodological independence. Thereby, systemic independence and individualism between various entities predominate. The systemic consequences ought otherwise to be explained in order to unravel the dynamics of consilience. This approach is of the *Tawhidi* nature and methodological logic and its formalism.

M. A. Choudhury (✉)
Faculty of Economics, Trisakti University, Jakarta, Indonesia
e-mail: masudc60@yahoo.ca

© Springer Nature Singapore Pte Ltd. 2019
M. A. Choudhury (ed.), *The* Tawhidi *Methodological Worldview*,
https://doi.org/10.1007/978-981-13-6585-0_6

The innovatively derived model of asset-valuation with its various participatory financing instruments and socioeconomic consequences arising from the primal *Tawhidi* ontological premise of unity of knowledge is of a substantively holistic nature. This analytical model that is centered in belief-driven knowledge-flows that embody the moral-material choices according to *Tawhid* as law of unity of knowledge is called the 'nearest point of valuation' model of asset valuation, understood as a multidimensional IIE-learning process model with knowledge-induced consciousness. The knowledge-centered description and choices of the IIE-learning process model is the essence of consciousness. It enters in the way of abstracto-empirical phenomenology in the evaluative wellbeing function. Such an evaluative criterion is organically linked with the inter-generational 'nearest point valuation' model with its many elements.

When critically examined and analytically formalized, the various so-called Islamic financing instruments are found to defy even the most basic of its axioms. That is annulment of *riba* (interest rate) and the pursuit of trade by its various forms of market exchange IIE-learning relations. In *shari'ah* such a well-derived analytical precept from the *Qur'an* is not of an analytical nature. The critical questions relating to annulment of *riba* is therefore based on the combination of intra-systemic valuation of capital, investment, and transactions; and simultaneously with the inter-systemic valuation question of such flows taken intertemporally. The *riba*-question is fully explained by the simultaneous treatment of intra-systemic and inter-systemic treatment. The 'nearest point valuation' model addresses the intertemporal issue thoroughly. *Shari'ah* approach being *aqd*-based is piecemeal over time. Such a *shari'ah* approach to the *riba*-question cannot offer an answer to *riba*-abolition in the intertemporal social contractual sense.

An in-depth study of all so-called Islamic financial instruments shows that, this existing portfolio according to *shari'ah* is fully debt-based. Various such instruments can be studied with this disturbing conclusion. Even though *shari'ah* is invoked yet it does not have sound methodological approach to the problem of *riba*-abolition, except just a divine ordainment, not its analytical explanation. *Tawhidi* methodological approach is of the holistic and organic nature. It is aimed at developing the pooled portfolio of diverse financing instruments in the midst of diversification and the role of money as resource interconnecting money, spending, and the real economy in the sense of continuity and institutional action by 100% reserve requirement monetary system. In this analytical context of *maslaha* and valuation as by the 'nearest point valuation' model the generalized model of evaluation of wellbeing with the selected inter-causal variables brings out the total outlook in pricing and prospects of inter-variable relations. Thereby, the 'nearest point valuation' model formalizes, evaluates, explains, and carries forward in simulacra the IIE-learning consequences along the historical conscious path of sustainability by continuity of evolutionary learning processes.

Introduction

The interconnectedness of intra-system and inter-system phases of asset valuation is of the nature of the TSR model. According to this model, the evaluation of the *maslaha* function of assets is done across every point in time and evolutionary learning process across intertemporality. Valuation of an asset in reference to the combination of intra-system and every evolutionary learning episode at inter-system points of time is done by the concept of the 'nearest point' of evaluation of an event concerning assets and the associated vectors of moral and material elements. In every case, whether with one system with multivariables or multiple systems of multivariable *maslaha* functions experiencing IIE-learning, the evaluation of the resulting *maslaha* function is done 'nearest' to that point of evaluation. The probabilistic nature of such a 'nearest point' exists but with decreasing degrees of uncertainty and subjectivity.

Indeed, the evolutionary learning world-system and the multifarious events in it of various sub-systems, like economics, finance, science, and society are ever probabilistic in nature caused by the incompleteness of knowledge. Yet such probabilistic systems always move by evolutionary convergences towards unity of knowledge. Knowledge thereby arises from but remains incomplete in reference to the primal ontology of *Tawhid*, guided by the episteme of the *sunnah* and the incompletely though explicated learning by discourse of the devoted authority. Thereby, via the evaluative wellbeing function, subject to circular causation relations, sustainability continues across knowledge, space, and time dimensions. The evaluative event with its wellbeing (*maslaha*) ensemble in historical consciousness is thus evaluated in the probabilistic sense of deriving evolutionary learning of unity of knowledge.

The approach to evaluation according to the *shari'ah* orientation in present 'Islamic' economics is riddled by two serious problems. Firstly, sheer use of any specific point of time to evaluate assets means to function in a given intra-stage of pricing in a state of valuation. Examples are of the nature of pricing in *ijara* (rents), *murabaha* (mark-up), *takaful* (Islamic insurance), *sukuk* (Islamic bonds), and the like. Thereby, the pricing formula is determined as agreed upon between partners at that point of time by a particular contract to manage financial collection. The same kind of cross-sectional pricing formula is subsequently applied for each subsequent point in time as separate points of asset-valuation. In the case of *ijara* (rental), a rate is set at and for that specific stage of valuation exclusively. Yet no intertemporal rate can be set as a future asset pricing viewed at the present time. That is when a spending decision is virtually made.

The pricing formula according to *shari'ah* approach results in nominal pricing relating to every segregated intra-system stage of valuation. The formalism of inter-system, and thereby, the meaning of intertemporal valuation remains non-existent in *shari'ah* based *aqd*-related phase-specific valuation. As well as the evaluation of *maslaha* subject to inter-variable circular causation relations is unknown to the *shari'ah*-based piecemeal approach in asset valuation. The rate of change of various situations in the intra-system event of *shari'ah aqd*-induction remains oblivious of the generalized *maslaha* implications. The TSR-based IIE-learning approach addressing the intertemporal case of asset valuation by the *maslaha* objective criterion transcends all piecemeal features of *shari'ah* approach to valuation. Thereby in *shari'ah*, a comprehensive moral-material embedded inter-causality approach to every kind of event valuation is unknown in the *shari'ah* approach. Separable contract approach based on possession of artefacts in exchange (*qabd*) is adopted. In this perspective moral and material consideration are treated in differentiated ways at the cost of moral-material embedded method using the episteme of *Tawhidi* unity of knowledge of TSR.

The mark-up Islamic financing called *murabaha* faces a worse problem as a category of *ijara* (rental) financing instrument. That is because the future incidents are unknown to price the expected value of risk and a stipulated fair rate of profit by mark-up pricing of assets as in leased *ijara* items. A problem interconnecting money, finance, and real economy arises. That is because in the disjoint valuation of risk and return *shari'ah* causes broken relationship with financing and real economy. Such linkages otherwise would determine the 'nearest point' of relationship between setting the mark-up and the determination of risk and return at and over knowledge, space, and time dimensions.

The overall result then would be this: The mark-up financing, risk-return condition, and the real economy remain disjoint events. Yet contrarily, this problem is resolved in the concept of 'nearest point' of evaluation, although the probabilistic nature of valuation exists even in the case of TSR-based evaluation. But the uncertainty in the probabilistic state of the occurrence of contingencies associated with an event in historical conscious time is reduced by the reduction of subjective probability of the occurrence of events.

Problem of *Takaful* Premium Pricing

Yet another similar deficiency of the pricing formula exists for Islamic insurance (*takaful*) in the case of *shari'ah* approach. The problem in the corresponding pricing arises with the assignment of insurance premium. The concept of the 'nearest point' of probabilistic incidence on events prevails. The *maslaha* evaluation, subject to inter-variable causal relations and the calculation of the quantitative form of the wellbeing function, altogether characterize the moral-material setting of premiums intertemporally along the IIE-learning trajectory of the knowledge-induced space and time dimensions.

The same irresolution exists between pricing and exchange in the absence of market venue. Thereby, shadow *riba* rate exists in such a mark-up pricing rule. According to Fig. 6.1, the following financing modes as debt instruments in *shari'ah* context relent to *riba*-like financing.

1. *ijara*;
2. the *musharakah* debt financing of *takaful*;
3. *sukuk* by its round-aboutness of production;

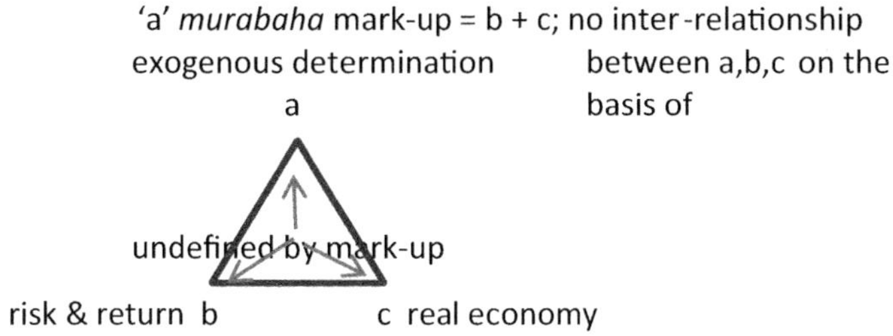

'a' *murabaha* mark-up = b + c; no inter-relationship
exogenous determination   between a,b,c on the
                a   basis of

undefined by mark-up

risk & return b   c real economy

Fig. 6.1 Undefined *murabaha* relations except by exogenously set contract & probability

4. absence of interdependent valuation with unity of knowledge [no methodology exists];
5. failure of statistical models in their absence of endogenous ethical parameterization; as also for *maslaha* (wellbeing) function.
6. financing of shareholder models opposed to social stakeholders' model of wellbeing.

'Nearest Point' Type Valuation by Overlapping Generation Model

In terms of the model of TSR by *Tawhidi* unity of knowledge the emergent valuation model takes the form of the overlapping generation model,

$$\text{Terminal Value, TV}_{\text{TSR}}, = A_0\big[(1+r)(1+g)\big]_p^T + A_1\big[(1+r)(1+g)\big]_{P+1}^{T=1} + \cdots$$
$$+ A_{T-1}\big[(1+r)(1+g)\big]_{P+(n-1))} + A_{P+n.}^T \qquad (6.1)$$

All variables are induced by the knowledge parameter, 'θ', and are evaluated by the circular causation model of wellbeing along with the market-institutional discursive medium that forms part of the model with n-number of IIE-learning processes, P, P + 1, …, P + n. 'r' is the nominal rate of return on *maslaha* 'g' is the rate of change in economic growth.

On the other hand, in the presently practiced exogenously determined intra-system rates distributed over given points of time (T), the valuation model is as follows:

$$\text{Terminal Value} = \text{TV} = \Pi_T A_{T-}(1+r)^T \qquad (6.2.)$$

For every intra-system stage, $T = 1, 2, \ldots$ of nominal intra-stage evaluation of A_T and rates of return 'r' determined over learning processes and time. There is no incidence of 'θ' on the variables. An implication of such results is that, the rate is exogenously assigned. Hence it the financial collection forms adhoc collection from the goodwill of willing contributors to finance the debt-bearing instruments as the need arises to finance occurrences of community contingencies. There is no organized way to raise funds on an intertemporal basis from those entities that would buy insurance policies according to probabilistic exigencies. Such an ad hoc approach of *shari'ah* towards financial collection to meet probabilistic contingencies makes all contributions to be ad hoc *aqd*-based community charities as collectively desired.

Mutually Inclusive Inter-system IIE-Learning Valuation Model

The multi-systems IIE-learning process implies the unity of relations between such systems as the meaning of unity of knowledge expressed by the aggregated wellbeing functions, as explained earlier. The mutually joint valuation of the inclusive projects by systems in the two cases of TSR and the present state of Islamic finance quantitative methods are as follows:

TSR approach to valuation of mutually inclusive projects (systems, S) yields:

$$TV_{TSR,PS} = \cap_P[\cap_S][TV_{TSR}](\theta_{PS}) \qquad (6.3)$$

The non-TSR approach to inter-project valuation yields,

$$TV = \cup_s[TV_S] \qquad (6.4)$$

A most disturbing consequence of the multi-system valuation of diverse assets exists in respect of the *aqd*-approach of *shari'ah-compliance*, rather than by *Tawhidi* methodology of unity of knowledge and its embedding in the participatory multi-systems, and thus in compounded systems by the IIE-learning property of TSR. The dissociative form of *aqd*-approach to inter-system valuation continues the hidden interest-based future pricing of assets. Each asset in the inter-system domain thereby yields its own issuance of hidden rental rates. In case of using the 'nearest-point valuation' approach as explained above, the valuation is only for the intra-system. The intertemporal valuation model combining intra-system and inter-system evolutionary perspective of intertemporal valuation and the consequential pricing formula is unknown. In the end, no formula financing by Islamic instruments is known to exist in *shari'ah-compliance* that can distribute or collect available funds in respect of probabilistic events with given contingencies. Consequently, sustainability of intertemporal pricing remains in question for both the financial firm and for the purpose of ethical valuation by means of *maslaha* function for society at large.

The nature and consequences of financing for asset valuation is different in the case of TSR-learning approach. The rates, (r, g), occurring in the evolutionary valuation formula at continuous points of time under the impact of $\{\theta(\varepsilon)\}$, with many disaggregations of these, are probabilistic expected rates estimated nearest to the point of occurrence of contingencies. If at such points the formula given by $TV_{TSR,PS}$ $= \cup_P [\cap_S][TV_{TSR}](\theta_{PS})$ does not match up with the value of risk and return at the points of valuation, then the adjustment of the difference is made by the financial firm for the benefit of shareholders. The expected rates are always estimated at the 'nearest points of valuation' across knowledge-induced space and time Intertemporal (ity). This is spread contingency-specific valuation along IIE-learning processes intra-systems and inter-system Events with valuation happening in evolutionary fashion by time.

Furthermore, continuous complementarities exist between the inter-variables in intra-systems and inter-systems in their joint wellbeing function for evaluation. Here the extensive existence of complementarities implies a continuous regeneration of resources by the use of the above-mentioned financial adjustment arising from valuation of assets in the real and productive economy. An example of such financial adjustment according to the terminal valuation at points over time is of complementarities between money, financial spending (Islamic financial instruments), and the real economy. At the end, all rates (r, g) and their disaggregations turn out to be objective rates satisfying the wellbeing objective of embedded unity of knowledge between material and moral inter-causal relations. One of the designs of such inter-system financial instruments and their relations with money and real economy can be derived by the model of portfolio financing instruments existing as securities. Contrarily, the instruments of such a portfolio are *aqd*-based in the *shari'ah-compliant* outlook.

The following formulas of valuation in terms of the notions held regarding the *maslaha* function make a substantive difference between TSR-approach and the *shari'ah-compliant* approach:

TSR-approach to inter-systemic valuation in terms of complementarities between them yields:

$$W(W_1, W_2, \ldots, W_n)[\theta(\varepsilon)] = A(\theta(\varepsilon)) \cdot [\prod_{i=1}^{n} W_i((\theta(\varepsilon)), \mathbf{x}(\theta(\varepsilon)))^{a_i \theta(\varepsilon))}]_{s,p} \quad (6.5)$$

Non-*Tawhidi* approach to cumulative intra-systemic valuation in terms of contracts (*aqd*) yields:

$$W(W_1, W_2, \ldots, W_n)[\theta(\varepsilon) = \cap_i \{\theta_i(\varepsilon)\} = \phi] = \sum_{i=1}^{n} a_i \cdot W_i(\mathbf{x}) \quad (6.6)$$

There is no presence of the evolutionary learning (that is nullified, ϕ) as the participatory (complementary) nature of ethics by the conception of wellbeing function evaluated subject to the circular causation between all endogenous variables. What results thereby is a linear utilitarian function rather then a non-linear and complex expression caused by evolutionary learning in knowledge-induced space and time, the historical consciousness sustaining in knowledge, knowledge-induced space. and knowledge-induced time.

The coefficients $a_i(.)$ are knowledge-induced in the TSR-valuation formula of inter-generational evaluation by learning with induction of inhering belief. This belief induction of knowledge flow is denoted by $(\theta(\varepsilon))$—expression (6.5). This is the main feature that conveys the non-linearity and complexity properties to TSR-valuation according to expression (6.5). Contrarily, the absence of $\{\theta(\varepsilon)\}$ in expression (6.6) makes this expression a non-dynamic and linear one. Such an expression is unable to explain non-linearity and complexity caused by evolutionary learning behaviour of decision-makers.

Evolutionary Learning in Unity of Knowledge Contrary to Risk-Return Economic Rational Behaviour with Different Forms of Mutuality of Relations

It is argued in Islamic economics that every venture is risky. Therefore, an expected profitable venture, necessarily meaning participation for productive engagement in ventures contrary to avoidance of *riba*, must incur risk. While this is true for risk-taking under subjective and objectified probability causing expected returns and subjectively measured returns, the true meaning of risk-return analysis in Islamic asset valuation has to do with risk-diversification. This approach to project selection and economy-wide extension of choices of projects in Islamic economics means that, such choices are determined positively by the increase in the number of stakeholders, and thereby with unit amounts of output held by each stakeholder's participation in the corresponding productive activity. This approach establishes the choice function of every project in terms of rewards (expected returns, $E(\mathbf{x}(\theta))$ and risk diversification $(D(\theta) = $ variance of return/expected return $= (\sigma^2/E(\mathbf{x}))[\theta])$. The multivariable functions can be further induced by the belief governing the knowledge variable, i.e. $\{\theta(\varepsilon)\}$. The result on risk and return under the impact of $\theta(\varepsilon)$-induction of the multi-variables points to complementary movements between expected rewards and risk-diversification $(D(\theta(\varepsilon))$ in response to $\theta(\varepsilon)$. We write this interrelationship as, $\{D, E(\mathbf{x})\}[\theta(\varepsilon)] \Leftrightarrow \{\theta(\varepsilon)\}$ in the sense of inter-variable complementarities caused by $\theta(\varepsilon)$-induction of variables and functionals.

We now formalize as follows the above-mentioned explanation of $\{D, E(\mathbf{x})\}[\theta(\varepsilon)] \Leftrightarrow \{\theta(\varepsilon)\}$ for the case of the *Tawhidi* (participatory = complementary) determination of choice of projects by treating the resulting wellbeing (*maslaha*) function:

$$\text{Evaluation } W(\theta(\varepsilon)) = W(D, E(\mathbf{x})\}[\theta(\varepsilon)] \qquad (6.7)$$

Subject to the circular causation relations regarding inter-variable endogeneity:

$$D(\theta(\varepsilon)) = (\sigma^2/E(\mathbf{x}))[\theta(\varepsilon)]) = f_1(E(x), \theta)[\theta(\varepsilon)] \qquad (6.8)$$

Fig. 6.2 Return and
risk-diversification in the
case of their
complementarities

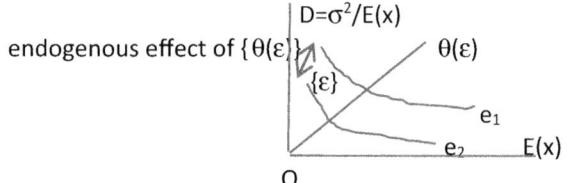

$$E(\mathbf{x}(\theta(\varepsilon))] = f_2(\sigma^2/E(\mathbf{x}))[\theta(\varepsilon)] \tag{6.9}$$

$$\vartheta(\theta(\varepsilon)) \approx \theta(\varepsilon) = F(D, E(\mathbf{x})\}[\theta(\varepsilon)] \tag{6.10}$$

Some analysis in risk and diversification as the Tawhidi methodological approach in project selection

We write expression (6.7) for multiple projects as,

$$W(\theta) = W(E(\mathbf{x}) = \sum_i E(\mathbf{x})_I, \sigma^2(\mathbf{x}))[\theta] \tag{6.11}$$

$\{\varepsilon\}$ is suppressed in these expressions.
Rewrite expression (6.11) as,

$$W(\theta) = W[E(\mathbf{x}) * (\sigma^2(\mathbf{x})/E(\mathbf{x}), 1))[\theta] = W(E(\mathbf{x}) \cdot D)[\theta] \tag{6.12}$$

Expression (6.12) implies that, $E(x)$ and $D(\theta)$ being complementary, $W(\theta) > 0$. This result can be summarized in Fig. 6.2.

Figure 6.2 explains that even if risk of the project increases, yet risk-diversification can increase with the increase in the level of returns. Thereby, risk-diversification increases by $D(\theta) = (\sigma^2/E(x))[\theta]$. There is a further implications in this relationship due to variations in $\{\varepsilon\}$-induction of θ-values that is caused by deepening conscious-ness in projects that enhance $(D, E(x))[\theta]$-complementarities. By writing, $E(x) = \Sigma_i E(q_i \cdot s_i)$, with unit output;$q_i$' for each corresponding unit of share of stakehold-ers ('i'), both being in tune with $i = 1, 2,..., n$ say, the expected value of returns increases. The complementarities between q_i and s_i thereby enhance the productive effect, and the depth of complementary effect between the variables is explained by $\{\theta(\varepsilon)\}$. Figure 6.2 shows such a learning effect on returns and risk-diversification by the shifts of the curves e_i and e_2.

Taking the expression, $E(x) = \Sigma_i E(q_i \cdot s_i)$, we can write the formulas,

$$D(\theta) = (\sigma^2/E(x))[\theta] = \text{either} \left[(\sum_i q_i^2 / \sum q_i) * (\text{Var}(s))/E(s) \right][\theta(\varepsilon)],$$

with unit quantity 'q' being parametric;

Or

$$\left[(\sum\nolimits_i s_i^2 / \sum\nolimits s_i) * (\text{Var}(q)) / E(q)\right][\theta(\varepsilon)],$$

with unit share 's' being parametric.   (6.13)

Thus, risk-diversification is deepened by $(\text{Var}(s)/E(s))[\theta(\varepsilon)]$ declining under the impact of $(\Sigma_i q_i^2 / \Sigma q_i) > 1$.

Likewise, risk-diversification is deepened by $(\text{Var}(q)/E(q))[\theta(\varepsilon)]$ declining under the impact of $(\Sigma_i s_i^2 / \Sigma s_i) > 1$. The vector of variables for the extended form of the wellbeing function in risk-diversification and expected return is this: $\{E(x), \sigma^2, q, s\}[\theta]_I, i = 1, 2,\ldots, n$. The details of evaluation of the contingent wellbeing function thereby follow.

Contrasting *Tawhidi* Valuation of Expected Return and Risk-Diversification with the Expected Utility Criterion of Rational Choice

Risk-return analysis in standard investor utility, $U(E(x), \sigma)$, of optimal decision-making under uncertainty assumes, $dE(x)/d\sigma > 0$,[1] based on the axioms of rational choice that, the decision-making utility function is an expression of aversion to risk and preference for returns, both taken in their purely economic forms, ignoring embedding between moral and material values. Thus there is no presence of $\{\theta(\varepsilon)\}$-induction. Consequently, the episteme of complementarities between variables, as in the wellbeing (*maslaha*) function of *Tawhidi* methodology, does not exist. Thereby, we have contrariety to the explanation underlying Fig. 6.2 regarding pervasive complementarities between the variables representing the good choices denoted by the variables $(D, E(x))[\theta(\varepsilon)]$. As the *Tawhidi* methodology would imply, there is no equivalence of such a result in mainstream economics and in *shari'ah*-based Islamic financial economics.

The difference in Epistemology (cal) interpretation between Figs. 6.2 and 6.3 is in respect of the *Tawhidi* methodological property of complementarity and contrarily of the marginal rate of substitution as in mainstream economic theory. We thereby note the following two opposite objective functions: $W(E(\mathbf{x}), D(\mathbf{x}))[\theta(\varepsilon)]$ and $U(E(\mathbf{x}), \sigma(\mathbf{x}))$. The further distinction between these two objective criteria is that of the presence of embedded moral and material elements in the *Tawhidi* wellbeing criterion existing in the abstracto-applied form; and the absence of endogenous moral and ethical criteria in the utility analysis. It is also noted that, the evaluation of wellbeing in the *Tawhidi* sense of evolutionary learning is never optimally realized. In the case of utility function optimality is necessarily assumed to explain optimal decision-making under uncertainty.

The above postulates result in the following consequences: We can rewrite the utility function as, $U = U(E(x), D)$. The optimality assumption still holds in this case. Thereby, $dU(E(x), D) = 0$, implying, $dE/dD = -(\partial U/\partial D)/(\partial U/\partial E) = -(E/D) < 0$,

---

[1]Obtained from the optimization formula, $dU(E(x),\sigma) = 0$, implying that by risk aversion axiom, $\partial U/\partial E(x) > 0$, $\partial U/\partial \sigma < 0$. Thereby, $dE(x)/d\sigma = -[\partial U/\partial \sigma / \partial U/\partial E(x)] > 0$.

Fig. 6.3 Risk, return, and risk-diversification relations in mainstream and conventional Islamic economics

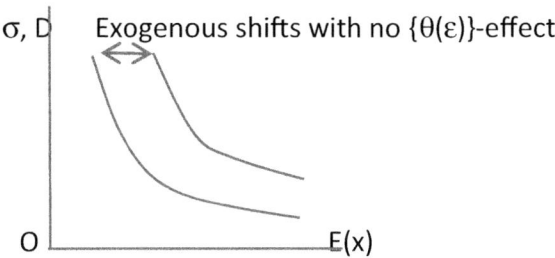

implying that, $\log(e) + \log D = \text{constant}$; $E^*D = \text{constant}$. This result is contrary to the one explained in Fig. 6.2. The essential reason for this contrariness is the difference in the postulates—one set for the case of evolutionary learning in *Tawhidi* unity of knowledge; and the other set for mainstream and non-*Tawhidi* Islamic economics in the absence of evolutionary learning. This latter case is of steady-state equilibrium marking the end of innovation in the optimal state. Exogenous relations between variables result. Circular causation characteristic of inter-variable complementary relations in the *Tawhidi* wellbeing evaluation fails to exist in the non-*Tawhidi* case.

Determination of Value According to the TSR Worldview in the Wellbeing Context

All of the above nature of analysis and its socio-scientific implications are unchanged in non-*Tawhidi* Islamic economics. The latter case abides to the ambivalence of *Tawhidi* methodology of unity of knowledge. An example of such contrasting cases is the stakeholder approach to wellbeing as formalized by *Tawhidi* methodology versus the mainstream and non-*Tawhidi* Islamic approach to shareholder formulation of optimal decision-making under uncertainty. In the case of multiple decision-makers with rational choice, the utility function converts into a utilitarian form of the welfare function, which is of the additive type in respect of individual utility functions.

Each of the additive utility functions is then governed by the rational choice property of steady-state optimality. The individual shareholder in this case reduces the effect of diversification on his expected return. Conversely, any increase in diversification in the portfolio reduces individual claim to expected return in either of these two cases of inverse relationship. Risk-aversion points to inverse risk-return relationship. Such shareholder relationship in the rational-choice construct of utilitarianism and rational choice theory of risk and return under uncertainty is fully imitated by non-*Tawhidi* Islamic financial economics and socio-scientific generality and details.

The consequences of capitalist methodological individualism in so-called 'Islamic' socio-scientific theory are evidently felt in the shareholders utilitarian perception in Islamic finance and socioeconomic development theory, except for grandiose ethical sounding. We note thereby, Islamic banks have mustered a great deal of financial capital mobilization by the so-called Islamic financial instruments that perforate financial contracts (*aqd*) of a separable nature and that are unintelligently approved by *shari'ah* as non-interactive *aqd*. Yet such a structure of portfolio is not conducive of the *Tawhidi* methodological worldview.

Contrary to the shareholder model, *Tawhidi* methodological worldview constructs a truly communitarian model of ethical interrelations between the defining complementary variables under the episteme of unity of knowledge (Lozano, 2000). This is the stakeholder model. It appears as a specific form of the generalized model of wellbeing (*maslaha*) with all its theoretical and applied properties as were explained earlier. The enriching point of the stakeholder model that the shareholder model cannot explain is its intra-system and inter-systemic nature. This expands from specific systems to all diversity of systems—ecological, cosmological, intertemporal widening of systems, moral and material orders of cultural and religious extendibility, etc. All of these expanding system and cybernetic inter-connectivity establish in respect of circular causation of unity of knowledge that the *Tawhidi* methodological worldview pronounces between the good things of life at the exclusion of the bad things of life.

The model of wellbeing is thereby the endogenous expression of the extended form of the *maslaha* function along with its theoretical formalism and empirical applications to generality and details of intra-system and inter-system diversity of being and becoming in embedded moral and material reality concerning 'everything'. The concept of 'everything' is the topological evolutionary learning super-space whose inter-systemic learning dynamics is subsumed and explained wholly by the elegant equation of the multiverse that comprises the holistic universe.[2]

In the utilitarian context of welfare, the concept of value follows the neoclassical idea of marginal rate of substitution between goods. In this case, groups of variables can exist as substitutes and convey the ends opposing social benefits, as for example, wellbeing contested between the rich and the poor. Likewise wages, interest rates, prices, and the like are determined by their corresponding marginal utility functions. Marginal utility functions as ceteris paribus expressions of economic value do not include ethical and moral effects in the system of multivariable welfare functions of the utilitarian genre that are benign of such effects (Buchanan, 1999).

In Ricardian theory, followed by Marxist theory of value, the surplus value is measured by the excess of prices and interest rates over the wages paid according to the value of labour time. In the case of the TSR-theory of *maslaha* (wellbeing), value is determined by the change in the wellbeing function by inter-causality between the endogenous IIE-variables of moral-material embedding. Such endogenous embedding between moral and material values is explained by the circular causal relations as indicated by, $W(\theta) \leftrightarrow \vartheta(\theta) \approx \theta \leftrightarrow \{x_i(\theta)\}$ ... sustainable continua. Consequently, all forms of prices are determined by their corresponding circular causation relations. In turn such price-values influence all other variables as the property of inter-variable

---

[2]*Tawhid* (Ω, S) as Beginning $\rightarrow$ World-System $\{\theta, x(\theta)\}$ $\rightarrow$ *Tawhid* as End ((Ω, S).

Unbounded and Open Supercardinal Universe comprising Open World-Systems within the Closure (Beginning, End) of the Unbounded and Open Universe.

endogeneity suggests. Now the change in the wellbeing criterion implies the changes that occur in the complementary interrelations between the variables to attain sustainability in knowledge-flows across knowledge-induced space and time dimensions.

In quantitative form the TSR-theory of value explained by the *maslaha* function is given by its total change under the impact of knowledge $\{\theta(\varepsilon)\}$ along its regenerative IIE-learning processes:

$$dW(\theta)/d\theta = \sum (\partial W(\theta)/\partial \mathbf{x}(\theta)) \cdot (d\mathbf{x}(\theta)/d\theta) > 0 \text{ identically by terms in multivariables.} \quad (6.14)$$

Expression (6.14) is true in both cases—of the good things of life induced by knowledge-flows; and of the bad things of life induced by 'de-knowledge'-flows. Figure 6.4 depicts such cases, pointing out the important result that, the *Tawhidi* primal ontology as the criterion of truth against falsehood,[3] acts as the methodological origin of both these opposite realities. Thereby, the opposite criteria leads to the differentiation by independence between the variables, as in the case of utilitarian models having exogenous and thereby competing exogenous relationship between the material values and moral values. There is no methodical possibility for the endogenous embedding between moral and material values (Hammond, 1989).

The TSR methodology governing good (*haqq*) and falsehood (*batil*) is universally and uniquely explained by Fig. 6.4:

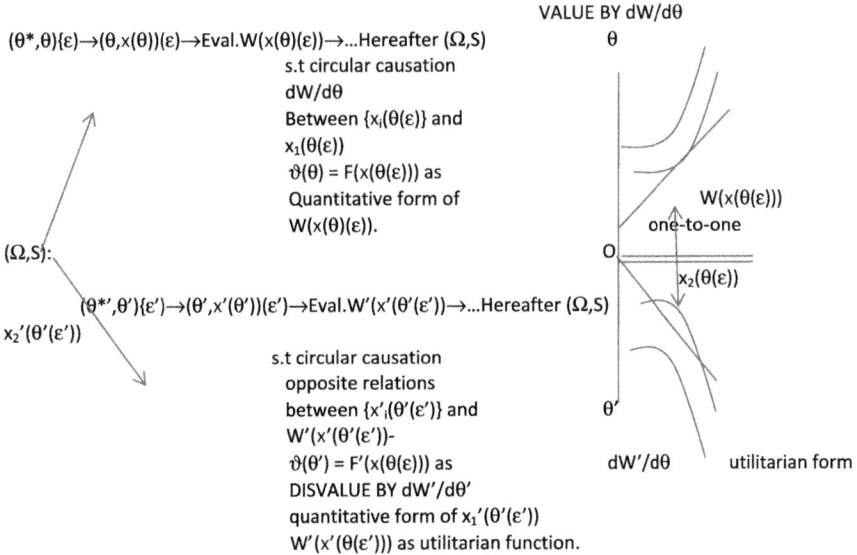

Fig. 6.4 Opposite TSR value-relations of truth and falsehood by unity of knowledge contra utilitarian differentiation

---

[3] *Qur'an* (25:1): "Blessed is He who sent down the Criterion upon His Servant that he may be to the worlds a warner-".

The importance in the two opposite meanings of 'value' and 'disvalue' is that value arising from the composite and complementary (participatory) form of *maslaha* (wellbeing) gives an estimable function that remains complex and inter-variable dependent in nature. This property is conveyed by the mathematical differentiation of the wellbeing criterion. Value is thus measured by,

$$dW(\theta)/d\theta = \sum(\partial W(\theta)/\partial \mathbf{x}(\theta)) \cdot (d\mathbf{x}(\theta)/d\theta) > 0.$$

In this expression interdependence between the variables is explained by $(d\mathbf{x}(\theta)/d\theta) > 0$. The further implication of this result is that, value incorporating moral and material abstracto-empirical embedding is the cause of interdependence between all the variables, all of which are thereby endogenously knowledge-induced by $\{\theta(\varepsilon)\}$. In the special case of price-variable in its various forms, the measure of price as value is dependent on the mathematical differentiated values of all other variables of the wellbeing function, which is continuously differentiable in all the variables being induced by $\{\theta(\varepsilon)\}$.

In the case of the welfare origin of value in the utilitarian sense,

$$dW'(\theta')/d\theta' = \sum(\partial W'(\theta')/\partial \mathbf{x}'(\theta')).(d\mathbf{x}'(\theta')/d\theta') > 0,$$

It is possible for $\{\theta(\varepsilon)\} = \{\phi\}$, implying ethical neutrality; or an existing measure of falsehood implied by additive meaning methodological independence and individualism between the welfare criteria of the independently allocated variables. Some or all of the circular causation equations may not exist. Thereby, $(d\mathbf{x}'(\theta')/d\theta') = 0$ for all or given $\mathbf{x}'(\theta')$. These points are all explained by $(d\mathbf{x}'(\theta')/d\theta') > 0$. This result occurs in terms of falsehood in respect of inter-variable marginalist relations and in terms of dialectical relations for ethically-benign evolutionary learning processes within the rationalist episteme of 'de-knowledge'. 'De-knowledge' is characterized by competition, differentiation, and methodological individualism between variables. These characteristics represent the conflicting behaviour of agents and agencies in the problems under study.

Contrasting Theories of Institutionalism in TSR and Mainstream Economic Theory: Consequences of Non-*Tawhidi* Islamic Economics

Institutionalism means the outlook of institutions according to the episteme of certain types of collectivity that together abide with and work towards attaining an objective criterion and given goals. In addressing this approach towards attaining the institution's and its organization's vision and mission, it adopts methods pertaining to its epistemic origin in the light of collective thought by means of appertaining methods of various kinds. Some such methods are qualitative and cross-sectional in type, based on primary data and information raised by surveys. Other methods are based on secondary data having quantitative methods of statistical analysis. Yet other forms of methods are a mix of primary and secondary data analysis. The statistical analyses using a variety of structural econometric models lead to policy analysis and recommendations for developing newer simulated approaches to policy-theoretic inferences

In the case of TSR method (epistemic) the resulting objective criterion is of wellbeing (*maslaha*). The *maslaha* function is continuously differentiable in respect of the variables that form knowledge-induced complementarities between them of the type that epistemically conform to the *Tawhidi* ontology of unity of knowledge. Thus in all cases of institutional and organizational variety only one episteme and its methodology, followed by application of methods and sustainability across continuum of systems prevails. This methodological origin followed by pertinent method was pointed out symbolically earlier in this text.

Epistemic derivation of institutional objective criterion is evaluation of $W(\theta) = W(\theta, x(\theta))$, subject to inter-variable circular causation relations to determine the degrees of existing inter-variable complementarities between the good things of life. Likewise, we can determine the negative complementarities (mainstream idea of marginalism) that are imitated by non-*Tawhidi* Islamic economics and socio-scientific studies) between the good things of life as in the case of the concept of 'prioritization' that non-*Tawhidi* economics uses.

Thereby TSR methodologies normatively examines the possibility of avoidance of the bad things of life; while simulating to revise statistical results for attaining greater degrees of complementarities and lesser degrees of marginal substitution between the recommended variables. The resulting circular causation equations are denoted by, $x_i = f_i(\theta, x_j(\theta))$, $I = 1, 2, \ldots, n$; and the measured wellbeing function, $\vartheta(\theta)$ linearized to $\theta = F(x(\theta))$. The estimated coefficients of these various relations are also θ-induced by virtue of simulated learning through institutional participation, mathematical continuity and differentiability. Thereby, only one unique and universal episteme abides throughout the multi-stage systemic operations and *maslaha* (wellbeing) objective of *Tawhidi* institution.

The Example of *Waqf* (Charitable Allocations) in Socioeconomic Development in the Perspective of *Tawhidi* Meta-science Methodology

As an example, we take the case of *waqf* (perpetual charitable endowment) in the socioeconomic development process. We define socioeconomic development as a continuously sustainable evolutionary learning process in respect of pervasive complementarities between recommended variables. In this way, the implications of wellbeing (*maslaha*) objective function are satisfied. The truly Islamic function of *waqf* in the *Tawhidi* meta-science epistemic sense is represented by the above-mentioned objective criterion of its multi-system *maslaha* model of socioeconomic development with moral-material embedding. Consequently, *waqf* is to be viewed as an embedded moral-material institution with its definitive complementary role in socioeconomic development across continuums of complementary variables and interrelated systems.

Examples in this respect are the social positioning and the role of *waqf*. Thereby, in educational *waqf* project, a central focus must be in devoting the project to human resource development for poverty alleviation, rather than simply assimilating advanced human resource development with the poor-due for addressing the objective of poverty alleviation. Yet, inter-system complementarities require such a blending of the two sections of human resource development. The implication is that all development regimes ought to be of the life-fulfillment type interconnecting all systems of human resource development. The focus is to be on life-fulfillment regimes of sustainability. In this way, all variables $\{x_i(\theta)\}$ are complementary across stages and systems of life-fulfillment regime of development. Parameterized $\{\theta\}$-values explain the complementarity focus according to the *Tawhidi* episteme of unity of knowledge between the good things of life-fulfillment regimes.

The same kind of dynamics would apply to organizations to realize life-fulfillment development regimes. Growth-oriented conception of human resource development that ignores the endogenous embedded nature of poverty-centered development in all of human resource development (World Bank, 2000; Streeten, 1981; Rawls, 1971) are to be replaced. In truly *Tawhidi* worldview of life-fulfillment regimes of development there is the entire *Qur'anic* scenario of human ecology.[4] Such a life-fulfillment form is emulated in the life-fulfillment model of Imam Shatibi (trans. Draz, n.d.). The Shatibi-basket comprises needs (dururiyath), comforts (hajiyath), and refinements (tahsaniyath).

Any *waqf* model as an endowment that addresses goals such as economic growth and secularization of knowledge cannot advance the nature of organic pairing across variety of elements of inter-variable and inter-system complementarities in life-fulfillment regime of development. Such a *waqf* project does not emulate the worldview of connectivity in charity of endogenous development by human consciousness that the *Qur'an* pronounces[5] and which the Prophet emphasised on perpetual charity. The fruition between all possibilities of human resource development by *waqf* as perpetual charity and in coterminous interrelationship would yield the true meaning of *waqf*.[6]

In the sense of *waqf* as perpetual charity, *waqf* can be defined as spiritual capital taken up in its complex and non-linear form as bestowal and bequeath with its intertemporal moral-material endogenous complementarities across historical con-

---

[4]*Qur'an* (14:24): "Seest thou not how Allah sets forth a parable?—A goodly word like a goodly tree, whose root is firmly fixed, and its branches (reach) to the heavens,—of its Lord. So Allah sets forth parables for men, in order that they may receive admonition."

[5]*Qur'an* (14:26): "And the parable of an evil Word is that of an evil tree: It is torn up by the root from the surface of the earth: it has no stability."

[6]*Qur'an* (57:11): "Who is it that will offer up unto God a goodly loan, which He will amply repay? For, such (as do so) shall have a noble reward."

sciousness of life-fulfillment regimes. Thereby, if one of the variables of the wellbeing (*maslaha*) function is θ-induced value of capital investment, then the corresponding circular causation equation of spiritual capital ($I(\theta)$ induced by spirituality variables 'θ') is, $I(\theta) = f(\mathbf{x}_j(\theta), \theta)$. This represents the moral-material embedding in the case of *waqf*-investment as spiritual capital. Recursively, every other variables is related by circular causation with $I(\theta)$.

That is, $x_i(\theta) = f_i(\mathbf{x}_j(\theta), I(\theta), \theta)$. In so formalizing the *maslaha* basis of *waqf* as perpetual charity with extended complementary relations, *waqf* enters a comprehensive process of evolutionary learning with a conscious sway of coordinated interrelations under the unique and universal episteme of *Tawhidi* unity of knowledge. Contrarily, even if *waqf* forms a contract in the portfolio of independently distributed Islamic financial instruments, it fails to be meaningful Islamic project under TSR, and thereby to be of the truly Islamic worldview.

It was the contractual and independently existing nature of *waqf* that made it fail in Islamic development history. Some of the large *waqf*, such as of Tunisia and Morocco,[7] reverted to control by their donors. In Malaysia, the emergence of *waqf* is predominantly a government activity, with few being in private sector initiative. Contrary to such institutional governance of *waqf*, this institution ought to be a widely participative social project. In that case, the financing of *waqf* should be contained within the portfolio with other Islamic participatory instruments. Such a complementary pooled portfolio of development financing instruments reflects the *Tawhidi* participatory worldview in the framework of unity of knowledge as the organically overarching epistemic worldview.

References

Buchanan, J. M. (1999). The domain of constitutional economics. *The logical foundations of constitutional liberty*. Indianapolis: Liberty Fund.

Hammond, P. J. (1989). On reconciling Arrow's theory of social choice with Harsanyi's fundamental utilitarianism. In G. R. Feiwel (Ed.), *Arrow and the foundation of the theory of economic policy* (pp. 179–221). London: Macmillan.

Lozano, J. M. (2000). *Ethics and organization, understanding business ethics as a learning process*. Dordrecht: Kluwer Academic.

Rawls, J. (1971). *A theory of justice*. Cambridge: Harvard University Press.

Streeten, P. (1981). From growth to basic needs. In P. Streeten (Ed.), *Development perspectives*. New York: St. Martin's Press.

World Bank. (2000). *World development report 2000–2001*. New York: Oxford University Press.

---

[7]"Giving to eternity", https://www.aljazeera.com/programmes/aljazeeraworld/2016/03/giving-eternity-160309083954994.html, visited May 9, 2018.

"*Waqfs*, Morocco", https://islamicmarkets.com/education/waqfs-morocco, Islamic Markets; visited May 9, 2018.

Chapter 7
Structure of Participatory Institution According to *Tawhidi* Unitary Worldview and Conversely

Masudul Alam Choudhury

Abstract The mind of participatory institutions is set at accomplishing the unitary methodological worldview in its positive programs and their applications. Thus the institutional wellbeing criterion (*maslaha*) forms the foundation of the wider field of valuation of the social contract. At once with this objective criterion the *Tawhidi* worldview of monotheistic unity of knowledge ought to be fused into true Islamic institutionalism. This expectation though is not realized by *shari'ah*, as in the case of Islamic banks. The cause of such deficiency is the failure of the emergent understanding under *shari'ah* that locks up the decision-making and valuation model in an *aqd*-contractual type. The intra-system and inter-system intertemporal valuation consequences must be brought into the conscious abstracto-empirical model of asset valuation, capital formation, and transactions in the interconnected present to future inter-generational sense. Thereby, all the financial instruments, which are presently debt-ridden in *shari'ah* must be transformed into debt-free ones. This is possible by the *Tawhidi* methodological worldview of monotheistic unity of knowledge in its systemic meaning of IIE-learning processes in continued sustainability.

A Non-technical Overview of the Chapter

Of utmost need for high erudition in Islamic socio-scientific methodology for inquiry into 'everything' is to study the inner meanings of the *Qur'an* in terms of its cardinal law of *Tawhid*. This is explained in increasing depth by the penetrating meaning of monotheistic unity of knowledge in the form of organic interrelations between all entities of creation. It is also necessary to learn by the depth of analytical knowledge the logic, nature, and consequences gained for inferences and continuity of simulacra

M. A. Choudhury (✉)
Faculty of Economics, Trisakti University, Jakarta, Indonesia
e-mail: masudc60@yahoo.ca

© Springer Nature Singapore Pte Ltd. 2019
M. A. Choudhury (ed.), *The* Tawhidi *Methodological Worldview*,
https://doi.org/10.1007/978-981-13-6585-0_7

of evaluation results of the wellbeing objective criterion across knowledge-induced space and time dimensions. Such an approach by its increasing heights of learning as by the IIE-learning processes assumes sustained historical consciousness.

The rest of the inner depths of *Tawhidi* explanation of the knowledge-induced world-system assume their multifarious properties and logical formalism to gain inroads into the systemic study of reality. The ultimate axiom that drives the entire *Tawhid* methodological worldview is irreducibly one. This is the inexorable foundation of the monotheistic unity of knowledge and its consequential generality and details of the knowledge-induced world-system intertemporality. Thereby, intra-system dynamics combine in rich and complex ways with inter-system dynamics to lay down the *Tawhidi* phenomenology of the abstracto-empirical investigation. *Tawhid* as the primal ontological premise of knowledge, and thereby reasoning, gives emanation to epistemology followed by phenomenology and sustainability of the IIE-learning processes in continuity. Such an analytical dynamic is to be understood as the observed, reasoned, and applied method that is manifest and configured in degrees of its abstraction, evaluation, application, and continuity. Such attributes of *Tawhid* as law are to be critically introduced and comprehended in the universal and unique theories of 'everything'. Islamic economics, finance, and socio-scientific inquiry are to be embedded and immersed in the form of relational causality within the diversely evolutionary learning systems described by the precept of unity of knowledge. Together with such a methodological approach the instruments like the financing ones and the knowledge-induced socioeconomic ones are to be studied in the same light of unity of knowledge. They are to be evaluated by the estimation and simulacra of the wellbeing objective criterion, subject to the evaluation of inter-causal relations of the multivariables in the wellbeing function. The configuration of the quantitative form of the wellbeing function and of the numerical coefficients of the inter-causal relations in respect of inquiring on the principle of inter-variable complementarities arise in the analytical process. Such relations are the cause and the regenerated cycles of effects and causes in the endogenous nature of the variables that read out degrees of unity of knowledge, or otherwise, for moral and material reconstruction.

The above-mentioned summary of *Tawhidi* law as methodology of unity of knowledge is universally unique to itself alone. The *shari'ah* approach to the same kinds of inter-causal logical questions immersed in unity of knowledge and its moral-empirical forms does not have any abstracto-empirical potentiality. Consequently, the entire realm of the *Tawhidi* methodological worldview in terms of unity of knowledge in 'everything' remains alien to the *aqd*-based contractual nature of *shari'ah* constricted as it is to earthly events alone taken up in piecemeal form.

The richly complex and non-linear form of logical formalism along with their functional ontologies that carry forward the entire *Tawhidi* methodology in abstracto-empirical form are required for study and development in advanced mathematical form. The relevance of such a methodological approach is found in *Tawhidi* law. Such a methodology and its emergent methods of evaluation are unknown to *shari'ah*. The *shari'ah* approach and the empirical works of the gurus pronounced in the *shari'ah* school have failed to derive logical formalism in any way similar to the *Tawhidi* methodological worldview.

Introduction

Figure 7.1 presents a unique and universal institutional structure according to the *Tawhidi* methodological worldview of unity of knowledge. This epistemic precept establishes the participatory institutional design of socioeconomic development of 'everything'. The model of participatory Islamic banking as an institution is now being actively sought in Turkey (2015). Yet the caution ought to be pointed out that participatory institution of the financial type in *Tawhidi* unitary perspective is conceived as a widening form of inter-systemic and inter-variable circular causation model of organic participation, beyond simply pooling of members' funds to attain a cluster of economic and financial performance. This would simply be a continuation of the shareholder model in national sustainable development within the global partnership concept of moral-material embedded form of transformation. This is the architecture of bringing about moral and ethical understanding within the hub of financial organic linkages. That would convey the evolutionary learning perspective of *Qur'anic* pairing between conforming entities. We define such entities as participating agents, agencies, and ever-widening parts of the evolutionary learning social economy at large. They all bear the ultimate objective of *maslaha* (wellbeing) connected with the design of life-fulfilling regime of endogenous growth and development (Romer, 1986).

In Fig. 7.1 we define the following symbols:

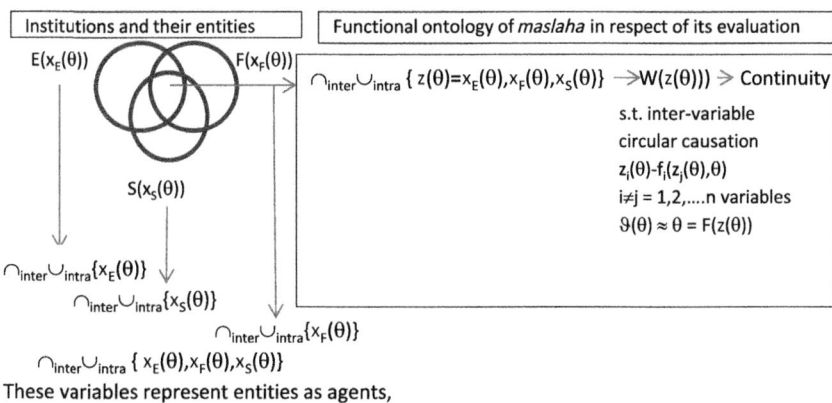

Fig. 7.1 The *Tawhidi* ontological Institutional perspective of wellbeing evaluation in IIE-learning process

F($\mathbf{x}_F(\theta)$): financial sector with its financing variables of the participatory type both within them and with other moral-material unison of variables all induced by the evolutionary learning parameter, $\{\theta\}$. Thus for intra-system endogenously combined with inter-system IIE-learning processes of preferences, menus of socioeconomic development entities, agents, and agencies are explained intertemporally.

Likewise, there are the vectors of variables similarly defined in light of circular causation by organic pairing between the diversity of intra-system and inter-system intertemporal experience as follows: Event coordinates are denoted by E($\mathbf{x}_k(\theta)$). $\{\mathbf{x}_k(\theta)\}$, k = E, F, S form combined with inter-system evolutionary learning in intertemporal processes and represent their participatory agents, agencies, and entities. Among these kinds are portfolios of participatory financing instruments that pair in organic sense of the IIE-learning processes with industry-specific sectoral development. These accounts further result in human resource development and resource mobilization, reformation of the monetary sector and policy in relation to the real economy (Choudhury & Hoque, 2017). Moral/ethical focus is given to the choices and product development of goods and services in a life-fulfillment regime of development. The comprehensive result of extensive participation between the variables of the vector, $\{\mathbf{x}_E, \mathbf{x}_F, \mathbf{x}_S\}(\theta)$, addresses poverty alleviation and the like. The inherent intra-system and inter-system dynamics are shown in Fig. 7.1. In the intertemporal sense of IIE-learning processes we note,

$$\{\mathbf{x}_E, \mathbf{x}_F, \mathbf{x}_S\}(\theta) = \cup_{\text{inter-syst}}[\{\mathbf{x}_E\} \cap \{\mathbf{x}_F\} \cap \{\mathbf{x}_S\}](\theta)_{\text{intra-system}}. \qquad (7.1)$$

The consequences on *maslaha* as the wellbeing criterion explain the conceptual and applied perspective of wellbeing with extensively participatory intra-system and inter-system intertemporally variables. The *maslaha* function maintains its continuously differentiable and monotonic positive transformation forms as implied by evaluation comprising estimation and simulation of the estimated coefficients of the quantitative form of the wellbeing function,

$$\vartheta(\theta) \approx \theta = F(\mathbf{x}_E, \mathbf{x}_F, \mathbf{x}_S\}(\theta), \qquad (7.2)$$

with, $d\vartheta(\theta)/d\theta$ as total differential in continuously participatory inter-causal relations between the variables.

The particular case of *Tawhidi* worldview in the study of *waqf* as a pairing institution in unity of knowledge with the expanding entities of the intertemporal evolutionary learning type socioeconomic intra-systems and inter-systems is equally applicable to the generalized theory of institutionalism according to *Tawhidi* methodological worldview. In one such particular case studied within the generalized *Tawhidi* worldview of paired world-system with unity of knowledge there is the financial instrument of so-called Islamic bond, *sukuk*; and the case of pricing of *takaful*. The case of *takaful* was discussed earlier.

Problem of *Sukuk* Revolving Around Debt Instruments

The example of *sukuk* as an instrument of participatory financial cooperation can be formalized under the same kind of organic structural worldview of *Tawhid* as explained above. In this attempt the approach once again is to formulate the *sukuk* contract (*aqd*) not as isolated financing case from the rest of the participatory instruments. Rather, the multi-stage and multi-system IIE-learning processes between diverse intra- and inter-system taken in intertemporal evolutionary learning under organic unity of knowledge implies a vast extension of interacting and integrating financial instruments and project outlets in socioeconomic development with the help, guidance, and direction of Islamic financing institution. An example of such a participatory instrument is the Islamic bank.

There are some critical points in *sukuk* financing of a mega-project. Mega-projects governed by shareholder conception ought to be diversified to link with grassroots development is of the case of life-fulfillment kind mentioned in the preceding sections. Circulating *sukuk* around debt-instruments is to be avoided, despite being referred to as *shari'ah-compliant* (*ijara, murabaha, musharakah* etc.) for raising funds by Special Purpose Vehicle (SPV) institution with the promise of assigned bond rates. Instead, the 'nearest-point valuation' rates determined intertemporal across intra-systems and inter-systems is to be used as the asset-valuation and returns model. Such a model was discussed earlier. The intertemporal ('t') evaluation of rates $\{r_t(\theta)\}$ is then done by the circular causation relation, $r_t(\theta) = f_t(x_j(\theta))$. Here '$x_j(\theta)$' denotes the vector of all circular causal variables except '$r_t(\theta)$'. Furthermore, the corrective in rates to bondholders through asset/bond-holding is to be exercised for equality and fairness of distributive ownership.

Debt is thereby avoided by 'nearest-point' rates to the lowest possible level, though probabilistic measure of the evaluated rates exists to the marginal extent depending upon the level of attainment of $\{\theta\}$-induction in debt-dissolution. This knowledge-flow can be further refined by the endogenous belief- parameter to yield the conceptual, though not measurable parameter $\{\theta(\varepsilon)\}$. By the fair distribution of excess or shortfall in the measured rate compared to the estimated rate of debt-reduction the distribution is evened off between the bondholder and the SPV. All so-called Islamic instruments are debt-instruments and *sukuk* revolves around these instruments. Thereby, both the theory and practice of Islamic financing in terms of such debt-instruments makes it questionable whether interest-rate avoidance is at all a central focus of non-*Tawhidi* Islamic finance. In the sense of intertemporal of resource allocation, as realized in the presently existing way, it is debatable whether the *riba*-problem has at all been addressed adequately well by *shari'ah*.

Problems of *Shari'ah-Compliance* Contra *Tawhidi* Methodological Worldview in Addressing *Maslaha* of Institutionalism Within the World-System

Neither *maqasid as-shari'ah* nor *shari'ah-compliance* as human concocted innovations to claim Islamic Law is acceptable in contrast to the universal and unique Law of *Tawhid* as the primal ontology upon and from which the design of the generality and particulars of 'everything' rests. If this duality was allowed, as is today the case with so-called 'Islamic' approach of *shari'ah* by a complete ambivalence regarding *Tawhid* as the primal ontology of Islamic worldview, that would be tantamount to assuming two primal laws contesting in the body framework of Islamic belief. This state would interfere with the universal precept of monotheism (*Tawhid*) upon which the supercardinal truth of unitary belief rests. Subsequently, the powerful worldview of unity of knowledge, the explicatory world-system (*a'lameen*) of signs of Allah (*Ayath Allah*) , and the design of the evolutionary learning world-system in terms of the principle of extensive complementarities between the good and the bad things of life, all taken in their separate folds, would be lost. The resilience of *Tawhid* in the enriched explanation of the generality and particulars of the world-system would be lost. Indeed, all this leads into a contradiction of the monotheistic worldview. That is what has happened in the entirety of so-called 'Islamic' connotation of law and its functioning.

According to the theory of law, Hart (1994, slightly edited) categorizes the field of law into two different kinds, the primary law and the secondary law. Hart writes, and our text gives an equivalent meaning with *Tawhid* as ontological law and the *shari'ah* as codified sub-law, as follows: Hart (1994, p. 92, see Starr, 1989) explained: [Secondary rules] (which is equivalent to *Tawhid* as Ontological Law of 'everything') may all be said to be on a different level from the primary rules, (which is the sub-law codification by *shari'ah*) for they are all about such rules, in the sense that, while primary rules are concerned with the actions that individuals must or must not do (*maqasid* choices), the secondary law (*Tawhid* as primal Ontological Law) is concerned with the primary rules. "They specify the ways in which the primary rules may be conclusively ascertained, introduced, eliminated, varied, and the fact of their violation conclusively determined". Thus there is the ultimate governance by *Tawhid* as the law of monotheistic unity of knowledge concerning 'everything'.

The often variegated nature of *shari'ah* in regional, and *madhab* (sects) context is found in the case of the emergence of such Islamic law in South-East Asia. An example is of the law that prevailed in Malacca (Hooker, 1984). In many cases there were non-conformity between the *Qur'anic* injunction and the human-concocted cultural influence of regional practices in the development of Islamic law. That is to say, the *shari'ah* is the sure result of assimilating *urf* and *adah* (culture and practices) into Islamic law. *Madhabs* (sects). An example here is of the Shafa'ie sect that had a distinct role to play in the formulation of certain economic reasoning that were different from those of other *madhabs* (Djibrilla, Buang, & Olayemi, 2017).

In general as noted by Hooker (op cit, p. 36), "Nowhere does the *shari'ah* alone determine the public or private obligations of Muslims."

This is a remark that reverberates across the observation regarding *shari'ah*. It was noticed also by Ibn Khaldun. That is Ibn Khaldun remarked, although *shari'ah* may be thought of as the best law, yet it was nowhere to be found in practice. Ibn Khaldun as a vizier of the sultan's court during his time and by his historical study of North Africa, found the *shari'ah* a legal system that lay at the determination of the ruling class (Mahdi, 1964 op cit).

A Summary Viewpoint on *Shari'ah*

In summary we note that, *shari'ah* as the human-concocted law despite its roots in the *Qur'an* and the *sunnah* (*maqasid as-shari'ah al-Tawhid*), has partitioned status relating to *Tawhid* as the revelatory law of 'everything'. No great work has been done to restore them together in religious, economic, social, political, ecological, or legal worldview of Islam. A unified worldview, as of *Tawhid* as law in 'everything', has not moved the Muslim mind over the entire span of historical consciousness, in the way as Hubner et al. (1985) states regarding historistic ensemble. Beyond the failure of *shari'ah* to uphold the unitary knowledge of the *Qur'an* and *sunnah* in living conception and world-system overarching experience, the same episteme of unity of knowledge and the world-system has escaped the rationalist reasoning, despite much endeavour in this evasive domain of thought for a long time now (Barrow, 1991; Hawking, 1988). This point of socio-scientific ontological, epistemological, and phenomenological dimensions is discussed below with respect to the problem of heteronomy in a priori and a posteriori demarcated reasoning according to Kant and Friedrich 1949.

A Mathematical Questioning of *Shari'ah* Contra *Tawhid* Regarding *Shari'ah* Inacceptability as Islamic Law

If one were to surmise that the epistemology of law and justice is premised on the realm of common global ethics that are acceptable and life-fulfilling for all of humankind, then the cultural and religious diversities must be first, ingrained in such an epistemology. Thereafter, such a universally well-defining epistemology must be able to overarch all details of human experience globally while embracing the medium of discourse.

On mathematical topological grounds the tenability of *shari'ah* as Islamic law can be questioned. Figure 7.2 explains the ontological, epistemological, and phenomenological status of TSR in contrast to the mainstream conception, which is shown to be emulated by the *shari'ah* methodology qua *fiqh* and *fatawa*. The real-

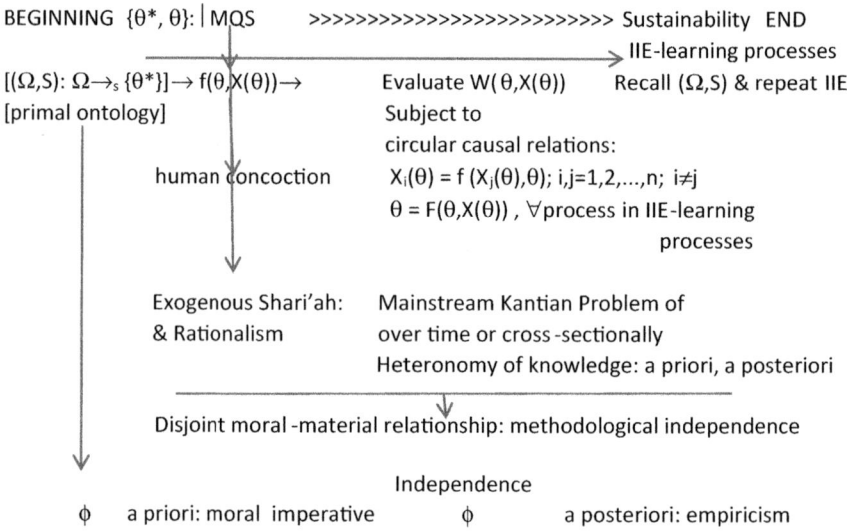

Fig. 7.2 Contrasting implications between *Tawhid* as the primal ontological law and rationalism and *shari'ah*

ity of the monotheistic worldview rests firmly and inextricably on the knowledge-induced process of the evolutionary learning world-system from the Beginning to the End. This also implies the Unbounded Closure of the entire creation from the End to the Beginning. That is, the two overwhelming relations abide: (i) Beginning ⇒ End as evolutionary learning process; AND (ii) End ⇒ Beginning as identity. Thereby, in topological sense, Beginning ≡ End, both as the unique Great Event of entire Creation.

Within this entire evolutionary learning process of Unbounded Closure rests the meaning and functioning of 'everything'. This entirety comprises two parts—The primal ontology of (Ω, S) germinating *Tawhidi* methodological worldview, which explains by its overarching inclusiveness the mind-space of both rationalism (falsehood) and *maqasid as-shari'ah*, denoted by MQS as rule-based perspectives (*ahkam*). Rationalism and MQS being both human concocted experiences of reality give rise to knowledge-flows that formalize their distinct model of reality from that of *Tawhid* as Law of unity of knowledge. Mainstream rationalism premises such a functional ontology explained by $\{\mathbf{f}(\theta, \mathbf{X}(\theta))\}$ along the dialectical process of evolutionary learning in its own precept of a conjectural world-system (Popper, 1965) and ever-repeating world-system of competition and bifurcation by methodological individualism (Wallerstein, 1998).

In MQS no such assumption of methodological individualism exists. But the derivation of the MQS rules from the nature of its functional ontology, epistemology, and phenomenology would be similarly implicated. For instance, although *Tawhidi* law determines MQS, MQS alone does not have any self-same approach to establish *Tawhidi* law as the primal ontology. *Tawhidi* law as primal ontology thus remains irreducible in the quiddity of oneness of Allah, expressed in methodological sense as the episteme of unity of knowledge and its induction of 'everything'. MQS like mainstream rationalism generates functional ontology derived from primal ontology as rules of earthly action. This is the result of the impossibility of MQS to endogenously embed the moral-material nature of reality and the resulting abstracto-empirical modulation of *Qur'anic* universal and unique reality. This otherwise is the highest domain of *Tawhid* as law of organic complementarities and participation of being and becoming in 'everything'.

Tawhid and *Shari'ah*: A Deepening Problem of Non-convergence

In the *Tawhidi* derived functional ontology, MQS as rules is devoid of some of the most critical properties as of the interactive, integrative, and evolutionary learning worldview of IIE-learning processes. *Maqasid as-shari'ah* inherits the *Tawhid* principle from *Tawhidi* primal ontological premise: $(\Omega, S) \to$ MQS. But it is monotheistic impossibility for MQS $\to (\Omega, S)$. The simultaneous occurrence of these two as conversant relationship would deny the primacy and sole exogeneity of *Tawhidi* ontological beginning as the sole universal and unique law of monotheism affecting the generality and particulars of 'everything'. The ultimate injunction of the *Qur'an* (8:18) thereby is this: "There is no god but He: That is the witness of Allah, His angels, and those endued with knowledge, standing firm on justice. There is no god but He, the Exalted in Power, the Wise." The whole of the *Qur'an* and *sunnah* is exaltation of this foundational and indispensable principle of *Tawhid* in the very first place as the law of primal ontological origin explaining 'everything'.

Consequently, the principle of pervasive complementarities, and thus systemic participation of TSR grounds the endogenous formulation of the *maslaha* function as the objective criterion of the truly Islamic order. *Maslaha* as the distinctive goal includes the extensive vector of variables of inter-causal relations. The *maslaha* function presents the substantive formulation of a generalized model of unity of knowledge (consilience) and its induction of the unified world-system in generality and particulars. All of these are consistently and analytically explained by the *Tawhidi* methodological worldview. On the other hand, they are not imminent in the *shari'ah* fold and not realizable except by the dialectics of differentiation and competition in rationalism. This property of the rationalist dialectical process is found in the demarcation between moral and material system of variables and values that characterize the world-system according to TSR in embedded continuity (Popper, 1988).

The nature of *Tawhid* contra *shari'ah*, as the primal ontological law, has occupied the debate and dissent between these vast disciplines over centuries, casting thereby fresh examination of the two domains of Islamic investigation. *Maqasid as-shari'ah* for instance has been overly concerned with personal rules and codes of conduct concerning earthly affairs known as *muamalat*. *Muamalat* comprises a secularized view of reality. It regulates interpersonal relations rather than the relationship to deity in the *Qur'anic* meaning of *Tawhid* as the Final Law (*sunnat Allah*).

MQS is not the extended study of earthly affairs and science, society, and other interacting domains in a most analytical way, which otherwise is the rich extant of the *Tawhidi* methodological worldview. This is particularly true of the advancing age of search and discovery as of the concurrent world of complexity and system and cyberneticconsilience. Thus *shari'ah* is of limited scope, whereas the *Tawhidi* methodological worldview and its concomitant emergences are of a vast nature. There is thereby considerable divergences of interpretation called juristic *fiqh* and *fatawa* by leaders of sects (*madhabs*) and their protege. During present times, there has arisen a plethora of interferences in socio-scientific disciplines by *shari'ah* rules. The result and controversies so arising from these divergent interpretations and use have put to question the degrees of reliability of such rules and on the questioning of such rules that originated by the utterances on *fiqh* and *fatwas* of medieval jurists.

Tawhid as the Law super-encompassing MQS and mainstream rationalism is thus the primal ontological law.[1] *Tawhid* cannot be compared in any shape and form with rationalism, which is by nature dissociative. *Tawhid* as law cannot be compared with *shari'ah* in all its terminological forms. *Shari'ah* thereby ceases to 0 be law in the light of the primal origin of *Tawhid* concerning 'everything'. Thereby, the functional ontology of MQS is of the following form: $f(\theta, X(\theta)) = f_1(\theta_1, x_1(\theta_1)) + f_2(\theta_2, x_2(\theta_2))$. Suffix '1' denotes the world-system of material composition. '2' denotes the world-system of moral composition. These are disjointly treated and are therefore exogenously related in *shari'ah*. The endogenous value created by the primal ontology of *Tawhid* as law is thus differentiated by the rationalist and MQS functional ontologies concerning disjoint moral and material values. The resulting deontological consequence in rationalism and MQS remains contrary to the preception of monotheistic worldview in *Tawhid* as the law of organic unity of knowledge in and across 'everything' in historical consciousness.

Tawhid Contra Rationalism and *Shari'ah* on Methodological Grounds

One critical difference between *Tawhid* as law and rationalism and MQS is their ways of understanding the inter-causal paired (unified by participative circular causation) world-system 'between the heavens and the earth'. If we denote the suffixes '1' for the earthly system and '2' for the heavenly system (cosmology), then the linear dichotomy means methodological independence (thus systemic individualism) between these domains. The 'starred heavens and the moral law within' mankind are not in interaction with each other in mainstream rationalism and MQS. Such a nature of mainstream rationalism and MQS delimits their capability to be universally

---

[1]*Qur'an* (6:101): "To Him is due the primal origin of the heavens and the earth: How can He have a son when He hath no consort? He created all things, and He hath full knowledge of all things."

the true and unitary worldview as is the overarching and all-comprehensive *Tawhid*. The *Qur'an* (13:3) declares regarding the unified systemic sense of universal pairing: "And it is He who spread the earth and placed therein firmly set mountains and rivers; and from all of the fruits He made therein two mates; He causes the night to cover the day. Indeed in that are signs for a people who give thought."

The absence of embedding the organic unity by complementarities and participation in *shari'ah* is a deep problem of irresolution in logical formalism. The unitary essence of *Tawhid* and thereby of the *Qur'an* and *sunnah* in Islamic economics, finance, science, society, and furthermore in the theory of a widest meaning of institutionalism are premised in the episteme of unity of knowledge. This is the grand meaning of the Islamic world-system of *ummah*.[2] The hidden worlds of non-physicalism and of physicalism comprise yet other organically embedded world-systems called *umamun* in the *Qur'an*. Together all the world-systems in their organic unity of being and becoming is called *a'lameen* in the *Qur'an*.

In Fig. 7.2 the difference between *Tawhid* and MQS in deriving knowledge and reasoning is seen in the functioning of these worldviews in describing the ontological nature of unity of knowledge in the diversified world-system. *Tawhid* has its unique origin in itself as the self-referencing quiddity expressed in terms of supercardinal topology by (Ω, S). Thereby, the ultimate topological proof of truth is found in the evolutionary learning framework of the open-ended Fixed Point (Nikaido, 1987) relationship, Beginning $\equiv$ End. This proof is established through the evolutionary learning processes of the generality and particulars of the world-system from aye to eternity.

On the other hand, MQS, if it is to be considered as primal ontological law must begin from itself, and thereby avoid the origin and functionality of *Tawhid* as the primal ontological of 'everything'. This kind of derivation of the nature of the world-system by MQS is thus left to the vagaries of human concoction of an incomplete nature of belief and knowledge that only in a cursory sense refer to *Tawhid* as the ontological beginning but does not use *Tawhid* by itsmethodological worldview of unity of knowledge and the world-system. How contrarily, MQS ought to be invoked continuously in the derivation of knowledge and reasoning to establish circularity between MQS and (Ω, S)—remains a void issue.

Yet this cannot be the case, for if this was to be an endogenously invoked case in reality, then topologically, MQS $\equiv (\Omega, S)$. This result would convey a form and shape of the world-system that is utterly haphazard, uncharted, and in disorder. (Ω, S) holds its own ultimately exogenous sway in the elegant relationship:

Beginning, $(\Omega, S) \rightarrow$ (IIE-world-system) $\rightarrow$ End $= (\Omega, S)$.

Along with this negation of *shari'ah* as law—only holding the position of a domain of choices by discourse and authenticated—the primal ordainment is by the ontology of (Ω, S).

---

[2]*Qur'an* (2:143): "Thus We have made you [true Muslims—real believers of Islamic Monotheism, true followers of Prophet Muhammad and his *Sunnah* (legal ways)], a just (and the best) nation, that you be witnesses over mankind and the Messenger (Muhammad) be a witness over you"

MQS cannot exist in duality with *Tawhid*. That would be sacriligious with the strict monotheism of Islam. The theory of derivation of knowledge and reasoning in MQS is thereby similar to rationalism in its exogenous separation between a priori (moral imperative) and a posteriori (inductive materiality) structure of reasoning. These two are otherwise organically unified in *Tawhidi* worldview. The absence of the cogently continuous mapping 'S' interconnecting 'Ω' with the unified world-system causes a priori to remain dichotomised from a posteriori and vice-a-versa in a systemic sense.

Contrarily, the endogenously embedded world-system of unified moral-material reality rejects the above-mentioned form of dichotomy on logical grounds. To enforce inseparable embedding between a priori and a posteriori realities is to contain them both with materiality (inductive reasoning) or to leave a priori disjoint from a posteriori in the moral order. To enforce belief in consilience between moral imperative (God) and the world-system (materiality) against an exogenous will of individuals and social systems is an unwanted enforcement against freedom and liberty. The resulting problem is called heteronomy. Heteronomy thereby means the loss of freedom of the human will caused by the a priori compulsion of God's Will (Law) in the world-system. The situation is contrary to *Tawhid* as the *Qur'an* (2:256) declares: "Let there be no compulsion in religion. Truth has been made clear from error. Whoever rejects false worship and believes in God has grasped the most trustworthy handhold that never breaks. And God hears and knows all things."

Conclusion: *Tawhid* Contra Rationalism and *Shari'ah*

The history of emergence of *shari'ah* is strewn with cases of the influence of dynastic rulers in the Muslim World over time. On this matter Hallaq (2005, p. 182) notes regarding the privileged state of the legists during the rule of Umayyad.[3] The *shari'ah* scholars were thereby bound by the desires of the rulers and governments in framing up the *shari'ah* as court law. In recent times the situation of acclaiming *shari'ah* in economic and social issues has intensified among scholars who are supervised by the government institutions to enact their viewpoints of *shari'ah-compliance* rules and juristic interpretations. Examples of such *shari'ah* forming rules on economic and financial matters are enacted by the central banks, government appointed boards, and private Islamic bank departments to adopt the government *shari'ah-compliant* rules.

The result throughout the history of secularization of *shari'ah* has been its compromise between traditionalism and rationalism. In the end, the essence of the primal ontological premise of *Tawhid* started to disappear. It is now a disinherited and disre-

---

[3]Hallaq (2005). *The Origins and Evolution of Islamic Law*. Cambridge University Press, Cambridge, Eng: "The legists depended on royal and government patronage, the single most important contributor to their financial wellbeing. They were often paid handsome salaries when appointed to a judgeship, but they also received generous grants as private scholars."

garded functional origin of *shari'ah*. *Tawhid* as law and methodological worldview is not even mentioned and discussed among contemporary authors of *shari'ah* such as by Attia (2008), Ashur (2013), Kamali (2008). By marginalizing its reference to *Tawhid* as the ontological law, except by mention only, *shari'ah* has been secularized to burden Islamic issues of theology, economics, finance, science, and society by the incursion of cumbersome system of rules of *shari'ah-compliance*. No authentic methodological worldview of Islamic economics, finance, science, and society could take roots and present the academic alternative to the world of learning. As an example, the continuation and defense of debt-ridden so-called 'Islamic' financial instruments has remained a contradiction to the theory of avoidance of interest (*riba*) and the emergence of productivity by trade. The continued *riba*-like pricing problem has deepened in regards to financialization of Islamic banks around debt-ridden product development instruments (Choudhury, 2018).

The absence of the principle of pervasive complementarities by organic meaning of unity of knowledge and its induced world-system according to *Tawhidi* methodological worldview prevails as foundational assumption in mainstream economics and non-*Tawhidi* Islamic economics. This oblivion in thought and application gives implied legitimacy to individuated contracts according to *shari'ah* as *aqd* in their separated forms. The resulting critical debility can be interpreted as the expression of methodological individualism, differentiation between contracts, and silence on the critical need for systemic unity of being and becoming.

An example in Islamic economics of this individuated consequence is the absence of a dynamic model of organic interaction, integration, and evolutionary learning in portfolio instruments matrix model of circular causation type. Another example of the inability of *shari'ah* in formulating the unitary model of circular causation in its various sophisticated dynamic and non-linear diversity is the continued use of exogenously endowed variables in linear econometric models. The essential complementary and participatory nature explained by the endogenous inter-variable relations with dynamic coefficients in circular causation relations and their various other mathematical representations is non-existent in and by the *shari'ah* invoked inter-variable individuated approach of the independently instituted contracts (*aqd*). Contrarily, the concept of *aqd* ought to be of social contract and a communitarian social arrangement that brings about collective wellbeing to neighbors, society, and the extended global order at large for the present and the future in the intertemporal sense of sustainability of theevolutionary learning processes of wellbeing (*maslaha*).

An example of such a moral and socially expanded concept of *aqd* in intertemporal wellbeing (*maslaha*) between self and other is the food that an individual family consumes in its contract of the *shari'ah* to attain goodness by way of permissibility of that food (*halal*). Yet this same food would not be *halal*, if consciously the family forgot the starving neighborly community. In a vaster implication of wellbeing social choice of widening *aqd* bestows an expanded concept of community and self. This carries the meaning of sustainability across evolutionary continuums (Busutill, Agius, Inglott & Macelli, 1990) of unity of being and becoming.

In regards to such a holistic creational worldview there is Professor Whitehead's encapsulated summary in Agius (1990, pp. 82–83): "Whitehead's philosophical understanding of the universe as an interconnected web of relations, as well as the ontological nature of the relational self offer a new paradigm of human society. In contrast to the individualism of the liberal tradition, process philosophy defines human society as a relational structure of experience …". "The present holds within itself the complete sum of existence, backwards and forwards".

References

Ashur, M. T. I. (2013). *Treatise on Maqasid as-Shari'ah*. Herndon, VA, U.S.A: International Institute of Islamic Thought.

Attia, G. E. (2008). *Towards realization of the higher intents of islamic law: A functional approach of Maqasid as-Shari'ah* (p. 2008). Herndon, VA: International Institute of Islamic Thought.

Barrow, J. D. (1991). *Theories of everything, the quest for ultimate explanation*. Oxford, Eng: Oxford University Press.

Choudhury, M. A. (2018). The ontological law of Tawhid contra shari'ah-compliance in Islamic portfolio finance. *International Journal of Law and Management, 60*(6), 1–22.

Choudhury, M. A., & Hoque, M. N. (2017). Shari'ah and economics: A generalized system approach. *International Journal of Law and Management, 59*(6), 990–1012.

Djibrilla, M. M., Buang, A. H., & Olayemi, A. A. M. (2017). The challenges of Shari'ah compliance in the Islamic banking practices: whether Ibn Qayyim's principles of muamalat be the panacea? *Journal of Muamalat and Islamic Finance Research, 14*(1), 73–85.

Hallaq, W. B. (2005). *The origins and evolution of islamic law* (p. 182). Cambridge University Press, Cambridge, UK.

Hart, H. L. A. (1994). *The concept of law* (p. 92). Oxford, England: Clarendon Press.

Hawking, S. W. (1988). *A brief history of time, from the big bang to black holes*. New York: Bantam Books, Inc.

Hooker, M. B. (1984). *Islamic law in South-East Asia*. Oxford, UK: Oxford University Press.

Hubner, K., Dixon, P. R., Jr., & Dixon P. R. (1985). Foundations of a universal historistic theory of the empirical sciences, in his *Critique of scientific reason* (pp. 105–122). Chicago, IL: The University of Chicago Press.

Inglott, P. S. (1990). *The rights of future generations: Some socio-philosophical considerations*; Agius (1990) as above S. Busuttill, E. Agius, P. S. Inglott & T. Macelli (Eds.), *Our responsibilities towards future generations* (pp. 17–27). Malta: Foundation for International Studies & UNESCO.

Kamali, M. H. (2008). *Shari'ah Law: An introduction*. Oxford, UK: Oneworld Publication.

Kant, I., Friedrich C. J. (1949). *The philosophy of Kant*. New York, NY: Modern Library.

Mahdi, M. (1964). *Ibn Khaldun's philosophy of history*. Chicago, IL: The University of Chicago Press.

Nikaido, H. (1987). Fixed point theorems. In J. Eatwell, M. Milgate & P. Newman (Eds.), *The new palgrave: General equilibrium* (pp. 139–44). New York, NY: W.W. Norton.

Popper, K. (1965). *Conjectures and refutations: The growth of scientific knowledge*. New York: Basic Books.

Popper, K. (1988). Natural selection and the emergence of mind. In G. Radnitzky & W. W. Bartley III (Eds.), *Evolutionary epistemology, rationality and the sociology of knowledge open court*. IL: La Salle.

Romer, P. M. (1986). Increasing returns and long-run growth. *Journal of Political Economy, 94*, 1002–1037.

Starr, W. C. (1989). Law and morality in H.L.A. Hart's legal philosophy. *Marquette Law Review, 67*(4), 673–689.

Wallerstein, I. (1998). Spacetime as the basis of knowledge. In O. F. Bordo (Ed.), *People's participation, challenges ahead* (pp. 43–62). New York, NY: Apex Press.

Chapter 8
Science, Society, and Technology in Institutionalism According to TSR Contra Other

Masudul Alam Choudhury

Abstract The inner construct of the *Tawhidi* wellbeing (*maslaha*) criterion function comprises a deeply analytical methodology followed by its phenomenological method in the philosophy of science. In the case of the *Tawhidi* socio-scientific methodology, the philosophy of science arises from the primal ontology of unity of knowledge as the foundational premise. This foundation of *Tawhidi* law translating into constructive emergence of knowledge and its opposite ('de-knowledge') then delineates the generality and details of the world-system premised in unity of knowledge. The substantive inner construct of this world-system according to *Tawhid* as law in the primal ontological worldview comprises the ineluctable inter-causal relationship between *tasbih* (intrinsic worshipping in creation) and *shura* (discursive medium of decision-making). *Tasbih* means the worshipping capability of the world-system, which is expressed in terms of its inherent submission to the divine law of meaning, substance, order, and continuity. The induction of *tasbih* in knowledge-formation enables discourse, search and discovery forms in the institutional process of evolutionary learning. The institutional aspects of the wellbeing function are brought together by the application of the IIE-learning process approach converging to wellbeing objective criterion (*maslaha*). This holistic worldview is shown to establish the *Tawhidi* ontology of complementarities between science and technology and other artifacts that inhere in the totality of institutions.

A Non-technical Overview of the Chapter

The generalization of *Tawhidi* law in generality and particulars includes its extension to 'everything'. The concept of 'everything' as the socio-scientific totality conveys the meaning of the formalism and application of *Tawhidi* primal ontology of unity of knowledge universally and uniquely across historical consciousness. A specific application of *Tawhid* as law within institutional totality is in the areas of science, technology, and society at large. The self-same *Tawhidi* methodology prevails with-

M. A. Choudhury (✉)
Trisakti University, Jakarta, Jakarta, Indonesia
e-mail: masudc60@yahoo.ca

© Springer Nature Singapore Pte Ltd. 2019
M. A. Choudhury (ed.), *The* Tawhidi *Methodological Worldview*,
https://doi.org/10.1007/978-981-13-6585-0_8

out any change along its ontological, epistemological, phenomenological, and sustainability completeness by the IIE-learning processes.

The holistic interactive domain of 'everything' in the *Tawhidi* sense of organic oneness invokes the inseparable embedding of *tasbih* in belief formation across the knowledge-induced space and time dimensions. The result of the inner induction of belief in 'everything' causes the nature, derivation, and application of knowledge formation. The emergent complementary result establishes the nature of *tasbih*, which embeds reasoning by discourse called the discursive process of determining knowledge-induced good choices while avoiding the bad choices. Such a process of discursive decision making is called *shura*. It is of the nature of embedding belief in knowledge formation. The knowledge induction by belief determines the moral-material endogenous interrelations between all the entities of experience. The endogenous embedding of *tasbih* in *shura* as discursive process of reasoning and choice together with the attribute of belief inducing knowledge formation form the *tasbih-shura* dynamics of the conscious world-system.

Thereby, the cognitive world-system abides and manages its endowed guidance and regulations automatically by the order and scheme of *Tawhidi* law. This kind of automaticity in abidance with rules, guidance, and regulations by the generalized and particularized framework of 'everything', with the knowledge embedded institutions and its IIE-evolutionary learning processes of *tasbih-shura* further establishes *Tawhid* as the law of 'everything'. The *tasbih-shura* dynamics has its detailed analytical features and unlimited applications.

Such a methodological worldview presents the organically inter-causal world-system. *Shari'ah* in any of its meaning, scheme, and form does not embody such a *Tawhidi* methodological worldview of unity of knowledge in anything. The *Qur'anic* meaning of *shari'ah* as the way arising from and leading towards *Tawhid* as law, thereby rests on the understanding and invoking of the *Tawhidi* law of unity of knowledge in the theory of 'everything' by the extant of its *Tawhidi* methodological worldview. The meaning of *shari'atan* in the *Qur'an* is thereby altogether different from the *shari'ah* jurisprudence of latter days along with its juristic *fiqh* and *fatawa* as human concocted innovations of varying Muslim sects (*madhabs*) and product development pursuit of *shari'ah-compliance*.

Abdullah Yusuf Ali writes in his seminal and immortal work on the *Qur'anic* meaning of *shari'ah*. Indeed, the verse mentioning the actual term *Shari'ah* was revealed during the Meccan period, when no laws, codes or even compulsory rituals had been revealed. Abdullah Yusuf Ali therefore points out in his seminal translation of the *Qur'an*: "*Shariah* is best translated the 'right Way of Religion', which is wider than the mere formal rites and legal provisions, which mostly came in the Medina period, long after this Meccan verse had been revealed." (Abdullah Yusuf Ali, The Holy *Qur'an*: Text, Translation and Commentary, New York: Tahrike Tarsile *Qur'an*, Footnote no. 4756).

Introduction

Science, society, and technology are inter-twined experiences in the world-system. Thereby, institutions that guide and govern such interrelations are examined by *Tawhidi* methodological worldview in the sense of the paired universe. This takes up a cybernetic and systemic nature as is the essential model of universal consilience. The consequential neuro-cybernetic model thereby invokes all the properties of the intra-system and inter-system nature of the compounded wellbeing function evaluated in reference to circular causation relations between the systems of representative endogenous variables. The search for the profound connectivity between all such evolutionary learning and uniquely interrelated systems has been the persistent endeavour by the most subtle minds.

Kant wrote regarding such consilience of neuro-cybernetic connectivity in the following words (Kant, trans. Friedrich, 1949, p. 261): "Two things fill the mind with ever new and increasing awe and admiration the more frequently and continuously reflection is occupied with them; the starred heaven above me and the moral law within me. I ought not to seek either outside my field of vision, as though they were either shrouded in obscurity or were visionary. I see them confronting me and link them immediately with the consciousness of my existence." While neither rationalism nor *maqasid as-shariàh* could attain the above-mentioned cognizance of self and other in a methodological context, it remains the positive functioning in the field of moral-material and abstracto-empiricism of *Tawhidi* methodology in 'everything'. The reason for dichotomous thinking on a segmented outlook of reality has been due to their separable worldview between a priori and a posteriori reasoning.

The above ontological nature of the worshipping (*tasbih*) universe with its multiverses (*a'lameen*) endowed by the Signs of Allah in terms of *Tawhidi* unity of knowledge (*Ayath Allah*) in the evolutionary learning design of the universe (*khalq in-jadid*) is not within the scope of MQS. Yet it is the inherent expansion across knowledge, space, and time dimensions that comprises the new extant of *maslaha* (wellbeing) in the universe of historical consciousness. In the mystic mind of the Sheikh al-Islam, Abdul Hameed al-Ghazali, *Tawhid* was foremost as the foundation of all of reality. Regarding Ghazali's comprehension of *Tawhid* as quiddity, Buchman (1998, p. xviii) writes regarding Imam Ghazali's masterpiece, *Niche of Lights*: "While the book could stand by itself with little or no introduction, it may be helpful to elucidate the general '*Tawhid*-centred' worldview of twelfth-century Islam. People today—Muslims and non-Muslims alike—usually hold drastically different assumptions on the nature of existence than those held by al-Ghazali and most of his contemporaries."

Ghazali (Karim, n.d., p. 245) combined the epistemic comprehension of reality with *Tawhid* in respect of the endless functioning of knowledge: "When knowledge was puffed up in his heart, his oil was enkindled. Then light upon light came to him. Then knowledge said to him: Value this moment greatly. Open your eyes, so that you may find the path. When he opened his eyes, he found the pen of God as described. It is not made of reed, it has got no head. It is incessantly writing in the mind or soul of men. He said being surprised at it: What a good thing is knowledge." This supremacy of knowledge has been established by the *Qur'an* even at the moment of creation.[1] The ultimate position of knowledge overarching belief with belief (ε) not being measurable but knowledge being measurable entity (θ), these together have been expressed in this manuscript by the symbol, $\{\theta(\varepsilon)\}$. Thereby the *maslaha* is explained as the measure of interdependence and inter-variable endogenous ('pairing') consilience by $W(\theta(\varepsilon), \mathbf{x}(\theta(\varepsilon)))$ as objective criterion signifying degrees of attaining wellbeing.

The problem attacking Ghazali's comprehension of *Tawhid* as the ontological law arose in its much latter days' usage among Muslims and sects (*madhabs*). But as the horizon of knowledge and discovery advanced over the ages, Ghazali's thought could have been once again subsumed in the primacy of *Tawhid* transcending MQS and all latter categories of *shari'ah-compliance* beliefs. Indeed, if the understanding and application of Ghazali's *maqasid as-shari'ah* was kept alive by latter days' Muslims as it was meant to be a domain of choice of the good things of life as approved by *Tawhid* as law, then a vista of potentiality in abstracto-empirical thought could have been enabled for global scholarship. This did not happen. Ghazali appraised *maqasid as-shari'ah* in terms of the primacy and exclusiveness of *Tawhid* as the primal ontology. Ghazali wrote (Karim, n.d., p. 237, edited): "What is *Tauhid*? Know O readers, that God–reliance is a door out of the doors of faith. All the doors of faith are not kept in order except with knowledge, condition, and action. Out of these three elements, God-reliance is born. Knowledge is the basis, action is its fruit."

Indeed, in his own peripatetic sense Ghazali can be considered to be a neuro-cybernetic thinker of an earlier age. This is where the transdisciplinary nature of science, society, technology, and institutionalism by way of Ghazali's *Tawhidi* perception of *maqasid as-shari'ah* can be studied as an embedded and unified study of neuro-cybernetic. Ghazali contemplated in regards to this worldview. Ghazali compares the gaining of knowledge of *Tawhid* by its unravelling in the heart, soul and mind to the kernel of a cocoanut (Karim, n.d., op cit). A man who simply hails God as the One (*Tawhid* in its initial expression) is a believer, yet he is in the lowest rungs of true belief. This state of belief is like the outer kernel of the cocoanut. In the second stage, the believer sees the inside of the cocoanut. Subsequently, the believer continues on to see the oil of the cocoanut. This stage marks the growing consciousness moving towards purity. The stages of cognitive evolution move across seventy stages of evolutionary knowledge of *Tawhid*. In the delineation of knowledge formation,

---

[1] *Qur'an* (2:30–33): And when your Lord said to the angels, "Verily I am going to make in the earth a vicegerent"; they said: "wilt thou place in it such as shall make mischief in it and shed blood while we celebrate Thy praise and extol Thy holiness?" He said: "Surely I know what you do not know" (30).

And He taught Adam the names, all of them, then presented them to the angels and He said: "Tell Me the names of those if you are right" (31).

They said: "Glory be to Thee! We have no knowledge but that which Thou hast taught us; surely Thou, Thou (alone), art the knowing, the Wise" (32).

He said: "O Adam! Inform them of their names. And when he had informed them of their names, He said: "Did I not say to you that I surely know the unseen (secrets) of the heavens and the earth and (that) I know what you manifest and what you were hiding?" (33).

our *Tawhidi* ontological, epistemological, and phenomenological, and sustainability model resembles that of Ghazali's.

Most traditionalists have adhered to a metaphysical understanding of *Tawhid*. Only in recent times, the socio-scientific challenges to Islamic understanding of the *Qur'anic* revivalist thinking on *Tawhid* and science have created resurgence of thought. Wikepedia (https://en.wikipedia.org/wiki/Tawhid#Unity_of_existence; visited January 2, 2019) writes: "The classical definition of *tawhid* was limited to declaring or preferring belief in one God and the unity of God. Although the monotheistic definition has persisted into modern Arabic, it is now more generally used to connote 'unification, union, combination, fusion; standardization, regularization; consolidation, amalgamation, merger'". Thereby, in meagre exceptions of a few *mujtahids*, the substantive elaboration of the socio-scientific meaning of *Tawhid* and the world-system cannot be found among the traditionalists. Regretfully, the *mujtahids* of the traditional school of Islamic sects (*madhabs*) could not expand in this most substantive area of *Tawhid* and the socio-scientific worldview.

Rare exception to this approach was significantly Muyiuddin Ibn al-Arabi. He wrote (Chittick, 1989, edited): "Useless knowledge is that which is disconnected from its source and origin, i.e. from the divine reality. Any knowledge outside of *tawhid* leads away from *Allah*, not toward Him. But knowledge within the context of *tawhid* allows its possessor to grasp the interconnectedness of all things through a vast web whose centre is the divine. All existent things come from *Allah* and go back to Him." This concept of knowledge also establishes the circularity and continuity of the E-O model of unified reality with *tawhid* as its axiomatic foundation.

Ibn Taimiyyah (1967) came close to using the meaning of *shari'ah* in accordance with the *Qur'anic* declaration in respect of *maqasid as-shari'ah al-Tawhid*. Yet in the usage of the implications of *Tawhid* in his *maslaha* concept, this was near to the Occidental meaning of social welfare rather than social wellbeing. Thereby the conception of *shari'ah* turned out to be a utilitarian one. This was despite the fact that he believed that *shari'ah* is meant to perceive those deeds that can benefit or hurt man in his economic and other worldly matters, for example, the oneness of Allah, justice, virtue, charity, good behaviour, and fulfillment of rights.

In the case of Imam Shafei, his focus was almost exclusively on the Doctrine of Islamic Jurisprudence and thus on *Usul al-Fiqh*. This focus was mostly from the juristic (*fiqh*) point of view. Hence the extant of his magnum opus, *Risalah* (Khadduri, 2011) had little to strike base with the theme of *Tawhid* and the dynamics of the world-system. The subsequent consequences of *Risalah* on Muslim societies of South-East Asia, Iraq, and East Africa have been on acts of opinions on *shari'ah* rules. This was the field of *fatawa* The field of *shari'ah* based on *fiqh* and *fatawa* have since countless many years drifted away from the *Qur'anic* meaning and into confusing human engineered and *madhab* driven jurisprudence. Today the resurgence of *shari'ah-compliance* doctrinaire in Malaysian Islamic product development field proves the stated facts here (Hooker, 1984).

An example of interconnectivity in a transdisciplinary sense between science, technology, society and institutions can be studied as neuro-cybernetic. Bangladesh, is an example of progressive change. Even as a poor developing country, Bangladesh recently acquired developed country status. She launched a space craft from Kennedy Space Center in Cape Canaveral, Florida (science and technology). From a flight at 22,000 miles above earth, the space craft, Falcon 9-Bangabondhu1, would transmit digital information to assist telecommunication coverage (technology) to surrounding area. Other benefits would be to assist in providing information technology and its benefits to agricultural development (economy), and thereby to the wellbeing of Bangladesh nation and her surrounding areas (society).

All of these functions and more taken together as paired complementarities represent the dynamic nature and objective of wellbeing (*maslaha*) reflected through organization of the interconnection as institutionalism. For more on institutionalism as a transdisciplinary complex but orderly experience in social reconstruction of globalization as a dynamic co-existing process of discourse and actions see Choudhury and Sarwath (2011).

Institutionalism and Global Integrated Community

The scientific basis of such holistic view of institutionalism is of the highest importance in understanding global integrated community wellbeing characterized by evolutionary learning. In this regard of the ultimate objective of science seen as a social contract globally, *Tawhid* presents that universal and unique methodological worldview contrary to the individuated contract (*aqd*) legitimation of *shari'ah* in its varied perspectives. On the theme of the ultimate goal of science as the overarching transdisciplinary investigation with a singular methodological worldview of theory and modes of application Stephen Hawking (1988, pp. 10–11) wrote: "The eventual goal of science is to provide a single theory that describes the whole universe. However, the approach most scientists actually follow is to separate the problem into two parts. First, there are the laws that will tell us how the universe changes with time .... Second, there is the question of the initial state of the universe. Some people feel that science should be concerned with only the first part; they regard the question of the initial situation as a matter for metaphysics or religion. They would say that God, being omnipotent, could have started the universe off any way he wanted. That may be so, but in that case he also could have made it develop in a completely arbitrary way. Yet it appears that he chose to make it evolve in a very regular way according to certain laws. It therefore seems equally reasonable to suppose that there are also laws governing the initial state."

The Discursive Universe of *Tawhidi* Methodology in Evolutionary Learning of Unity of Knowledge: *Shura* and *Tasbih*

Derivation of knowledge from the primal ontological premise of *Tawhid*, then mapped onto the world-system by the *sunnah* via discourse of the enlightened community forms a vastly discursive society without end. The interrelationship between the various categories of sub-systems in the cybernetic world-system implies that the interactive, integrative, and evolutionary learning processes of consciously comprehending and instilling consilience of *Tawhid*, exists and is manifest in the order and scheme of 'everything'. This is the unravelling that the *Qur'an* refers to as *tasbih*.[2] Human mind and the interconnected entities of being and becoming in its endless varieties, extracts the essential and overarching meaning of consilience as unity of knowledge acquired by the discursive process of evolutionary learning. Human engagement in discussion by discourse called *shura* is thereby interconnected endogenously by pairing and symbolism of variables reflecting the nature of IIE-learning processes in the construction of the world-system. This latter experience in 'everything' is the *Qur'anic tasbih*. The organic discursive interrelations between *shura* and *tasbih* to discover the most extensive understanding of *Tawhidi* unity of knowledge can be referred to as *shura-tasbih*.

Shura-tasbih as inner experience of consciousness is also expressed by the vector $\{\theta(\varepsilon), \mathbf{x}(\theta(\varepsilon)), t(\theta(\varepsilon))\}$. This value then enters the wellbeing (*maslaha*) function to measure the degree of evaluated and reconstructive unity of knowledge as endogenous pairing between the selected variables in intertemporal framework, $t(\theta(\varepsilon))$. The embedding of $\{\varepsilon\}$ in knowledge-flows and these together induced in symbolized variables has a universally unified moral-material meaning as belief and consciousness across transdisciplinarity of systems. That is the knowledge qua belief induction of the *shura-tasbih* order, and thereby of neuro-cybernetics of worshipping systems in *Tawhidi* worldview of unity of knowledge.

The neuro-cybernetic nature of complementary relations between variables belonging to evolutionary learning systems in dynamic form applies within and between all forms of such systems. They are animate or inanimate in nature, subject to human investigation or independently of this. The neuro-cybernetic approach to evaluation of the resulting inter-systemic 'paired' (complementary) relations would be an unfathomably difficult one. To reduce the plethora of system interrelations the method of circular causation between the variables leading to measured form of the wellbeing function becomes cogently usable and simplifying. This is a novel discovery of the application of *Tawhidi* methodology in endogenous nature of unity of knowledge between the knowledge-induced variables. We will show later on the

---

[2]*Qur'an* (3:191): "Men who celebrate the praises of Allah standing, sitting, and lying down on their sides, and contemplate the (wonders of) creation in the heavens and the earth (with the thought): "Our Lord! thou hast not created (all) this for nothing! Glory to thee! give us salvation from the penalty of the fire."

empirical evaluation of the wellbeing function by the use of the circular causation relations.

Yet another method that is equivalent to the circular causation method is the dynamic coefficients form of the matrix arrangement of the inter-variables relational model. This is similar to the dynamic coefficients form of the input-output model. This method will be presented in the empirical form later on. Such richly endowed abstracto-empirical applications have remained unknown to the *shari'ah* approach in so-called 'Islamic' economics and finance. Consequently, the theory of *maslaha* function (wellbeing) has remained unexplored and undeveloped.

On the other hand, even in societies other than those garnered by *shari'ah-compliance* by institutionalism the place of {ε} as conscious organizational spirit reigns high. The implication of this is that, moral-material realization must be put into its abstracto-empirical and institutional policy and organizational realities on an extensive scale. The approach cannot be piecemeal as is the futile case of individuated *aqd* (contract) in *shari'ah* that has been used at the ambivalence of the meaning of *aqd* as the wider field of social valuation using the meaning of social capital formation and social wellbeing. Western societies have flourished on this very grand philosophy of self and other in recent times (Sztompka, 1991); but the Muslim World remains subdued.

Conclusion

The rise of heterodox economic worldview is charting new landscape different from mainstream orthodoxy. The example of complementary and participatory relations is thus rising as far as methodological individualism in decision-making and utilitarianism in institutionalism are both rejected. The new participatory approach is gaining grounds in the West, contrary to its decadence in the disintegrating Muslim World at large. Consequently, present days' situation points to the *Tawhidi* methodological worldview of consilience being better poised on the side of western society, while Muslim societies have failed to uphold the same. This contrary result is found to unbare the disintegrating state in its emptiness of so-called 'Islamic' thought and chaotic Muslim institutional arrangements all over the world today. Contrarily, the *Tawhidi* worldview is unique and universal for rejuvenation of scholarship in all the worlds.[3]

---

[3]*Qur'an* (2:115). "Unto Allah belong the East and the West, and whithersoever ye turn, there is Allah's countenance. Lo! Allah is All Embracing, All Knowing."

References

Buchman, D. (Trans.) (1998). *Al-Ghazzali niche of lights*. Provo, UT: Brigham University Press.

Chittick, W. C. (1989). *Sufi path of knowledge*. Albany, NY: State University of New York Press.

Choudhury, M. A., & Sarwath, L. (2011). Sustainability by interrelating science, society and economy in embedded political economy—An epistemological approach. In *The systemic dimension of globalization*.

Hawking, S. W. (1988). *A brief history of time, from the big bang to black holes*. New York, NY: Bantam Books, Inc.

Hooker, M. B. (1984). *Islamic law in South-East Asia*. Oxford, UK: Oxford University Press.

Ibn Taimiyyah (1967). *Al-Hisbah Fil Islam*. Beirut, Lebanon: Dar al-Kutb al-Arabiyyah.

Kant, I. (1949). In C. J. Friedrich (Ed.), *The philosophy of Kant*. New York, NY: Modern Library.

Karim, M.F. (Trans.) (n.d.). Imam Ghazali's *Ihya Ulum-Id-Din in 5 vols* (esp. Vol. 4), Lahore: Sh. Muhammad Ashraf.

Khadduri, M. (2011). *Translation of al-Shāfi'i's Risāla—Treatise on the foundations of Islamic jurisprudence*. England: Islamic Texts Society.

Sztompka, P. (1991). *Society in action, the theory of social becoming*. Chicago, IL: The University of Chicago Press.

Chapter 9
Winding Up the TSR Lectures of Part I

Masudul Alam Choudhury

Abstract TSR stands for *Tawhidi* String Relations. It forms the groundwork of the primal ontological emanation of *Tawhid* as law and carried sequentially through epistemology, phenomenology, and sustainability by means of the IIE-learning processes into all possibilities of the socio-scientific theory of 'everything'. The essential methodological worldview of *Tawhid* as law that is explained by TSR as a theoretical construct is fairly simple. Yet TSR generates substantive foundational knowledge and reasoning. They feed into the construction of the total reality. Total reality as explained by the *Qur'an* in its light of *Tawhidi* law as monotheistic unity of knowledge overarches the distinguishing of truth from falsehood. This precise distinguishing is used to describe and evaluate the nature of the opposite forms of the world-system. Truth establishes and sustains the world-system that presents the universal and unique meaning of wellbeing in the generalized and particularized cases of 'everything'. The emergent wellbeing function is referred to as *maslaha*. Oppositely the precept of unity of knowledge degenerates into falsehood nature by differentiation, competition, methodological independence and individualism in the variables of the emergent *mafasid* (falsehood) functional criterion. The entire realm of *Tawhidi* methodological worldview addresses the evaluation of either of these functions by its unique and universal method comprised in TSR.

A Non-technical Overview of the Chapter

Unlike in *shari'ah* in all its forms, it is essential to derive the logical formalism, consistency, application, and sustainability of an imminent methodology integrated with method that applies to 'everything'. This invincible challenge could not be accomplished by *shari'ah* as jurisdiction standing on its juristic interpretations—*fiqh* and *fatawa*. Yet the universal and unique methodological approach combined with its appropriate method of an analytical nature to measure and generate inference with is inherent in the theory of *Tawhidi* String Relations (TSR).

M. A. Choudhury (✉)
Trisakti University, Jakarta, Jakarta, Indonesia
e-mail: masudc60@yahoo.ca

© Springer Nature Singapore Pte Ltd. 2019   115
M. A. Choudhury (ed.), *The* Tawhidi *Methodological Worldview*,
https://doi.org/10.1007/978-981-13-6585-0_9

The universality and uniqueness of *Tawhidi* methodological worldview applies invariably to the opposite fields of Truth and Falsehood. The emergent goals of these two opposite realities in creation are indicated by their *maslaha* and *mafasid* functions. The *Tawhidi* ontological foundations uniformly apply to both these goals of opposite realities. This moral grounding is at once also measured in their *maslaha* functions (Truth) and *mafasid* function (Falsehood). The entire gamut of analytical interpretations, the nature of the underlying dynamics, inferences, and applications for continuity in the two opposite cases of disjoint realities proceeds on.

Systemic unity of knowledge is upheld in the *Tawhidi* worldview of the organically interlinked and evolutionary learning world-system of 'everything'. It is possible by inferential consequences of reading the coefficients of the *maslaha* and *mafasid* functions to reconstruct a degenerate function into the *Tawhidi* uplift. Such moral reconstruction is possible both from the *maslaha* function by attaining heights of moral transformation and applying dialectical change towards Truth out of the Falsehood of the *mafasid* function. This is to mark the attainment of the *Qur'anic* worldview—to bring humanity out of darkness into light. This is the lesson of the *Qur'an* in its entirety prevailing for 'everything'. It is the mapping of the meaning of the glorious *Qur'an* into living experience via the medium of *sunnah* and the discourse of the learned ones. Such is the nature of TSR in its full construction, application, and sustainability.

Introduction

TSR unbares a revolutionary methodology by its theory of 'everything'. This means the derivation of unity and knowledge from the primal ontology of *Tawhid*, which is carried into epistemology and thereby into phenomenology by an elegant equation of the learning universe by its consciousness (Kafatos & Nadeau, op cit). TSR yields this elegant expression along with its methodological generality and details. TSR as the elegant equation of creation is uniquely and universally formalized, empirically applied, and continued across multiverses by analytic study of 'everything' across knowledge, and knowledge-induced space and time dimensions. Indeed, the same TSR methodology and its imminent model and analytical framework is applied to both the moral-material reconstruction of reality and to the study of false kinds of things and their extended relations with either of its kinds or its opposites in the framework of the true and the good. The methodology of unity of knowledge as reflection to the structure of the good things of life is expressed by the permanent and sustained complementarities as organic pairing between the representing variables signifying the good things in the framework of unity by organic complementarities (*Qur'an*, 36:36, symbiotic pairing). The opposite of this reality is that of complementarities leading to differentiation and dissension between the bad things of life and with the good things as identified by the *maqasid* choice in light of *Tawhid* as Law.

The nature and conception of falsehood are unravelled by permanent and sustained methodological individualism and independence between such things that cause relational oppositeness, competition, and denial of pervasive complementarities at large. Thereby, while the false things unite between them, its nature of being results in dissociation of mutual self-interest and coexistence by independently formed groups. In the case of the good and false sets of representative variables, the truth and false cases are studied by the TSR methodology either by inversion of the falsehood variables in relation to the good choices; or the mix of good and falsehood variables are separated in contrary evaluative criterion functions. The variables of the good choices enter the wellbeing function as *maslaha* evaluation. The falsehood variables enter the criterion opposite to *maslaha* function of unity of knowledge induced in the variables. Such a contrary function to *maslaha*, appearing as a linear utilitarian model in form is called here as *mafasid* function—'dis-wellbeing' function.

The various functions between *maslaha* and *mafasid* and their TSR evaluation are shown below:

1. *Maslaha function*

Choices are by *maqasid as-shari'ah* in the light of *Tawhidi* methodology of unity of knowledge[1]:

$\mathbf{x}(\theta) = \{x_1, x_2, \ldots, x_n\}[\theta]$, '$\theta$' provides parametric representation of unity of knowledge. In the sections on the method of valuation of 'θ', the derived models will be taken up in respect of particular examples. The *maslaha* model is then given by $W(\mathbf{x}(\theta), t(\theta))$, which is evaluated subject to circular causation relations, $x_i = f_i(x_j(\theta), \theta, t(\theta))$, $i = 1, 2, \ldots, n$; plus $\theta = F(\mathbf{x}(\theta), t(\theta))$. The moral/ethical choices are possible as long as MQS is continuously and permanently in circulatory relationship with (Ω, S) along with discourse in the light of *Tawhidi* methodology of unity of knowledge.

---

[1]This statement means that MQS in the light of *Tawhid* acquires strictly its circular path between the variables chosen as an epistemic derivation in terms of the primal ontology of (Ω, S). All matters return back to the *Qur'an* for continued discursive determination between truth (*maslaha*) and falsehood (*mafasid*). Thus MQS as the domain of *maslaha* choices and the avoidance of *mafasid* is a set of rules in reference to the purpose and objective of truth while avoiding falsehood by *Tawhidi* Law. Truth in the context of the infallibility of *Tawhid* means evolutionary knowing by learning of the *Qur'anic* principle of organic unity of knowledge by pervasive complementarities between the good things of life that *Tawhid* implicates in the choice function of *maqasid as-shari'ah*. Such complementarities represent themselves in the *maslaha al-Tawhid* criterion of truth. Contrarily, falsehood according to the law of *Tawhid* is the permanent representation of contrariness, methodological independence and individualism, competition and the imminent characters that imbue the cult of rationalism qua marginalism and rationality. Some examples of these falsehood (*mafasid*) characters are the postulates of economic rationality; rationalism of a priorism contra a posteriorism, dialectical bifurcation contra organic unity of convergence and evolution of knowledge. *Maslaha* and *mafasid* properties of events can combine but must bifurcate absolutely or by evolutionary learning in an aggregate *maslaha* criterion function.

The analytical potentiality of the aggregate *maslaha* function in this sense differentiates truth and falsehood (T, F) by the principle of *Tawhidi* unity of knowledge. Such a quantitative form of the *maslaha* function is denoted by, $\vartheta(\theta(\varepsilon)) = F(T, F)[\theta(\varepsilon)]$, plim $\theta(\varepsilon)$, in given processes of events. We write in terms of inter-causality property, $\vartheta(\theta(\varepsilon)) = F(T, F)[\theta(\varepsilon)]$, plim $\theta(\varepsilon) \leftrightarrow \{T \cap F\}[\theta(\varepsilon)] \approx \phi$, with the property of asymptotic differentiation between Truth and Falsehood: $[dT((\varepsilon))/d\theta(\varepsilon)]\uparrow$, $[dF(\theta(\varepsilon))/d\theta(\varepsilon)]\downarrow$. Likewise, $[dT(\theta'(\varepsilon'))/d\theta'(\varepsilon')]\downarrow$, $[dF(\theta'(\varepsilon'))/d\theta'(\varepsilon')]\uparrow$; the T and F being opposite monotonic movements in respect of $\{\theta(\varepsilon)\}$ and $\{\theta'(\varepsilon')\}$, respectively.

One can set up and carry forth in detailed steps of *maslaha* evaluation, meaning estimation and simulation, by taking into account the positive or near-positive signs of the coefficients of the circular causation relations and the quantitative form of the *maslaha* function, $\theta = F(\mathbf{x}(\theta), t(\theta))$. The example could be of the five items of choice of the *maqasid as-shari'ah*. These are namely, protection of *Tawhid* in belief, protection of life, protection of intellect, protection of family and progeny, protection of property rights. Expanding upon these there would be more *maslaha* variables.

2. *Mafasid function*

Let the same definitions of symbols as given above apply to all the false choices identified by *maqasid as-shari'ah* in reference to *Tawhid* as law of unity of knowledge. The resulting *mafasid* (falsehood) function is similarly constructed and subjected to evaluation, as in the above case (1). However, the nature of utilitarianism arising from the property of methodological individualism results in the wellbeing function to be linear in form. This is equivalent to the concept of welfare function (Harsanyi, 1955) in terms of a class of utility functions of the various variables or in terms of all the variables for independently distributed individual cases (Lange, 1942). The *mafasid* 'de-knowledge' parameters, say $\{\theta'\}$, are calculated in the reverse way to the knowledge parameters: The smallest value of the corresponding *mafasid* variable, say $x'(\theta')$ can be set at $\theta' = 10$. The rest of the variables, say $\{\mathbf{x}''(\theta')\}$ are prorated in reference $(x'(\theta' = 10), \theta' = 10)$, as being worse *mafasid* variables than the minimal value. The entire set of $\{\theta'\}$-parametric values is calculated by, $\{x''(\theta')/x'(\theta' = 10)\}$ * 10}. $x'(\theta' = 10) = \min\{\mathbf{x}''(\theta)\}$. Increasing $\{\theta'\}$ values corresponding to increasing $\{\mathbf{x}''(\theta')\}$-values imply worsening *mafasid* values.

3. *Evaluation of functional mix of truth (maslaha) and falsehood (mafasid) variables*

The choices of *maslaha* and *mafasid* variables being pre-determined according to the *maqasid as-shari'ah* in reference to *Tawhid* as law of unity of knowledge, these two functions form separable functions in their respective domains. The operations (1) and (2) are then applied in the *maslaha* and *mafasid* separable functions. Such a bifurcation of the two separately evaluative functions is declared by the *Qur'an*.[2] The resulting additive function can be referred to as *mutashabihat* function (indecisive). The evaluation of *mutashabih* function follows the same methodical rules of circular causation as in case (1) and case (2). The two separate *maslaha* and *mafasid* functions are individually evaluated. Policies on moral and social reconstructions based on such separate evaluation of the functions can then follow.

---

[2]*Qur'an* (9:102): "Others (there are who) have acknowledged their wrong-doings: they have mixed an act that was good with another that was evil. Perhaps Allah will turn unto them (in Mercy): for Allah is Oft-Forgiving, Most Merciful."

4. *Evaluation of maslaha function by inverting mafasid variables in the integrated maslaha function*

If the inversion of the *mafasid* variable, either individually or in conjunction with *maslaha* variables is meaningful in an analytical study then the *mafasid* variables can be combined as inverts with corresponding *maslaha* variables. Wellbeing evaluation can continue as in case (1). Examples of such combined variables are (r/i), where 'r' denotes rate of return; 'i' denotes interest rate of any kind. Other examples are ratios of a quantity of *halal* to a quantity of *haram* in consumption, production, and distribution. Other examples are prices of *maslaha* good as ratios of prices of *mafasid* item, and so on. It is not acceptable to have a ratio of two *mafasid* variables. That is because there is no marginal rate of substitution as opportunity cost between *mafasid* variables, which are both unacceptable, and thus minimized by learning. Yet such situations can be social problems at any time, but would then be subject to reformation or rejection in their falsehood condition. The *Qur'an* provides the straight rule on such matters.[3] Furthermore, the *Qur'an* (41:34) declares in regards to moral transformation away from duration of evil.[4]

Case (4) is the most plausible one in the case of evolutionary organismic learning processes, where optimality, stead-state equilibrium, and perfection cannot exist. A specific formulation of the resulting wellbeing function follows in relation to international trad as an example:

$$\text{Evaluate } W(\theta) = W(y, \pi, NX, r/i, NX/I)[\theta] \tag{9.1}$$

Subject to circular causation relations,

$$y = f_1(\pi, NX, r/i, NX/I)[\theta]$$
$$\pi = f_2(y, NX, r/i, NX/I)[\theta]$$
$$NX = f_3(y, \pi, r/i, NX/I)[\theta]$$
$$(r/i) = f_4(y, \pi, NX, NX/I)[\theta]$$
$$(NX/I) = f_5(y, \pi, NX, r/i)[\theta]$$
$$\vartheta(\theta) \approx \theta = F(y, \pi, NX, r/i, NX/I)[\theta]$$

is the quantitative form of the wellbeing function that can be evaluated with data for all the variables, $(y, \pi, NX, r/i, NX/I, \theta)[\theta]$.

y denotes real GDP; π denotes profits; NX denotes net export revenue; r/i denotes rate of return relative to interest rate; NX/I denotes net export revenue relative to interest income (I). 'θ' inducing all of these variables points to the choices in *maqasid*

---

[3](*Qur'an*, 16:36): "For We assuredly sent amongst every People a messenger (with the Command), "Serve Allah, and eschew Evil": of the People were some whom Allah guided, and some on whom error became inevitably (established). So travel through the earth, and see what was the end of those who denied (the Truth)."

[4]Nor can goodness and Evil be equal. Repel (Evil) with what is better: Then will he between whom and thee was hatred become as it were thy friend and intimate!

as-shari'ah under the *Tawhidi* law of unity of knowledge. Using a variable like (i/I) is impermissible, if it is meant to convey marginal rates of substitution between the component variables of the relatives, as shown. This state of moral transformation (*maslaha*) and eschewing of *mafasid* (falsehood) is particularly pointed out by the signs of the coefficients of interrelated variables in the circular causation relations and the quantitative form of the wellbeing function. Negative coefficients imply partial marginal rates of substitution. *Maslaha* transformation of such an unacceptable situation is indicated by simulation into positivity or near positivity of the negative coefficients. Policy implications and institutional reconstruction of instruments of *Tawhidi* unity of knowledge are then implicated in respect of the empirical results.

The overarching extensiveness of *Tawhid* as methodology of unity of knowledge between the good things of life, avoidance of the bad things of life, and establishing the evolutionary learning processes in sustainability over knowledge and knowledge-induced space and time is a unique worldview explaining the theory of 'everything'. The *Qur'an* affirms that *Tawhid* as the universal essence is the law that governs 'everything' between the heavens and the earth. The concept of 'everything' is that of the continuity of the elegant *Tawhidi* String Relation that establishes the universal worldview as, Beginning $\approx (\Omega, S) \rightarrow$ world-system $\rightarrow (\Omega, S) \approx$ End.

The description of the generality and details of things stretching out across the heavens and the earth assumes a topological mathematical form. One way of explaining the interrelationship between coplanar intra-systems and the intertemporal inter-systems in mathematical form with supercardinality of *Tawhid* in its dimension is by the method of multivariate analysis. This rich potentiality of the *Tawhidi* methodological worldview proves the fact that, similar methodological approach has not been realized in mainstream socio-scientific discipline and thereby not in so-called 'Islamic' approach using *shari'ah*. *Shari'ah* thereby remains limited to the methodological independence of earthly affairs only, *muamalat*.

As a consequence of the vastness and limitless expanse of the domains that are covered by the episteme and methodological applications in their vastness, the socio-scientific methods responding uniquely and universally to endless diversity of issues and problems open up gates to the deepest recesses of analytical inquiry and fresh discoveries. Such methods also investigate 'everything'. The likeness of such vast capability and never-ending potentiality is not to be found in the field of mainstream dichotomous fields of inquiry and in the field of *shari'ah*. *Shari'ah* has traditionally remained constricted to *muamalat* only independently of the cosmic totality.

By keeping in view a tripartite IIE-learning process interrelationship in terms of the compounded wellbeing (*maslaha*) function and its evaluation by means of circular causation relations we note the central role of abstraction, as of *Tawhid* in the Beginning and *Tawhid* at the End of creation, in the construction of the non-physicalist and physicalist objective design of the moral-material universe in its meta-scientific totality. Thereby, this embedded unified nature of the domain of *muamalat* and of scientific domain in their non-physicalist and physicalist composition is primordially induced by the ontological abstraction of the meta-scientific universe.

The wellbeing (*maslaha*) thereby compounded by the wellbeing components of every part of the tripartite composition leads to the abstracto-empirical form of the describable universe in its totality. The totality comprises each and every one of the composition of creation comprising the heavens and the earth, all that is under and above these, and the induction of abstracto-empiricism in the worshipping world-system by its generality and particulars. Such an entirety of being and becoming by the *Tawhidi* methodological worldview causes all of other human concocted socio-scientific reasoning to be of a delimited and subdued nature. This includes the limited domain of *shari'ah* in all its forms in the face of the vastness of mathematical and analytical maturity offered by TSR in 'everything'.

The greatest problem of *shari'ah* over a long period of time now has been how to assimilate the *Qur'an* as the defining foundation of law that would prevail over the acquired regions of 'everything'. On the contrary, instead of assimilating the *Qur'an* as an intellectual body of episteme and law, the local cultures and practices remained the order of the day in the acquired lands. This state of social existence caused the Muslims over ages to accept the environing modes of life and thought of the regions over which they ruled. Thus no *Tawhidi* roots arising from the *Qur'an* could be instilled as a true content of the vast Islamic worldview.

Here then is the foundational problem of *shari'ah* that was explained in the TSR lessons: Over the long period of Islamic history, the historical consciousness has increasingly swayed away from the very foundation of *Tawhid* as the supercardinal primal ontology of 'everything'. The Muslim mind could not comprehend this depth of methodological worldview, while constricting a limiting bound of thought to *shari'ah*.

We pointed out in the text that even if Islamic intellection was to follow the *maqasid as-shari'ah* of Imam Ghazali, that would result in turning wholly towards the infallibility of *Tawhid* as the vastest worldview. This would mean to premise all of Islamic thought and its expanding law explaining 'everything' in the understanding of the following ontological beginning and to abstract this by the deepest of analytics.

The relationship of *maqasid as-shari'ah* to *Tawhid* as primal ontology is encapsulated in $[(\Omega, S) \rightarrow \{\theta^*, \theta\}](\varepsilon) \equiv MQS$. We argue that it is important to free the knowledge of the learned ones (*ulul-amr*), $\{\theta^*\}$ from the jurisprudence of *fiqh* and *fatawa*, and instead to let it emanate exclusively from the *Qur'an* mapped by the *sunnah*. The result would be the safest way to identify MQS with *Tawhidi* methodological worldview of unitary dynamics in 'everything'. If this is the logical and inevitable truth that is the ultimate reality, then *Tawhid* must prevail over MQS and not vice versa.[5]

The way towards such reformation of knowledge, life, progeny, and society in their generality as the world-system and in all particulars of it, it is necessary to uphold and inculcate *Tawhidi* precept of unity of knowledge and its methodological unified expression in 'everything'. This would encompass the fields of education, its socio-scientific generalization, and a new scope of Islamization of knowledge in the global scale of learning. Is this distinctive approach not what the sages have contemplated on across the socio-scientific vastness? The mathematical philosopher, Alfred North Whitehead (1911) wrote, "The progress of science consists in observing

---

[5] *Qur'an* (69:1): "The inevitable reality".

interconnections and in showing with a patient ingenuity that the events of this ever-shifting world are but examples of a few general relations, called laws. To see what is general in what is particular, and what is permanent in what is transitory, is the aim of scientific thought" (Whitehead, an Introduction to Mathematics 1911, p. 7). Is this ideal not the ultimate quest of and by *Tawhid* as the primal ontological worldview as meta-science of 'everything'?

And on the evident universality of the supercardinal value of Islam the Muslim convert philosopher-poet Goethe wrote regarding *Tawhid* and its role in the entire global order in space and time dimensions:

> …Only by the term of the One
> He (Muhammad) mastered the whole world.

References

Harsanyi, J. C. (1955). Cardinal welfare, individualistic ethics, and interpersonal comparisons of utility. *Journal of Political Economy, 63*.
Lange, O. (1942). The foundations of welfare economics. *Econometrica*, 10.
Whitehead, A. N. (1911). *An introduction to mathematics*. Project Gutenberg. www.gutenberg.org. Also see his explanation of the science of ontology in Whitehead, A. N. (1978). *Process and reality*. In D. R. Griffin, & D. W. Sherburne (Eds.). New York, NY: The Free Press.

Part II
Selected Abstracto-Empirical Applications of TSR

Introduction to Part II

Part II of the two parts of the work bears out the empirical applications of Part I, which treats the *Tawhidi* methodology and its conceptual implications in unification by organic interrelations between entities expressed as multivariables. The extensiveness of the conceptual content of the *Tawhidi* methodological worldview is found to apply theoretically to the generality and particulars of an ever-expanding domain of issues and problems. Thus, the completeness of such a vast domain as the mathematical topology of inter-variables relations is referred to as meta-science. The *Tawhidi* methodological worldview applies to both the unity of knowledge of the evolutionary learning world-system and the 'de-knowledge' of dissociative relations of individualism, competing individuation, and marginalist substitution by competition and displacement of one against another of the variables. The resulting empirical treatment of *Tawhidi* methodology commencing from the primal ontology of monotheism is established by what has been referred to as the evaluation of the wellbeing function (*maslaha*), subject to the system of circular causation relations between the selected endogenous variables pertaining to the specific problems under study.

The *Tawhidi* methodological Part I along with Part II together establishes the socio-scientific ontological, epistemological, and phenomenological components of any study to belong to full scientific inquiry. Rather, the elegant totality of the methodological foundations is combined with the resulting analytical viability of the unitary world-system (and the opposite in 'de-knowledge'). This unique symbiotic organism is empirically studied by the objective criterion of evaluation of wellbeing (*maslaha*) in the framework of inter-variables relations of the unity of knowledge (oppositely in 'de-knowledge'). Such an evaluation of the wellbeing objective criterion is followed by large-scale evolutionary learning properties of closure with unboundedness of the never-ending range of sustainability of historical consciousness. Altogether, these procedures assume the universality and uniqueness of consistency and viability of socio-scientific holism in *Tawhidi* law.

Part II completes the phenomenological part of the ontological and epistemo-logical foundations of Part I. The socio-scientific requirements of a consistent, analytical, and empirical meta-science in its holism are thus cogently completed. In respect of this totality of the theory and application of *Tawhidi* methodological worldview, Part II provides a number of empirical works in a variety of socioe-conomic problems as the phenomenological exemplification. These problems are empirically studied, and the *Tawhidi* methodology established in moral–material, abstracto-empirical applications by the use of the central method of evaluating the wellbeing function (*maslaha*) quantitatively. The wellbeing objective criterion is evaluated (estimated and simulated by coefficients and dependent predictor vari-ables), subject to circular causation relations between selected endogenously interrelated participatory variables pertaining to the specific problems under study in terms of organic unity of knowledge (oppositely 'de-knowledge'). In this sense of participative dynamics, the moral and material values emanating from the *Tawhidi* methodological origin are embedded in circular causation relations and the special θ-induced method of evaluating the *maslaha* objective function (also the *mafasid* function).

From the *Tawhidi* methodological formalism and its moral–material organis-mically unified method of evaluation of the wellbeing criterion, subject to circular causation relations, arise extended mathematical functions, models, and analytical forms. They apply cogently to the underlying quantitative results of evaluation of the wellbeing objective criterion in sustainable continuity. From such results arise policy directions, programs, and institutional developments. New theoretical per-spectives in meta-science are derived that belong to meta-socio-scientific heterodoxy.

Upon heterodoxy of thought, new extensions of meta-socio-scientific reality can be erected. No vista of thought and methodological application of the existing and new visions are left out from *Tawhidi* methodological worldview. This type of universality and uniqueness combined with its most elegant chain of evolutionary learning from the beginning to the end of sustainable realism establishes the *Tawhidi* methodological application to 'everything.' The ultimate reference to *Tawhid* as the primal ontological law transcending *shari'ah*, *fiqh*, and *fatawa* as human-concocted judgment is the conclusive supremacy of *Tawhidi* abstracto-empirical worldview. Exception is to the common premise of *Tawhid* as the ultimate be all and end all of the *Qur'an* and *sunnah*.[1]

Each chapter in Part II of this book is self-inclusive in terms of its numbering of tables, figures, and equations. The focus of all these chapters is to prove the application of the methodology of TSR by means of evaluating the wellbeing function, subject to circular causation relations between the selected endogenous

---

[1]*Qur'an* (4:59): O you who have believed, obey Allah and obey the Messenger and those in authority among you. And if you disagree over anything, refer it to Allah and the Messenger, if you should believe in Allah and the Last Day. That is the best [way] and best in result.

Qur'an (4:61): And when it is said to them, 'Come to what Allah has revealed and to the Messenger,' you see the hypocrites turning away from you in aversion.

variables. The search is for the existing state of complementary relations between the variables so as to evaluate the wellbeing objective criterion for the specific problems under study. From the empirical results on estimation follows simulation to construct more unified interrelationships by means of the organic complementarities between the variables. Pervasive complementarities between the variables representing the good and blessed choices of life and avoiding the false and evil things of life mark the sure representation of the unity of knowledge that *Tawhidi* methodological worldview explains by its theory of truth prevailing over falsehood in the unified nature of the goodly world-system.

This moral–material reconstruction of the unity of knowledge and its implications and impact on the unified world-system with generality and particulars is derived from the highest value of the *Quranic* world-system. The *Quran* (14: 24, 26) declares: 'Seest thou not how Allah sets forth a parable?—A goodly word like a goodly tree, whose root is firmly fixed, and its branches (reach) to the heavens,—of its Lord. So Allah sets forth parables for men, in order that they may receive admonition. (*Qur'an* 14: 24). And the parable of an evil word is that of an evil tree: It is torn up by the root from the surface of the earth: it has no stability. (*Qur'an* 14: 26).

Chapter 10
Empirical Method (Formalism) for Islamic Social and Charitable Financing Derived from the Epistemic Unity of Knowledge and the Wellbeing Objective Function

Masudul Alam Choudhury, Ari Pratiwi and Mohammad Shahadat Hossain

Abstract The tersely theoretical content of Part I of this work is now led into the methodological application in the principal objective criterion function, the *maslaha*. This is estimation and simulation of the wellbeing function (*maslaha*) resulting in empirical inferences. The general system model of *maslaha* is widely applicable and the empirical results are explainable to the widest class of problems of the theory of 'everything'. In this chapter the financial sub-class of IIE-learning properties of circular causation relations is examined. The idea thereby is to establish how the *maslaha* objective criterion can be explained as the representative measure of unity of knowledge conveyed by the inter-variable circular causality in the *Tawhidi* sense and the empirical results thereby interpreted so as to enable further simulation of the results to yield better scenarios of possible organic complementarities between the variables. Thus a coterie of empirical methods is used for simulation of the estimated coefficients, pointing out further simulacra of evaluation exercise of the wellbeing function, subject to its system of inter-causality relations that can be derived and used.

This paper is extracted in abridged form from Choudhury, M.A. Pratiwi, A. & Hossain, M.S. (2018). "From the ontology of *tawhid* to Islamic social finance conceptualization", in *Islamic Social Finance: Entrepreneurship, Cooperation and the Sharing Economy*, ed. Valentino Cattelan. Routledge, London, England.

M. A. Choudhury (✉)
Faculty of Economics, Trisakti University, Jakarta, Indonesia
e-mail: masudc60@yahoo.ca

A. Pratiwi
Postgraduate Program in Islamic Economics and Finance, Faculty of Economics, Trisakti University, Jakarta, Indonesia

Graduate Program of Human Resource Development, Paramadina University, Jakarta, Indonesia

M. S. Hossain
Department of Computer Science, Chittagong University, Chittagong, Bangladesh

© Springer Nature Singapore Pte Ltd. 2019
M. A. Choudhury (ed.), *The Tawhidi Methodological Worldview*,
https://doi.org/10.1007/978-981-13-6585-0_10

A Non-technical Overview of the Chapter

The *Tawhidi* String Relation (TSR) as an abstract-empirical model is the universally unique one that is methodologically derived from the *Tawhidi* law of primal ontology and is applied to all classes of socio-scientific problems. The TSR model thus explains the holism of intra-systemic and inter-systemic IIE-learning processes across various systems that exist and flower in the midst of evolutionary organic learning by unity of knowledge along the historical consciousness of sustainability. The limitless methodological implications and their methodical applications to complete the phenomenological worldview of the entire field of *Tawhid* and its applications prevail in the generality and particulars of all world-systems.

In this chapter the embedding of moral values signified by charity-giving in Islam called *Zakah* along with the financial variables is studied with the help of the dynamics of the wellbeing function and its circular causation relations. The methods of evaluation, subject to the system of inter-causal relations between the *zakah* (Z), *mudarabah* (M), 'financing' (F) variables are used between statistical estimation method and the method of Spatial Domain Analysis (SDA) of Geographical System (GIS) to obtain the coefficient estimation and simulation of the evaluated wellbeing function and its circular causal inter-variable relations. Thereby, the results are derived as the basis for policy recommendations in the field of moral-material embedding between the Z-variable and the selected financial variables (M, F).

The combination of the *Tawhidi* methodological premise with the appropriate methods of evaluation of the wellbeing function, subject to the inter-variable causality relations represent the much vaster class of phenomenological model of TSR. Several such empirical examples are taken up in the rest of this work.

Introduction

The TSR model in its details denotes the primal ontological form that is derived from the epistemic methodology shown in the chain of unity of knowledge and its impact on the generalized and particular world-systems. We take the latter in the form of an example of modelling the ethico-financial economics in the light of Islamic social finance. We explain and evaluate this illustrative empirical case below.

The explanation made here is that, in the Islamic case of charitable financing within a total portfolio, the methodology of consilience (episteme of unity of knowledge) leads the empirical model to test out the degree to which inter-variable complementarities exist or can be constructed by changes in the coefficients of the circular causation relations between the selected variables and thereby in the wellbeing function. The wellbeing function is thus defined as an ethico-financial economic index. It reads the degree of complementarities (participation) between the selected variables in accordance with the ethico-financial economic implication of the epistemic unity of knowledge.

The variables of the applicable vector for the study at hand that are selected represent some key ethical indicators of Islamic charity for grassroots development. The institutions that engage in such financing have traditionally practiced such philanthropic giving as individual modes of financing. The argument contrarily made is that a jointly interactive model of financing between the philanthropy variables would be more effective in generating better measures of wellbeing index as opposed to pursuing independent financial dealings (individuated *aqd*-based).

The following variables are selected for this illustrative empirical work: F denotes Islamic bank financing, with M referring to *mudarabah* financing as model for profit-sharing. Z denotes *zakah* as the philanthropy of a 2.5% (according to *sunnah*) taken on the net value of wealth of individuals, shareholders, and firms in any Islamic fiscal year. 'θ' denotes the average degree as ranks of the philanthropy variables. The method of computation of such 'θ'-values is shown in Table 10.1, which also computes the average 'θ'-column to estimate the circular causation relations.

Estimating Ethically Induced Inter-causal Relations of Financing Variables

The symbols in Table 10.1 in natural logarithmic form (ln) are defined as follows:

lnF: natural logarithm of Islamic banking financing
lnM: natural logarithm of Islamic banking profit-sharing (*mudharabah*) financing
lnZ: natural logarithm of charitable (Z known as *zakah*) disbursement
lnθ: natural logarithm of wellbeing value (See data table for ranked computation)
Monthly data are used for the period Jan 2013–Dec 2015.

Circular Causation inter-variable log-linear relations to test for positive complementarities

The OLS estimated equations of the circular causation relations are

$$\ln F = 0.519 * \ln M - 0.132 * \ln Z + 0.686 * \ln \theta + 6.005$$
$$[2.837064] \quad [-3.934903] \quad [3.683182]$$
$$\left(R^2 = 0.929303, \text{Durbin}-\text{Watson} = 1.053491 \right) \tag{10.1}$$

$$\ln M = -0.077 * \ln Z + 0.505 * \ln \theta + 0.387 * \ln F + 3.942$$
$$[-2.373022] \quad [2.968778] \quad [2.837064]$$
$$\left(R^2 = 0.929303, \text{Durbin}-\text{Watson} = 1.053491 \right) \tag{10.2}$$

$$\ln Z = 5.271 * \ln \theta - 2.472 * \ln F - 1.940 * \ln M + 39.398$$
$$[21.90296] \quad [-3.934903] \quad [-2.373022]$$
$$\left(R^2 = 0.945103, \text{Durbin}-\text{Watson} = 2.017945 \right) \tag{10.3}$$

Table 10.1 Statistical data and computation of estimation θ-values as ranks

	Islamic banking financing (F)	lnF	θ_F	Islamic banking mud-harabah financing (M)	lnM	θ_M	Zakah distributed (Z)	lnZ	θ_Z	θ
Jan-13	149,672.38	11.9162041	7.03	12,027.11	9.39	7.65	2.16	0.77	2.19	5.620521
Feb-13	154,072.07	11.9451757	7.23	12,055.75	9.40	7.66	2.53	0.93	2.56	5.81877
Mar-13	161,080.55	11.9896599	7.56	12,101.58	9.40	7.69	2.98	1.09	3.01	6.090051
Apr-13	163,406.82	12.0039982	7.67	12,026.43	9.39	7.65	2.54	0.93	2.57	5.964319
May-13	167,259.47	12.0273016	7.85	12,168.04	9.41	7.74	2.56	0.94	2.59	6.060542
Jun-13	171,227.42	12.0507479	8.04	12,628.62	9.44	8.03	2.67	0.98	2.70	6.256648
Jul-13	174,486.36	12.0696019	8.19	13,281.33	9.49	8.44	7.19	1.97	7.28	7.972108
Aug-13	174,537.18	12.069893	8.19	13,299.10	9.50	8.46	2.92	1.07	2.96	6.535747
Sep-13	177,319.57	12.0857089	8.33	13,363.86	9.50	8.50	3.58	1.28	3.63	6.815963
Oct-13	179,283.81	12.0967254	8.42	13,663.97	9.52	8.69	6.07	1.80	6.15	7.751267
Nov-13	180,832.53	12.1053266	8.49	13,877.80	9.54	8.82	3.94	1.37	3.99	7.101494
Dec-13	184,121.93	12.1233535	8.64	13,625.27	9.52	8.66	5.23	1.65	5.30	7.534328
Jan-14	181,397.77	12.1084475	8.52	13,322.46	9.50	8.47	2.40	0.88	2.43	6.472049
Feb-14	181,772.18	12.1105094	8.53	13,299.99	9.50	8.46	2.87	1.05	2.90	6.631498
Mar-14	184,964.30	12.1279181	8.68	13,498.13	9.51	8.58	4.13	1.42	4.18	7.149841

(continued)

Table 10.1 (continued)

	Islamic banking financing (F)	lnF	θ_F	Islamic banking mud-harabah financing (M)	lnM	θ_M	Zakah distributed (Z)	lnZ	θ_Z	θ
Apr-14	187,884.80	12.1435843	8.82	13,802.15	9.53	8.78	2.30	0.83	2.33	6.642824
May-14	189,689.65	12.1531446	8.91	13,868.60	9.54	8.82	2.24	0.81	2.27	6.664078
Jun-14	193,136.03	12.1711501	9.07	14,311.67	9.57	9.10	3.68	1.30	3.73	7.298306
Jul-14	194,078.90	12.1760201	9.11	14,559.44	9.59	9.26	6.48	1.87	6.56	8.310814
Aug-14	193,983.12	12.1755264	9.11	14,276.67	9.57	9.08	2.55	0.93	2.58	6.92062
Sep-14	196,563.48	12.1887407	9.23	14,355.61	9.57	9.13	9.87	2.29	10.00	9.451841
Oct-14	196,490.58	12.1883698	9.23	14,370.71	9.57	9.14	6.12	1.81	6.20	8.18597
Nov-14	198,375.54	12.1979172	9.31	14,307.35	9.57	9.10	2.81	1.03	2.85	7.085753
Dec-14	199,329.75	12.2027158	9.36	14,354.06	9.57	9.13	1.09	0.09	1.11	6.531021
Jan-15	197,279.24	12.1923755	9.26	14,207.18	9.56	9.03	2.53	0.93	2.56	6.953005
Feb-15	197,543.17	12.1937124	9.27	14,147.49	9.56	8.99	3.43	1.23	3.48	7.248759
Mar-15	200,712.16	12.2096271	9.42	14,136.43	9.56	8.99	3.58	1.27	3.62	7.344834
Apr-15	201,526.15	12.2136744	9.46	14,388.31	9.57	9.15	5.35	1.68	5.42	8.008619
May-15	203,894.15	12.2253563	9.57	14,906.42	9.61	9.48	3.39	1.22	3.44	7.495294
Jun-15	206,056.46	12.2359055	9.67	15,667.31	9.66	9.96	3.00	1.10	3.04	7.558113

(continued)

Table 10.1 (continued)

	Islamic banking financing (F)	lnF	θ_F	Islamic banking mud-harabah financing (M)	lnM	θ_M	Zakah distributed (Z)	lnZ	θ_Z	θ
Jul-15	204,842.60	12.2299972	9.62	15,728.66	9.66	10.00	6.43	1.86	6.51	8.709581
Aug-15	205,873.62	12.2350178	9.67	15,676.15	9.66	9.97	2.98	1.09	3.02	7.551213
Sep-15	208,142.91	12.2459802	9.77	15,143.63	9.63	9.63	6.53	1.88	6.61	8.670316
Oct-15	207,767.83	12.2441765	9.75	14,924.94	9.61	9.49	3.88	1.36	3.93	7.725662
Nov-15	209,123.91	12.2506822	9.82	14,680.38	9.59	9.33	2.19	0.79	2.22	7.124398
Dec-15	212,996.47	12.2690309	10.00	14,819.94	9.60	9.42	3.30	1.20	3.35	7.589472

Source Otoritas Jasa Keuangan (OJK), Indonesia (2016), Badan Amil *Zakah* Nasional (Baznas), Indonesia (2016)

Sources 1. OJK: Otoritas Jasa Keuangan—Financial Services Authority, http://www.ojk.go.id/, 2. BAZNAS: Badan Amil *Zakah* Nasional—National *Zakah* Management Agency, http://pusat.baznas.go.id/ the data collected from this web sites: http://pusat.baznas.go.id/laporan-bulanan/, http://www.ojk.go.id/id/kanal/syariah/data-dan-statistik/statistik-perbankan-syariah/Default.aspx

Quantitative evaluation of the wellbeing function in terms of empirical knowledge-function

$$\ln\theta = 0.434 * \ln F + 0.428 * \ln M + 0.178 * \ln Z - 7.606$$
$$[3.683182] \quad [2.968778] \quad [21.90296]$$
$$\left(R^2 = 0.974572, \text{ Durbin–Watson } = 2.131067 \right) \qquad (10.4)$$

The estimated 'θ'-values are derived from the fitted Eq. (10.4) over all values of the financing variables.

Interpretation of OLS Statistical Results

The interpretation of the estimated coefficients in terms of the variables under consideration points out that, Islamic charitable spending as *zakah* (Z) is negatively related with finance (F). The estimation shows that, every 1% change in Z has a negative 0.132 of 1% change in Islamic financing oppositely. Hence, Z and F have opposite movements. An increase 0.00132 of F results from a diversion of 1% in Z; and vice versa. Although the numerical value of the negative relationship between Z and F is small, the result shows a worrisome performance of Islamic financing that has otherwise been claiming to have a charitable impact on the social economy at large. Contrarily, Z as purely charitable social financing to alleviate poverty and deprivation does not have a positive complementary relationship with F financing. Rather, Islamic financing F and charitable Z financing ought to be integrated together to finance commerce as well as social goals to foster poverty alleviation.

The positive relationship between F financing and profit-sharing (M) is a plausible result, as M is a primary mode of Islamic financing in F. However, the impact of M on the increase (or decrease) of F is small, to the level of 0.00519 of M financing. The implication is that M, although being a primary source of Islamic financing, is losing its grounds.

Total Islamic finance still bears the highest positive relationship with the wellbeing scale (θ), at the level of F gaining 0.00686 of wellbeing (θ). This implies that Islamic wellbeing results most predominantly from the total Islamic financing aspect of the economy than should be the case of sharing in the ethico-economic order. This is an outcome that reaffirms the poor relationship between Z charitable spending and total Islamic financing F.

Despite observing this result, the principle of complementarity between economic and financial effects to promote an Islamic socioeconomic order aimed at integrating charitable and commercial financing activities is still lacking. The above analysis of one set of results of a circular causation equation is consistent with the other circular causation equation results and in relation to the quantitative form of the wellbeing function shown by 'θ' as a linear approximation of the conceptual wellbeing function

$W(\theta)$ in terms of the non-parametric induction of the parametric variables, namely of F, M, and Z.

The Islamic approach to socioeconomic development in the Indonesian economy and society (to which the data of Table 10.1 refers) is still impacted mainly by the total Islamic financing activity of the Islamic economy. In such activities, the charitable role of Z has a substituting relationship with F and vice-a-versa. The measure of this negative relationship is substantive. The negative intensifying effect is shown at the level of 2.472 of 1% negative change in Z caused by a 1% change of F, and 1.940 of 1% negative change in Z caused by a 1% change in M. The relationship between F and M as θ-induced variables is of the complementary nature. However, the complementary relationship is subdued. The estimation results of all the circular causation equations are consistent with different elasticity coefficients in the inter-variable relations. Despite the diminished and opposite impact of charitable spending Z and commercial financing F, the aggregate contribution to social wellbeing remains slightly increasing in the economy of scale. These variant effects are shown in expressions (10.1)–(10.4). The total of the elasticity coefficients of each variable to social wellbeing, denoted by 'θ', being equal to 1.04 implies a 4% higher contribution of the charitable and financing variables than would be the case of constant returns to scale.

Inter-variable elasticity coefficients showing their interrelated coefficients to the Islamic social financial economy

$$\text{Elasticity Matrix} = \begin{array}{c|cccc} & F & M & Z & \theta \\ \hline F & 1.000 & 0.519 & -0.132 & 0.686 \\ M & 0.387 & 1.000 & -0.077 & 0.505 \\ Z & -2.472 & -1.940 & 1.000 & 5.271 \\ \theta & 0.434 & 0.428 & 0.178 & 1.000 \end{array} \qquad (10.5)$$

Simulation of the Wellbeing Model Subject to Circular Causation Relations by the SDA Method

On the topic of desired simulation of coefficients of estimated statistical equations of evaluation (estimation followed by simulations) of the wellbeing function, subject to circular causation, the Spatial Domain Analysis (SDA) helps out. The underlying computer software method generates a vast scale of possible ranks of the coefficient values to signify better complementarities between the inter-causal variables of specific equations. Following the estimator values of the specific equations, the new simulated values of the dependent inter-causal variables and the quantitative form of the wellbeing θ-function are computed. From the estimated and the simulated results of the evaluated wellbeing function subject to circular causation relations and the quantitatively evaluated wellbeing θ-function, strategic and policy oriented results can be generated. These results lend much insight in social and financial engineering

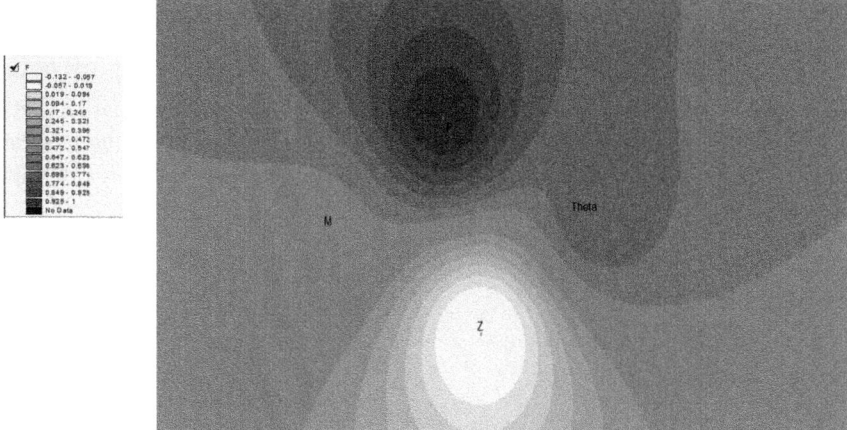

Fig. 10.1   SDA Interaction between F and M, Z and θ

keeping in view the essential goals of ethics arising from the episteme of *Tawhidi* unity of knowledge that are embedded in financial and economic variables.

The following Spatial Domain Analysis (SDA) of the social adaptation of the Geographical Information System (GIS) algorithm operation (Fig. 10.1) on the evaluated quantitative form of the wellbeing function is an example of the algorithmic result. The SDA map is generated to show how simulated selection of the coefficient (bold −0.132) can be made to reduce its negative value or convert it into a small positive value. The choice of the simulated value of the coefficient is indicated by the shades of colours between the regions of lnF, lnM, lnZ in relation to lnθ. The denser colored region around lnF shows higher complementarities between lnθ and lnF. The same is true for the relationship between lnF and between lnZ and lnF, and lnF and lnM. All these degrees of complementarities are in respect of the direction of relationship from (lnM, lnZ, lnθ) to lnF. In this given equation any simulation will also be maintained in this direction. Such simulations can be extended to positive coefficients as well.

$$\ln F = 0.519 * \ln M - \mathbf{0.132} * \ln Z + 0.686 * \ln\theta + 6.005 \ (\text{e.g.} -0.132 \rightarrow +0.019)$$

The two-dimensional map is generated by applying Spatial Domain Analysis (SDA) technique, allowing the demonstration of the interaction among the variables as shown in the above equation. It can be observed that the positive interaction (0.519) between the variable F and M can be understood from the intense color map. This can also be true for the interaction (0.686) between the variables F and θ as it is positive. However, the negative interaction (−0.132) between the variables F and Z is demonstrated in the SDA domain by using lighter color. Thus, the SDA approach enables the demonstration of both positive and negative interactions among the variables in the two-dimensional space, which is difficult to achieve by applying statistical method, where the interaction only on a certain point can be demonstrated. Eventually, the decision makers can perceive the degree of interaction among the variables and this allows taking the appropriate decision, especially to change the negative interaction among the variables. Indeed, how the complementarity or the bonding or the friendship between the variables can be formulated as the problem can be analysed from different perspectives in the SDA domain, which is not the case with the statistical approach.

Chapter 11
Empirical Results of Application of *Tawhidi* Methodology to *Waqf* (Perpetual Charity as Endowment) in Wellbeing Function

Masudul Alam Choudhury

Abstract The combination of *Tawhidi* methodology and its method of application in the context of monotheistic unity of knowledge is of a simgulat nature in its own field of econometrics involving pervasively continuous endogenous relations between circularly causal variables. This approach forms a universally unique model of the wellbeing function in anything and 'everything' of the world-system study, One such world-system of critical study in the framework of *Tawhid* as law that is distinctly different from the benign methodology and thereby absence of any precise approach in *shari'ah* is the Islamic financial system. In this system there has now been a burst of interest in the study of perpetual charity (also endowment) called *waqf*. In its vast meaning of charity as a social contract *waqf* and its vast extant of inter-causal relations in the *Tawhidi* methodological and applied context forms a generalized system-study. The underlying approach is afforded by *Tawhid* as law with its primal ontology of unity of knowledge and the supporting theory of *Tawhidi* String Relations (TSR).

A Non-technical Overview of the Chapter

The study of the moral-material unity of the world-system in its generality and details is unique and universally grounded in the methodology of *Tawhid* as law. The theory of *Tawhidi* law in its primal ontological form is unraveled by the theory of *Tawhidi* String Relations. It integrates and brings to a continuous fruition the methodological part with the methodical applied part of the *Tawhidi* ontological law in sustained continuity. The emergent methodological worldview along with its applied method in simulacra of evaluation of the wellbeing function, subject to the extensive system of inter-causal relations between the selected variables forms a new emergent field of econometrics. The exogenous partitioning of conventional econometrics as methodologically induced groundwork of rationalism and economic rationality has been completely replaced and explained by the continuously endogenous holism of

M. A. Choudhury (✉)
Faculty of Economics, Trisakti University, Jakarta, Indonesia
e-mail: masudc60@yahoo.ca

© Springer Nature Singapore Pte Ltd. 2019
M. A. Choudhury (ed.), *The* Tawhidi *Methodological Worldview*,
https://doi.org/10.1007/978-981-13-6585-0_11

Tawhid as law. The completeness and explanation carried through in TSR is fed into and evaluated by the objective of wellbeing (*maslaha*), Yet for this central monothe-istic worldview of the *Qur'an* in relation to 'everything', *shari'ah* has been unable to understand and formalize this.

Shari'ah has thus been unable to establish the methodological worldview of the like of *Tawhid* as law due to its limited philosophical speculation of human concoction nature. *Shari'ah* has thus failed to be a socio-scientific inquiry. An analytical inquiry that is either empty of methodological foundation, or is unable to fuse methodology with applied methods of evaluation of a problem-solving idea, and thereby derive its inferential application remains muddle-headed. Thus it is of no avail to quest for a socio-scientific theory of 'everything' in *shari'ah* by the combination of a cogent methodology and its application in the abstracto-empirical framework. This socio-scientific worldview is truly attainable by the *Tawhidi* law via the framework of its primal ontological foundation in terms of monotheistic unity of knowledge. The proof of the vastly resilient implication of *Tawhid* as law and the evaluation of the generality and particulars of the world-system is extolled in endlessly many cases of the moral-material fruition. One such example is the study of *waqf* in Malaysia in respect of its vast potential for systemic study.

Introduction

The choice of the variables in Table 11.1 has been on the basis of limited statistical information available for *waqf* in Malaysia to address our problem of socioeconomic and ethically embedded circular causation relations to evaluate the wellbeing function of *waqf*. The choice of these variables implies that, *waqf* is an effective Islamic institution in realizing both social economic and moral returns out of a number of inter-variable interactions, though not for all the variables. This fact is proved by the signs of the coefficients of some of the variables in the evaluated circular causation relations.

Table 11.2 shows in a cursory way that, a substantial amount of *waqf* charitable donations is outlaid in Malaysia per unit acre of land. The socioeconomic develop-ment contribution per unit of *waqf* value is low to moderate. In financial terms, the percentage ratio of development contribution to *waqf* value is diverse in terms of the various provincial states in Malaysia. But as a total development financing per unit of *waqf* value this is impressive. This implies that an effective *waqf* valuation is realized in its socioeconomic development contribution. This indicator also points to economies of scale in the use of *waqf* in Malaysian socioeconomic development contributed by *waqf*-wellbeing value.

Table 11.1 Data on *WAQF*

Malaysian states	Total (Acres) X_1	Waqf value (MYR Millions) X_2	Development financing effect of *waqf* (MYR Million) X_3
Kelantan	305	52	30
Federal Territories	28	20	20
Terengganu	247	236	42
Pahang	3,985	129	15
Johor	5,928	1,043	8
Melaka	843	601	25
Kedah	843	1,472	2
Selangor	1,063	295	66
Perak	5,122	1,749	17
Total	18,364	23,961	24,186

Source Department of *Wakaf, Zakah dan Haji* (JAWHAR), Malaysia
Sources Laporan Tahunan MAIS, Laporan Tahunan MAIk, Laporan Tahunan MAIps, Laporan Tahunan MAIP

Table 11.2 Inter-variable development contributions

Selected states	waqf value per acre	waqf develop. effect per acre	Development finance effect per unit of *waqf* value
	(MYR $= X_2/X_1$)	(MYR $= X_3/X_1$))	(% ratio $= X_3/X_2$)
Johore	175,944	1349	0.767
Perak	341,468	3378	0.989
Pahang	32,371	3764	11.63
Selangor	277,516	62,088	22.37
Total	2.622 million	1.317 million	100.9

Evaluation of *Waqf* Related Empirical Model of Wellbeing and Circular Causation Equations Reflecting the Methodology of *Tawhidi* Unity of Knowledge

The endogenous embedding of the knowledge parameter ('θ') implies the possibility of pervasive inter-variable complementarities. Degrees of complementarities convey the quantitative meaning of unity of knowledge between ethical and socioeconomic values. This phenomenon also conveys the quantitative form and evaluation of the wellbeing function and its circular causation between the endogenous vectors of variables for degrees of complementarities between the selected variables. The matter of such degrees of complementarities in terms of the *Tawhidi* methodological world-

Table 11.3 Computation of ranked θ-values by pro-rata of X-values

θ_1 for X_1	θ_2 for X_2	θ_3 for X_3	$\theta = (\theta_1 + \theta_2 + \theta_3)/3$
(10/5928) * 305 = 0.5145	(10/1749) * 52 = 0.2973	(10/66) * 30 = 4.5455	1.7857
0.0017 * 28 = 0.0476	0.0057 * 20 = 0.114	0.1515 * 20 = 3.03	1.0639
0.0017 * 247 = 0.4199	0.0057 * 236 = 1.3452	0.1515 * 42 = 6.363	2.7094
0.0017 * 3985 = 6.7745	0.0057 * 129 = 0.7353	0.1515 * 15 = 2.2725	3.2608
*0.0017 * 5928 = 10.00*	0.0057 * 1043 = 5.9451	0.1515 * 8 = 1.212	5.7190
0.0017 * 843 = 1.4331	0.0057 * 601 = 3.4257	0.1515 * 25 = 3.7875	2.8821
0.0017 * 843 = 1.4331	0.0057 * 1472 = 8.3904	0.1515 * 2 = 0.303	1.7206
0.0017 * 1063 = 1.8071	0.0057 * 295 = 1.6815	*0.1515 * 66 = 10.00*	4.4962
0.0017 * 5122 = 8.7074	*0.0057 * 1749 = 9.9693*	0.1515 * 17.3 = 2.6209	7.0992

$\theta_1 = 10$ for the best selected X_1-value; $\theta_2 = 10$ for the best choice of X_2-value; $\theta_3 = 10$ for the best choice of X_3-value

Thereby, $(10/\text{selected } X_1) * (X_{1i}\text{-values}) = \theta_{1i}\text{-values}$, $i = 1, 2, \ldots$, X-values of column 1

view of unity of knowledge between the recommended life-fulfillment variables conveys the organic unified relationships between the recommended variables, and the unity of relations between morality, ethics, and life-fulfillment choices. Empirical policy-theoretic inferences can then be derived. Simulacra of changes and policy recommendations can thereby be carried out.

The final 'θ'-values are generated in accordance with the trend in the selected socioeconomic variables as life-fulfillment ones in the following steps: Firstly, values in each of the X-variable columns are ranked by the measure of $\theta = 10$ (could be another ordinal number) for the best selected value. Secondly, rest of the θ-values of the specific columns are pro-rated according to the X-values. Table 11.3 shows such computation of θ-values.

Likewise it is the case with θ_{2i}-values; and θ_{3i}-values. Finally, by row, the θ-values are averaged to yield the final column of θ-values corresponding to the X-values across rows. X-values are in natural logarithm. Thus values in Table 11.1 appear in the natural logarithm form along with the last column of the generated θ-values.

The following circular causation relations are evaluated to statistically determine the degree of inter-variable complementarities as signified by the statistical level of significance and the coefficient signs. Positive sign of the coefficients as elasticity coefficients between the endogenously related variables in circular causation relations means complementary relationship in the sense of partial elasticity values. Negative signs mean lack of complementarities, and thereby marginal rates of substitution between the endogenously related variables in the partial sense. This latter case implies the abandonment of unity of knowledge in statistical degrees between the good things of life (implied by choice of specified variables). Marginal rate of substitution is also the sign implying the neoclassical economic theory that can be underlying *waqf* organization.

The Evaluated Equations Appear in the Following Forms

Circular causation relations to evaluate degrees of inter-variable endogenous relations of unity of knowledge:

$$X_1 = a_0 + a_1 \cdot X_2 + a_2 \cdot X_3 + a_3 \cdot \theta.$$
$$X_2 = b_0 + b_1 \cdot X_1 + b_2 \cdot X_3 + b_3 \cdot \theta$$
$$X_3 = c_0 + c_1 \cdot X_1 + c_2 \cdot X_2 + c_3 \cdot \theta$$

X's are taken in the natural logarithmic form to include the relevance of non-linearity and complexity of the log-linearized equations in which all the variables including the coefficients remain evolutionary by learning caused by θ-induction. This allows for evaluation of the wellbeing criterion in terms of estimation followed by simulacra of estimations of the variable predictors and the coefficients to develop moral-material embedded reconstruction of endogenous complementarities between the variables. Such an empirical exercise signifies the empirical unraveling of unity of knowledge by the cogent combination of *Tawhidi* methodology of unity of knowledge and the empirical method of evaluating the wellbeing function and its system of inter-causal relations. The inter-related dynamics are represented by the selection of the endogenous variables and their degrees of complementarities conveyed by the θ-induced coefficients.

The quantitative form of the conceptual wellbeing function shown in the chapter by $W(\theta, X(\theta)) \equiv \vartheta(\theta) \approx \theta$ *(linearly approximated).*

This is given by,

$$\theta = d_0 + d_1 \cdot X_1(\theta) + d_2 \cdot X_2(\theta) + d_3 \cdot X_3(\theta)$$

Estimated circular causation equations with one set of simulation are given by:

1. *Without θ-term in circular causation relations (estimated)*

$$\ln X_1 = 0.8758949 \ln X_2 + 0.16288223 \ln X_3 + 1.28663456$$
$$R^2: \ 0.552710173$$
$$\text{t-stats: } 2.559526799, 0.315992693, 0.435201355 \tag{11.1}$$

$$\ln X_2 = 0.59591305 \ln X_1 - 0.4196131 \ln X_3 + 2.87306838$$
R^2: 0.617878957
t-stats: 2.559526799, 1.067777954, 1.317083242   (11.2)

$$\ln X_3 = 0.10049886 \ln X_1 - 0.3805446 \ln X_2 + 4.35836284$$
R^2: 0.213740022
t-stats: 0.315992693, 1.067777954, 2.814962982   (11.3)

2. *With θ-term in circular causation relations (simulation)*

$$\ln X_1 = 0.14816067 \ln X_2 - 0.1457056 \ln X_3 + 0.64791604 * \theta + 3.97258957$$
R^2: 0.712803855
t-stats: 0.279876177, −0.29811193, 1.669486057, 1.301067329   (11.4)

$$\ln X_2 = 0.10410653 \ln X_1 - 0.4818005 \ln X_3 + 0.52689595 * \theta + 4.4639981$$
R^2: 0.746601128
t-stats: 0.279876177, 1.365943643, 1.59371016, 2.041118613   (11.5)

$$\ln X_3 = -0.11198564 \ln X_1 - 0.5640363 \ln X_2 + 0.37270085 * \theta + 5.54081495$$
R^2: 0.326940901
t-stats: − 0.29811193, 1.365943643, 0.917029488, 2.72807182   (11.6)

3. *Quantitative form of the wellbeing function in terms of θ (functional form of θ)*

$$\theta = 0.55241625 \ln X_1 + 0.63933361 \ln X_2 + 0.3862987 \ln X_3 - 4.8562873$$
R^2: 0.798012129
t-stats: 1.669486057, 1.59371016, 0.917029488, 1.995406884   (11.7)

Conclusion: Statistical Inference

Statistical estimation of circular causation relations without inclusion of θ-parameter in them points to the first level estimation results. Although a neo-classical *waqf*-orientation is shown to exist by the negative endogenous relationship between $\ln X_2$ and $\ln X_3$ in the partial differential sense, yet interrelationship between $X_1 \leftarrow (X_2,$

X_3) is positive.[1] Thus complementarity abides in this case, establishing the existing of unity of knowledge.

The other estimation and results with θ-parameter in the circular causation equations can be taken as one possible simulation out of a family of simulacra. The interpretation of the empirical results follows as in the previous case. However, results show X_3 is negatively related with (X_1, X_2). This conveys the neoclassical implication of partial marginal rate of substitution that opposes the *Tawhidi* pervasive principle of complementarity of unity of knowledge. This is not acceptable in respect of improving the socioeconomic and ethical effects of *waqf*. There is also substitution between these two-variables (X_1, X_2) and X_3.

Yet there exists positive relationship between all the variables and θ-parameter. This conveys the result of existence of economy of scale between the ethical and socioeconomic variables in the perspective of the ontological law of *Tawhid* in spite of the existence of some inter-variable neoclassical features of marginalism.

In the case of the quantitative form of the wellbeing function in terms of θ-function, positive coefficients with the θ-induced socioeconomic variables are found to exist in both the estimated and the simulated cases. The estimated form of the wellbeing function points to the existence of economy of scale, because of the result that, sum of elasticity coefficients $= 1.57804856$ points to a good wellbeing indicator value for *waqf* in Malaysia contributed by the total effect of all the variables, in spite of the existence of some degrees of inter-variable marginal rates of substitution. Such deepening effects would otherwise imply the existence of neoclassical approach to the absence of complementarities by unity of knowledge.

Complementary interface of ethical development in respect of the *Tawhidi* methodology of organic unity of knowledge between the variables is thus established. The marginal substitution effect of some of the variables can be changed to positive coefficient complementary effects by further simulations. One such family of simulations of the wellbeing evaluation relations is done by the Spatial Domain Analysis of Geographical Information System (Choudhury & Hossain, 2006).

Reference

Choudhury, M. A., & Hossain, M. S. (2006). *Development planning in the sultanate of Oman*. Lewiston, New York: Edwin Mellen Press.

---

[1]Partial Elasticity Coefficient, $(\partial \ln X_2/\partial \ln X_3) = (X_3/X_2) * (\partial X_2/\partial X_3) = -0.4196131$, implying, partial marginal rate of substitution of X_3 for X_2, $(\partial X_2/\partial X_3) = -(0.4196131/100.9) = -0.004159$, a small value of a marginal change in X_2 per unit of a marginal change in X_3. Likewise, Partial Elasticity Coefficient $(\partial \ln X_3/\partial \ln X_2) = -0.3805446$; and $(\partial X_3/\partial X_2) = -(0.3805446/(1/100.9)) = -38.3970$, a significant value of marginal change in X_3 caused by a marginal change in X_2.

Chapter 12
The Contrast Between the Law of *Tawhid* and the Ideas of *Shari'ah-Compliance* and *Maqasid As-Shari'ah* and Its Extension: An Empirical Work

Masudul Alam Choudhury

Abstract Contrary to *Tawhidi* way of organizing and formalizing unity of knowledge by the portfolio of inter-related financing instruments that gain their relational inter-causal dynamics, the way of *shari'ah* in financing is one of separable contracts (*aqd*). Thereby, two opposite pictures are attained regarding the mode of financing. The *shari'ah* approach cannot address the central ontology of unity of knowledge explained by inter-variable endogenous relationship unraveling pervasive complementarities in and between 'everything'. Contrarily, *Tawhid* is indispensably premised in its primal ontology of monotheistic unity of knowledge and its replication in the unified world-system by way of using the organic inter-causal meaning of endogenous relationship between the variables. The difference between these approaches in respect of the gains that can be obtained from Islamic financing in the case of applying *Tawhidi* methodological worldview can be noticed. This is contrary to the case of *aqd*-based approach of *shari'ah* in all its forms. Such empirical differentiation arising from the *Tawhidi* methodological origin contrary to the *shari'ah* approach is brought out by the abstracto-empirical study of the principle financing instruments.

A Non-technical Overview of the Chapter

A comparative study of Islamic financing modes between *Tawhid* as law immersed in monotheistic unity of knowledge and on the other hand by the exercise of *shari'ah* contractual *aqd*-rules is important to understand the moral-material embedded difference between these two modes of thought and applications. The *Tawhidi* construct of pooled portfolio comprising various participatory instruments has proved to be superior in its methodological explanation and empirical evaluation of the inter-variable endogenous relationship. The wellbeing function of *Tawhidi* genre is found to yield

M. A. Choudhury (✉)
Faculty of Economics, Trisakti University, Jakarta, Indonesia
e-mail: masudc60@yahoo.ca

© Springer Nature Singapore Pte Ltd. 2019
M. A. Choudhury (ed.), *The* Tawhidi *Methodological Worldview*,
https://doi.org/10.1007/978-981-13-6585-0_12

higher economy of scale and better degrees of explainable inter-variable complementarities with the composition of the collection of participatory instruments pooled together.

In terms of the precision, consistency, universality, and uniqueness of the *Tawhidi* String Relations as the theory underlying *Tawhidi* law prevailing in 'everything', this methodological worldview is found to be firmly established. This aspect of socio-scientific validation characterizing the universal and unique model arising from *Tawhidi* ontological law confronts as a permanent challenge to the contractual *aqd*-based characterization of *shari'ah* in all its forms. The latter category remains undefined and therefore impossible in tracking along any precise empirical direction by a precisely underlying methodological orientation. This is a proved accomplishment of TSR. It is moral-material embedded and thus abstracto-empirical viability contrary to *shari'ah*.

Modeling the Financing Instruments in the Contrasting Meanings of *Shari'ah-Compliance* and *Maqasid As-Shari'ah* with *Tawhid* as the Primal Ontological Law

A striking example of the consequences of a systemic approach to the study of *maqasid as-shari'ah* in a broad and extended meaning encompassing complementary dynamics between the entities ought to be the approach to the modeling of Islamic financing. In the meaning of *shari-ah-compliance* there is no compelling need to think of a systemic understanding of *shari'ah*. This is the case that was critically observed by Hassan (2002). On the other hand, the res extensa and res cogitans perspectives of universality call for a systemic understanding of the objective and purpose of the *shari'ah*, which does not exist.

We exemplify here these two contrasting consequences in respect of the two different ways of modeling Islamic financing instruments. In the case of *shari'ah-compliance*, the financing instruments stand independently of each other outside the portfolio of the total number of financing instruments that otherwise enables inter-instruments interaction. Thereby, interactions between the underlying real assets enable development in an inter-variables complementary development regime. The greater domain of *maqasid as-shari'ah* as this ought to be res extensa and res cogitans is to be found in the generalized system modeling of interaction and integration between the socioeconomic and financing activities.

In what follows we exemplify the contrasting scenario for the case of Islamic financing. It forms systemic organism in the case of the holistic treatment of complementary relations within the total portfolio as the meaning of systemic holism. Instead, independent status of the financing instruments outside the generalized systemic view of the totality denies the *maqasid* approach.

The computations for generating the ranked financing values by degrees of their intra- and inter- financing values are shown in Table 12.2.

For each of the years we take only MUR ($X_{4,t}$), MUSH ($X_{5,t}$), MUD ($X_{6,t}$), TOTAL ($X_{8,t}$). We run the log-linear regression equations, t = 2006, 2009. 2010, 2011, 2014:

$$\ln X_{4,t} = a_0 + a_5 \cdot \ln X_{5,t} + a_6 \cdot \ln X_{6,t} \tag{12.1}$$

and recursively,

$$\ln X_{5,t} = a_0 + a_4 \cdot \ln X_{4,t} + a_6 \cdot \ln X_{6,t} \tag{12.2}$$

$$\ln X_{6,t} = a_0 + a_4 \cdot \ln X_{4,t} + a_5 \cdot \ln X_{5,t} \tag{12.3}$$

$$\ln \theta = A_0 + A_4 \cdot \ln X_{4,t} + A_5 \cdot \ln X_{5,t} + a_6 \cdot \ln X_{6,t} \tag{12.4}$$

θ-values are generated by the formula, (i = 4, 5, 6, 8)

$$\theta_i = \{[\text{values of} (x_{4,t}; x_{5,t}; x_{6,t}, x_{8,t} \text{ resp. corresponding to } \theta = 10)]/10\}$$
$$\times [\text{individual values of} (x_{4,t}; x_{5,t}; x_{6,t}, x_{8,t} \text{ resp.}] \tag{12.5}$$

$$\theta = \text{Avg.} (\theta_1, \theta_2, \theta_3, \theta_4); \text{ each } \theta_i \text{ calculated by (12.1)} \tag{12.6}$$

We re-estimate:

$$\ln X_{4,t} = a_0 + a_8 \cdot \ln X_{8,t} + b \cdot \ln \theta \tag{12.7}$$

and recursively,

$$\ln X_{5,t} = a_0 + a_8 \cdot \ln X_{8,t} + b \cdot \ln \theta \tag{12.8}$$

$$\ln X_{6,t} = a_0 + a_8 \cdot \ln X_{8,t} + c \cdot \ln \theta \tag{12.9}$$

$$\ln X_{8,t} = a_0 + a_4 \cdot \ln X_{4,t} + a_5 \cdot \ln X_{5,t} + a_6 \cdot \ln X_{6,t} + d \cdot \ln \theta \tag{12.10}$$

$$\ln \theta = A_0 + A_4 \cdot \ln X_{4,t} + A_5 \cdot \ln X_{5,t} + A_6 \cdot \ln X_{6,t} + A_8 \cdot \ln X_{8,t} \tag{12.11}$$

θ-values are calculated as below.

$\theta_i = \{[\text{values of } (x_{4,t}; x_{5,t}; x_{6,t}, x_{8,t}, \text{ resp. corresponding to } \theta = 10 \text{ for highest financing value})]/10\} \times [\text{individual values of } (x_{4,t}; x_{5,t}; x_{6,t}, \text{ resp. along their columns})]$ (12.12)

$$\theta = \text{Avg. } \{\theta_i\} \text{ as above} \qquad (12.12)$$

Statistical Results

Independent financial values of major categories (MUR, MUSH, MUD)

$$\ln X_4 = 3.74 + 0.597 \ln X_5 + 0.281 \ln X_6$$
$$\quad (3.13) \qquad (12.64) \qquad (1.37)$$
$$R^2 (\text{adjusted}) = 97.5 \qquad (12.13)$$

Sum of inter-variable elasticity coefficient is less than 1. Hence the inter-variable relations do not have economy of scale.

$$\ln X_5 = -6.05 + 1.65 \ln X_4 - 0.470 \ln X_6$$
$$\quad (-2.71) \quad (12.64) \qquad (-1.34)$$
$$R^2 (\text{adj}) = 97.6 \qquad (12.14)$$

Sum of inter-variable elasticity coefficient is marginally greater than 1. Hence the inter-variable relations have weak marginal economy of scale.

$$\ln X_6 = -3.61 + 1.72 \ln X_4 - 1.04 \ln X_5$$
$$\quad (-0.54) \quad (1.37) \qquad (-1.39)$$
$$R^2 = 0.49 \qquad (12.15)$$

Sum of inter-variable elasticity coefficient is less than 1. Hence the inter-variable relations do not have economy of scale.

Each financing value with the total portfolio

$$\ln X_4 = 5.45 + 0.219 \ln X_8 + 1.32 \ln \theta$$
$$\quad (2.41) \qquad (0.95 \qquad (4.57)$$
$$R^2 = 99.9 \qquad (12.16)$$

The inter-variable sum of elasticity coefficients is greater than 1. This indicates the existence of economy of scale in the relationship.

$$\ln X_5 = -32.4 + 3.70 \ln X_8 - 2.00 \ln \theta$$
$$(-3.99) \quad (4.49) \qquad (-1.93)$$
$$R^2 = 99.7 \tag{12.17}$$

The inter-variable sum of elasticity coefficients is greater than 1. This indicates the existence of economy of scale in the relationship.

$$\ln X_6 = 45.1 - 4.05 \ln X_8 + 5.06 \ln \theta$$
$$(2.13) \quad (-1.88) \qquad (1.87)$$
$$R^2 = 63.9 \tag{12.18}$$

The inter-variable sum of elasticity coefficients is greater than 1. This indicates the existence of economy of scale in the relationship.

$$\ln X_8 = 16.3 - 1.01 \ln X_4 + 0.310 \ln X_5 - 0.0175 \ln X_6 + 2.03 \ln \theta \tag{12.19}$$

$\Rightarrow$ highest elasticity coefficient value to X_8 is contributed by θ.

$$\ln \theta = -8.02 + 0.494 \ln X_4 - 0.152 \ln X_5 + 0.00863 \ln X_6 + 0.492 \ln X_8 \tag{12.20}$$

Conclusion: Explanation of Inference

The above estimated equations point out that, the economy of scale caused by inter-variables relations occurs in the case of their relations with the total financing variable X_8. In this case as well the degree of complementarities between the variables indicated by $\ln \theta$ is found to have the largest impact on the economy of scale. Contrarily, in the case of independent status of the financing variables (X_4, X_5, X_6) without the complementing total financing portfolio variable (X_8), there is no trace of economy of scale. The conclusion then is that, immersion of every financing instrument in the portfolio of all financing together as a coordinated and interactive system causes greater gains and security for the existence of the individual instruments. The same is true of the total of all instruments taken together by virtue of the elasticity effect of $\ln\theta$ in the system of interactive relations among the financing instruments in the total financing portfolio.

Independent treatment of financing instruments is the message of *shari'ah-compliance*. The holistic interactive treatment of all and every instruments in the total portfolio is the message conveyed by the generalized system idea of *maqasid as-shari'ah al-Tawhid* by its imminent inter-variables interaction. Yet the latter case has escaped comprehension by the present-days *shari'ah* scholars. It is a much needed perspective to establish stability with extension and growth of the organic comple-

Table 12.1 Islamic Bank Financing, Malaysia, Millions Ringgit

End of period	Bai Bithaman Agil	Ijara	Ijara Bai	MUR	MUSH	MUD	Istisna	Total
	$X_{1,6}$	$X_{2,6}$	$X_{3,6}$	$X_{4,6}$	$X_{5,6}$	$X_{6,6}$	$X_{7,6}$	$X_{8,6}$
2006 (Dec)	15,822	499	9,518	3,501	157	148	494	30,139
% share	52.50	1.65	31.58	11.62	0.52	0.49	1.64	100
	$X_{1,9}$	$X_{2,9}$	$X_{3,9}$	$X_{4,9}$	$X_{5,9}$	$X_{6,9}$	$X_{7,9}$	$X_{8,9}$
2009 (Dec)	42,732	4017	38,353	23,016	1,875	376	1487	111,856
% share	38.20	3.59	34.28	20.58	1.68	0.34	1.33	100
	$X_{1,10}$	$X_{2,10}$	$X_{3,10}$	$X_{4,10}$	$X_{5,10}$	$X_{6,10}$	$X_{7,10}$	$X_{8,10}$
2010 (Dec)	52,642	2,834	43,487	23,296	3,958	275	1,615	128,107
% share	41.09	2.21	33.49	18.18	3.06	0.21	1.26	100
	$X_{1,11}$	$X_{2,11}$	$X_{3,11}$	$X_{4,11}$	$X_{5,11}$	$X_{6,11}$	$X_{7,11}$	$X_{8,11}$
2011 (Dec)	83,148	6,332	62878	56,940	15,817	146	696	260,476
% share	26.07	2.43	24.14	21.85	6.07	0.05	0.26	100
	$X_{1,14}$	$X_{2,14}$	$X_{3,14}$	$X_{4,14}$	$X_{5,14}$	$X_{6,14}$	$X_{7,14}$	$X_{8,14}$
2014 (Jan)	83,452	6,526	63,812	58,746	16,636	148	900	284,616
% share	29.32	2.29	22.42	20.64	5.84	0.05	0.31	100

Sources Bank Negara Malaysia 2014
http://www.bnm.gov.my/index.php?ch=en_publication_catalogue&pg=en_publication_msb&
eId=box1&mth=1&yr=2011&lang=en
Bai Bithaman Agil: hire purchase financing
Ijara: rental
Murabaha (MUR): cost-plus pricing
Musharakah (MUSH): equity participation
Mudarabah (MUD): profit-sharing
Istisna: prepayment to enable production of manufacturing

mentary inter-relationship between financing instruments and their extended relationships with the real sectoral socioeconomic activities.

In the same light, estimated equation (12.8) shows that the largest elasticity effects
are contributed almost equally by X_4 and X_8 (total). We also note from Tables 12.1 and
12.2 that the primal Islamic financing instruments under their independent treatment
shows MUD and MUSH to be almost extinct. These results point out the absence of
interactive support between the primal financing instruments namely, MUR, MUSH,
and MUD that ought to exist in the sense of *maqasid as-shari'ah*.

Table 12.2   Computations of ranking by θ-values (degrees of complementarities) of the selected financing values {x_4, x_5, x_6, x_8, θ} for studying the contrast between the res extensa and res cogitans of *maqasid as-shari'ah* (the domain of *Tawhid* as Law) and the independent status of *shari'ah-compliance*

X_4	X_5	X_6	X_8	$\ln X_4$	$\ln X_5$	$\ln X_6$	$\ln X_8$
3,501	157	148	30,139	8.160804	5.056246	4.997212	10.31358
23,016	1,875	376	111,856	10.04394	7.536364	5.929589	11.62497
23,296	3,958	275	128,107	10.05604	8.283494	5.616771	11.76062
56,940	15,817	146	260,476	10.94975	9.668841	4.983607	12.47027
58,746	16,636	148	284,616	10.98098	9.719324	4.997212	12.5589
θ_4	θ_5	θ_6	θ_8	θ	lnθ		
0.595955	0.094374	3.93617	1.058936	1.421359	0.351613		
3.917884	1.127074	10	3.930067	4.743756	1.556829		
3.965547	2.379178	7.31383	4.501047	4.5399	1.512905		
9.692575	9.507694	3.882979	9.15184	8.058772	2.086761		
10	10	3.93617	10	8.484043	2.138187		

Reference

Hassan, H. (2002). Contracts in Islamic law: The principles of commutative justice and liberality. *Journal of Islamic Studies, 13*(3), 257–297.

Chapter 13
Circular Causation for Population and Economic Growth and Development Issues of Bangladesh

Masudul Alam Choudhury

Abstract The knowledge-induced databank for estimating the wellbeing function and its endogenous inter-variable circular causation relations has various ways for its development. The most critical point in the development of the databank is the calculation of the knowledge parameters (θ-values). This chapter suggests an alternative way slightly different from the pro-rata and averaging approach to calculating the knowledge parameters in concert with the socioeconomic variables. The conclusion at the end is that, the computation of such values is necessary in evaluating the wellbeing function (*maslaha*). In this regard it is important only to maintain the monotonic relations that the various approaches generate in the θ-calculation in relation to the socioeconomic variables within the purview of *Tawhidi* methodological worldview and its phenomenological use in the empirical modeling context. Thus this chapter is like an addendum to the rest of the work suggesting acceptability of alternative ways of calculating the θ-values in relationship with the socioeconomic variables to make up the full databank for empirical evaluation of the *Tawhidi* wellbeing criterion, subject to the system of endogenous inter-variable circular causation relations.

A Non-technical Overview of the Chapter

The proficiency and abstracto-empirical viability of the *Tawhidi* methodological worldview feeding into the empirical evaluation model of wellbeing followed by the inferences and further IIE-learning reconstruction under sustainability of simulacra is a vastly open exercise. No problem-solving and the design of issues and problems in light of the *Tawhidi* worldview is left out in this endless socio-scientific coverage. The result then is to further impress the meaning of universality and uniqueness of the *Tawhidi* methodological worldview as crystallized by its underlying *Tawhidi* String Relations (TSR). This evidence is explained by extending the application of TSR to issues of economic growth.

M. A. Choudhury (✉)
Faculty of Economics, Trisakti University, Jakarta, Indonesia
e-mail: masudc60@yahoo.ca

© Springer Nature Singapore Pte Ltd. 2019
M. A. Choudhury (ed.), *The* Tawhidi *Methodological Worldview*,
https://doi.org/10.1007/978-981-13-6585-0_13

153

The databank, particularly the computational formulas of the θ-parameters connected with socioeconomic variables, is important to set up for empirical work that carries within it the *Tawhidi* methodological worldview. This undertaking goes across two critical stages. Firstly, the pro-rating of computational θ-values in respect of the sequencing of the various endogenous socioeconomic (socio-scientific) variables pertaining to the *Tawhidi* worldview of life-fulfillment choices is necessary. The pro-rata computation then follows corresponding to the various variables. The second critical approach is regarding the averaging (or aggregation) of the computed θ-values into one set of aggregate values by columns. The databank is then completed with the socioeconomic (socio-scientific) variables and their calibration by means of the averaged (aggregated) θ-values linked with the various columns of socioeconomic (socio-scientific) values.

A third critical question pertaining to the use of the aggregated θ-values in the databank is to make the empirical decision whether or not the column of aggregated θ-values is to be used in the system of endogenous inter-variable circular causation model. This choice follows the robustness of the empirical evaluations. Thus the methods of evaluation out of a vast range of statistical methods and mathematical formalism follow in the TSR abstracto-empirical study of *Tawhidi* genre.

Introduction

These values are targeted because of development sustainability and realism around these points (Table 13.1).

Formulas applied for estimating θ_1 and θ_2 values:

(1) $\theta_1 = (g_{1\text{-}2}) \pm 10$, subject to an inverted curve-values for g_1 on either side of the 2% optimal value of g_1.
(2) $\theta_2 = (g_{2\text{-}8}) \pm 10$, subject to the values $\theta_2 = 10$ for $g_2 > 8$; and $\theta_2 = 0$ for $g_2 < 0$.

Summary Results for Bangladesh Data

Model 1: Regression Analysis: g_2 and θ on g_1

$$g_1 = 2.64 + 0.0206g_2 - 0.0730.\theta$$
$$t = (9.59) \quad (1.57) \quad (-1.76)$$
$$R^2 = 9.6\%, \quad SE = 0.43 \tag{13.1}$$

g_2 is statistically significant at 10% level.
θ is statistically significant at 5% level.
Durbin-Watson statistic $= 0.226865$.
D-W statistic indicates high positive autocorrelation.

Table 13.1 Bangladesh annual rates of growth and assignment of wellbeing (ethical) values, 1971–2009

Year	Population rate of growth (%) (g_1)	GDP per capita (USD)	Rate of growth of GDP per capita (%) (g_2)	θ_1	θ_2	θ Average
1972	2.71	89.72	14.23	9.29	10.00	9.645
1973	2.72	89.98	0.29	9.28	2.29	5.785
1974	2.73	104.67	16.32	9.27	10.00	9.635
1975	2.73	106.96	2.18	9.27	4.18	6.725
1976	2.73	116.34	8.77	9.27	10.00	0.635
1977	2.72	119.28	2.53	9.28	4.53	6.905
1978	2.72	148.82	24.77	9.28	10.00	9.640
1979	2.72	167.69	12.68	9.28	10.00	9.640
1980	2.71	185.06	10.36	9.29	10.00	9.645
1981	2.71	182.75	−1.25	9.29	0.00	4.645
1982	2.69	161.96	−11.38	9.31	0.00	4.655
1983	2.66	161.01	−0.59	9.34	0.00	4.670
1984	2.61	183.93	14.24	9.39	10.00	4.695
1985	2.54	186.12	1.19	9.46	3.19	6.325
1986	2.47	191.59	2.94	9.53	4.94	7.235
1987	2.40	212.58	10.96	9.60	10.00	9.800
1988	2.34	224.36	5.54	9.66	7.54	8.600
1989	2.28	238.28	6.20	9.72	8.2	8.960
1990	2.22	243.33	2.12	9.78	4.12	6.950
1991	2.16	254.52	4.60	9.84	6.6	8.220
1992	2.10	254.45	−0.03	9.90	0.00	4.950
1993	2.06	257.41	1.16	9.94	3.16	6.550
1994	2.02	268.15	4.17	9.98	6.17	8.075
1995	1.99	295.63	10.24	2.00	10.00	6.000
1996	1.97	304.69	3.06	9.97	5.06	7.515
1997	1.94	309.20	1.48	9.94	3.48	6.710
1998	1.91	314.51	1.72	9.91	3.72	6.815
1999	1.87	323.78	2.94	9.87	4.94	7.405
2000	1.85	323.01	−0.24	9.85	0.00	4.925
2001	1.79	317.07	−1.84	9.79	0.00	4.895
2002	1.75	323.70	2.09	9.75	4.09	6.920
2003	1.70	348.60	7.69	9.70	9.69	9.695

(continued)

Table 13.1 (continued)

Year	Population rate of growth (%) (g_1)	GDP per capita (USD)	Rate of growth of GDP per capita (%) (g_2)	θ_1	θ_2	θ Average
2004	1.65	371.20	6.48	9.65	8.48	9.065
2005	1.59	376.35	1.39	9.59	3.39	6.490
2006	1.53	387.93	3.08	9.53	5.08	7.305
2007	1.47	434.85	12.09	9.47	10.00	9.735
2008	1.42	493.75	13.54	9.19	10.00	9.595
Average: **2.23**			**4.31**			
	($\theta^*_1 = 10$ for avg. rate $= 2.00\%$)		($\theta^*_2 = 10$ for avg. rate $= 8\%$)			

Source Database, Statistical, Economic and Social Research and Training Center for Islamic Countries, Ankara, Turkey

Model 2: Regression Analysis: g_1 and θ on g_2

$$g_2 = -15.5 + 3.29g_1 + 1.87.\theta$$
$$t = (-2.52) \quad (1.57) \quad (4.22)$$
$$R^2 = 35.3\%, \quad SE = 5.45 \tag{13.2}$$

g_1 is statistically significant at 10% level.
θ is statistically significant at less than 1% level.
Durbin-Watson statistic $= 2.22584$.
D-W statistic indicates almost no autocorrelation.

Model 3: Regression Analysis: g_1 and g_2 on θ [Quantitative Wellbeing]

$$\theta = 8.75 - 1.14g_1 + 0.184g_2$$
$$t = (5.98) \quad (1.76) \quad (4.22)$$
$$R^2 = 36.4\%, \quad SE = 1.71 \tag{13.3}$$

g_1 is statistically significant at 5% level.
g_2 is statistically significant at less than 1% level.
Durbin-Watson statistic $= 2.01858$.
D-W statistic indicates no autocorrelation.

Chapter 14
Society's Attitude to Pay *Zakah* Relating to Employment and Income Variables Seen from *Tawhidi* Perspective in South Sumatera: A Cross Sectional Study Based on Survey

Lily Rahmawati Harahap and Masudul Alam Choudhury

Abstract The socioeconomic development question continues concerning society's attitude to uphold its moral duty in paying Islamic charity to positively affect employment and circularly interrelate with income generation. The TSR model of circular causation relations between the three variables, namey social attitude to pay the mandatory charity called *zakah*, and its interrelationship with income, and employment in affecting social wellbeing (*maslaha*) is used. This adaptation of the TSR-model brings out the effectiveness of *Tawhidi* methodological worldview of unity of knowledge and its affective reconstruction of social wellbeing and deontological reformation of the society of South Sumatera in Indonesia. The empirical effectiveness of the TSR-model under the primal *Tawhidi* methodology of unity of knowledge between the selected variables and thereby the social consequences continues. One more example of moral-material embeddedness of deontological social attitude is thus borne out of this study.

A Non-technical Overview of the Chapter

Social attitude concerning the consciousness of redistributing its financial resources to attain wellbeing is an Islamic duty. The principal instrument that attains this moral objective is by utilization of the mandatory charity called *zakah*. The social uplift is thus measured by the effectiveness followed by its moral reconstruction to realize positive relationship between the payment of *zakah* and the attainment of employment and recursively generating income in the circular causation model of

L. R. Harahap
Faculty of Economics, IBA University Palembang, South Sumatera, Indonesia

M. A. Choudhury (✉)
Faculty of Economics, Trisakti University, Jakarta, Indonesia
e-mail: masudc60@yahoo.ca

© Springer Nature Singapore Pte Ltd. 2019
M. A. Choudhury (ed.), *The* Tawhidi *Methodological Worldview*,
https://doi.org/10.1007/978-981-13-6585-0_14

social wellbeing (*maslaha*). *Tawhidi* methodological worldview becomes effective in understanding the moral-material embedding in the abstracto-empirical model of wellbeing. Such social realization is centered in both the citizens' consciousness to pay their duty of *zakah* and together the Government's activity to mobilize the *zakah* resources towards the ends of income and employment generation. A *zakah* social model under the generalized TSR-modeling approach is thereby essential for the social and economic uplift of the society in South Sumatera, Indonesia.

Introduction

The obligation of paying *zakah*, an Islamic requisite take on wealth above a legal exemption level, is an important Islamic duty. It is intended to resolve the gap between the rich and the poor in society at large. As stated in the *Qur'an* (58:13), the importance of paying *zakah* is equated with the importance of prayer. *Zakah* and *sadaqah* are main charity instruments in Islamic scheme to alleviate poverty. Sarea (2012) viewed *zakah* as contributing to generating economic growth. The collection and disbursement of *zakah* funds cannot therefore be separated from society's obligation to pay *zakah* for establishing wellbeing (*maslaha*).

Indonesia as the largest Muslim population country in the world has a great potential in collecting and disbursing *zakah* funds. According to Vice-Chairman of National Amil *Zakah* Board, Zainulbahar Noor, Indonesian *zakah* potential rises to 217 trillion rupiah. With this potentiality, *zakah* fund will be able to help government to alleviate poverty.

Unfortunately, the collecting of *zakah* funds so far reaches only about 3 trillion rupiah or about 1.2% (https://m.tempo.co.: 2016) of the potential *zakah* payment.

South Sumatera is a province located in the southern part of Sumatera island. It is rich in natural resources such as petroleum, natural gas, and coal. Besides, the province has many attractive tourist destination to visit. This aspect of tourism indirectly influences the culture of society in South Sumatera. With 91,592.43 km^2 area, South Sumatera is the largest province in Sumatera island. Its economic performance continues to strengthen each year. Economic growth is supported by the magnitude of regional gross domestic product, which continues to increase. Data shows that, South Sumatera has the rating of 11 of 34 provinces in Indonesia in regional real gross domestic product. But on the contrary, it is also among the poorest province, ranked 18 out of 34 provinces in Indonesia. This fact indicates that the provincial riches have not been distributed evenly and have not been able to improve the wellbeing of society. Therefore, seen from the data, *zakah* should positively correlate with the ability of society to be able to share in total wellbeing.

From these explanations it can be stated that, local government is not fully able to handle the poverty problem. The question then is this: Why increase in regional income could not automatically increase the wellbeing of society, which has failed to fulfill the need for poverty alleviation? *Zakah* fund can therefore be an alternative and a principal support in poverty alleviation. Society's role can be expected to assist the collection and distribution of *zakah* to alleviate poverty.

Literature Review

Definition and the Basic Concept of Zakah

The term *zakah* upholds many meanings, that are sacred duties conducive of growth, blessings, praises to Allah, and socioeconomic development (Mardhani, 2013). In addition, the *zakah* charity could also mean a certain amount of blessed assets assigned to a particular person (Sholihin, 2010) for spending in the good cause. Indeed, Sumatera Government has the Law No. 23 Year 2011 on the Management of *zakah*. It declares that, *zakah* as an asset must be issued by a Muslim or a business entity to be given to those who deserve it in accordance with the law of the *Qur'an* (www.sumsel.kemenag.go.id). Az-Zuhaili (2011) writes that *zakah* ought to be paid regularly. This practice applies both to the person who pays (*muzakki*) and to the person who receives *zakah* (*mustahiq*).

Relationship Between the Variables Explaining Social Inclusiveness

Human beings cannot be separated from the things that affect their lives. Two variables of many variables that influence society attitude are employment and income. This chapter reviews the relationship between these two variables on society's attitude to pay *zakah*.

Employment

Islam gives guidance and teachings for its prescribed way of life on earth. These teachings encourage the people to work hard and in spirited ways; avoid laziness, and always practice charity. The *Qur'an* declares in its chapter At-Taubah (9:103), about the importance of paying *zakah* to purify and cleanse self and ownership in earth. Thus, everyone will be trying to replenish themselves and sharing with others by *zakah* according to the ways to work and try as much as possible to contribute to the righteous path of earning and redistributing *zakah*.

Income

The meaning of income is the gross inflow of financial-economic benefits arising from a company's normal activity during a period when those inflows result in increase in equity that does not come from the contribution of capital investment. To obtain income, every human must work hard and seriously. The *Qur'an* in its Chapter Al-Furqaan (26:47) explains about Allah's gift to human being, and about the time allocated to them to look for sustenance and for the time to rest. Yogatama (2010) in his research concluded that income level factor showed positive and significant effect on the probability of adherence to fulfill the obligation paying *zakah*. Rouf (2011) explains that income is one factor that influences significantly society's interest in giving *zakah* at Semarang *Zakah* House, South Sumatera. The respondents agree that the more the income the stronger the desire to give *zakah*.

Tawhidi String Relation (TSR) Concept

See Fig. 14.1.

For Muslims, belief in *Tawhid*, oneness of Allah holds the cardinal place. The principle of oneness of Allah explained in the *Qur'an* as organic complementary (participatory) and unifying interrelations is the foundation and is at the root of

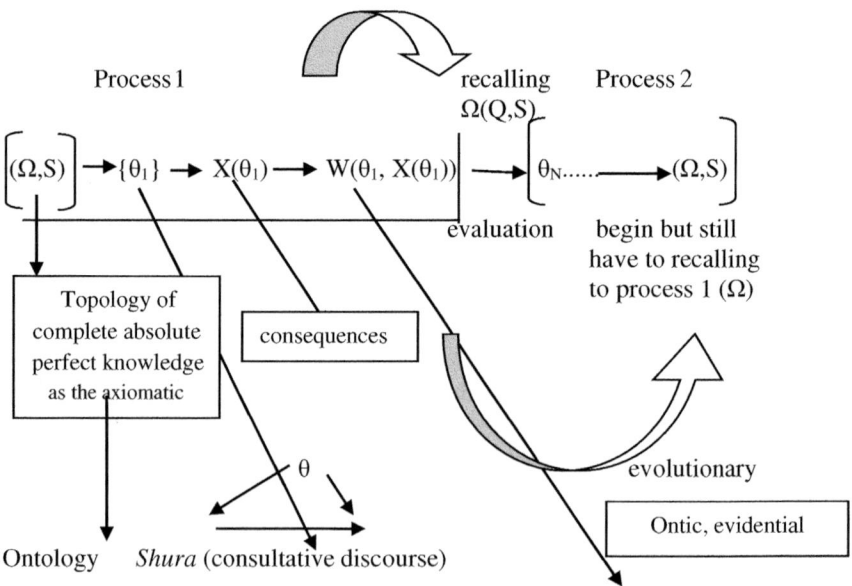

Fig. 14.1 The formal concept of unity of knowledge (*Tawhid*): The IIE or *Shuratic* process

all sciences. Essentially, the understanding of *Tawhid* covers all matters relating to oneness of Allah with varied opinions of the unitary precept of knowledge. *Tawhid* was the centerpiece of the lessons and life of the Prophet (*sunnah*) in all activities in the entire world system.

The source of knowledge derived from the *Qur'an* is symbolized by 'Ω'. As a guidance for mankind, the implementation is done by the Prophet's *sunnah*. This is denoted by 'S'. TSR precept is thus derived from the *Qur'an* and *sunnah*. This ontological foundation of knowledge according to *Tawhid* as law is derived from (Ω, S). Discourse by the learned ones in Islam over the generality and particulars of world-system results in derivation of organic unity of knowledge (θ). In the broadest worldview of unified world-system, all activities, learning processes, social interaction systems, integration, cooperation, realization of complementary and subsistence are structured in respect of organic unity of knowledge in being and becoming.

TSR formalism commences the beginning process of unity of knowledge (contrarily identifies the opposite, 'de-knowledge') until the end of every continuous event of conscious history of reasoning, comprehension, application and consequences. This entire knowledge-forming discursive process is done via *shuratic* (consultation, discussion, discursive) process with participation and complementary (pairing) attitude using amenable methods. In such *shuratic* knowledge-deriving process, the discursive activities are marked by interaction (I) between all entities. From interaction arises systemic integration (I), which shows consensus arising from discursive interaction. Interaction and integration yield evolutionary learning (E) through the evaluation of the wellbeing function, subject to circular causation between the selected endogenous variables. The *maqasid as- shari'ah al-Tawhid* plays a role here in choices and decision-making in conformity to *Tawhid* as law of unity of knowledge with its endowed methodological worldview. Following the evaluation of the wellbeing function (*maslaha*), processes of evolutionary learning in respect of the IIE-learning processes continue.

Methodology

The research conveyed in this chapter was done on social ordering for four regencies in South Sumatera, namely OKU Timur, Muara Enim, Banyu Asin, Musi Bayu Asin. One city is included, namely, Palembang in South Sumatera province. 592 respondents were surveyed. The statistical test yielded validity with a loading factor of 0.30 (Hair, Black, Babin, & dan Anderson, 2016). Reliability test was carried out by using Alfa Cronbach's index.

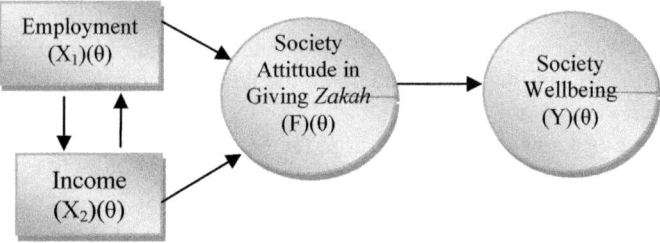

Fig. 14.2 Conceptual framework

Conceptual Framework

Figure 14.2 explains the inter-relationship model between variables that influence society's attitude to pay *zakah* and generate social wellbeing. The model estimates the relations between variables that significantly influence society's attitude to pay *zakah*. TSR stands to test the degree of pervasive complementarities between the selected variables. The relations stand to normatively questioning when negative inter-variable coefficients are found empirically. The latter case implies marginal rate of substitution between the specific variables. The estimation is carried out by applying Ordinary Least Square Method applied to the inter-variable relations in circular causation system of equations:

Empirical Work

$$
\begin{aligned}
\text{SA} &= f(\text{EMP, INC})(\theta) \\
\text{WB} &= (\text{SA, EMP, INC})(\theta)
\end{aligned}
\tag{14.1}
$$

Evaluation is done by estimation and simulation in the light of the underlying system of circular causation relations between the selected variables as follows:

$$
\text{SA} = f_{\text{SA}}(\text{EMP, INC})(\theta) \tag{14.2}
$$

$$
\text{EMP} = f_{\text{EMP}}(\text{SA, INC})(\theta) \tag{14.3}
$$

$$
\text{INC} = f_{\text{INC}}(\text{SA, EMP})(\theta) \tag{14.4}
$$

$$
\theta = W(\text{SA, EMP, INC})(\theta)\text{in the empirical form.} \tag{14.5}
$$

SA   denotes Society Attitude
EMP   denotes Employment
INC   denotes Income
W   denotes Wellbeing Function.

The empirical model used is,

$$SA = \alpha_{1.0} + \beta_{1.1}EMP + \beta_{1.2}INC + \beta_{1.3}\theta \tag{14.6}$$

$$EMP = \alpha_{2.0} + \beta_{2.1}SA + + \beta_{2.2}INC + \beta_{2.3}\theta \tag{14.7}$$

$$INC = \alpha_{3.0} + \beta_{3.1}SA + \beta_{3.2}EMp + \beta_{3.3}\theta \tag{14.8}$$

$$\theta = \alpha_{4.0} + \beta_{4.1}SA + \beta_{4.5.2}EMp + \beta_{4.3}INC + \beta_{4.4}\theta \tag{14.9}$$

The endogenous nature of every variable and thereby of equations is explained by the circular inter-causal affects between all the variables. The change of percentage in one variable will change another variable. The resulting relationships between the variables are expected to be positive according to TSR methodology. But such relationships may also result in negative values due to social reality. If the result shows negative value of the coefficients then simulation is done to change negative value into positive or progressively less negative values of the coefficients. The simulated coefficients are set by observing the factors relating to the improvement of coefficients of the problematic variables in the midst of a discursive *shuratic* process of exchange of views. The revised coefficient values between variables describes a reconstructed social attitude to pay *zakah*.

Figure 14.3 shows inter-causality between two explanatory variables on society's attitude to attain wellbeing. If the estimated coefficients of the variables are positive, this implies inter-variable complementarities. This avoids oppositeness as marginal rate of substitution between the variables. Such a result according to *Tawhidi* law of unity of knowledge is referred to as systemic pairing according to organic principle of unity of knowledge. Inter-causality between the variables explains the existing and potentially revised status of complementarities between the variables arising from the IIE-learning process-oriented nature of inter-causality. The IIE-learning processes

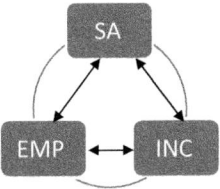

Fig. 14.3 Inter-causality between SA, EMP and INC

continue indefinitely by means of evaluation of the wellbeing (*maslaha*) function, subject to circular causation relations between the selected variables.

Discussion and Results

Hyphotesis Test

Table 14.1 shows $F_{value}(663,634) \geq F_{table}(2.312)$. H_{a1} 'is accepted', meaning employment variable and income variable influence society attitude to pay *zakah* in 4 regents and 1 city at South Sumatera simultaneously.

Table 14.2 shows employment variable has t-value (9.358) > t table (1.647) and income variable has t-value (27.957) > t table (1.647). H_a accepted, meaning employment variable and income variable influence society's attitude to pay *zakah* in 4 regents and 1 city at South Sumatera partially.

Table 14.3 shows $R^2 = 0.693$. This means employment variable and income variable influence society's attitude in paying *zakah* about 69.30% and about 30.70% of the influence by other variables. Employment variable influences society's attitude about 17.30% and income variable influences society attitude about 52%.

Table 14.1 Simultaneously hypothesis test

Model	Sum of squares	df	Mean square	F	Sig.
Regression	84.796	2	42.398	663.634	0.000
Residual	37.630	589	0.064		
Total	122.426	591			

Table 14.2 Partially hypothesis test

Model	t	Sig.
(Constant)	9.066	0.000
Employment (X_1)	9.358	0.000
Income (X_2)	27.957	0.000

Dependent Variable is Attitude (Y)

Table 14.3 The influence of employment and income variables to society's attitude

Model	R	R^2	Adjusted R^2	Std. error of the estimate
1	0.832[a]	0.693	0.692	0.253

[a]Predictors: (Constant), Employment (X_1), Income (X_2)

TSR Analysis

From the results of the questionnaire survey using a Likert scale of 5 points the average rate of society's attitude to pay *zakah* in South Sumatera is found to be influenced by 2 variables. Tables 14.4 and 14.5 explain the coefficient regression value between variables according to the TSR method.

From Table 14.4 the first linear equation is:

$$Empl = \alpha_{1.0} + \beta_{1.2} \, Inc + \beta_{1.3} SA \tag{14.10}$$

$$Empl = 1.594 - 0.019 \, Inc + 0.660 \, SA \tag{14.11}$$

From Table 14.5 the second linear equation is:

$$Inc = \alpha_{1.0} + \beta_{1.1} \, Emp + \beta_{1.3} SA \tag{14.12}$$

$$Inc = 0.164 - 0.009 \, Emp + 0.968 \, SA \tag{14.13}$$

From Table 14.6 the third linear equation is:

$$SA = \alpha_{1.0} + \beta_{11} \, Emp + \beta_{1.2} Inc \tag{14.14}$$

$$SA = 0.853 + 0.196 \, Emp + 0.589 \, Inc \tag{14.15}$$

Table 14.4 Linear regression income variable coefficients

Model	Unstandardized coeff.		Standardized coeff.
	B	Std Error	Beta
(Constant)	1.594	0.172	
Income	−0.019	0.059	−0.019
Social_attitude	0.660	0.070	0.549

Dependent Variable: Employment
Source Processed Data (2018)

Table 14.5 Linear regression society's attitude variable coefficients

Model	Unstandardized coeff.		Standardized coeff.
	B	Std error	Beta
(Constant)	0.164	0.129	
Social_attitude	0.968	0.035	0.809
Employment	−0.009	0.029	−0.009

Dependent Variable: Income
Source Processed Data (2018)

Table 14.6 Linear regression employment variable coefficients

Model	Unstandardized coeff.		Standardized coeff.
	B	Std Error	Beta
(Constant)	0.853	0.094	
Employment	0.196	0.021	0.236
Income	0.589	0.021	0.705

Dependent Variable: Social Attitude
Source Processed Data (2018)

Table 14.7 Regression result

Item/Y	EMP	INC	SA
constant	1.594	0.164	0.853
$a_2 = EMP$		−0.009	0.916
$\theta_2 = X_2$		4.062	4.062
$a_3 = INC$	−0,019		0.589
$\theta_3 = X_3$	4.193		4.193
$a_8 = SA$	−0.660	0.968	
$\theta_8 = X_4$	4.126	4.126	

Source Processed Data (2018)

Table 14.7 explains how much every coefficient value of explanatory variables generates a value for explained variables. For example, value of −0.019 explains that income variable generates employment as the value shown. While coefficient value −0.009 explains that employment variable generates income variable as the value shown. These inter-variables linkages generate circular causation relations.

Equations of the Corresponding TSR Model

These equations are made to find the estimated-$(\theta^{\hat{}})$ result, i.e. by embedding (θ) with each variable-coefficient regression value of the variables. $\{\theta\}$-values are actual data values, while $\{\theta^{\hat{}}\}$-values give evaluated values.

Equation 1: employment variable as an explained variable.

$$X_1 = 1.594 - 0.019\,\theta_2 + 0.660\,\theta_3$$
$$= 1.594 - 0.019(4.193) + 0.660(4.126) = 4.101. \quad (14.16)$$

From equation like (14.9) we obtained $\{\theta^{\hat{}}\}$-values or estimation data value of 4.101 against an actual data value 4.062 meaning a decrease of X_1 by 0.039.

Equation 2: income variable as an explained variable.

$$X_2 = 0.164 - 0.009\,\theta_1 + 0.968\,\theta_3$$
$$= 0.164 - 0.009(4.062) + 0.968(4.126) = 4.121.$$

From Eq. 14.9 is obtained $\{\theta^{\wedge}\}$-value or estimation data value of 4.121 against an actual data value of 4.193, meaning a decrease of 0.072.

Society attitude variable as an explained variable.

$$X_3 = 0.853 + 0.196\,\theta_1 + 0.589\,\theta_2$$
$$= 0.853 + 0.196(4.062) + 0.589(4.193) = 4.119.$$

From obtained $\{\theta^{\wedge}\}$-value or estimation data value of 4.119 against an actual data value 4.126 is obtained meaning a decrease of 0.007.

Other tabular values of X's can thus be generated.

The above results show that the actual data show respondents' opinion relation to the variables that form an attitude to pay *zakah*. Using the TSR method with embedded θ-values in each variable will generate an assessment toward attaining a good value. It proves that, even though respondents give a lower than best assessment according to TSR approach to estimation of wellbeing, a simulation by the *shuratic* discursive approach of simulation can result in better wellbeing and estimation values of the various predictors and complementarities signified by the coefficients.

Conclusion

From the statistical test according to TSR-methodology and model formalism it can be concluded that, employment and income variables simultaneously and partially influence society's attitude in paying *zakah*. It is also seen from the value of R^2 that, income variable influences social attitude in paying *zakah*. This relationship is more significant than the case of employment on the propensity towards *zakah* payment. If income increases then respondents' attitude to pay *zakah* will also increase in value more than the change of employment on attitude to pay *zakah*.

TSR approach shows that, every variables is an organic pairing, and thereby, there exists complementary relationships between SA, INC, and EMP and in an acceptable positive value of the wellbeing function. This simulated result is found despite the statistical result showing that employment variable does not influence social attitude in paying *zakah* as significantly as income does. Yet these two variables relate in complementary ways with the attitude to pay *zakah* according to the wellbeing function.

References

Az-Zuhaili, W. (2011). *Fiqih Islam Wa Adillatuhu. Puasa, I'tikaf, Zakah, Haji, Umrah*. Jilid 3. Jakarta: Gema Insani.

Hair, J. F., Black, W. C., Babin, B. J., & dan Anderson, R. E. (2016). *Multivariate data analysis* (7th ed.). E-book. Retrieved March 15, 2016, from www.pearsonhighered.com.

Mardani, (2013). *Fiqh Ekonomi Syariah: Fiqh Muamalah*. Jakarta: Kencana PrenadaMedia Group.

Rouf, M. A. (2011). *Analisis Faktor-Faktor Yang Mempengaruhi Minat Masyarakat Membayar Zakah Di Rumah Zakah Cabang Semarang*. Retrieved February 26, 2017, from http://eprints.walisongo.ac.id.

Sarea, A. (2012). *Zakah as a benchmark to evaluate economic growth: An alternative approach*.

Sholihin, A. I. (2010). *Buku Pintar Ekonomi Syariah*. Jakarta: PT. Gramedia Pustaka Utama.

Yogatama, R. A. (2010). Variabel-Variabel Yang Mempengaruhi Kepatuhan Menunaikan Zakah, Pendekatan Kontijensi. Retrieved March 17, 2015, from www.academia.edu.

Chapter 15
Omanization (Development Transformation of the Sultanate of Oman) as an Economic and Social Wellbeing Goal: Application of TSR Circular Causation Method

Masudul Alam Choudhury, Saeed Al-Muharrami and Saleh Ahmed

Abstract The *Tawhidi* methodological formalism reaches its empirical climax in the evaluation of the imminent wellbeing function, subject to its system of inter-variable circular causation relations. The resulting quantitative strategic policy implications are thereby derived. It is essential for full socio-scientific acceptability of a theory and idea to carry the underlying methodological origin of thought to its empirical validation, quantitative inferences, and continuity of the IIE-learning dynamics for anything in the completeness of the theory of 'everything'. Thus far it can be seen, as empirically studied in this work that, the TSR-model emerging from *Tawhidi* methodology and its empirical application, does not fail. Socioeconomic development and social systemic study is one such vastly applied area. In this chapter this generalized area of *Tawhidi* ontological study is particularized to the sectoral development of Oman under the ethical reconstruction of Omanization as explained and measured by its social wellbeing perspective.

Masudul Alam Choudhury, Saeed Al-Muharrami & (Late) Saleh Ahmed—This research was completed for Daleel Oil Corporation and Oman Ministry of Oil and Gas in December 2014. Professor Dr. Saeed Al-Muharrami is in the Department of Economics and Finance, College of Economics and Political Science, Sultan Qaboos University, Muscat, Sultanate of Oman.

M. A. Choudhury (✉)
Faculty of Economics, Trisakti University, Jakarta, Indonesia
e-mail: masudc60@yahoo.ca

S. Al-Muharrami
Department of Economics and Finance, College of Economics and Political Science, Sultan Qaboos University, Muscat, Sultanate of Oman

S. Ahmed (Deceased)
Department of Mathematics and Statistics, Sultan Qaboos University, Muscat, Sultanate of Oman

© Springer Nature Singapore Pte Ltd. 2019
M. A. Choudhury (ed.), *The* Tawhidi *Methodological Worldview*,
https://doi.org/10.1007/978-981-13-6585-0_15

169

A Non-technical Overview of the Chapter

There is an abstracto-empirical automaticity in *Tawhidi* methodology driven from its ontological foundations to the empirical validation of the *Tawhidi* worldview of unity of knowledge and its organic unity of being and becoming in the generality and details of the world-system. This inherent nature of the *Tawhidi* methodological worldview has been effectively established in this work in respect of various specific studies. As an additional one it is now extended to the study of In-Country Valuation, which is a development valuation investigation taking account of the inter-sectoral relationships between critical sectors. The approach of ICV is a combination of microeconomic and macroeconomic studies using imminent statistical models that generate quantitative policy analysis. The focus of the *Tawhidi* methodology feeding into organic interrelated studies for inter-sectoral analysis becomes a resilient groundwork for the use of the wellbeing model of *Tawhidi* String Relations (TSR). Its properties of inter-variable organic relations of circular causation model are articulated to make the abstracto-empirical nature of TSR-model of wellbeing a universally and uniquely valid one to study diverse issues and problems of 'everything'.

In the present special case it is the organic inter-sectoral study of ICV for Oman in the light of the Omanization wellbeing index that is studied as the problem-issue. Various microeconomic and macroeconomic equations of the attenuating model are thereby used and quantitative policy analysis undertaken. The abstracto-empirical focus leads to the quantitative policy analytic evaluation of the ICV development problem. This points out how cogently the *Tawhidi* methodology could be integrated with its automaticity in the computerised version of the ICV-model. The result is in generality for all types of ICV-development problems. The particular case is of Oman and the Omanization Wellbeing Index.

Introduction

The holistic goal of national socioeconomic wellbeing by creating, supporting, and sustaining a productive transformation of the economy within an increasing Omanization perspective is the strategic goal referred to as Omanization of Oman's national economy As well, Omanization means maintaining the complementary needs for achieving such goals between labour and all productive sectors. Thereby, the entire gamut of economic activity measured by productivity and distributive equity in wages, salaries and employment within the Omanization program becomes a field of complementary relations. This means also that, sustainability of the Omanization program in terms of economic and social goals of wellbeing must proceed on without substantial replacement (or substitution) between Omani and non-Omani participation in Omani national development.

The Omani Wellbeing Index of Social and Economic Complementarities

By the Omani wellbeing index of social and economic complementarities between the critical goals represented by their variables we mean sustainability of the extensively inter-sectoral complementarities between the critical socioeconomic variables. The Omani index as objective function is defined by the pervasiveness of complementarities between the requisite variables of a participatory socioeconomic development. Such inter-variable complementarities may not exist, may be negative, can be weak, medium or strong in any development process. Negative and weak levels of inter-variable complementarities are improved to generate better levels of simulated wellbeing out of the circular causation results inter-relating the variables (Toner, 1999). Complementarities also signify endogenously evolutionary learning properties of the multivariate interacting, integrating, and evolutionary (IIE) systems of socioeconomic variables. Consequently, all of the following properties of the wellbeing model are coterminous: Participation (complementarities), endogenous nature of evolutionary relations, discursive patterns of inter-entity learning, and simulacra property of circular causation relations spanning over complexity of inter-relations, but simplifying this by specific empirical methods for predictive purposes.

The Development Target of Omani Economy

The Sultanate of Oman is poised to take off in its 2020-vision of accelerated growth and development by a selection of strategic and policy approaches. Of these approaches an important one is diversification of the economy into non-oil sector (Choudhury & Al-Sahlawi, 2000). On the expectation of sectoral diversification in respect of the development diversification program, Oman aims at interfacing development with higher employment and economic conditions, especially of Omanis. This obviously means that, the development process in the Sultanate of Oman is aimed at achieving its important wellbeing goal of increasing the Omani composition of productive employment. Towards achieving this goal there has to be significant inter-sectoral complementarities in productive activities. In all therefore, sustainability by way of maintaining complementary trend in Oil/Gas activities and its enhancement of sectoral employment, marks the important socioeconomic development focus.

Objective: Focusing the Macroeconomic Modeling of the Oil and Gas Sector for In-Country-Valuation (ICV)

Underlying the completed ICV macroeconomic modeling (Tordo, Warner, Monzano, & Anouti, 2013) of the oil and gas sector and extended to the ICV macro-micro interface, of which this is the report, the principal objective is to study the existing state of interrelations between some key indicators affecting oil and gas activities. The national development perspective is kept in view. Omanization is a goal understood in its broad context of economic and social wellbeing for the nation arising from the oil and gas sector. This chapter recommends strategies and policies towards enhancing the strengths and correcting the weaknesses of the actual state of the economy 'as is' in respect of the end-all of Omanization goal as defined above (Choudhury, Al-Muharami, Ahmed, & Hossain, 2015). The underlying wellbeing model with its circular causation relations between critical variables is estimated with the background of TSR methodology and imminent empirical method.

Methodology 1: The Conceptual Version: Generalized ICV Model Structure that Can Be Further Computerized for the Oman National Economy

In this chapter only the oil and gas sector is the focus of study. However, the model developed for empirical estimation of Eq. (15.1) impact study of various critical variables in the oil and gas sector in respect of the Omanization goal. Equation (15.2) examines strategies and policies for inter-sectoral complementarities where this remains weak. Likeness of such equations can be extended to formulate national development. The ICV model of Omanization in terms of socioeconomic Omani index would then be formalized as follows. The emergent model is next extended to the ICV-micro data with macro-micro interface in the second part of this chapter.

Let the wellbeing simulation function defined as above be denoted by,

$$\text{Evaluate } W(x) \tag{15.1}$$

Simulation of expression (15.1) is performed subject to the circular causation system of equations,

$$x_j = f_i(x); \ \forall i \neq j = 1, 2, \ldots, n \tag{15.2}$$

with $x = \{x_1, x_2, \ldots, x_n\}$

The 'measured Omani index' as being different from the conceptual form given in expression (15.1) is the Omanization Index. It is given by,

$$\theta = F(x) \tag{15.3}$$

Expression (15.3) represents the socioeconomic Omani index. The x-vector components are the critical ICV-variables of the problem under study. These variables are firstly taken up in their macroeconomic version. In the second part of this chapter they are extended to ICV-micro data and the ICV macro-micro interface model is re-evaluated.

In its simplest form the Omani index is given by,

$$W \approx \theta = F(x) = \prod_{i=1}^{n} x_i \qquad (15.4)$$

To allow for non-linearity of the wellbeing function and its circular causation equations and to readily interpret the estimated (simulated) coefficients, we take these functional relations in their log-linear forms for the special case of the oil and gas sector in Oman, but in relation to the national economy via the nominal Gross Domestic Product (GDP).

Methodology 2: The Empirical Version of Macroeconomic ICV-Model for Oil and Gas Sector in Oman

The estimated log-linear equations for the data on the variables $(X_1, X_2, X_3, X_4, X_5)$ corresponding to the data shown in appendix are given below. The interpretations of the estimated and simulated results follow. The estimated results are for the actual state of inter-variable results implied by the actual data. The simulated results on new estimators of the variables and comparative trends point out the induced impact results of the inter-variable relations. In either case, the work done here represents a macroeconomic perspective of the ICV study. Consequently, certain areas of policy and strategy arising from the 'simulation' results compared with the 'estimation' results are examined. The second part of this chapter further extends the policy and strategic issues. A fresh trend in the simulated variables (estimators) compared to the estimated (fitted) values displays the strategy and policy effects.

The equations that we will study in terms of the estimated form and the simulated form relating to the oil and gas sector are as follows:

$$\widehat{\ln X_1} = 2.35 - 0.766 \ln X_2 + 0.224 \ln X_3 + 0.183 \ln X_4 + 1.24 \ln X_5 \qquad (15.5)$$

$$\widehat{\ln X_2} = 2.01 - 0.759 \ln X_1 + 0.164 \ln X_3 + 0.121 \ln X_4 + 1.35 \ln X_5 \qquad (15.6)$$

$$\widehat{\ln X_3} = -6.02 - 2.92 \ln X_1 + 2.17 \ln X_2 + 0.380 \ln X_4 - 3.50 \ln X_5 \qquad (15.7)$$

$$\widehat{\ln X_4} = -10.0 + 3.90 \ln X_1 + 2.61 \ln X_2 - 0.620 \ln X_3 - 4.28 \ln X_5 \qquad (15.8)$$

$$\widehat{\ln X_5} = -1.59 + 0.633 \ln X_1 + 0.698 \ln X_2 - 0.137 \ln X_3 - 0.103 \ln X_4 \qquad (15.9)$$

where X_1 = Total GDP, X_2 = Oil and Gas Exports, X_3 = Wages and Salaries, X_4 = Total Gross Capital Formation and X_5 = Total Petroleum Activities (GDP Oil and Gas).

Findings

Interpreting the estimated equations

We associate the term 'estimation' with the empirical form and study of the regression equations in the actual 'as is' state of data and socioeconomic situation. This term is different from 'simulation'. By 'simulation' we mean the induced (impact) change in the coefficients of the estimated equations under conditions of strategy and policy perspectives pertaining to the Omanization goal as an 'ought to be' socioeconomic situation.

The equation system (15.2) is said to comprise the circular causation system of inter-relations between the variables. In it, every variable is endogenously related to all other variables so as to make all these variables inter-causal in nature. In the estimation form, the coefficients are subject to interpretation of the state of inter-variable relations 'as is' with actual data. Circular causation is the method of examining the level of existence or absence of complementarities between the variables.

The equations with every variable being dependent on the rest of the variables imply extensive complementarities or absence of these among all the variables. Positive coefficients denote corresponding inter-variable complementarities. Such complementarities are good indicators of general prosperity of the national economy via the oil and gas sector.

Interpreting the Simulated Equations

The term 'simulation' will mean reforming the 'estimated' system of equations to attain better and more desired degree of complementarities when certain independent and dependent variables are not found to show positive complementarity. Absence of inter-variable complementarities is shown by the negative estimated values of the inter-variable coefficients. The selection of new replacing coefficient values is done through strategy and policy discourse. Hence while estimated coefficients give the actual state of inter-variable relations; their revisions towards simulated better values of complementarities point out the normatively strategic and policy changes.

The simulated values also represent the induced effects via choice and discourse as the inter-variable relations 'ought to be'. The inter-variable relations are between dependent and independent variables and are signified by the coefficients of the model. Choices of multiple values of the coefficients for simulation can be made from the tables of the method called Spatial Domain Analysis. These ensuing methods are explained later on. Multiple 'simulated' coefficient values point out variously different choices and discursive scenarios of sectoral relationships between the variables. This means that, each process of strategic and policy change leads to further more of such changes. The multitude of 'simulation' is called simulacra.

Thus for instance, it would be desired that oil and gas exports ought to affect national GDP positively or in better degrees. Likewise, all the variables ought to have positive or better relations to each other, indicating the positive complementarities between the variables in respect of the goals of national development through the impact of the oil and gas sector activity.

Evaluating the Oil and Gas Sector Macroeconomic ICV-Model

In-Country-Valuation of the oil and gas sector and the critical variables shown here ought to show positive or better results ensuing from the oil and gas sector in terms of all the variables. This though is not always the case. That is because inter-variable (dependent to independent) substitutions rather than their inter-variable complementarities shift oil and gas related resources away from their expected effects into either leakages or structural development problems of substitutions in the development process. Policies for not correcting such marginal substitution incidence of oil and gas resources can accentuate the problems of misallocation of resources for balanced development as the goal of Omanization.

The actual state of resource allocation and inter-variable relationships can show the existence of marginal substitutions between critical variables. When this happens, the ICV component emanating from oil and gas sector may be less than effective in engendering balanced development in the economy at large. Such results are unraveled by the statistical estimation of the natural log-linear set of Circular causation equations.

Figure 15.1 shows that, the circular causation equations are really inter-variable organic relationships between all the variables taken one at a time to regress on the rest of the variables. The objective of such statistical estimation is to detect where marginal substitution instead of degrees of complementarities between the variables are found. Positive or better signed estimated coefficients show complementarities (relative degree of complementarities) between the dependent and the corresponding independent variables. Complementarities between the variables that are conducive to national wellbeing, as in the broader meaning of Omanization, are desired. Contrarily, negative-signed coefficients of variables mean the existence of marginal substitutions between the dependent variables and the corresponding independent variables.

When the undesired situation of inter-variable marginal substitutions is found to be present, then simulations of the coefficients are done under reasonably possible degrees of inter-variable complementarities. Such simulated changes in the value of the corresponding coefficients point out the normative transformation of the existing estimated inter-variable relationships into better states of complementarities or lower degrees of substitution. One of the important cases is to aim at the empirical value of the effect that oil and gas sector development ought to play in generating employment and wages and salaries, and investment in capital goods as indicators of Omanization as wellbeing objective taken in its broader meaning. A high negative coefficient value

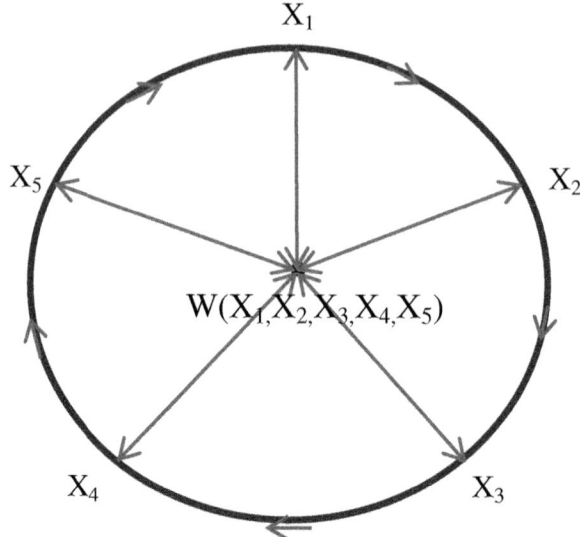

Fig. 15.1 Circular causation organic inter-variable relations to evaluate the wellbeing function

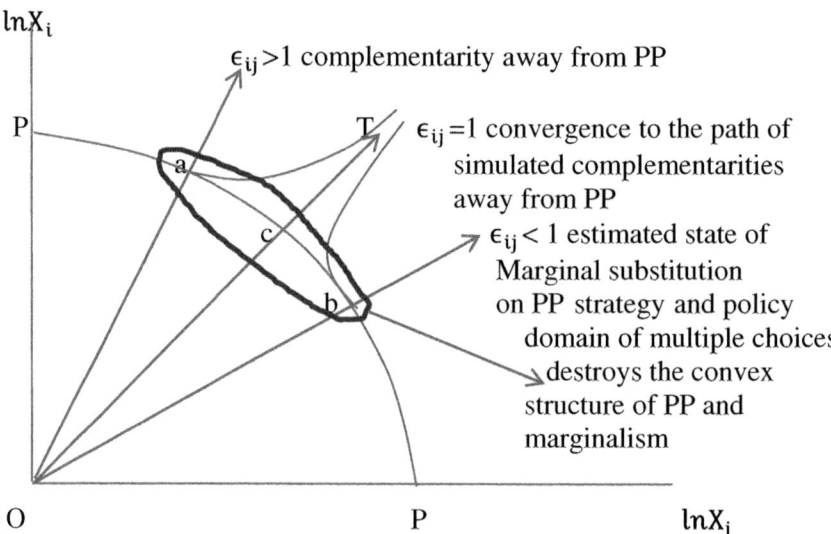

Fig. 15.2 Complementarities versus marginal substitution in explaining strategy and policy towards Omanization as Omani social index

between wages and salaries and the other variables cannot be acceptable in the sense of Omanization as the Omani index. See Fig. 15.2.

In Fig. 15.1, the method of circular causation is explained by double-arrows between all the variables in terms of each one as a dependent variable regressed against the rest of the variables as independent ones. The double-sided arrows denote the feedback between the social Index of Omanization and the circular causation variables in the sense of sustainability over stages of simulation towards improving the plausible degrees of complementarities between the critical variables.

The plausible re-simulations can be done by selecting coefficients as listed in the multitude of values in the table of Spatial Domain Analysis, shown later on. Implicitly, such choices arise via a mix of empirical work and discourse on strategies and policies. These in turn determine the coefficients of the selected variables to generate new sets of simulated circular causation estimators. Thereby the new sets of social wellbeing indexes of Omanization appear as denoted by complementarities between the critical variables.

The smooth PP surface in Fig. 15.2 is the effect and cause of marginal substitution between the variables. The region covering 'abc' along with its varied expansion denotes the discursive decision-making on choices to select simulated coefficients as the slopes, $\ln X_i / \ln X_j$. Consequently, such a surface becomes corrugated. Marginal substitution is then replaced by complementarities. Thereby, points like abc are discursively changed by strategies and policies to cause convergence along paths of complementarities, such as OT, and Oa away from Ob. As such, dynamics can exist everywhere along PP, and therefore, in the case of pervasive complementarities between $\ln X_i$ and $\ln X_j$ (and therefore, X_i, X_j due to monotonicity). The entire convex to the origin surface is now turned into corrugated domains of complexity caused by inter-variable learning dynamics.

Such kinds of corrugation cannot be smoothened by probabilistic correction. That is because simulations continue on ad infinitum. Such a system of evolutionary simulations is referred to as simulacra. The surface PP is thus continuously corrugated over simulacra. Every probabilistic surface would be corrugated as soon as complementarities appear and more so evolve in continuity of simulacra.

Interpreting the Estimated Equations

Interpreting Eq. (15.10)

$$\widehat{\ln X_1} = 2.35 - 0.766 \ln X_2 + 0.224 \ln X_3 + 0.183 \ln X_4 + 1.24 \ln X_5 \qquad (15.10)$$

The elasticity coefficient is interpreted as follows. As an example, the elasticity coefficient of X_2 to X_1 is given by,

$$\in_{12} = \frac{\partial \ln X_1}{\partial \ln X_2} = -0.766. \qquad (15.11)$$

This means that, every 1% increase (decrease) in X_2 results in -0.766% of 1% negative change in X_2. This form of a negative movement between the variables X_1 and X_2 in the partial equilibrium sense of the relationship between these variables implies the existence of marginal substitution rather than complementary effect between the variables in the sense of partial equilibrium, while all other variables remain fixed when this particular relationship between X_1 and X_2 exists.

A casual attention to the variables in the estimated Eq. (15.10) points out that, oil exports do not have positive effect on the total national nominal GDP. Why this would be the case, is a matter to be studied. One reason for such (X_1, X_2) substitution result in respect of total GDP is the oil and gas sector diversification into non-oil sector according to national development policy. Another reason could be the lower world oil prices that can depress oil and gas export revenue in contributing to GDP. There is need for better human resource development and technological choice in the oil and gas sector.

Such effects through the existing case revealed by estimation with actual data should be subjected to restructuring by examining the policy and strategy of oil and gas sector to non-oil sectoral diversification. Such a strategy can be pursued by examining how much of a multiplier effect of oil and gas exports can be improved to account for complementarities or a lower degree of substitution in the diversification case. It is always a wise policy not to replace oil and gas sector by non-oil sectoral development. Rather, the two sectors should proceed in complementary ways in national development signified by GDP-variable.

For instance, if $\epsilon_{12} = \frac{\partial \ln X_1}{\partial \ln X_2} = -0.766$ was changed by policy discourse to the coefficient value of $+1.00$, that would mean differential of ϵ_{12} by $+1.766$. The implication is that, the percentage change in GDP by the differential improvement in the export revenue effect would be 1.766 of this differential value. This means as well that, a 1.766 of one percent $(0.01766 \times \ln X_2)$ increase in export revenue will establish complementarities in the economy showing an increase in the GDP-effect of oil and gas and non-oil sector inclusively by this same amount.

Interpreting Eq. (15.12)

The same kind of strategic and policy implications also holds for the case of

$$\widehat{\ln X_2} = 2.01 - 0.759 \ln X_1 + 0.164 \ln X_3 + 0.121 \ln X_4 + 1.35 \ln X_5 \qquad (15.12)$$

with, $\epsilon_{21} = \frac{\partial \ln X_2}{\partial \ln X_1} = -0.759$

The implications of the inter-variable causal relationship in this case are from X_1 to X_2 in expression (15.12). It means that, a one percentage change in X_1 causes $|1.759|$ of differential percentage change in X_2. This is a reversibility result to expression (15.10): That is, the implication of the estimated Eq. (15.12) is from the side of X_1 to X_2. Consequently now, if there could be a simulated choice of $\epsilon_{21} = +1.00$; then a change in the elasticity coefficient of X_2 to X_1 of 1.759 would be required. Thereby, to realize a strategic improvement towards complementarity between GDP and export revenue, 1.759 of one percent of GDP should be mobilized into the oil and gas sector to establish complementary change between export revenue and GDP.

Interpreting Eq. (15.13)

X_4 as total petroleum activity measures the nominal GDP of the oil and gas sector. In this case of $(X_3$ to $X_4)$ negative relationships of circular causation estimations are noticed. This is an important relationship in terms of the goal of Omanization as a total wellbeing objective. The estimated result points out that, the oil and gas sector being traditionally capital intensive, it causes labor- saving techniques. Much of the capital formation goes into fixed assets in the oil and gas sector. In a situation of fixed resource budget, the budgetary resource allocation between capital and labor causes marginal rate of substitution between these productive factor inputs.

$$\widehat{\ln X_3} = -6.02 + 2.92 \ln X_1 + 2.17 \ln X_2 - 0.380 \ln X_4 - 3.50 \ln X_5 \qquad (15.13)$$

A differential change in $\in_{34}$ for 1% in capital formation would cause 1.380 of differential change in wages and salaries. That is, $\Delta \left(\frac{\partial \ln X_3}{\partial \ln X_4} \right) = \Delta \in_{34} = 1.380$. The implications here are that, the capital intensity of the oil and gas sector needs to be re-structured to form capital and labor augmentation type of oil and gas production process. The technology causing the distribution of oil and gas GDP between labor and capital should also complement with the productive factor-wise distribution of oil and gas GDP. In the interest of distributive equity in the allocation of GDP of the oil and gas sector there is good reason to maintain an equitable distribution of wages and salaries among various occupational categories of workers and managerial and technical staff. Such restructuring would bring about release of resources of the oil and gas sector GDP towards capital and labor complementarities in the production process.

In general, for development planning in respect of particular reasons of Omanization as a comprehensive goal of wellbeing, there is need for a positive policy and strategy to establish and sustain capital-labor complementarities (Choudhury & Hossain, 2006). This can be indicated by simulation of the estimated results connecting (X_3, X_4).

Interpreting Eq. (15.14)

$$\widehat{\ln X_4} = -10.0 + 3.90 \ln X_1 + 2.61 \ln X_2 - 0.620 \ln X_3 - 4.28 \ln X_5 \qquad (15.14)$$

When we set, $\in_{43} = 1.00$, a differential value of $\Delta \left(\frac{\partial \ln X_4}{\partial \ln X_3} \right) = \Delta \in_{43} = 1.620$, between the estimated and simulated value of the coefficient of $\ln X_3$ in Eq. (15.14) is required. Now by way of explanation as before, it would require a differential of 1.620 of 1% differential change in logarithmic wages and salaries to re-allocate oil and gas sector GDP to generate capital-labour complementarity in wages and salaries by the budgetary expenditure in oil and gas sector. This would signal a better scenario towards Omanization of wellbeing through complementarity between capital efficiency and distributive equity of wages, salaries and productive employment.

On the other hand, the marginal substitution condition between (X_4, X_3), does not convey an acceptable sign of Omanization in terms of wellbeing based on complementarity between the selected development variables as shown. The marginal substitution condition needs to be changed to a complementary situation. As it stands, the estimated result shows that, a percentage decrease in wages and salaries will cause an increase in the budgetary allocation into capital formation to optimize production but not wellbeing. Consequently, an acceptable state of Omanization as wellbeing interpreted by the balance and complementarities between $(X_3 X_4)$ is not attained.

To establish such needed complementarities strategic and policy restructuring is required. As a similar example setting $\in_{34} = 1.00$ via policy and strategy discourse medium implies a 1.620 of the change in the estimated elasticity coefficient via a differential in the percentage change of X_3 to result in a differential positive value of $\ln X_4$ equal to $1.620 \times \ln X_4$.

The negative impacts of X_3 and X_5 on X_4, but more significantly in the latter case, points to a deep strategic and policy restructuring on the side of the relationship between oil and gas GDP negatively affecting capital formation. But at the same time, wages and salaries also bear negatively on capital formation. These show the existence of marginal substitutions between wages and salaries, and oil and gas GDP on the one side; and capital formation as a substitute on the other side.

Such a result implies that, although low productivity and misallocation of oil and gas sector GDP between capital and labor (in the sense of wages, salaries, and employment) are noted, the capital productivity of the oil and gas sector is suspect. In this respect, the oil and gas sector GDP is found not to support the capital formation positively.

On the assumption that, through strategy and policy discourse the elasticity $\in_{43}$ is improved to $\in_{43} = 1$, the consequential strategic and policy restructuring would require a differential improvement in $\in_{43}$ to a value of 1.620. That is, there is now need to increase the percentage change of $\ln X_3$ to $\ln X_4 \left(\Delta \left(\frac{\partial \ln X_3}{\partial \ln X_4} \right) \right)$ to 1.620. With such transformation in the inter-variable relationship (X_3, X_4), it would be possible to obtain complementarity between wages and salaries (and thus employment) and capital formation.

(X_5, X_4)-*marginal substitution relationship*

Likewise, on a similar assumption borne out of discourse around strategy and policy, if we set $\in_{54} = 1$, then the differential increase in percentage change of X_5 impacting upon the percentage differential change in X_4 would be in the tune of $4.28 \times$ (percentage change in X_5). It would then be possible to attain productivity increases in both capital and labor by their complementary and positive or better effects on oil and gas GDP and conversely. Such induced complementary effects would be conducive of Omanization as an overall wellbeing scenario caused by complementarities between all the critical variables.

Interpreting Eq. (15.15)

$$\widehat{\ln X_5} = -1.59 + 0.633 \ln X_1 + 0.698 \ln X_2 - 0.137 \ln X_3 - 0.103 \ln X_4 \quad (15.15)$$

Equation (15.15) shows the reversible effects of wages and salaries (thus employment and productivity) and of capital formation on oil and gas sector GDP. While the negative impacts of these variables on oil and gas sector GDP is unwanted in the role of the oil and gas sector in national development, the strategic and policy induced transformation to generate complementarities all over, i.e. between labor, capital, and oil and gas sector GDP, would point to a sure way of sustaining the oil and gas sector in the Omanization goal as both an economic and social focus of complementarities.

Such transformations would require the following numerical impacts:

(i)   a differential percentage change in $\in_{35}$ of 1.137. This would then imply a differential percentage change in X_5 equal to $1.137 \times$ differential percentage change in X_3.

(ii) a differential percentage change in $\in_{45}$ of 1.103. This would then imply a differential percentage change in X_5 equal to $1.137 \times$ differential percentage change in X_4.

Such changes in the independent variables and their effects on the dependent variables convey the measure of multiplier impacts (induced effects) of each and all the variables in the circular causation equations. The coefficients are taken for both the estimation and the simulated forms. Estimated coefficients and the fitted variables (estimators) convey the state of the oil and gas development in terms of the Omanization goal 'as is'. The simulated coefficients convey the state of the Omanization goal 'as it ought to be'. The sum-total of the coefficients in the two cases shows respectively, existence of positively signed sum-total for economies of scale; or dis-economies by non-positive sign of scale in the wellbeing function.

Simulating Empirical Impact Study: Inter-sectoral Variable-Relations by Selecting 'simulated' Coefficients

While we have exemplified a discursive way of selecting simulated coefficients and then measuring the impacts of differential elasticity effects on the dependent variables to attain complementarities, the Spatial Domain Analysis provides greater machine generated freedom for such coefficient selection. This leads to generating simulacra of coefficients for further socioeconomic interpretations. We adopt the SDA method of generating simulacra now.

Figure 15.3 demonstrates the conversion of Eq. (15.10) in the SDA domain, which is more interactive and user-friendly method in perceiving simulation sensitivity than the statistical method. In this figure it can be seen that, there is negative interaction between petroleum activities and wages and salaries as shown by the lighter intensity of the color. In the same way, the negative interaction between total gross capital formation and petroleum activities can be understood, as this is represented by the lighter intensity of the color. This type of representation of the degree of interaction between the sectors cannot be demonstrated in the statistical domain. The statistical domain only represents the interaction at a certain point in space, while in SDA domain simulation can be represented in large number of points in extended geometrical space. There is a positive interaction between petroleum activities and oil exports. This is shown using the deeper intensity of the color in the SDA figure.

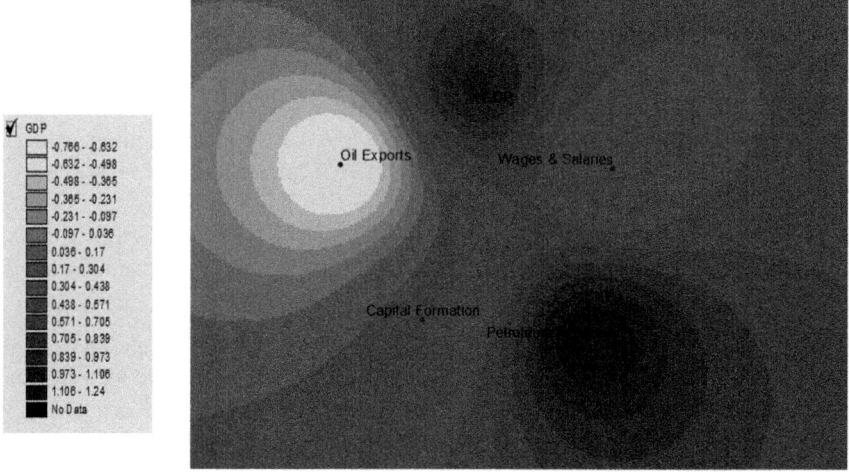

Fig. 15.3 Interaction between GDP (X_1) and oil exports (X_2), wages and salaries (X_3), total gross capital formation (X_4), total petroleum activities (X_5)

Importantly, the tables by the side of the SDA diagrams list the machine-generated numerical values of simulacra of coefficients that can be selected to justify for chosen levels of complementarities. Such simulated coefficient values are once again discoursed. They are used to generate new values of the simulated $\ln X$'s as estimators. Thereafter, similar strategic and policy analysis can be done as was shown above.

One example in each of the circular causation equations can be taken up in this regard. The remaining exercises would be similar. It is thereby appropriate to cast the entire analysis into computerized forms (see later). For Eq. (15.16) let the selected $\in_{12}$ elasticity coefficient be 0.036. See below the simulated coefficient for all possibilities as generated by SDA.

Thereby, the simulated equation is,

$$\widehat{\ln X_{1_s}} = 2.35 - 0.498 \ln X_2 + 0.224 \ln X_3 + 0.183 \ln X_4 + 1.24 \ln X_5 \qquad (15.16)$$

Now rest of the analysis can be carried out as was done earlier. For Eq. (15.17) a similar alternative choice can be discoursed in the strategy and policy meeting:

$$\widehat{\ln X_{2_s}} = 2.01 - 0.337 \ln X_1 + 0.164 \ln X_3 + 0.121 \ln X_4 + 1.35 \ln X_5 \qquad (15.17)$$

For Eq. (15.18) an alternative similar equation for strategy and policy analysis can be,

$$\widehat{\ln X_{3_s}} = -6.02 + 2.92 \ln X_1 + 2.17 \ln X_2 - 0.076 \ln X_4 - 2.644 \ln X_5 \qquad (15.18)$$

For Eq. (15.19) an alternative simulated form for strategic and policy analysis via discourse can be,

$$\widehat{\ln X_{4_s}} = -10.0 + 3.90 \ln X_1 + 2.61 \ln X_2 - 0.463 \ln X_3 - 1.553 \ln X_5 \quad (15.19)$$

For Eq. (15.20) the alternative form for strategic and policy analysis via discourse can be,

$$\widehat{\ln X_{5_s}} = -1.59 + 0.633 \ln X_1 + 0.698 \ln X_2 - 0.015 \ln X_3 - 0.090 \ln X_4 \quad (15.20)$$

Spatial Domain Analysis (SDA) Simulation Results to Identify Impact Coefficients

See Figs. 15.4, 15.5, 15.6 and 15.7.

$$\widehat{\ln X_{1_s}} = 2.35 - 0.7 \ln X_2 + 0.224 \ln X_3 + 0.183 \ln X_4 + 1.24 \ln X_5$$
$$\widehat{\ln X_{2_s}} = 2.01 - 0.7 \ln X_1 + 0.164 \ln X_3 + 0.121 \ln X_4 + 1.35 \ln X_5$$
$$\widehat{\ln X_{3_s}} = -6.02 - 2.92 \ln X_1 + 2.17 \ln X_2 + 0.380 \ln X_4 - 3.4 \ln X_5$$
$$\widehat{\ln X_{4_s}} = -10.0 + 3.90 \ln X_1 + 2.61 \ln X_2 - 0.620 \ln X_3 - 4.2 \ln X_5$$
$$\widehat{\ln X_{5_s}} = -1.59 + 0.633 \ln X_1 + 0.698 \ln X_2 - 0.134 \ln X_3 - 0.102 \ln X_4$$

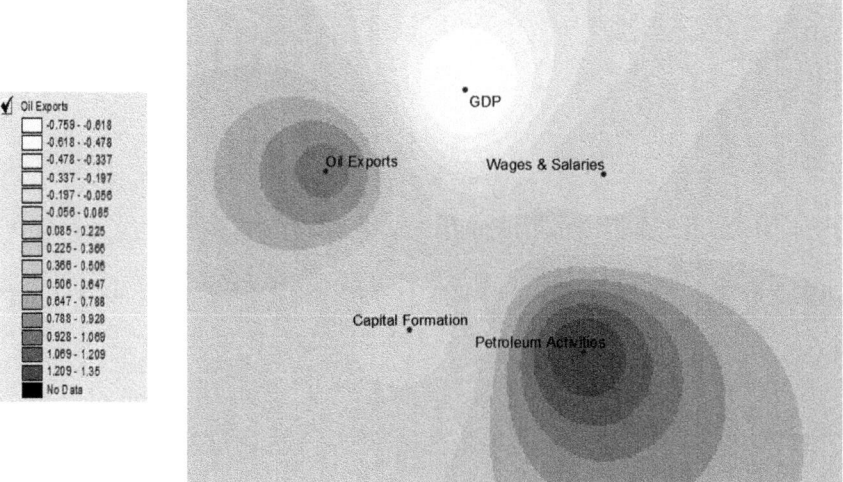

Fig. 15.4 Interaction between oil exports (X_2) and GDP (X_1), wages and salaries (X_3), total gross capital formation (X_4), total petroleum activities (X_5)

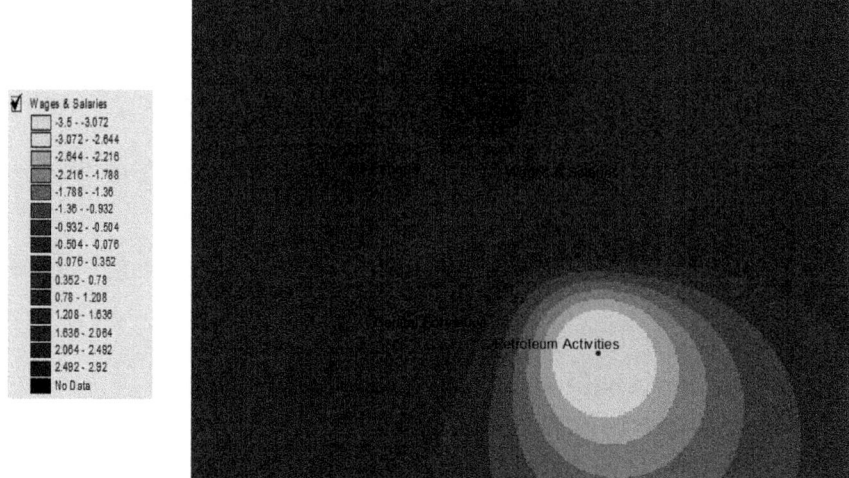

Fig. 15.5 Interaction between wages and salaries (X_3), and GDP (X_1), oil exports (X_2), total gross capital formation (X_4), total petroleum activities (X_5)

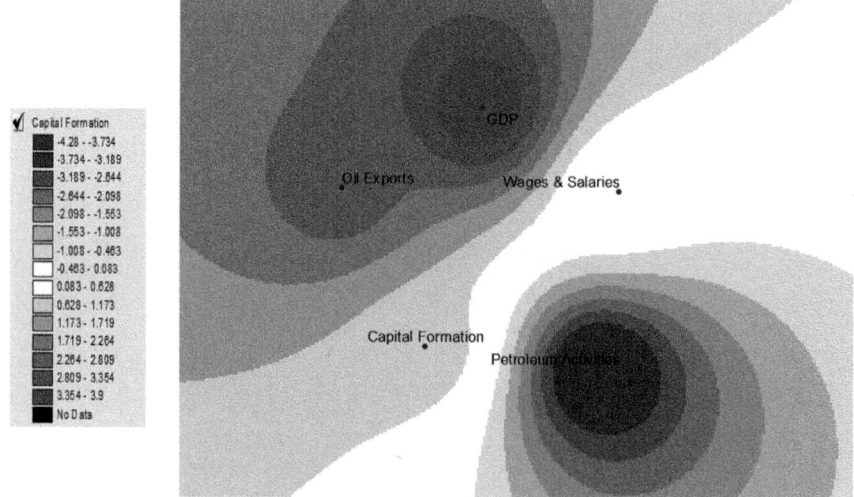

Fig. 15.6 Interaction between total gross capital formation (X_4), and GDP (X_1), oil exports (X_2), wages and salaries (X_3), total petroleum activities (X_5)

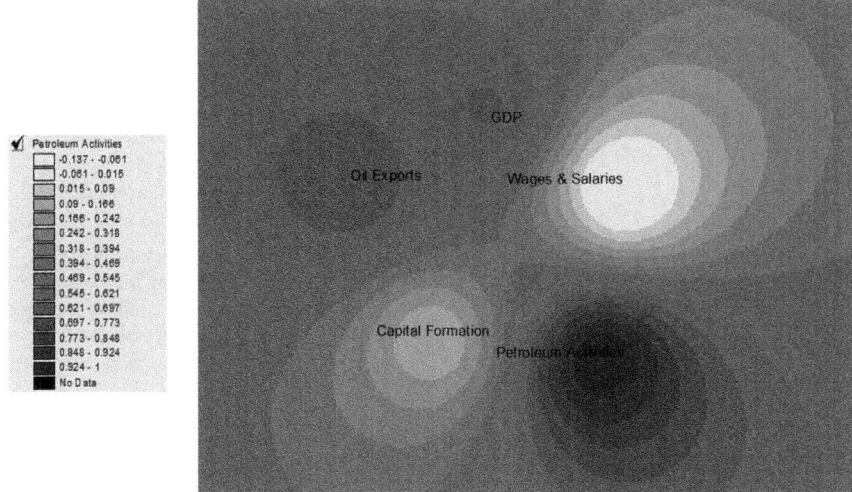

Fig. 15.7 Interaction between total petroleum activities (X_5) and GDP (X_1), oil exports (X_2), wages and salaries (X_3), total gross capital formation (X_4)

Macroeconomic Empirical Results

Total actual and induced effects (impact) of all variables on Omanization by the Omani Index

$$W(X_1, X_2, X_3, X_4, X_5) = \prod_{i=1}^{5} X_i \qquad (15.21)$$

From the study of the circular causation equations the message of socioeconomic development transformation towards building up complementarities between all the variables point out a number of principal strategic and policy directions. In reference to Fig. 15.1 we infer that the complementary relationships between oil and gas sector GDP, the total GDP, capital formulation, wages and salaries (thereby employment), and export revenue need to be constructed. For instance, the following inference can be deduced from Table 15.1:

Observations and Recommendations: Macroeconomic Inference

The Omani national economy shows a fairly good deal of complementarities in respect of the GDP-variable interaction. But the oil and gas sector is internally less receptive to issues of complementarities between capital and labor distribution of oil and gas GDP and their factor-productivities. A good deal of strategic and policy efforts ought to be launched in restructuring the oil and gas sector in these directions

Table 15.1 Inferences from the 'estimated' equations requiring 'simulated' improvements towards inter-variable complementarities

	X_1	X_2	X_3	X_4	X_5	Implications
GDP (X_1)	1	–	+	+	+	GDP shows complementary relations with X_3, X_4, X_5 implying favorable national development impacts of total GDP in these sectoral variables
Oil and gas exports (X_2)	–	1	+	+	+	Oil and gas exports plays complementary role with its own sectoral variables but not in GDP. Restructuring of sectors and resource induction are needed
Wages and salary (X_3)	+	+	1	–	–	X_3 has complementary relations with national GDP and Oil and Gas export. But not so within the Oil and gas sector activity. There is need to induce the wages, salaries, and labor market adaptation in the oil and gas sector
Capital formation in oil and gas sector (X_4)	+	+	–	1	–	X_4 has favorable complementary relations with the national economy and oil and gas export revenue but not so with oil and gas internal activity. oil and gas restructuring and induction of the resources are necessary
Oil and gas GDP (X_5)	+	+	–	–	1	Oil and gas GDP is complementary with the national economy but is not so with capital and labor activity internal to oil and gas sector. Induction is needed to improve the productivity of factor inputs to contribute to oil and gas sector GDP

in order to play greater role in Omanization as a complementary social wellbeing goal.

The Estimated and Simulated Comparative Trends in the Variables and Wellbeing Indexes

The variables are taken in their estimated (estimators) form and in their simulated forms. The comparative time trends are shown for the variables and the wellbeing function over the given time-period. These time trends are explained in relation to the estimated and simulated variables correspondingly. For details regarding all trends in the variables and the Oman Index see Graphs 15.1 in the appendix.

Computerizable generalized matrix model of the macroeconomic circular causation

The circular causation results on elasticity coefficients can be represented in a matrix form as follows.

$$
A = \begin{pmatrix}
\in_{11} & \in_{12} & \in_{13} & \in_{14} & \in_{15} \\
\in_{21} & \in_{22} & \in_{23} & \in_{24} & \in_{25} \\
\in_{31} & \in_{32} & \in_{33} & \in_{34} & \in_{35} \\
\in_{41} & \in_{42} & \in_{43} & \in_{44} & \in_{45} \\
\in_{51} & \in_{52} & \in_{53} & \in_{54} & \in_{55}
\end{pmatrix}
=
\begin{pmatrix}
1 & \in_{12} & \in_{13} & \in_{14} & \in_{15} \\
\in_{21} & 1 & \in_{23} & \in_{24} & \in_{25} \\
\in_{31} & \in_{32} & 1 & \in_{34} & \in_{35} \\
\in_{41} & \in_{42} & \in_{43} & 1 & \in_{45} \\
\in_{51} & \in_{52} & \in_{53} & \in_{54} & 1
\end{pmatrix}
$$

$$
= \begin{pmatrix}
1.00 & -0.77 & 0.224 & 0.183 & 1.24 \\
-0.76 & 1.00 & 0.164 & 0.121 & 1.35 \\
2.92 & 2.17 & 1.00 & -0.38 & -3.50 \\
3.90 & 2.61 & -0.62 & 1.00 & -4.28 \\
0.633 & 0.698 & -0.14 & -0.103 & 1.00
\end{pmatrix}
\tag{15.22}
$$

The matrix form (15.21) can be re-written as,

$$
[E_{ij} - I][X_i] + [A_i] = 0
\tag{15.23}
$$

where, $E_{ij}(\theta) = \begin{pmatrix}
1 & \in_{12} & \in_{13} & \in_{14} & \in_{15} \\
\in_{21} & 1 & \in_{23} & \in_{24} & \in_{25} \\
\in_{31} & \in_{32} & 1 & \in_{34} & \in_{35} \\
\in_{41} & \in_{42} & \in_{43} & 1 & \in_{45} \\
\in_{51} & \in_{52} & \in_{53} & \in_{54} & 1
\end{pmatrix}$

$[X_i]$ is the column vector of variables, I is the identity matrix, $[A_i]$ is the column vector of technological parameters of the model; $i = 1, 2, 3, 4, 5$.

The theoretical form of the matrices of coefficients is empirically written down as,

$$
\begin{pmatrix}
1 & \in_{12} & \in_{13} & \in_{14} & \in_{15} \\
\in_{21} & 1 & \in_{23} & \in_{24} & \in_{25} \\
\in_{31} & \in_{32} & 1 & \in_{34} & \in_{35} \\
\in_{41} & \in_{42} & \in_{43} & 1 & \in_{45} \\
\in_{51} & \in_{52} & \in_{53} & \in_{54} & 1
\end{pmatrix}
=
\begin{pmatrix}
1.00 & -0.77 & 0.224 & 0.183 & 1.24 \\
-0.76 & 1.00 & 0.164 & 0.121 & 1.35 \\
2.92 & 2.17 & 1.00 & -0.38 & -3.50 \\
3.90 & 2.61 & -0.62 & 1.00 & -4.28 \\
0.633 & 0.698 & -0.14 & -0.103 & 1.00
\end{pmatrix}
$$

The simulated coefficient matrix can be readily written down.

Observations on Simulated Values of the Macroeconomic Model Coefficients

The selection of the simulated values of coefficients is done judiciously and by technical discourse within the perspectives of development planning and wellbeing criterion of Omanization in respect of the principle of inter-variable degrees of complementarities. By adopting this methodical approach, the feasible circular causation equations of estimators (simulated coefficients) yielded the following results. These comprise the induced or normative perspectives of the contributions of the oil and gas sector in national socioeconomic development including importantly the Omani index studied by the Omanization objective goal.

The attached EXCEL tables indicate the final estimated and simulated values, and the Omanization wellbeing indexes with their respective graphs. From these results using the circular causation method the final impacts in terms of multiplier coefficients can be studied. Thereby, the inter-variable elasticity coefficients can be computed in both the estimated and the simulated cases. The corresponding matrixes of the form indicated in this chapter can be computed.

The final set of results points out the need for a substantively higher simulated value of wages and gross capital formation (likewise ln(wages) and log-linear(gross capital formation), respectively) in providing good simulated values of the Omanization criterion wellbeing function. These and similar differences between the simulated values of the various variables estimated above the estimated ($\approx$actual) values are the induced and prescriptive values for strategic reconstruction of the ICV effects.

Comparative Simulation and Estimated Values of the ICV Macroeconomic Variables

On a summary basis the final estimated and simulation circular causation results are given below:

Here

$X_1 =$ Total GDP,
$X_2 =$ Oil and Gas Exports,
$X_3 =$ Wages and Salaries,
$X_4 =$ Total Gross Capital Formation and
$X_5 =$ Total Petroleum Activities (GDP oil and gas).

1. **Estimation results**

$$\widehat{\ln X_1} = 2.35 - 0.766 \ln X_2 + 0.224 \ln X_3 + 0.183 \ln X_4 + 1.24 \ln X_5$$

$$\widehat{\ln X_2} = 2.01 - 0.759 \ln X_1 + 0.164 \ln X_3 + 0.121 \ln X_4 + 1.35 \ln X_5$$

$$\widehat{\ln X_3} = -6.02 - 2.92 \ln X_1 + 2.17 \ln X_2 + 0.380 \ln X_4 - 3.50 \ln X_5$$

$$\widehat{\ln X_4} = -10.0 + 3.90 \ln X_1 + 2.61 \ln X_2 - 0.620 \ln X_3 - 4.28 \ln X_5$$

$$\widehat{\ln X_5} = -1.59 + 0.633 \ln X_1 + 0.698 \ln X_2 - 0.137 \ln X_3 - 0.103 \ln X_4$$

Matrix of elasticity (multiplier impact) coefficients of 'estimated' equations:

$$\begin{pmatrix} \in_{11} \in_{12} \in_{13} \in_{14} \in_{15} \\ \in_{21} \in_{22} \in_{23} \in_{24} \in_{25} \\ \in_{31} \in_{32} \in_{33} \in_{34} \in_{35} \\ \in_{41} \in_{42} \in_{43} \in_{44} \in_{45} \\ \in_{51} \in_{52} \in_{53} \in_{54} \in_{55} \end{pmatrix} = \begin{pmatrix} 1.00 & -0.77 & 0.224 & 0.183 & 1.24 \\ -0.76 & 1.00 & 0.164 & 0.121 & 1.35 \\ 2.92 & 2.17 & 1.00 & -0.38 & -3.50 \\ 3.90 & 2.61 & -0.62 & 1.00 & -4.28 \\ 0.633 & 0.698 & -0.14 & -0.103 & 1.00 \end{pmatrix}$$

It is noted that, the difference between the actual and the estimated values of the variables is very small. Consequently, no difference in the impacts can exist significantly. This calls for simulation of the estimated equations. But the simulated values of the variables are significantly sensitive to changes in the coefficients (impacts read as multipliers).

Matrix Forms in the Estimated and Simulated Macroeconomic Circular Causation Relations

The computerizable matrix form of the circular causation that has led to the theoretical and applied aspects of the macroeconomic modeling of Oman Oil and Gas Sector ICV can be written down as follows:

CONSTANTS		COEFFICIENTS OF C.C.	VARIABLES		EVALUATED VARIABLES
$\begin{vmatrix} A_0 \\ B_0 \\ C_0 \\ D_0 \\ E_0 \end{vmatrix}$	$+$	$\begin{vmatrix} 0 & \in_{12} & \in_{13} & \in_{14} & \in_{15} \\ \in_{21} & 0 & \in_{23} & \in_{24} & \in_{25} \\ \in_{31} & \in_{32} & 0 & \in_{34} & \in_{35} \\ \in_{41} & \in_{42} & \in_{43} & 0 & \in_{45} \\ \in_{51} & \in_{52} & \in_{53} & \in_{54} & 0 \end{vmatrix}$	$*$ $\begin{vmatrix} X_1 \\ X_2 \\ X_3 \\ X_4 \\ X_5 \end{vmatrix}$	$=$	$\begin{vmatrix} X_1' \\ X_2' \\ X_3' \\ X_4' \\ X_5' \end{vmatrix}$

1. *Numerically in the estimated form*

$$\widehat{\ln X_1} = 2.35 - 0.766 \ln X_2 + 0.224 \ln X_3 + 0.183 \ln X_4 + 1.24 \ln X_5 \quad (15.24)$$

$$\widehat{\ln X_2} = 2.01 - 0.759 \ln X_1 + 0.164 \ln X_3 + 0.121 \ln X_4 + 1.35 \ln X_5 \quad (15.25)$$

$$\widehat{\ln X_3} = -6.02 - 2.92 \ln X_1 + 2.17 \ln X_2 + 0.380 \ln X_4 - 3.50 \ln X_5 \quad (15.26)$$

$$\widehat{\ln X_4} = -10.0 + 3.90 \ln X_1 + 2.61 \ln X_2 - 0.620 \ln X_3 - 4.28 \ln X_5 \quad (15.27)$$

$$\widehat{\ln X_5} = -1.59 + 0.633 \ln X_1 + 0.698 \ln X_2 - 0.137 \ln X_3 - 0.103 \ln X_4 \quad (15.28)$$

2. Simulation results

$$\widehat{\ln X_{1_s}} = 2.35 - 0.7\ln X_2 + 0.224\ln X_3 + 0.183\ln X_4 + 1.24\ln X_5 \tag{15.29}$$

$$\widehat{\ln X_{2_s}} = 2.01 - 0.7\ln X_1 + 0.164\ln X_3 + 0.121\ln X_4 + 1.35\ln X_5 \tag{15.30}$$

$$\widehat{\ln X_{3_s}} = -6.02 - 2.92\ln X_1 + 2.17\ln X_2 + 0.380\ln X_4 - 3.4\ln X_5 \tag{15.31}$$

$$\widehat{\ln X_{4_s}} = -10.0 + 3.90\ln X_1 + 2.61\ln X_2 - 0.620\ln X_3 - 4.2\ln X_5 \tag{15.32}$$

$$\widehat{\ln X_{5_s}} = -1.59 + 0.633\ln X_1 + 0.698\ln X_2 - 0.134\ln X_3 - 0.102\ln X_4 \tag{15.33}$$

Matrix of elasticity (multiplier impact) coefficients of 'simulated' equations:

$$
\begin{pmatrix}
\epsilon_{11} & \epsilon_{12} & \epsilon_{13} & \epsilon_{14} & \epsilon_{15} \\
\epsilon_{21} & \epsilon_{22} & \epsilon_{23} & \epsilon_{24} & \epsilon_{25} \\
\epsilon_{31} & \epsilon_{32} & \epsilon_{33} & \epsilon_{34} & \epsilon_{35} \\
\epsilon_{41} & \epsilon_{42} & \epsilon_{43} & \epsilon_{44} & \epsilon_{45} \\
\epsilon_{51} & \epsilon_{52} & \epsilon_{53} & \epsilon_{54} & \epsilon_{55}
\end{pmatrix}
=
\begin{pmatrix}
1.00 & -0.7 & 0.224 & 0.183 & 1.24 \\
-0.7 & 1.00 & 0.164 & 0.121 & 1.35 \\
2.92 & 2.17 & 1.00 & -0.38 & -3.4 \\
3.90 & 2.61 & -0.62 & 1.00 & -4.2 \\
0.633 & 0.698 & -0.134 & -0.102 & 1.00
\end{pmatrix}
$$

The matrix form given above for the simulated coefficients of circular causation equations can be repeated.

Graphical representations of the actual versus the estimated and the simulated results of circular causation relations show that, the objective of attainment of Omanization by complementarities between certain critical variables requires substantive changes in the actual values of variables. Such simulated coefficient values are indicated in red in the simulated equations and multiplier impact matrix of the simulated coefficients. The graphical representations show these significant results for all the variables except oil and gas GDP and the steady change in the Omanization index.

The statistical results and as represented by the graph on oil and gas GDP imply that there is unutilized potential for oil and gas sector to contribute to the rest of the variables. The consequence in such a case would also reflect on further increase in the Omanization index.

Microeconomic Application of Estimated and Simulated Equations

Having completed the macroeconomic general equilibrium computational model and methodology underlying circular causation idea, and bringing these into applications to ICV issues, we now apply the completed macroeconomic model to the microeconomic level of ICV variables.

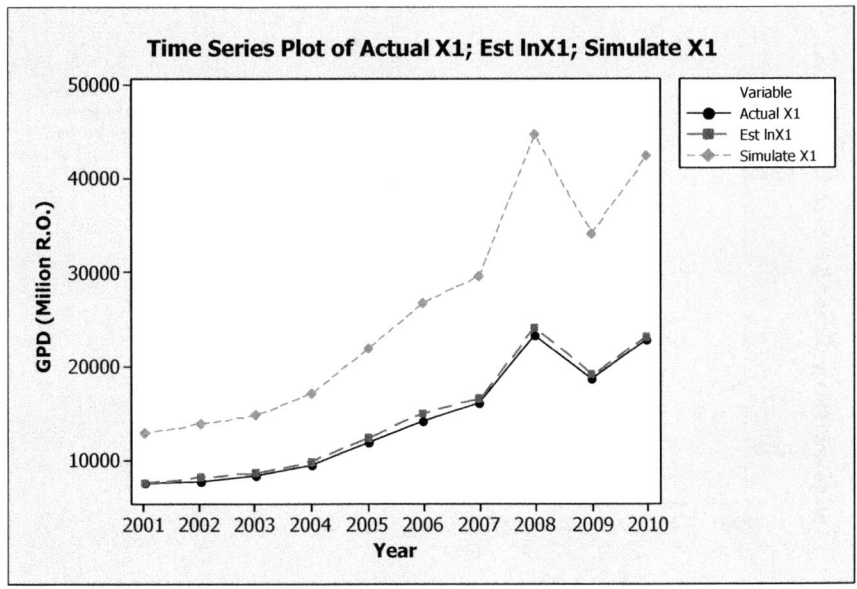

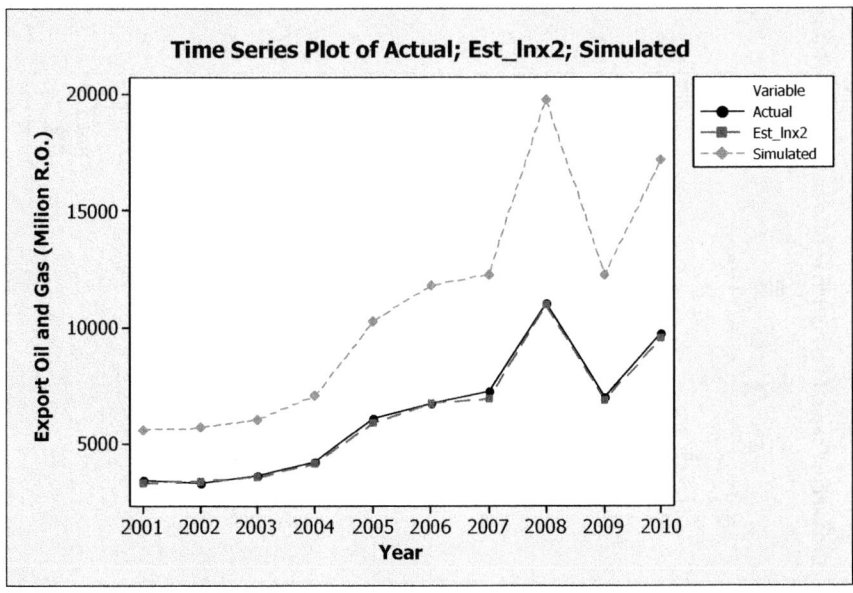

Graph 15.1 Actual, estimated and simulated omani oil and gas macroeconomic results

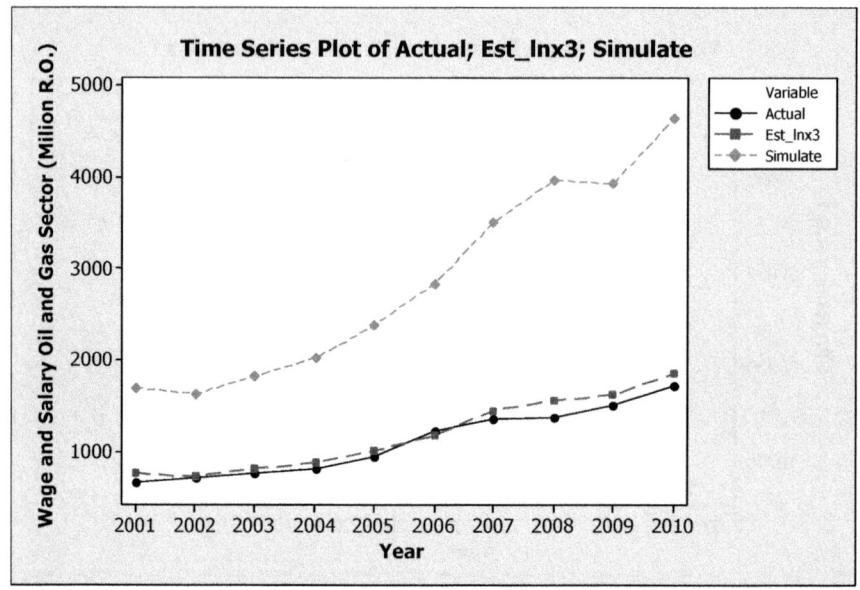

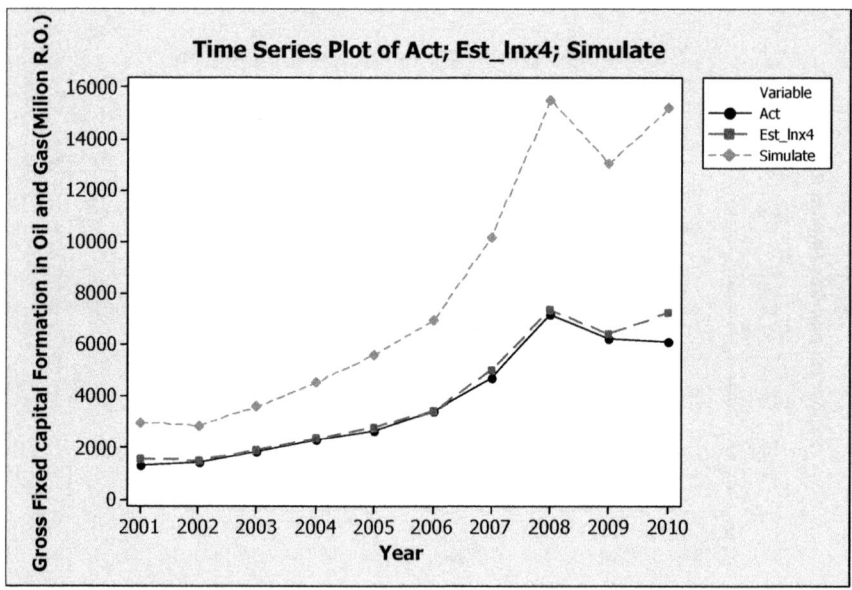

Graph 15.1 (continued)

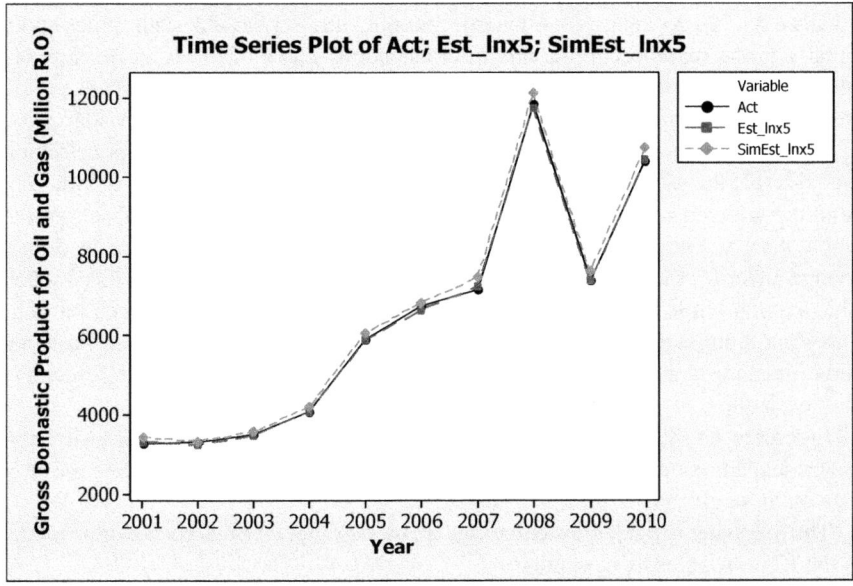

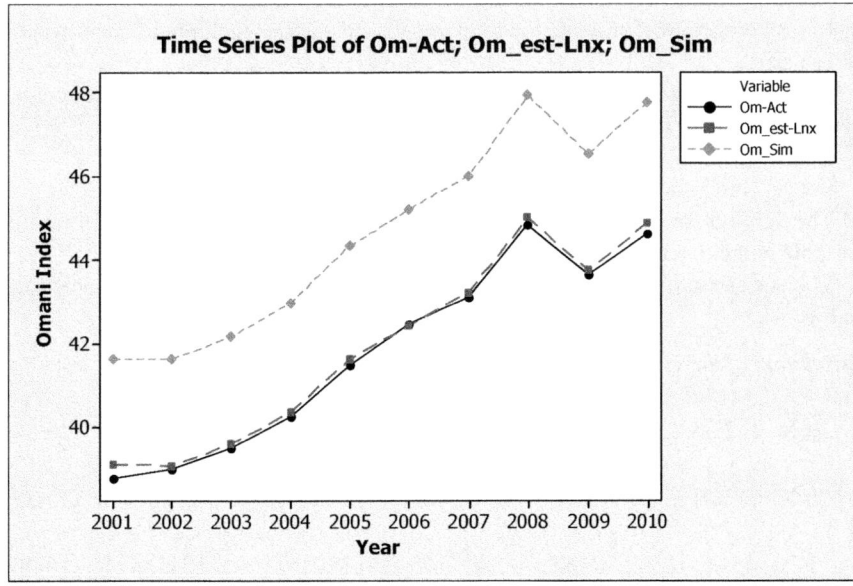

Graph 15.1   (continued)

Since X_1, X_2, X_5 are given as macroeconomic time-series data, such values apply equally to the macroeconomic and microeconomic cases of the ICV. Because X_3 and X_4 can be derived from the microeconomic ICV model we simply change these variables to their microeconomic values. The assumption underlying such adaptation of the estimated and simulated versions of the matrix form of the circular causation model is that the estimated/simulated coefficients remain unchanged for the microeconomic selected companies, operations, and contracts as these are subsets of the whole macroeconomic domain of observations. Therefore, such coefficients do not change either for the macroeconomic ICV model or the microeconomic ICV model. This assumption is borne out also by the similarity of the shapes between the estimated and simulated trends in the graphed variables. Besides, in the case of the actual and estimated values several of such variables, as shown in the graphs, are coincident with each other.

In reference to the microeconomic data provided by Oman Oil and Gas Ministry, the critical equations are on wages and salaries and capital formation. See the ICV data on these given later on in the appendix.

The following variables and equations are used to apply the macroeconomic model to the ICV-variables by operators:

Let X_3' (hence $\ln X_3'$) denote wages and salaries for Omanis.

Let X_3'' (hence $\ln X_3''$) denote the total wages and salaries including Omani wages and salaries.

Both of these two cases represent the X_3 ($\ln X_3$) variables in the macroeconomic model comprising Eqs. (15.5)–(15.9).

Likewise, let X_4' ($\ln X_4'$) denote the ICV-sourcing for Omanis.

Let X_4'' ($\ln X_4''$) denote the ICV-total sourcing.

The ICV-outsourcing data in the two cases comply with the capital formation variable in the macroeconomic model as, X_4' ($\ln X_4'$); (X_4'', $\ln X_4''$).

The corresponding structural equations for these three categories of variables are as follows:

Estimators of the estimated equations with $\ln X_3'$ (and respectively, $\ln X_3''$)

$$\widehat{\ln X_1} = 2.35 - 0.766 \ln X_2 + 0.224 \ln X_3' + 0.183 \ln X_4' + 1.24 \ln X_5 \qquad (15.34)$$

$$\widehat{\ln X_2} = 2.01 - 0.759 \ln X_1 + 0.164 \ln X_3' + 0.121 \ln X_4' + 1.35 \ln X_5 \qquad (15.35)$$

$$\widehat{\ln X_3} = -6.02 - 2.92 \ln X_1 + 2.17 \ln X_2 + 0.380 \ln X_4' - 3.50 \ln X_5 \qquad (15.36)$$

$$\widehat{\ln X_4} = -10.0 + 3.90 \ln X_1 + 2.61 \ln X_2 - 0.620 \ln X_3' - 4.28 \ln X_5 \qquad (15.37)$$

$$\widehat{\ln X_5} = -1.59 + 0.633 \ln X_1 + 0.698 \ln X_2 - 0.137 \ln X_3' - 0.103 \ln X_4' \qquad (15.38)$$

Estimators of the simulated equations

$$\widehat{\ln X_{1_s}} = 2.35 - 0.7 \ln X_2 + 0.224 \ln X_3' + 0.183 \ln X_4' + 1.24 \ln X_5 \quad (15.39)$$

$$\widehat{\ln X_{2_s}} = 2.01 - 0.7 \ln X_1 + 0.164 \ln X_3' + 0.121 \ln X_4' + 1.35 \ln X_5 \quad (15.40)$$

$$\widehat{\ln X_{3_s}} = -6.02 - 2.92 \ln X_1 + 2.17 \ln X_2 + 0.380 \ln X_4' - 3.4 \ln X_5 \quad (15.41)$$

$$\widehat{\ln X_{4_s}} = -10.0 + 3.90 \ln X_1 + 2.61 \ln X_2 - 0.620 \ln X_3' - 4.2 \ln X_5 \quad (15.42)$$

$$\widehat{\ln X_{5_s}} = -1.59 + 0.633 \ln X_1 + 0.698 \ln X_2 - 0.134 \ln X_3' - 0.102 \ln X_4' \quad (15.43)$$

Interpretation of the Estimated and Simulated Relations

The following computational methods were used to estimate and simulate the distribution of wages and salaries and the sourcing of goods and services on the basis of limited data obtained from Oman Petroleum Development and Daleel Petroleum Corporation. These microeconomic data were used to generate the estimates and simulation of the macroeconomic results across all the selected variables reflecting the effect of oil and gas ICV in the economy as a whole.

Appendix 15.1 Macroeconomic Data (Oman Statistical Yearbook Millions of OMR)

Year	GDP	Oil Export	Wages and salaries	TG Capital	GDP_OG
	X_1	X_2	X_3	X_4	X_5
2001	7459	3414.601313	650.827	1275.84562	3279.587
2002	7708	3307.203726	716.374	1444.000453	3300.282
2003	8283	3581.740077	759	1823.081108	3481.078
2004	9487	4186.474749	805.658	2320.377695	4077.692
2005	11883	6047.883221	938.058	2631.123618	5875.824
2006	14151	6720.289661	1227.49	3415.58113	6739.887
2007	16111	7199.876245	1347.84	4671.599056	7139.021
2008	23352	11024.30707	1369.23	7172.772596	11844.15
2009	18559	6947.897766	1506.45	6196.7202	7383.457
2010	22773	9703.321185	1722.71	6091.593146	10388.39

X_1, X_2, X_3, X_4 and X_5 are Total GDP, Oil and Gas Exports, Wages and Salaries, Total Gross Capital Formation and Total Petroleum Activities (GDP Oil and Gas) of Oman respectively

Appendix 15.2 Excel Tables and Graphs (Macro Interface Results)

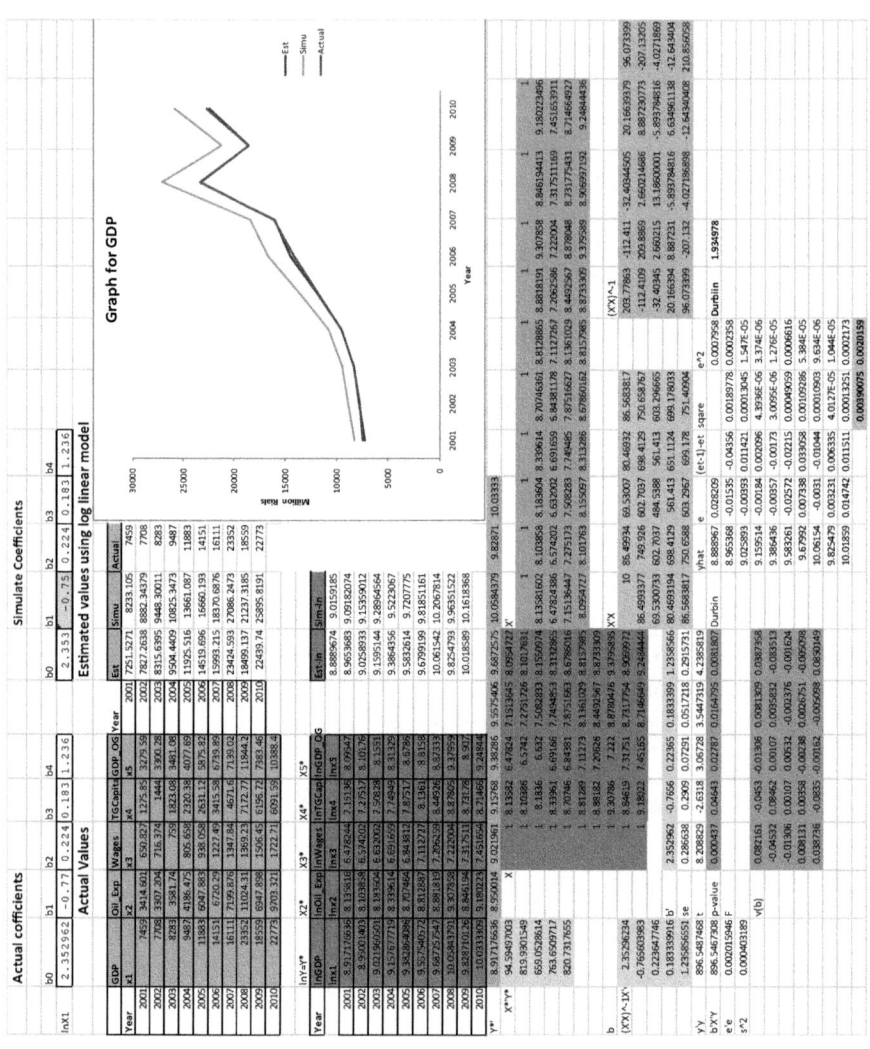

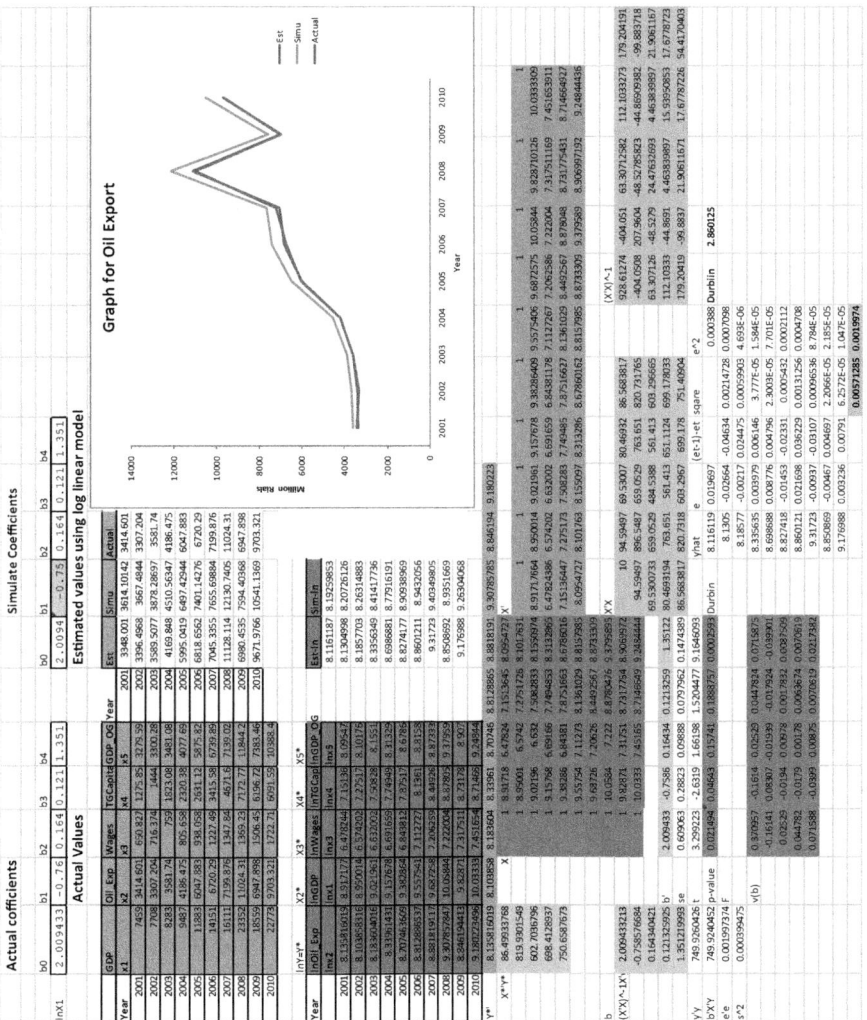

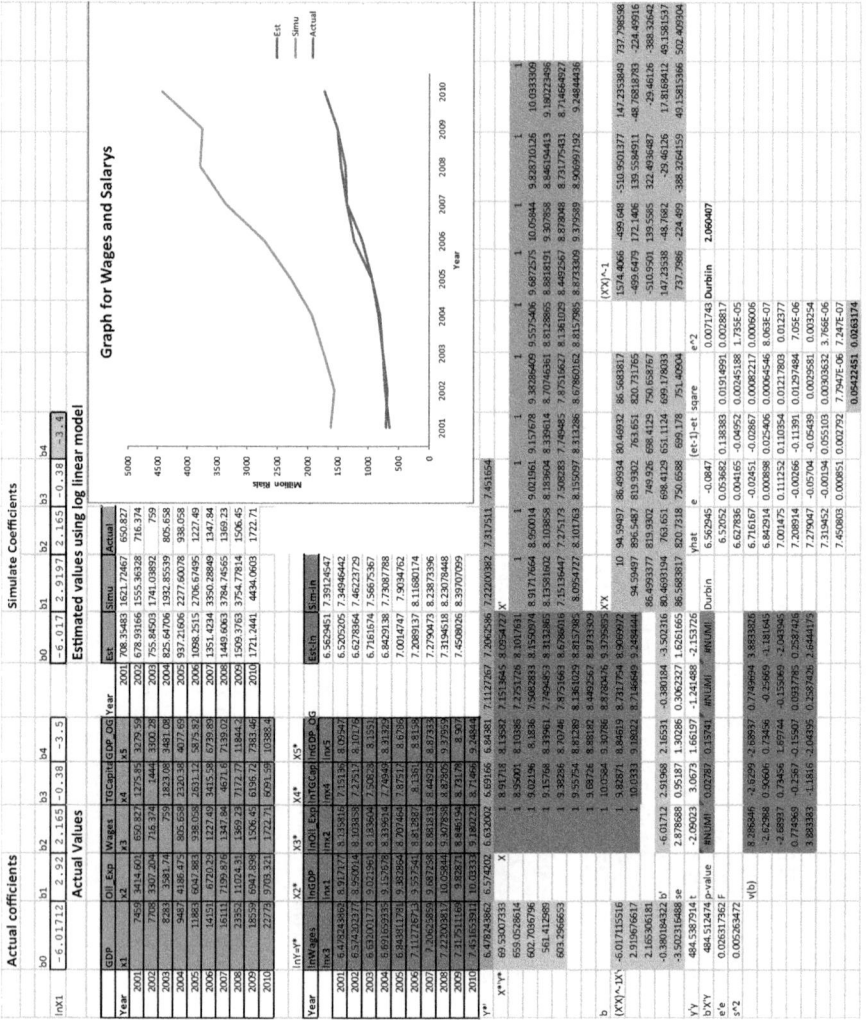

Graph for Wages and Salarys

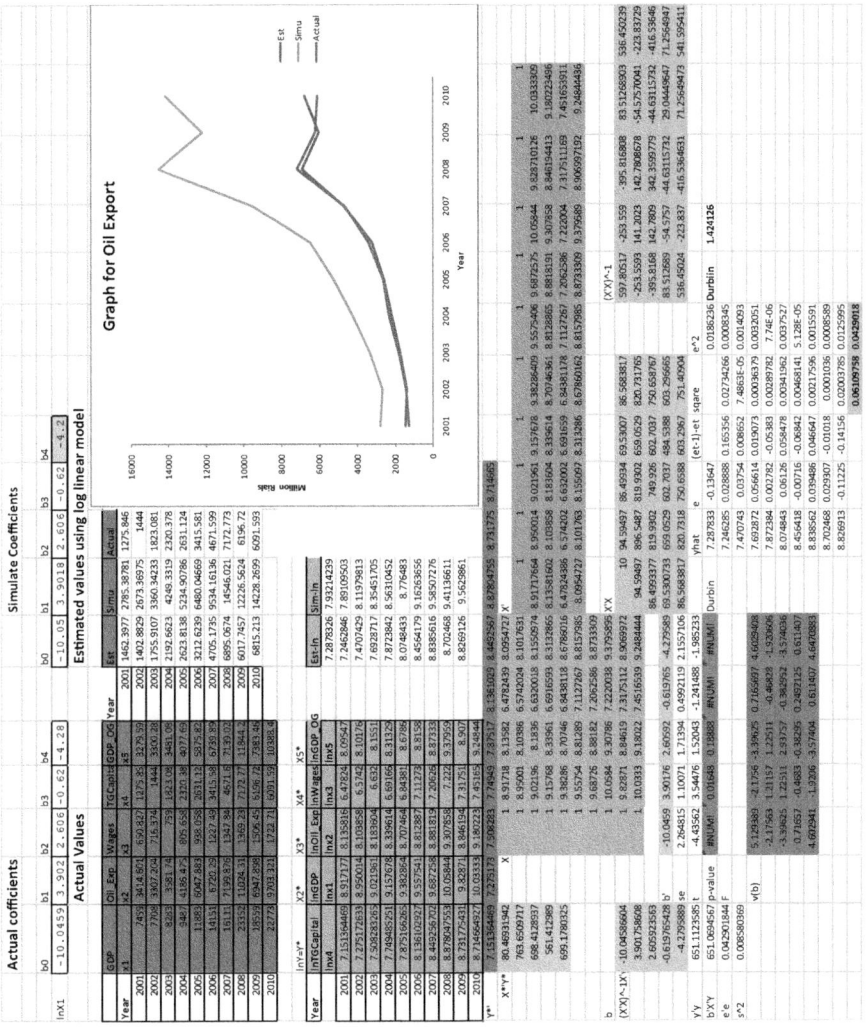

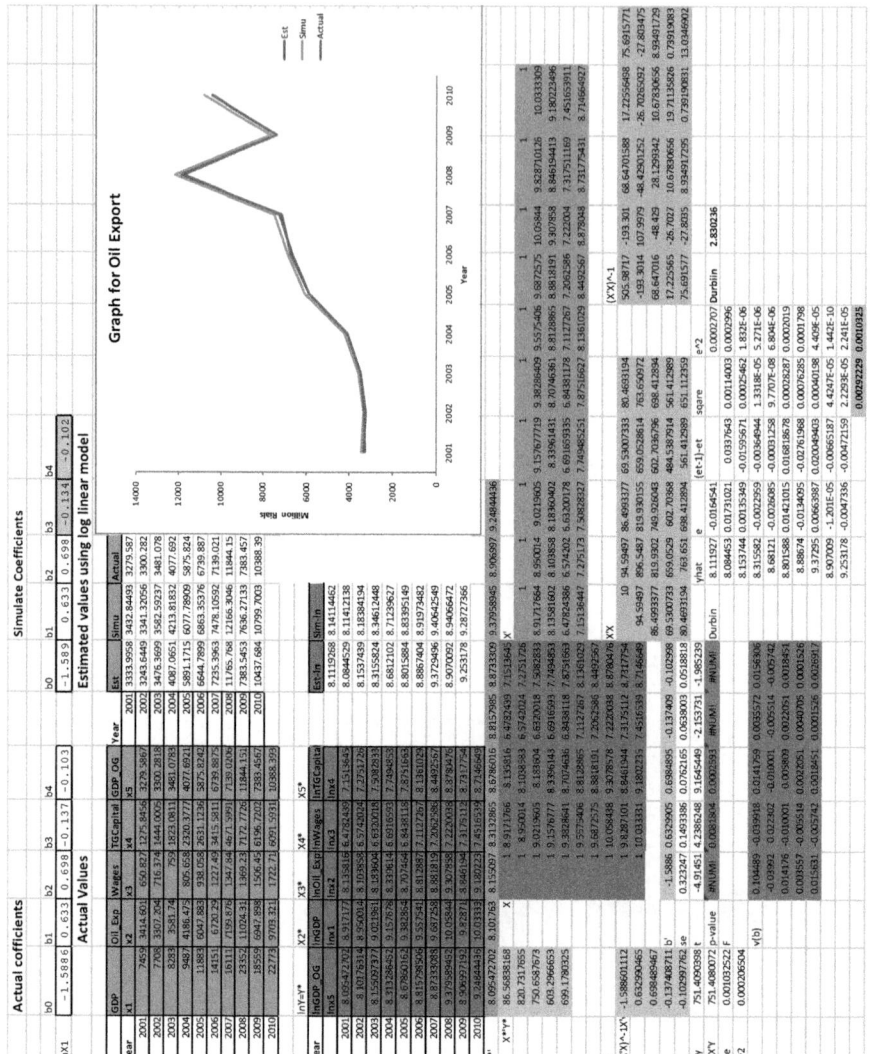

Actual cofficients

	b0	b1	b2	b3	b4
lnX1	2.353	-0.7656	0.2236	0.18334	1.2359
lnX2	2.0094	-0.75858	0.1643	0.12133	1.3512
Log-linear lnX3	-6.017	2.919677	2.1653	-0.3802	-3.502
lnX4	-10.05	3.901759	2.6059	-0.6198	-4.28
lnX5	-1.589	0.63299	0.6985	-0.1374	-0.103

Simulate Coefficients

	b0	b1	b2	b3	b4
	2.352962	-0.75	0.22365	0.18334	1.2359
	2.009433	-0.75	0.16434	0.121326	1.3512
	-6.01712	2.92	2.16531	-0.38018	-3.4
	-10.0459	3.902	2.60592	-0.61977	-4.2
	-1.5886	0.633	0.69849	-0.134	-0.102

Actual Values

Year	GDP x1	Oil_Exp x2	Wages x3	TGCapital x4	GDP_OG x5
2001	7459	3414.601	650.827	1275.84562	3279.586748
2002	7708	3307.204	716.374	1444.00045	3300.281807
2003	8283	3581.74	759.18	2308.111	3481.07828
2004	9487	4196.475	805.658	2320.3777	4077.692128
2005	11883	6047.883	938.058	2631.12362	5875.824208
2006	14151	6720.29	1227.49	3415.58113	6739.887458
2007	16111	7119.876	1347.84	4671.59906	7139.020637
2008	23352	11024.31	1365.23	7172.7726	11844.15117
2009	18559	6947.998	1506.45	6196.7002	7383.456677
2010	22773	9703.32	1722.71	6091.9935	10388.39254

Estimated values using log linear model

Year	GDP A-logX^1	Oil_Exp A-logX^2	Wages A-logX^3	TGCapital A-logX^4	GDP_OG A-logX^5
2001	7251.5271	3348.00101	708.354829	1462.398	3333.995777
2002	7827.2638	3396.49678	678.931657	1402.883	3243.644864
2003	8315.6395	3589.50767	755.845033	1755.911	3476.369851
2004	9504.4409	4169.84798	825.64706	2192.662	4087.065058
2005	11925.516	5995.04187	937.216057	2623.814	5891.171486
2006	14519.696	6818.65619	1098.25152	3212.624	6644.789941
2007	15993.215	7045.33555	1351.4234	4705.173	7235.396322
2008	23424.593	11128.1144	1449.60635	6895.067	11765.76809
2009	18499.137	6980.45347	1509.37632	6017.746	7383.545327
2010	22439.74	9671.97664	1721.24414	6815.213	10437.68359

Simulation by changing coefficient

GDP A-logX^1	Oil Exp A-logX^2	Wages A-logX^3	TGCapital A-logX^4	Year
8233.105	3614.10142	1621.724672	2785.3878	1521.446
8882.344	3667.4844	1555.363283	2673.3697	1590.501
9448.3	3878.28697	1741.03892	3360.3423	1840.606
10825.35	4510.56347	1932.855394	4249.3319	2362.311
13661.09	6497.42944	2277.600778	5234.9079	3545.682
16660.19	7401.14276	2706.674949	6480.0467	4307.079
18870.69	7655.69884	3350.288492	9534.1614	4961.709
27086.25	12130.7405	3784.74565	14546.021	8560.543
21137.32	7594.40368	3754.778143	12226.562	5534.82
25895.82	10541.1369	4434.060305	14228.27	7168.216

Omani index

Year	Om-Act	Om_est-ln	Om_Sim
2001	38.77807	38.96779	39.8593215
2002	39.00501	38.94713	39.911446
2003	39.50095	39.46399	40.5166245
2004	40.25172	40.21977	41.3924896
2005	41.48791	41.48163	42.7689367
2006	42.43506	42.28859	43.678141
2007	43.09792	43.09211	44.550661
2008	44.84594	44.86933	46.4890051
2009	43.63119	43.60528	45.1596471
2010	44.62832	44.72647	46.2623467

Om_Act — Omani index from estimated x values
Om_est-x — Omani index from estimated lnx values
Om_ex_lnx — Omani index from estimated antilog x values

Omani Index

Appendix 15.3 Excel Tables and Graphs (Micro Interface Results)

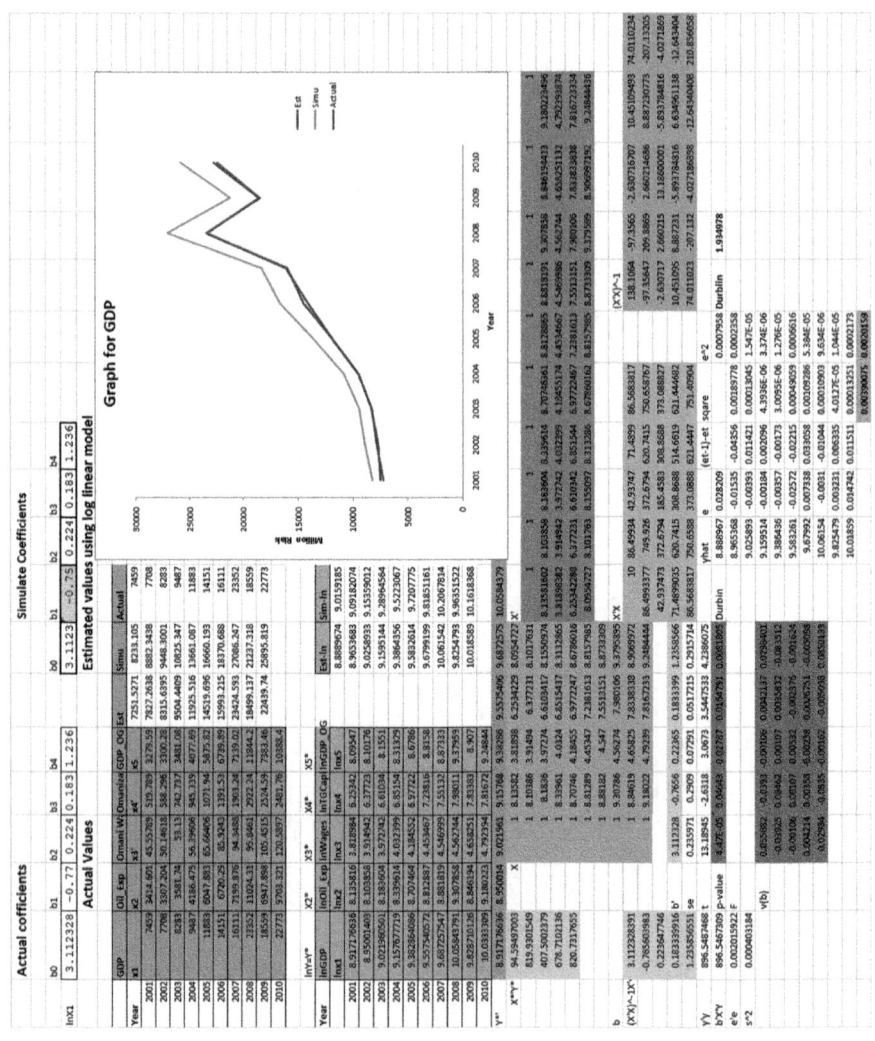

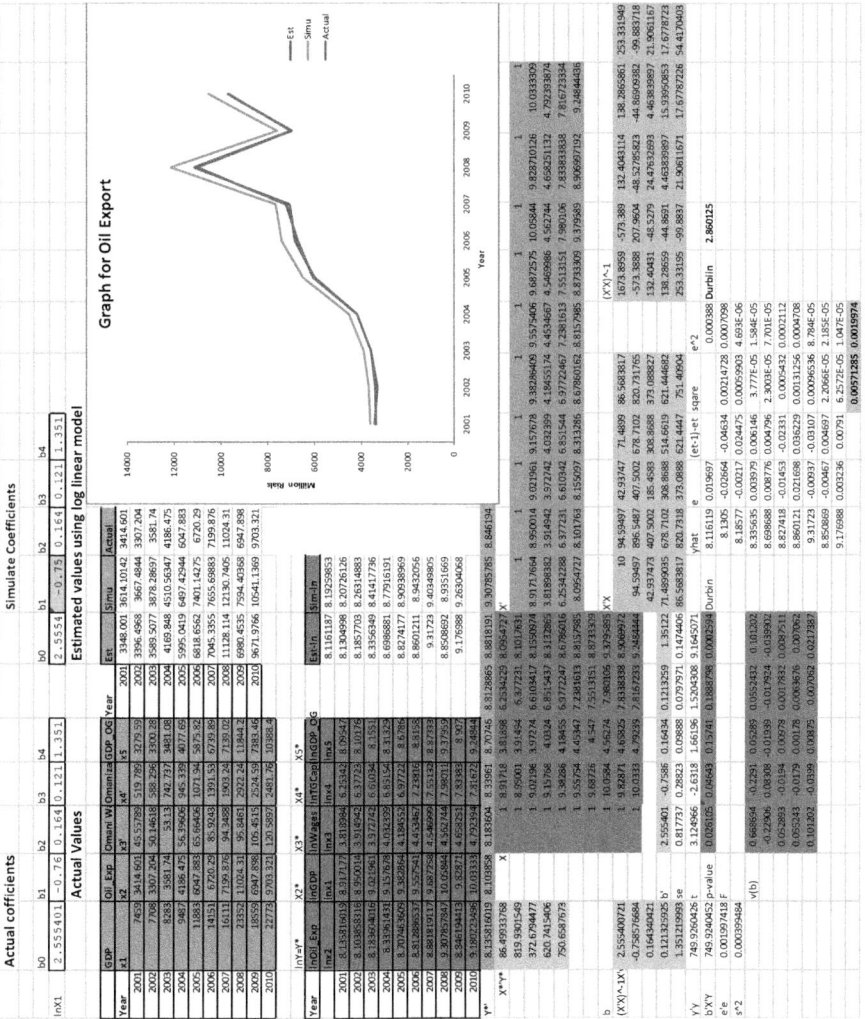

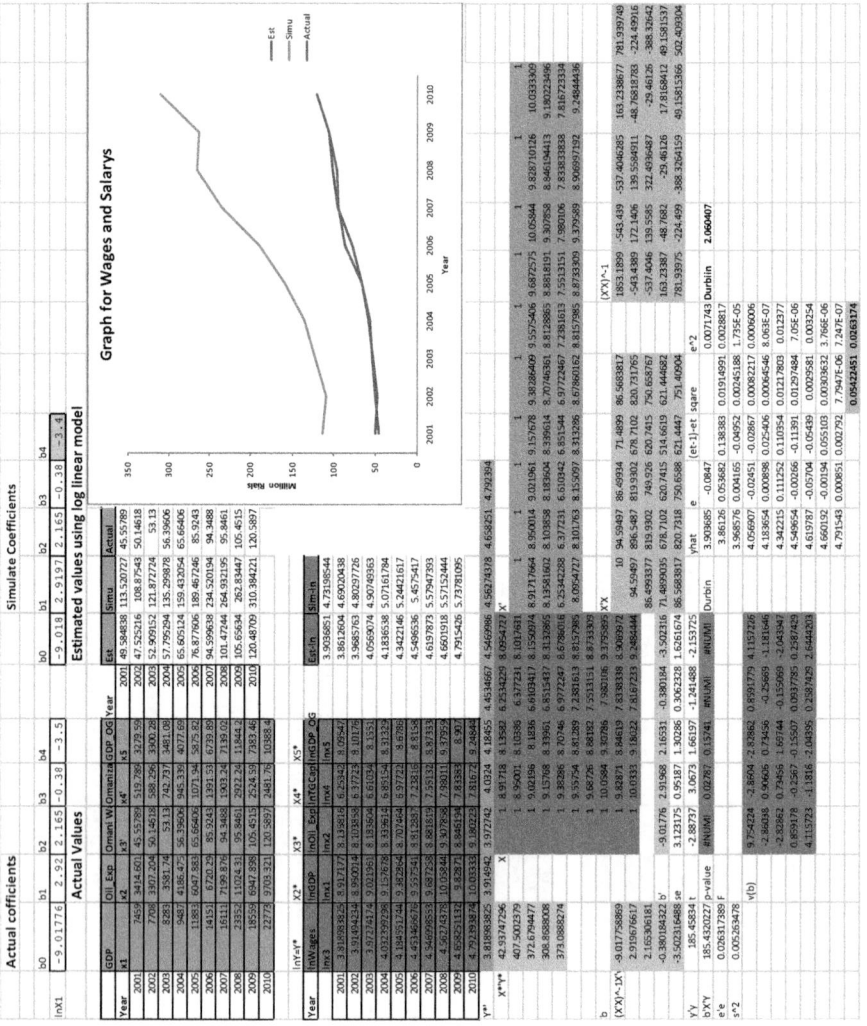

Graph for Wages and Salarys

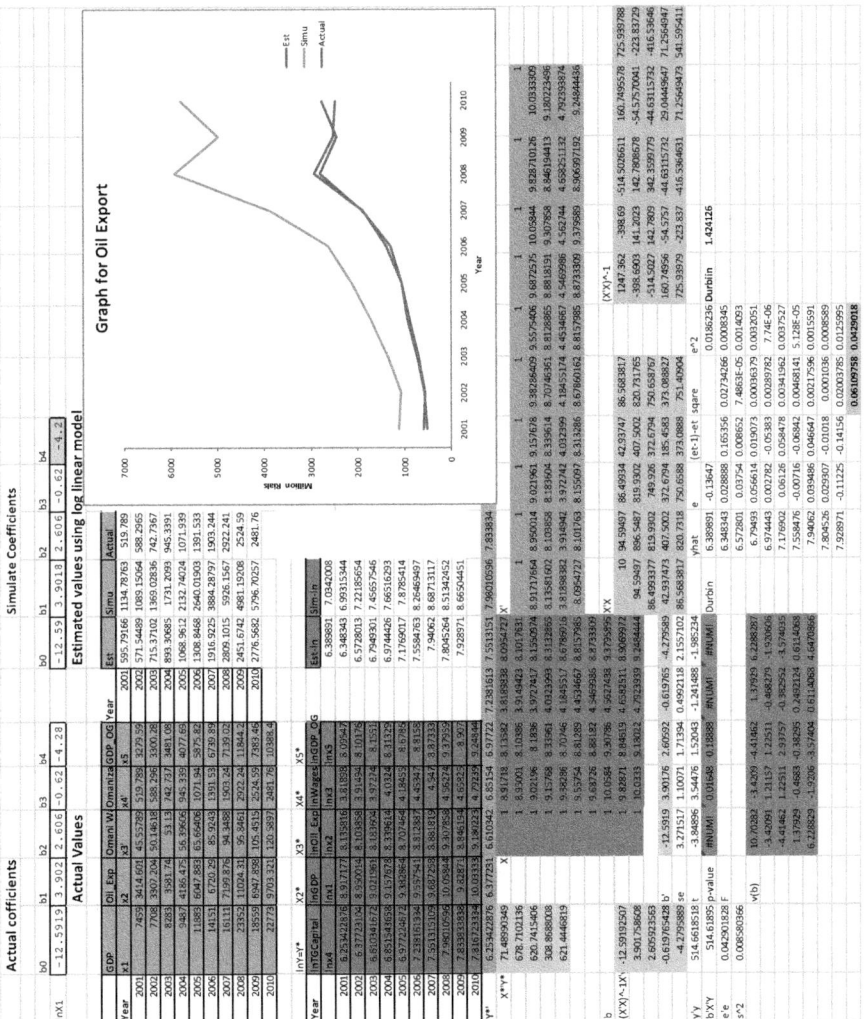

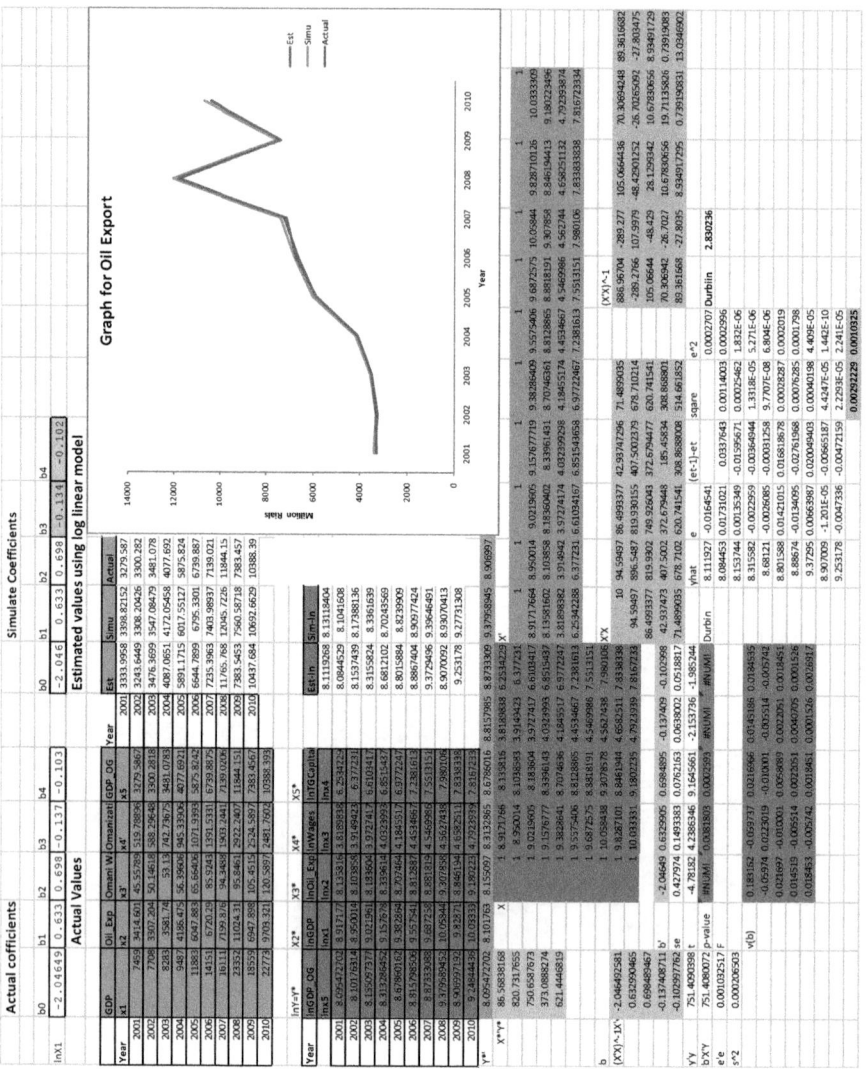

Graph for Oil Export

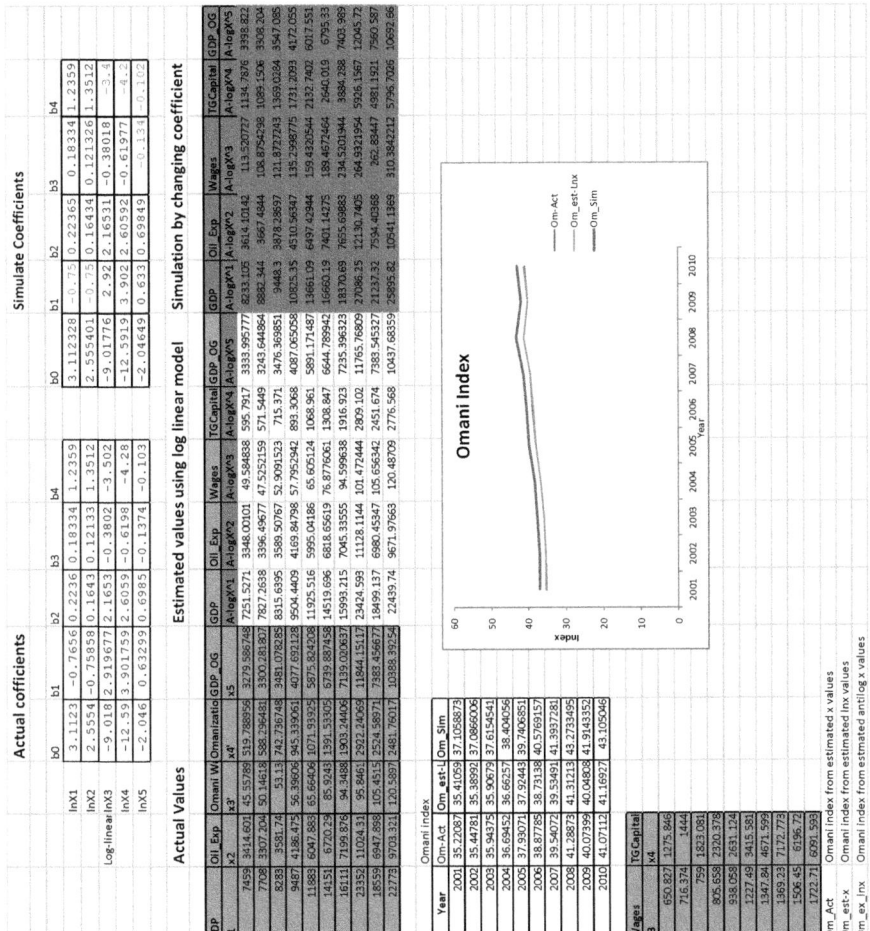

References

Choudhury, M. A., & Al-Sahlawi, M. (2000). Oil and non-oil sectors in Saudi Arabia. *OPEC Review, XXIV,* 3.

Choudhury, M. A., & Hossain, M. S. (2006). *Development planning in the Sultanate of Oman.* Lewiston: Edwin Mellen Press.

Choudhury, M. A., Al-Muharrami, S., Ahmed, M. S., & Hossain, M. S. (2015). Circular causation model of the oil and gas sector relative to the non-oil sector in the Sultanate of Oman. *International Journal of Management Studies, 21,* 1.

Toner, P. (1999). Gunnar Myrdal (1898–1987): Circular and cumulative causation as the methodology of the social sciences. *Main currents in cumulative causation, the dynamics of growth and development.* Hampshire: Macmillan Press Ltd.

Tordo, S., Warner, M., Monzano, O. E., & Anouti, Y. (2013). *Local content policies in the oil and gas sector,* World bank study. Washington D.C: World Bank.

Chapter 16
Conclusion

Masudul Alam Choudhury

Abstract Mathematics is logical language. In the context of the inner and explained dynamics of *Tawhid* as law pertaining to the theory of 'everything', mathematics proves as a profound medium of thought. In such a projection of the study of socio-scientific philosophy of 'everything' the inner details of *Tawhid* as law extends beyond sheer mechanical usage. In the *Tawhidi* methodological worldview mathematics as logical formalism becomes the medium of construction of the thoughtful mind. In the most extensive of studies in the area of *Tawhid* and *shari'ah* in respect of Islamic studies in economics, finance, science, and society, mathematics has proved to be mechanical tool of use in quantification. In this book we have soared to advanced heights of mathematical formalism in our study of *Tawhid* as law contrary to the weak foundation of *shari'ah* in the true sense of universal methodology and analysis. Thus we have addressed the issue of abstracto-empiricism and its sustained continuity across knowledge, space, and time dimensions in the generality and details of the theory of 'everything'. The attained limit of our mathematical formalism is now the advanced field of contravariant and covariant tensor applied to the theory of conjoint intra-system and inter-system intertemporality. Much more can proceed thereon.

A Non-technical Overview of the Chapter

The resilience of *Tawhidi* methodology combined with its substantive approach to empirical application stands as true challenge to *shari'ah* in all its forms. That is because the basis of *shari'ah* as human concocted area of jurisprudence does not bear the possibility of addressing the holistic domain of *Qur'anic* universe of the Signs of Allah. This field of critical investigation to unravel the true and substantive meaning of the universal and unique of law is not to be found in the jurisprudential context of *shari'ah* as it is limited to earthly law and having no organic dynamics of unity of knowledge in it.

M. A. Choudhury (✉)
Faculty of Economics, Trisakti University, Jakarta, Indonesia
e-mail: masudc60@yahoo.ca

© Springer Nature Singapore Pte Ltd. 2019
M. A. Choudhury (ed.), *The Tawhidi Methodological Worldview*,
https://doi.org/10.1007/978-981-13-6585-0_16

The important areas derived in this book from the *Tawhidi* primal ontology of unity of knowledge and its application to the generality and details of the world-system are as follows: The substantive methodology is derived from the *Tawhidi* ontological, epistemological, phenomenological, and sustainability stages in the form of the theory of *Tawhidi* String Relations (TSR). An extensive area of application of the resultant abstracto-empiricism is proved in substantial details. The detailed structures, as of the nature of organic unity of knowledge of the world-system over knowledge, space, and time dimensions, are formalized. One important analytical form derived from *Tawhidi* law is the formulation and empirical evaluation of the wellbeing function. The emergent quantitative criterion in its formal and applied form with derived inferences in socioeconomic development studies is utilized in its substantive form. Various real experience problems are studied. Cogent levels of mathematical logic are used to render the intra-system and inter-systemic dynamics of various ingredients of analytical functions in their context of continuity, sustainability, and internal consistency of logical arguments.

Introduction

In this book chapters on *Tawhid* as the law contrary to a historically erroneous belief of *shari'ah* as law have centered on the *Tawhidi* methodology in terms of *Tawhidi* String Relations (TSR). Being the first of scholarly publications in expounding the methodological worldview of monotheistic unity of knowledge and reconstruction of the design of the unifying world-system in generality and particular this forms a especially analytical work. It lays down the essential foundation of the greater transdisciplinary domain of socio-scientific inquiry that overarches the theory of 'everything' from the viewpoint of monotheistic holism. The emergent *Tawhidi* methodology of unity of knowledge thus encompasses the fields of the essential methodology of Islamic economics, finance, science, and society. The chapters presented in this book along with their many scholarly contributions by the co-authors lay down the missing and much sought for methodological foundations of these fields of analytical formalism pointing further to an expanse of potentiality that can be studied in generality and details. The result of such analytical investigation in the derivation, formalism, and rendering of the abstract and applied form of the emergent theory and methodology of TSR is consequently a study in heterodox scholarly thought. This comprises the socio-scientific philosophy of knowledge of the theory of 'everything' and its applications. A bold challenge is thus the logical outcome of such heterodox scholarship to scrupulously venture beyond and into the domain of knowledge and reasoning that reject the mainstream embodiments. In fact the result of such bold and over-turning findings in theory and applications is a challenge to the conceptions of mainstream 'Islamic' economics, finance, science, and society.

TSR is ever new in its monotheistic *Tawhidi* explication of visionary thought that is most often contrary to the mainstream Islamic approaches that have remained inextricable in their wrappings of *shari'ah* as Islamic law by human concoction. An example of such a flawed exposition can be found in Tag el-Din's book (2013) and the unquestioned revelation of *shari'ah* as the infallible law contrary to the essentiality of *Tawhid* as law establishing the primal ontological foundation of the *Qur'anic* worldview. The present work on TSR-lectures along with its complementary publications on *Tawhidi* unity of knowledge and the evolutionary learning world-system rejects this traditionally held human concocted belief on *shari'ah* as law. Instead, TSR invokes the *Qur'anic* logical formalism to supplant *shari'ah* by *Tawhid* as the law with its methodological systemic holism in primal ontology, the emergent epistemology, and convergence to phenomenology of unity of knowledge in abstracto-empirical form. On the other hand, *maqasid as-shari'ah*, given a thorough criticism of rejecting the recently human concocted idea of *shari'ah-compliance*, is treated as a historical example of social ordering based on rules, customs, and cultural vintages of space-time variations. These fields form *fiqh* (jurisprudence) and *fatawa* (opinions).

In such a theocratic experience while the *Qur'anic* primal ontology premise of *Tawhid* is referred to, this only implies that, *Tawhid* is the permanent law to which 'everything' is referred. No Islamic reasoning, and thereby the universality and uniqueness of Islamic law can commence in the first place from any aspect of *shari'ah—maqasid as-shari'ah, shari'ah-compliance*. The subservience of Islamic thought and reasoning 'everything' it has touched has been the great impediment to Muslim scholarly advancement over time. This decadence is not seen to end. *Tawhid* thereby, stands unquestionably as the singular universal and unique law for 'everything'. Contarily, *shari'ah* is an experience in discourse of rules of choices, good against bad. This choices must firstly be determined by the application of *Tawhid* as the law of 'everything' in respect of unity of knowledge (consilience).

The beginning and end of TSR in its abstracto-empirico-applied explications through the processes of unitary evolutionary learning as the reconstructive base of the world-system forms the completeness of the unitary geodesic of the theory of 'everything'. Geodesic is the complex evolutionary learning and confirmatory path ascribing *Tawhidi* unity of knowledge as the law. The emergent goal out of TSR-model results in the evaluation and reconstruction of the theory of 'everything'. The geodesic being an expression for the measure of the shortest distance on a curvilinear surface, the TSR-geodesic means that the methodology and formalism of the TSR-evolutionary learning and complex path applies everywhere along events of historical consciousness. Consequently, the ensuing abstracto-empirical method from the TSR-formalism, namely evaluation meaning estimation followed by simulation in simulacra possibilities of the coefficients of the quantified wellbeing criterion, subject to circular causation relations between sets of endogenous variables to test unity of knowledgebetween variables, pervades across historical consciousness. The micro-aspect of geodesic, spanning the moral-material knowledge-induced continuity across the domain of knowledge, and knowledge-induced space and time dimensions of conscious historicism, implies that every event along such continuums must be sensitive to moral and ethical actions and responses.

Such an ideal of historical consciousness was discussed in a deeply intellectual way by Ortega (Gonzalez, 2005, p. 24) as the experience of interiority and exteriority being integrated together. That is the construct of subjectivity of consciousness and its spanning of all of creation: "The reality of life consists, then, not in what it is for him who sees it from without, but in what it is for him who is it from within, for him who is living it and in the measure that he lives it." The *Tawhidi* worldview projects such an idea of phenomenological consciousness in greater extant and depth of meaning by its bestowal of unity of being and becoming defining concrescence and reality of self and other. In this regard the *Qur'an* (43:4–10) affirms Prophet Muhammad's experience of true reality by his heart and vision in the unitary holism of monotheism: "It is but a revelation revealed; taught to him by the Extremely Powerful—the one of vigor. He settled, While he was at the highest horizon. Then he came near, and hovered around. He was within two bows' length, or closer. Then He revealed to His servant what He revealed." On the same phenomenological message of goodness pervading the material order in sustaining the unified and embedded moral-material continuum in universal historicism, the *Qur'an* (6:11) declares: "Say, 'Travel through the land; then observe how was the end of the deniers (of truth).'"

TSR has studied this fact as an analytical causation that explains the dynamics of the emergent geodesics by means of $\{\theta(\varepsilon), \mathbf{x}(\theta(\varepsilon))\}$ in the wellbeing function (*maslaha*) $W(\mathbf{x}(\theta(\varepsilon)))$. This objective criterion is subject to the circular causation relations spanning the entirety of the geodesics in the intra-system and inter-system continuums denoted by $(\Omega, S) \rightarrow$ Multiverse World-System, $WS\{\theta(\varepsilon), \mathbf{x}(\theta(\varepsilon)\} \rightarrow (\Omega, S)$. The bracketed term $\{.\}$ denotes spanning over multiverse continuums. TSR-formalism explained the role of $\{\varepsilon\}$ as intrinsic belief-induction in knowledge-formation, $\{\theta(\varepsilon)\}$, and thereby its induced embedding of the multiverse world-system, $\{\{\theta(\varepsilon), \mathbf{x}(\theta(\varepsilon))\}$. The lectures presented in this book explained every event along evolutionary learning. The lectures presented in this book explained every event along evolutionary learning historical geodesics of continuums as a super-topological Closure. That is, (Ω, S) is in the Beginning $\leftrightarrow (\Omega, S)$ in the End. The Closure is thereby Unbounded by the Supercardinal measure of (Ω, S).[1]

In conclusion and in what follows, a multivariate, non-linear (Gel'fand, 1961) mathematical explanation is made of the *Tawhidi* geodesic in relation to continuums encompassing the entirety of intra-systems and inter-systems. Since such occurrences happen at every event in knowledge, space, and time dimensions of historical consciousness, so the multivariate representation of the structure of *Tawhidi* multiverses in the unity of knowledge, space, and time dimensions of the universe of 'everything', envelops creation in the form of supercardinal completeness. This phenomenon is explained in Fig. 16.1 of this Conclusion chapter. This figure explains that, even though creation assumed an irregular shape of emanation in mind (seemingly the complex appearance of *Qur'anic* text), and physicalism (creation started off in murky smoke), order and harmony as the wider meaning of just balance ensued.[2]

---

[1] The precept of Closure and Unboundedness is expounded in the majestic *Qur'an* (112:1–4) as the central meaning and essence of creation: "In the name of Allah, the Most Compassionate, the Most Merciful, say: He Allah is One. Allah is He on whom all depend. He begets not, nor is He begotten. And none is like Him." Al-Shaykh al-Saduk (2009) writes a detailed commentary on these verses.

[2] *Qur'an* (20:2): "We have not sent down the *Qur'an* to thee to be (an occasion) for thy distress."

Qur'an (41:11): "Then He directed Himself to the heaven while it was smoke and said to it and to the earth, "Come [into being], willingly or by compulsion." They said, "We have come willingly."

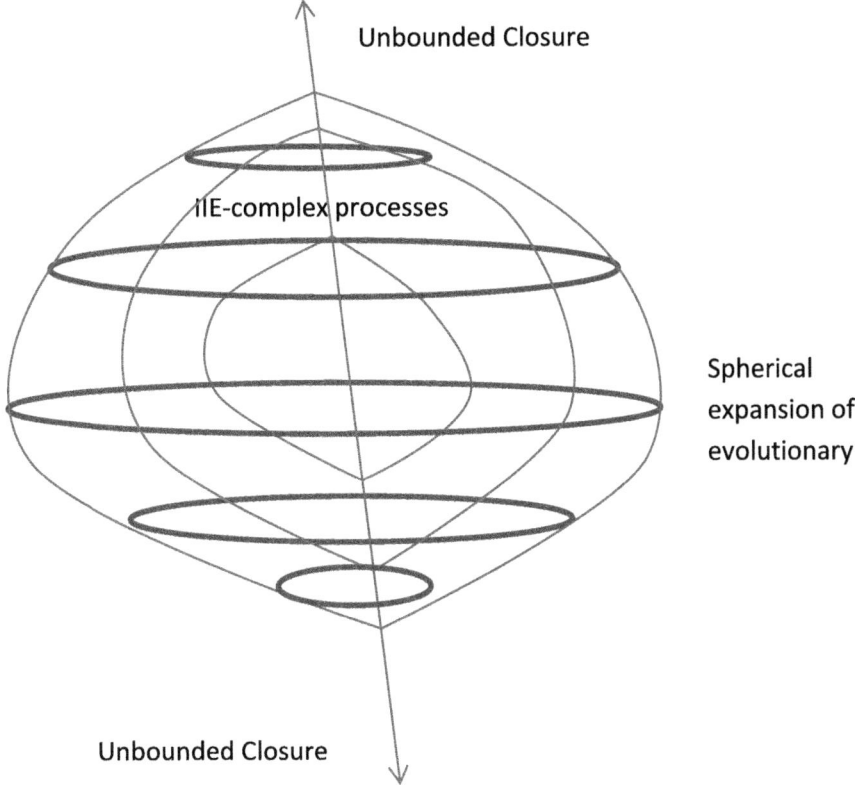

Fig. 16.1 Uniformity of evolutionary learning in all directions from the beginning to the end of *Tawhidi* methodological worldview of equivalence and completion of the evolutionary learning universe

The nature of *Tawhidi* geodesic is thereby one of order out of chaos to assume meaning and explanation in 'everything'. Figure 16.1 depicts the uniform and logical self-containment of 'everything' in the ultimate order of Closure and Unboundedness.

The expansion of the intra-system into continuums of inter-system, explained below as covariant-contravariant tensor across evolutionary learning spanned by knowledge, and knowledge-induced space, and time dimensions is a corrugated solid surface in the small scale dimension; and tend into uniformity in the very large scale evolutionary learning tensor systems (see below). Such a uniformity of spherical universe comprising all multiverses is a never-ending phenomenon. Hence creation is Unbounded in terms of knowledge, space, and time (dhar) across the world-system. The advance of creation is towards the differentiated realms of truth (Heaven = Jannah) and falsehood (Hell). As well as the Closure of moral-material experience is attained by the evolutionary learning process along the *Tawhidi* geodesic of Beginning and End of evolutionary learning.

The mathematical formulation of this multivariate explanation of *Tawhidi* geodesic is a logical outcome of the analytics of TSR. The result makes it possible to bring out the precepts of universality and uniqueness of *Tawhidi* methodological worldview prevailing in generality and particulars of knowledge, space, and time dimensions. Thereby, the economic, finance, science, and society as transdisciplinary studies are located with the particulars of the generalized *Tawhidi* world-system.

Tawhidi Geodesic Theorem of Tensor Calculus

We now formalize the *Tawhidi* geodesic theorem as follows:

Let $WS\{\theta(\varepsilon), \mathbf{x}(\theta(\varepsilon)), t(\theta(\varepsilon))\}$ denote the generalized universe, and the generality of multiverses as particulars. The multiverses are formed by the IIE-learning processes of evolutionary learning as governed by the precept of unity of knowledge (*Tawhid*) and its construct of the knowledge-induced world-system. Such a construct of continuums of intra-systems simultaneously evolving into inter-system stages of events denoted by $\{\{\theta(\varepsilon), \mathbf{x}(\theta(\varepsilon)), t(\theta(\varepsilon))\} = \mathbf{z}\{\theta(\varepsilon)\}_{ij}^{IIE}; i, j = 1, 2, \ldots, n$. The IIE-learning processes and endogenous inter-variable relations denote circular causation between variables of finite number 'n' occurring at every point in time within given processes where new knowledge-flows emerge, as explained in the TSR-figure in this book. At each of such event points in continuum, IIE-learning processes span across intra-systems qua inter-systems, sustaining themselves ever after, over processes denoting time $(t = P)[\theta(\varepsilon)\}_{ij}^{IIE}]$.

Using matrix notation [.] we write,

$$[\mathbf{z}\{\theta(\varepsilon)\}_{ij}^{IIE}]_{t_1=P_1} \rightarrow [\mathbf{z}\{\theta(\varepsilon)\}_{ij}^{IIE}]_{t_2=P_{21}} \rightarrow \ldots \rightarrow [\mathbf{z}\{\theta(\varepsilon)\}_{ij}^{IIE}]_{t=P}, \qquad (16.1)$$

in continuum by sustainability of knowledge-induced transformation.

A further monotonic transformation of expression (16.1) is the wellbeing (*maslaha*) function evaluated over IIE-learning processes, compounded across intra-systems leading to inter-systems $(s_k, k - 1, 2, \ldots n)$ in time identical with processes $(t = P)$ by the corresponding sets of ccircular causation relations between variables governed by *Tawhidi* unity of knowledge:

$$\left[\prod_{s_1} W_{s_1}(\mathbf{z}\{\theta(\varepsilon)\}_{ijs_1}^{IIE})\right]_{t_1=P_1} \rightarrow \left[\prod_{s_2} W_{s_2}(\mathbf{z}\{\theta(\varepsilon)\}_{ijs_2}^{IIE})\right]_{t_2=P_2} \rightarrow \ldots \rightarrow \left[\prod_{s_n} W_{s_n}(\mathbf{z}\{\theta(\varepsilon)\}_{ijs_n}^{IIE})\right]_{t=P},$$
$$(16.2)$$

Each term within expression (16.2) is evaluated by the corresponding circular causation relations in processes over time, like,

$$z_i = f_i((\mathbf{z_j}\{\theta(\varepsilon)\}_{js_1}^{IIE}$$

$$\prod_{s_1} \theta(\varepsilon)_{s_1}^{IIE} = \prod_{s_1} F(\mathbf{z}\{\theta(\varepsilon)\}_{ijs_1}^{IIE}) \tag{16.3}$$

$i, j = 1, 2, .., n; i \neq j.$ s_k denotes inter-systems for $k = 1, 2, ..., n$
$t = P$ in continuity of $\{\theta(\varepsilon)_{s_1}^{IIE}\}$.

The expressions (16.1)–(16.3) form the generalized form of multidimensional system model with its particulars, such as economics, finance, science, and society represented by s_k, $k = 1, 2, ..., 3$ etc. The uniform methodological formulation and application of the model comprising (16.1)–(16.3) to all sub-systems in the multidimensional system-space establishes the concept of generality, and thus of generality with its particulars. *Tawhidi* methodological worldview enables this result to actualize; and it prevails over the multidimensional entirety.

The resilience of the emergent methods from *Tawhidi* methodology is incredibly vast. One of the ways by which analytical resilience is realized for further extensions is the imminent mathematics connected with expressions (16.1)–(16.3). The mathematical nature of *Tawhidi* multiverses of 'everything' projects the delineation of truth. Therefore, the nature of the learning and construction of the conscious universe is indeed mathematical in nature by logical property. That is, not simply in how mathematics is used overtly as the invention of man. Rather, mathematics conveys the logic of truth contrary to falsehood. In this regard writes Lewis (2014): "Some people argue that math is just a tool invented by scientists to explain the natural world. But Tegmark contends the mathematical structure found in the natural world shows that math exists in reality, not just in the human mind." (visited 6/9/2018) (https://www.livescience.com/42839-the-universe-is-math.html).

Tensor Formulation of Wellbeing Evaluation Intra-system and Inter-system

So on a humble deduction from the Eqs. (16.1)–(16.3) we can suggest the tensor characterization of *Tawhidi* methodological reality of unity of knowledge (truth) embedded in 'everything' along with its contradistinction of 'de-knowledge' as the oppositely (i.e. falsehood of dualism and multipolarity) co-existing. We formulate a tensorial expression in the *Tawhidi* model of a complex type from which human mind can derive elegant mathematical forms as follows.

For simplification we rewrite expression (16.1) as a multivariate vector over which the function 'y' can be defined as (Smirnov, 2004),

$$y = f(x^1, x^2, \ldots, x^n)[\theta(\varepsilon)] \tag{16.4}$$

Each x^i, $i = 1, 2, .., n$ is evaluated by estimation followed by simulation as shown by expression (16.3). $(x^1, x^2, \ldots, x^n)[\theta(\varepsilon)]$ denotes the multivariate vector wherein each element is induced by the covariant continuum of $\{\theta(\varepsilon)\}$-ethical values in respect of parametrized values of unity of knowledge by inter-variable complementarities. Complementarity as ethical moral-material unity of knowledge is the property derived from the meaning of organic pairing declared in the *Qur'an* (36:36).

The gradient form of expression (16.4), 'g', explaining the curvature of the covariant-contravariant nature of evolutionary intra-system to inter-system multistages as evolutionary distancing (d), is written as,

$$\mathbf{g} = \left[\frac{\partial y}{\partial x^1}, \frac{\partial y}{\partial x^2}, \cdots, \frac{\partial y}{\partial x^n} \right] \quad \mathbf{d} = \left[dx^1, dx^2, \ldots, dx^n \right] \qquad (16.5)$$

'$\mathbf{g}$' denotes covariant tensor of the transformation of 'y' in the manifold around vector (16.4). '$\mathbf{d}$' is the contravariant tensor of 'y' in the manifold around vector (16.4). Such a manifold comprise the evolutionary learning stages across knowledge, space, time dimensions.

Each of the terms of expression (16.5) is induced by $\{\theta(\varepsilon)\}$. Thereby, the equation of geodesic as multivariate transformation of 'dy' is, $dy(\theta(\varepsilon)) = (\mathbf{g} \cdot \mathbf{d})[\theta(\varepsilon)]$. This value gives the covariant-contravariant transformation of intra-system and inter-system manifolds convoluted together along the continuum of knowledge, and knowledge-induced space and time dimensions of evolutionary learning in 'everything'.

The convoluted covariant-contravariant structure of the evolutionary learning universe of IIE-learning processes in *Tawhidi* unity of knowledge is given by the convoluted mathematical integral over induction of knowledge in knowledge, space, and time dimensions. The result is also of the evaluated circular causation relations:

$$\text{Convoluted} \int dy(\theta(\varepsilon)) d\theta(\varepsilon) = \text{Convoluted} \int (\mathbf{g} \cdot \mathbf{d})[\theta(\varepsilon)] d\theta(\varepsilon) \qquad (16.6)$$

Expression (16.3) in a simplified form represents a functional transformation of expression (16.4). We write the transformed vector of expression (16.1) as,

$$\mathbf{X}(\theta(\varepsilon)) = F(w_1(x_1), w_2(x_2), \ldots, w_n(x_n))[\theta(\varepsilon)] \qquad (16.7)$$

The covariant-contravariant tensor transformation of the function defined on vector (16.5) along the multivariate wellbeing functions in evolutionary learning dimensions is given by,

$$dy = \sum_{k=1}^{n} \left(\frac{\partial x^1}{\partial X^k} \frac{\partial y}{\partial x^1} + \frac{\partial x^2}{\partial X^k} \frac{\partial y}{\partial x^2} + \cdots + \frac{\partial x^n}{\partial X^k} \frac{\partial y}{\partial x^n} \right) dX^k \qquad (16.8)$$

Every variable shown in expression (16.8) is $\{\theta(\varepsilon)\}$-induced. Expression (16.8) in its vastly extended form over evolutionary learning multidimension of intra-system and inter-system in multistages is the true result in covariant-contravariant tensor analysis applied to the study of *Tawhidi* wellbeing functionals (*maslaha*). Expression (16.8) is also equivalent to a non-linear and complex transformation of expression (16.6) in the form of convoluted mathematical integration.

Winding up

This book has been the study of *Tawhidi* String Relation (TSR) in reference to *Tawhidi* methodological worldview of unity of knowledge (monotheistic consilience) in its extended dynamics of the multivariate functional analysis in multidimensional knowledge, and knowledge-induced space and time dimensions. In this way, the critical objective criterion of simulacra of wellbeing (*maslaha*) functions, rejecting all notions of optimality and steady-state equilibrium and of linear functional forms, overarches the dynamics and meaning of *Tawhid* as *the Law* over systemic transdisciplinarity in contradistinction to the limited scope of *shari'ah* that is narrowed to earthly affairs (*muamalat*), and this only to the limits of human concocted interpretations. Even when *shari'ah* refers to *Tawhid* as its functional origin, it is illogical to consider *shari'ah* as *law* and to abandon the primordial *LAW of Tawhid* in its richest form. This is the methodological worldview of TSR for deriving a rigorous theory of meta-science of 'everything'.

The theory of TSR is thereby an original contribution in the field of monotheistic worldview that is strictly contained in the *Qur'an* and explained by *sunnah* for the study of the world-system in its generality and diversity of particulars. The studies of economics, finance, science, and society are thereby complemented within the generalized system theory of unity of knowledge as a heterodox scientific originality. The example is presented thereby of the inter-causal relationship of socio-scientific theory of economics, finance, science, and society as much as between them in a unified way of *Tawhidi* methodology, as also between these and the cosmological entirety.

An example in this case is to place the *Qur'anic* precept of evolutionary learning and reorigination of consciousness (*taqwa* and *tasbih*) by the meaning of *khalq in-jadid*. This is a principle that is descriptive of the universal entirety of balance, creativity, and connectivity by organic complementarities between the heavens and the earth. Within such a holistic principle there emerges and prevails the function of Justice as Balance as critical embedding assuming the fullness of application. Thereby, while the *Qur'an* is the Book of guidance and not a Book of science, this implies that, the *Qur'an* and *Tawhid* as law comprise the path to convey and sustain guidance in the scientific explanations of the Signs of Allah. In this regard the *Qur'an* (2:225) declares: "His knowledge extends over the heavens and the earth." This knowledge is of *Tawhid* and its bestowing is the explanation of the Signs of Allah by the primordial law of unity of knowledge of *Tawhid* in 'everything'.

The question in the end will be asked: How can *Tawhid* as law replace the juristic origin of Muslim thought after the latter has prevailed in Muslim surrender of reasoning to *shari'ah* by *taqlid* for almost fourteen hundred years. The conclusive answer to this question by this book is to reconstruct the meaning, methodology, application, and sustainability of *Tawhid* as law in terms of its primal ontological unity of knowledge in the study of 'everything'. Thereby, the original thought around *maqasid as-shari'ah* and its genre would be cast fully in the originative framework of *Tawhid* and its methodological worldview. This is indeed how the *Qur'an* refers to *shari'atan* as the way that emanates from *Tawhid* and directs itself to *Tawhid* along the elegant understanding of the straightpath—*siratal-mustaqim*. This is also how Imam Ghazali thought of *maqasid as-shari'ah* in terms of *Tawhid* and *Tawakkul*. We refer to its attainment in TSR-orientation of the *Tawhidi* methodological worldview as *maqasid as-shari'ah al-Tawhid*.

References

Al-Shaykh al-Saduk (2009). In J. A. Morrow, A. R. Rizvi, L. A. Vittor, & B. Castleton (Eds.), *The Savor Foundation*, Paradstesh (pp. 177–180; 255–264; 265–280). Also see in this, Morrow, J. A., & Vittor, L. A. Tawhid in theological mode (pp. 35–49).

Gel'fand, I. M. (1961). *Lectures on linear algebra*. New York: Interscience Publishers, Inc.

Gonzalez, P. B. (2005). *Ortega Y Gasset's philosophy of subjectivity: Human existence radical reality*. St. Paul, Madison, USA: Paragon House.

Lewis (2014). Retrieved Sept 6, 2018, from https://www.livescience.com/42839-the-universe-is-math.html.

Smirnov, A. V. (2004). Introduction to tensor calculus. Internet version: http://www.nptel.ac.in/courses/105108072/mod03/hyperlink2-.pdf.

Tag el-Din, S. I. (2013). *Maqsid foundations of market economics*. Edinburgh, Scotland: Edinburgh University Press.

Glossary of Arabic Terms

Madhab Sect

Maqasid as-shari'ah Purpose and objective of *shari'ah*

Muamalat Worldly mundane affairs

Sunnah Teachings of the Prophet Muhammad including his sayings and actions

Khalq in-jadid Reorigination

Iqlas Purity

Ijara Rent

Shura Social consultation; but also social discourse at individual, community, and societal levels

tasbih The conscious creation in its worshipping of God as Creator in monotheism

murabaha Mark-up pricing as Islamic financial instrument

Ayath al-kursi The *Qur'anic* meaning of the Throne of Allah (God)

Dhat Divine essence

Sifat Attributes of Allah

Istawa The exclusive reign of Allah

Akhira Hereafter

Mukhtalifan Diversity

Ahkam Legal rule

Aqad Contract

Mudarabaha Profit-sharing as Islamic financial instrument

© Springer Nature Singapore Pte Ltd. 2019
M. A. Choudhury (ed.), *The Tawhidi Methodological Worldview*,
https://doi.org/10.1007/978-981-13-6585-0

Musharakah Equity-participation as Islamic financial instrument

Takaful Islamic insurance

Waqf Islamic endowment as perpetual charity

Ulema Learned religious persons

mujtahid The learned ones who carry out original extraction of meanings from *Qur'an* and *sunnah* (*ijtihad*)

Halal at-tayyabah Good things of life

Al-maslaha al-Tawhid Wellbeing in the context of Oneness of Allah in the form of its divine law of unity of knowledge

maslaha Wellbeing function as measure of blessing

masalih That which generates wellbeing (*maslaha*)

ulul amr The truly learned in Islam on the basis of *Qur'an* and *sunnah* as source of knowledge

haram Forbidden things in every form

halal Permissible things in every form

riba Financial interest

mafasid Harmful value contrary to wellbeing

arsh al-Azim The Highest stature of Allah's Throne

khabisa Evil

sirathal mustaqim Straight path of righteousness

qabd Possession of entitlement

haqq Reality of truth

batil Falsehood

dururiyath Necessities of life-fulfilling needs

hajiyath Comforts of life as part of life-fulfilling needs

tahsaniyath Refinements of life as part of life-fulfilling needs

Ayath Allah Signs of Allah (God)

urf Cultural practices

adah Regional customs of people

wahada Unity of Being (monotheism)

zakah Mandatory payments for social wellbeing of specific categories of the needy by enabling Muslims

muzakhi Those who qualify for receiving *zakah*

mustahiq Deserving, rightful

Jannah Heaven in its eight categories for the believers

Taqwa God-consciousness

Bibliography

Al-Faruqi, I. R. (1982). *Tawhid: Its implications for thought and life*. Herndon, VA: International Institute of Islamic Thought.

Al-Faruqi, I. R. (1982). *Islamization of knowledge: General principles and Workplan*. Herndon, VA: The International Institute of Islamic Thought.

Al-Shāṭibī, Abū Isḥāq Ibrāhīm b. Mūsā trans. A. Draz (n.d.). *al-Muwāfaqāt fī uṣūl al-sharī'a*, Cairo (on the Islamic conception of social well-being, *al-maṣlaḥa*).

Bakar, O. (1991). *Tawhid and science, essays on the history and philosophy of Islamic Science*. Kuala Lumpur, Malaysia: Secretariat for Islamic Philosophy and Science.

Bakar, O. (2014). *Islamic civilisation and the modern world*. Darassalam, Brunei: University of Brunei Darassalam Press.

Blaug, M. (1993). *The methodology of economics*. Cambridge, Eng.: Cambridge University Press.

Choudhury, M. A. (2017b). Tawhid, al-wasatiyyah, *and* maqasid as-shari'ah. In: *Absolute reality in the Qur'an*. Palgrave Series in Islamic Theology, Law, and History. New York: Palgrave Macmillan.

Choudhury, M. A. (forthcoming). A theory of justice in Islam. In T. Azid (Ed.), *Justice in Islam*. Routledge, London, UK.

Embedded Political Economy—An Epistemological Approach. In P. Pachura (Ed.), *The systemic dimension of globalization*, Chapter 1. Rijeka, Croatia: InTech.

Daud, W. M. N. W. (1998). Metaphysical worldview. *The educational philosophy and practice of Syed Muhammad Naquib Al-Attas, an exposition of the original concept of Islamization* (pp. 33–68). Kuala Lumpur, Malaysia: International Institute of Islamic Thought and Civilization.

Fox, G. (1997). *Reason and reality in the methodologies of economics*. Cheltenham, UK: Edward Elgar.

Hubner, K. (trans. Dixon Jr., P. R., & Dixon, H. M.). (1985). Foundations of a universal historistic theory of the empirical sciences. In *Critique of scientific reason* (pp. 105–122). Chicago, IL: The University of Chicago Press.

Inglott, P. S. (1990). The rights of future generations: Some socio-philosophical considerations. Agius (1990) as above S. Busuttill, E. Agius, P. S. Inglott & T. Macelli (Eds.), *Our responsibilities towards future generations* (pp. 17–27). Malta: Foundation for International Studies & UNESCO.

Karim, M. F. (trans.) (n.d.). Imam Ghazali's *Ihya Ulum-Id-Din in 5 vols* (esp. Vol. 4). Lahore: Sh. Muhammad Ashraf.

Lucaks, J. (1968). *Historical consciousness*. New York, NY: Harper & Row Publishers.

© Springer Nature Singapore Pte Ltd. 2019
M. A. Choudhury (ed.), *The Tawhidi Methodological Worldview*,
https://doi.org/10.1007/978-981-13-6585-0

Maritain, J. (1973). *On the philosophy of history* (Ed. J. W. Evans). Clifton, New Jersey: Augustus M. Kelley Publishers.

Myrdal, G. (1958). The principle of cumulation. In P. Streeten (Ed.), *Value in social theory, a selection of essays on methodology by Gunnar Myrdal* (pp. 198–205). New York, NY: Harper & Brothers Publishers.

Nasr, S. H. (1978). *An introduction to Islamic Cosmological Doctrines.* Shambhala, Boulder, CO, USA.

Nusseibeh, S. (2017). The nature of truth. *The theory of reason in Islam* (pp. 167–168). Stanford, California: Stanford University Press.

Pheby, J. (1988). *Methodology and economics, a critical introduction.* London, Eng.: Macmillan.

Rahman, R. (1988). Islamization of knowledge: A response. *American Journal of Islamic Social Sciences, 5,* 1.

Rahman, T. (n.d.). *Social justice in Western and Islamic Thought (A comparative study of John Rawls's and Sayyid Qutb's theories of social justice, n.d. internet version).*

Index

© Springer Nature Singapore Pte Ltd. 2019
M. A. Choudhury (ed.), *The Tawhidi Methodological Worldview*,
https://doi.org/10.1007/978-981-13-6585-0

225

Printed by Printforce, the Netherlands